CNOR® EXAM PREP

Revised First Edition

CCI® The Leader in Perioperative Certification

CNOR® Exam Prep, Revised First Edition

Copyright © 2018 by Competency & Credentialing Institute

All rights reserved. Printed in the United States of America.

CCI's educational materials, in print and electronic form, are protected under federal copyright law. No part of this publication may be reproduced, stored, modified, or transmitted in any form by any means, electronic or otherwise, without the prior written permission of the publisher; except in the case of brief quotations within critical articles and reviews. Any unauthorized use of CCI materials is strictly prohibited. Violation of CCI's intellectual property rights may incur substantial damages, including statutory damages of up to $150,000 for a single willful violation of CCI's copyright.

©CCI

Competency & Credentialing Institute
2170 South Parker Road
Suite 120
Denver, Colorado 80231

Disclaimer: CCI has attempted to ensure all information in this publication is accurate and consistent with current patient guidelines. However, nothing in this book should be construed as medical or legal advice or opinion and readers should make their own independent practice decisions based on the particular circumstances and the advice of a licensed professional, as appropriate. CCI does not make any warranties of merchantability or fitness for a particular purpose and is not liable for any claims or damage resulting from use of the information in this publication.

As a certification organization, CCI's role is developing and administering certification examinations. CCI does not require or endorse any specific study guides, review products, or training courses. Candidates may prepare for certification examinations with any educational materials they choose. Purchase of CCI review materials is not a requirement for testing, nor does use of any review materials (CCI or otherwise) imply successful performance on the certification examinations. No study resources are prerequisites for the certification examinations.

CNOR is a registered trademark of the Competency & Credentialing Institute. All rights reserved.

ISBN 978-0-9986576-3-9

For information about purchasing CCI books, please call 888.257.2667 or visit www.cc-institute.org.

CONTENTS AT A GLANCE

1 Preoperative Patient Assessment and Diagnosis *1*

2 Plan of Care *21*

3 Intraoperative Care *47*

4 Communication *111*

5 Transfer of Care *135*

6 Instrument Processing and Supply Management *155*

7 Emergency Situations *181*

8 Management of Personnel, Services, and Materials *207*

9 Professional Accountability *227*

CONTENTS

Foreword ix
Introduction xi

1 Preoperative Patient Assessment and Diagnosis   1

    Overview of the Nursing Process 3
    Steps of the Preoperative Assessment 3
    Conducting an Assessment 5
    Performing the Physical Examination 5
    Completing the Medical Record Review 6
    Performing Medication Reconciliation 7
    Preprocedure Verifications: The Universal Protocol 8
    Identifying Applicable Nursing Diagnoses 10
    Documentation 10
    Key Concepts and Review: Case Study 11
    Practice Exam 16

2 Plan of Care   21

    Identifying Desired Patient Outcomes 23
    Developing a Patient-Centered Perioperative Plan of Care 24
    Preoperative Patient Preparation 36
    Patient and Family Education 38
    Collaboration with Interdisciplinary Team Members 40
    Legal and Ethical Implications 40
    Key Concepts and Review 41
    Practice Exam 44

3 Intraoperative Care   47

    Universal Protocol 49
    Patient and Personnel Safety 50
    Patient Positioning 54
    Procedure-Specific Protective Materials and Equipment 58
    Environmental Factors 60
    Anesthesia Management 61
    Hemodynamic Needs 63
    Physiological Responses 65
    Pain Management 68
    Behavioral Responses 70
    Cultural, Spiritual, or Ethical Patient Beliefs 72
    Perioperative Asepsis 78
    Ensure the Sterility of Surgical Products and Instrumentation 85

Specimen Management. 87
Surgical Counts. 89
Perioperative Documentation 90
Hemostasis and Wound Management 92
Key Concepts and Review: Case Study 97
Practice Exam 103

4 Communication 111

Factors That Influence Effective Communication. 114
Nonverbal Communication. 114
Assertiveness 115
Authenticity 116
Emotional Intelligence. 116
Communication Tools 116
Culture of Safety 117
Barriers to Effective Communication 117
Communicating in the Perioperative Area 121
Health Care-Information Management in the Perioperative Setting 125
Key Concepts and Review: Case Study. 127
Practice Exam 130

5 Transfer of Care 135

Perioperative Transfers of Care. 139
Patient-Centered Transfer of Care Through Discharge Planning 144
Regulatory Guidelines for Discharge Planning 146
Documentation of Transfer of Care 147
Transitions of Care: Engaging Patients and Families 149
Key Concepts and Review. 149
Practice Exam 151

6 Instrument Processing and Supply Management 155

Perioperative Infection Prevention and Control Principles 157
Cleaning and Disinfecting Instruments, Equipment, and Endoscopes 157
Packaging 163
Sterilization of Instruments and Supplies 165
Physical Monitors for Sterilization 168
Transporting Contaminated Instruments 170
Conditions for Storing Sterilized Instruments and Supplies. 170
Commercial Instruments and Supplies Provided by Industry Representatives. 171
Key Concepts and Review. 174
Practice Exam 177

7 Emergency Situations — 181

- Perioperative Crises 183
- Surgical Classifications: Elective, Emergent, Urgent 189
- The ABCs of Preparing for Emergencies 189
- Environmental Hazards and Natural Disasters 192
- Diagnostic Tools 193
- System-Specific Situations, Complications, and Their Immediate Actions ... 193
- Perioperative-Specific Considerations 196
- Key Concepts and Review 199
- Case Study 199
- Practice Exam 203

8 Management of Personnel, Services, and Materials — 207

- Management of OR Personnel 209
- Management of Non-OR Personnel 211
- Management of Supplies, Equipment, and Implants 214
- Environmental Cleaning 218
- Key Concepts and Review 221
- Practice Exam 224

9 Professional Accountability — 227

- Perioperative Nurse Scope of Practice 229
- Sources of Professional Standards 229
- Traits Exhibited by the Nursing Professional 233
- Professional Growth 234
- Quality Improvement 236
- Culture of Safety 236
- Risk Management 237
- Patient Rights and Advocacy 237
- Delegation 238
- Key Concepts and Review 238
- Practice Exam 241

100-Question Practice Exam — 245

Appendix: Taking the CNOR Exam 277
List of Contributors 283
Index 285

FOREWORD

I was very pleased to be asked to write the Foreword to this edition of the *CNOR® Exam Prep*. AORN supports the mission of the Competency & Credentialing Institute (CCI), and I know this book will provide you with a tool to assist in successfully passing the certification exam.

Licensure and registration are granted for meeting minimal professional requirements, while certification is an objective measure to validate that a nurse has the knowledge required to provide an optimal level of care to the patient undergoing operative or other invasive procedures. In addition, certification contributes to nursing's social contract with society. As nursing evolved from an occupation into a profession, we accepted a social contract with society. Within the social contract, society has expectations for the obligations that nursing must meet as a profession.[1] The contract acknowledges professional rights and responsibilities as well as mechanisms for public accountability. Much of society's faith in nursing rests on its perceived and real faithfulness in meeting these obligations. One of the expectations includes that the profession will "ensure the knowledge, skill, and competence of new practitioners entering practice (licensure and registration) and those in practice, at every level and in every role."[1(p20)]

The Code of Ethics for Nurses identifies that nurses have a moral responsibility to promote effective health outcomes, to protect the public from harm, and to maintain and advance competencies beyond the basic level. The third provision of the Code of Ethics speaks to this responsibility as being inherent in professional nursing. This process involves the ongoing acquisition and development of knowledge, skills, dispositions, practice experiences, commitment, rational maturity, and personal integrity, all of which are essential for professional practice.[2]

The process of certification in nursing was developed as a mechanism to provide formal recognition of advanced excellence in the practice of nursing. Certification contributes to the social contract with society and to meeting our responsibilities to patients as identified in the Code of Ethics in the following ways:

- Certification demonstrates that as a professional registered nurse (RN), you accept accountability to the public to practice at a higher level of nursing practice.
- Certification is not static—it requires that the practitioner recertify to validate current evidence-based knowledge, thus enhancing the quality of patient care.

- Certification provides health care facilities a method of validating the professional achievement of individual practitioners.
- Certification provides personal satisfaction for practitioners.

Both AORN and CCI are committed to lifelong learning and continuing education for the specialty of perioperative nursing.

Thank you for studying to take the CNOR exam. This is an important step toward achieving excellence and assuring your patients that you are delivering optimal care that meets evidence-based standards of practice for perioperative nursing.

Linda K. Groah, MSN, RN, CNOR, NEA-BC, FAAN
Executive Director and Chief Executive Officer
AORN, Inc
Denver, CO

References

1. Fowler DM. Social contract theory. In: *Guide to Nursing's Social Policy Statement: Understanding the Profession from Social Contract to Social Covenant*. Silver Spring, MD: American Nurses Association; 2015:1-28.
2. American Nurses Association. *Code of Ethics for Nurses with Interpretive Statements*. Silver Springs, MD: American Nurses Association; 2015.

INTRODUCTION

Welcome to the elite group of perioperative nurses interested in attaining the next step in their professional development—certification as a perioperative registered nurse (RN). By holding the CNOR certification, perioperative nurses acknowledge a commitment to lifelong learning as an important component in providing competent, safe patient care. To become a certified perioperative nurse requires passing an exam based on what a nurse with two years of perioperative experience is expected to know regardless of clinical setting or specialization. Whether you are a nurse seeking guidance in those areas in which you have limited exposure to update your current knowledge base or wishing to review best practices, guidelines, and evidence-based standards, the Competency & Credentialing Institute (CCI) wants to be an active partner in your exam preparation. CCI administers the CNOR exam, and this exam prep book was developed to assist you in understanding and mastering the material you will need to know to pass the exam.

Background on the CNOR Certification and Exam

The CNOR certification documents validation of professional achievements of identified standards of care provided by the perioperative RN. The CNOR credential is currently accredited by two, independent accrediting bodies: the National Commission for Certifying Agencies (NCCA) and the American Board for Specialty Nursing Certification (ABSNC). As an accredited program administered by CCI, the CNOR exam demonstrates knowledge of the highest standards of practice in the professional certification and nursing communities.

SUBJECT AREAS OF THE CNOR EXAM

The CNOR exam is meant to evaluate competent practice and thus is directed toward what a nurse with two years of experience is expected to know and do. The exam contains 200 multiple-choice, single-answer questions that pertain to nine subject areas based on formal, in-depth job analysis conducted by CCI. Members of the job analysis committee include certified perioperative nurses representing the

TABLE I.1 CNOR Exam Subject Areas and Corresponding Percentage of Questions

	SUBJECT AREA	PERCENTAGE OF QUESTIONS
1	Preoperative Patient Assessment and Diagnosis	12%
2	Plan of Care	10%
3	Intraoperative Care	27%
4	Communication	10%
5	Transfer of Care	6%
6	Instrument Processing and Supply Management	9%
7	Emergency Situations	11%
8	Management of Personnel, Services, and Materials	6%
9	Professional Accountability	9%
	Total	100%

perioperative community in terms of education, experience, demographics, length of time in practice, years holding the CNOR credential, and age. Together with CCI's testing partner, this job analysis committee determines the subject areas on which the exam is built. Although the major subject areas may remain unchanged from one job analysis to the next, the weight, or the amount of time a perioperative nurse may spend in each subject area, may shift with changes in practice. This will affect the percentage of questions covering each subject area, and ultimately, may help determine how much time you want to spend studying a topic. These subject areas are listed in Table I.1 along with the corresponding percentage of test questions allocated for each subject.

CCI'S JOB ANALYSIS: THE FOUNDATION OF THE CNOR EXAM

The job analysis, including CNOR test specifications, is developed by the Test Specifications Committee of CCI in cooperation with its testing agency. The purpose of the job analysis is to capture the overall functions and responsibilities, as well as the underlying knowledge and skills, that are essential to proficiency as a perioperative nurse. The test specifications were developed on the basis of external ratings, and constitute a plan on which the job-related certification exam was constructed for nurses functioning in the perioperative role. CCI intends this document to act as a guideline for development of the certification exam. It is recognized that the job analysis may not reflect all of the specific tasks performed by an individual perioperative nurse.

How to Use This Guide

The chapters in this book are organized by subject areas of the CNOR exam. Each chapter covers a subject area and its corresponding key terms and concepts and nursing skills and tasks, as established by CCI's job analysis. Such components put competent nursing practice into manageable "chunks" to make it easy to prepare and study for the exam. The tables and figures provided throughout this book provide an efficient way to grasp concepts and aid in retention. An overview of everything you need to know to be ready for test day is provided in the Appendix.

> **Learn More about CCI's Job Analysis**
>
> More information about CCI's job analysis may be found online by accessing the *CNOR Candidate Handbook*, available on CCI's website. Launch the online handbook to access detailed information about the exam and its corresponding job analysis. Several of the subject areas are sequential in nature to build on the knowledge and skills specified in the findings of the job analysis. Also included are policies and procedures pertaining to certification and recertification of the CNOR credential.

🖉 KEY TERMS

A list of key terms appears at the beginning of each chapter. These terms identify key concepts and topics that will be discussed. Each key term is listed in boldface when discussed in the chapter. Understanding key terms is an important component of preparing for the exam.

☑ REQUIRED NURSING SKILLS

These are skills expected for competent practice by a perioperative nurse with two years of experience. A list of the nursing skills that correspond with an exam subject area are listed at the beginning of each chapter. Discussion of these skills is included in each chapter. In addition to using this exam prep book, aligning personal practice as closely as possible to recommended standards and guidelines is the best way to operationalize the knowledge necessary to perform well on the exam.

➤ EXAM TIPS

Exam tips are provided throughout each chapter to highlight practical information to help you prepare for the exam.

KEY CONCEPTS AND REVIEW

This section contains a snapshot of key points and takeaways for each chapter. Some chapters conclude with a case study to help you apply the information using scenarios based on what nurses encounter in the practice setting.

REFERENCES AND ADDITIONAL RESOURCES

In an effort to provide the highest-quality information, references used in this study guide reflect the most current evidence found in the literature. Additional resources are included to supplement the information found in the chapter. Handy tips for analyzing multiple-choice questions, applying for the exam, and the actual test-day experience are provided in the Appendix.

PRACTICE EXAM QUESTIONS, ANSWERS, AND SUPPORTED RATIONALES

Sample multiple-choice questions and their answers and supported rationales have been included at the end of each chapter to give you ample opportunity to apply your knowledge and become familiar with the specific format of the test questions. There is also a 100-question practice exam at the end of the book. Each question on the exam is multiple-choice with one single correct answer; and for each question, there are four possible answers (ie, A, B, C, or D). There is only *one correct answer* for every question, and there are no multiple correct answers. The sample questions found in this exam prep guide (and in CCI's other test preparation products) follow this same format (see the Appendix for more discussion on question format and how to prepare for the exam).

It is important to understand the purpose of practice questions and how they can be used to maximize their effectiveness as a study aid. Sample test questions provide an experience similar to the actual test-taking event and can be used to evaluate knowledge of a particular topic. Although the practice questions in this book are similar in form and content to the types of questions found on the actual CNOR certification exam, they will not be found on the actual test.

Because performing well on a practice question does not transfer to equal success on the exam, practice questions should not be used as the sole method of study. Answering the same questions multiple times may improve your score of correct answers, but is the result of memorization of the correct answer rather than a true reflection of knowledge. Ways to extract additional benefits from sample questions include

- analyzing the incorrect options to understand why they were wrong,
- looking for trends in missed answers to identify areas needing additional study or experience, and
- being able to answer a question in a minute or less.

Replicating the actual testing experience when answering practice questions is a good strategy for decreasing the anxiety typically encountered during the testing experience.

Putting It All Together

By now you are probably excited, and maybe a little anxious, about realizing your goal to become a CNOR. Just remember that you have multiple resources available to you, both in your work setting and here at CCI. Everyone at CCI, your employer, your peers, and most importantly your patients want you to be successful. After all, passing the exam is just one part of your continued commitment to competent practice and providing safe, quality patient care.

CNOR® EXAM PREP

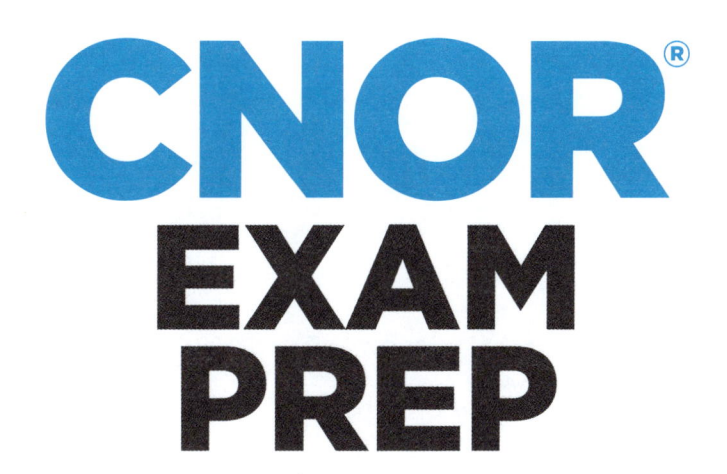

Revised First Edition

1 Preoperative Patient Assessment and Diagnosis

✎ KEY TERMS

- Advance directive
- Anatomy and physiology
- Approved nursing diagnoses
- Assessment
- DNR
- Informed consent
- Medication reconciliation
- NANDA International
- Nursing process
- Pathophysiology
- Perioperative Nursing Data Set (PNDS)
- Pharmacology
- Surgical Safety Checklist
- Universal Protocol

✓ REQUIRED NURSING SKILLS

- Documentation of preoperative assessment
- Participating in the nursing process
- Preoperative assessment
  - Collecting, analyzing, and prioritizing patient data
  - Conducting a physical assessment
  - Reviewing medication reconciliation
  - Using age and culturally appropriate health assessment techniques to evaluate patient status
- Verifying correct procedure, operative site, and side/site marking

Nursing students are taught how to apply the six components of the nursing process—assessment, diagnosis, outcomes identification, planning, implementation, and evaluation—to all patients they encounter.[1] These basic skills are continually applicable to perioperative registered nurses (RNs) in the perioperative setting. To deliver safe care to patients, as well as to be successful on the CNOR examination, nurses must master the nursing process. This chapter discusses the first two steps of the nursing process: completing a preoperative patient assessment and selecting applicable nursing diagnoses (additional components of the nursing process are reviewed in later chapters of this book).

Overview of the Nursing Process

It is a common misperception that perioperative care of the patient undergoing an operative or other invasive procedure occurs only in the surgical suite and is limited to the act of performing the procedure. In fact, the perioperative nurse's care of the patient begins the moment the patient comes through the doors of the surgical department. A perioperative nurse must be able to understand and apply the nursing process in delivering care. The nursing process comprises six steps (Figure 1.1). To provide the level of care outlined in these steps, nurses must view each patient as an individual with unique care needs that must be satisfied to achieve that patient's desired outcomes. This focus informs the nurse's ability both to successfully perform a baseline assessment as the patient enters the surgical department and to reassess the patient throughout his or her entire stay.

FIGURE 1.1 The Six Steps of the Nursing Process

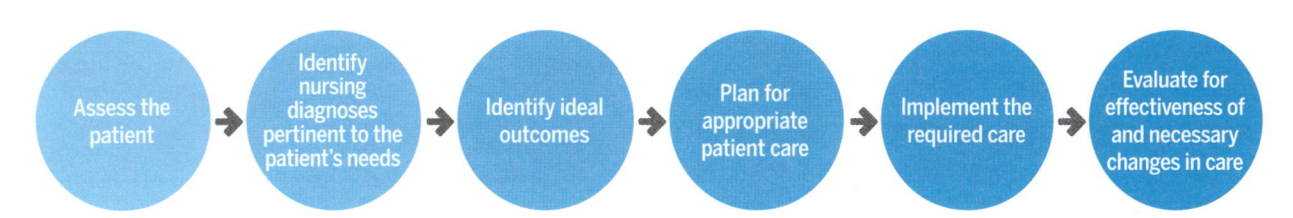

Assess the patient → Identify nursing diagnoses pertinent to the patient's needs → Identify ideal outcomes → Plan for appropriate patient care → Implement the required care → Evaluate for effectiveness of and necessary changes in care

Steps of the Preoperative Assessment

"Assessment is the collection and analysis of relevant health data about the patient."[1(p3)] Thorough preoperative assessment is essential for all patients entering the surgical environment. A complete assessment not only allows for gathering of essential data but also leads the way for the preoperative nurse to start identifying areas of opportunity for postoperative teaching of the patient. The steps of the preoperative assessment may be distinguished between patient assessment and the process of preprocedure verification (ie, Universal Protocol). The Universal Protocol was created to prevent wrong-person, wrong-procedure, and wrong-site surgery in hospitals and outpatient settings. The Universal Protocol consists of three steps: a preoperative/preprocedure verification process, marking the operative/procedure site, and a time out (final verification), which is performed immediately before starting the operation/procedure.

Patient assessment includes

- conducting an assessment,
- performing the physical examination,
- completing the medical record review (eg, assessing laboratory and diagnostic test values), and
- performing the medication reconciliation process.

The process of preprocedure verification includes

- confirming the patient's identity,
- verifying the scheduled surgical procedure,
- site marking, and
- performing the time out (eg, regional blocks, line placement, before incision).

GATHERING PATIENT INFORMATION

When performing the preoperative assessment, the nurse gathers data from a variety of sources. These sources include, but are not limited to,

- the patient;
- the medical record, including the physician's physical examination;
- the surgeon, anesthesia professional, and other health care personnel; and
- the perioperative nurse's knowledge of the planned surgical procedure.

Good communication skills and interviewing techniques are essential when gathering information from the patient (see Chapter 4). The nurse must endeavor to establish a trusting relationship with the patient and his or her family members so that open communication can occur. The nurse must

> **EXAM TIP**
>
> The patient and family should be actively engaged during the assessment phase because they are an excellent source of health care information.

provide for patient privacy during this phase of the assessment. This can be particularly difficult in some facilities where patients are only separated by curtains.

Actively involving the patient in the preoperative assessment makes information collection easier, and it can also decrease the patient's anxiety by allowing him or her to have a say in the plan of care. It is imperative for the nurse to give the patient the opportunity to ask questions and provide answers during the preoperative assessment. Open and honest communication with patients can help improve their expectations of the preoperative, intraoperative, and postoperative experiences.

Conducting an Assessment

When conducting an assessment, the nurse must use assessment techniques that are age and culturally appropriate. For example, if assessing an infant or small child, the nurse would call the child by his or her first name and ask any pertinent history questions of the parent(s) rather than the patient. When assessing adolescents, questions can often be asked of the patients themselves, but remember to provide for confidentiality. Recognize that older adults often have sensory and/or physical limitations, but use caution not to stereotype age and decreased level of cognition. Being culturally appropriate and sensitive is important as well. Avoid stereotyping on the basis of race or gender. Learn to recognize common practices of ethnic populations within your own community. (See Chapter 2 for more discussion of age- and culturally appropriate techniques.)

Regardless of the method of data collection used, the focus of the preoperative assessment is on the following key elements:

- obtaining the patient's current diagnosis and physical and psychosocial status;
- obtaining the patient's medical history, to include previous illnesses and surgical procedures; and
- validating patient's understanding of the procedure.

Additional information the nurse should obtain during the assessment includes NPO status; nutritional status (eg, body mass index [BMI]); loose teeth, dentures, or caps; eyeglasses or contact lenses; hearing aids; unexplained family death while under anesthesia; adverse response to previous surgeries or anesthesia; and travel to countries with infectious disease outbreaks.

Nurses must recognize that the format used to perform the preoperative assessment adheres to the health care institution's policies and procedures, and that these can vary among health care facilities. For some patients undergoing an operative or other invasive procedure, the preoperative assessment may begin with the nurse conducting a face-to-face or phone interview before the day of surgery, followed by a brief recap of the preoperative information with the patient on the day of admission. For other patients, the nurse may not perform the preoperative assessment until the patient arrives in the surgical department. There are pros and cons of doing this either way.[2] Some pros of beginning the assessment ahead of the patient's arrival may include that intraoperative care is more individualized, preoperative baselines are established, and a good patient/nurse relationship is started; whereas some cons may include the cost factor of staff and time as well as the redundancy that can occur if patients are repeatedly asked the same question. Regardless of the procedures that nurses will adhere to when conducting the preoperative assessment, the assessment must be thorough and accurate so that the appropriate nursing diagnoses can be made, appropriate patient outcomes can be identified, and applicable interventions can be planned and executed during the patient's continuum of perioperative care.

Performing the Physical Examination

The next step of the nursing assessment is performing the physical examination. The physical exam is the hands-on part of the preoperative assessment and includes a quick head-to-toe review of the patient's current health status. To complete this task a perioperative nurse needs to be aware of basic anatomy, physiology, and **pathophysiology**. The nurse should take note of the patient's general appearance, such as:

- Does the patient appear anxious or calm?
- Is the patient alert and oriented or drowsy?
- Is the patient's color expected for ethnicity or is he/she pale or flushed?
- When touching the patient, is the patient cool or hot, dry or sweaty?
- In assessing lung sounds and respirations, what is the patient's breathing status?

During the physical assessment, the perioperative nurse must also identify physical factors that will need to be taken into consideration during intraoperative planning:

- Does the patient have any joint immobility (eg, is hip or shoulder immobility pertinent when assessing for procedure-specific patient positioning)?
- What is the condition of the patient's skin? Are there any current areas of breakdown?
- What are the patient's heart rate and rhythm?

Additionally, the nurse must ask the patient about body piercings which will need to be removed for patient safety and current implants, because intraoperative positioning or electrosurgical unit dispersive pad placement may be hindered by the presence of artificial joints and the patient may require an additional preoperative antibiotic.

The nurse will record the patient's current vital signs and assess the patient's level of pain, as well as identify any allergies the patient may have to food, prep solutions, tape, latex, or medications.

> **EXAM TIP**
>
> Information gathered during the assessment facilitates prioritization of care and may reveal information that should be shared with other health care disciplines participating in the care of the patient.

The nurse must understand the **pharmacology** of any medications that are administered to the patient, including how the medication acts on the human body, what conditions the medication is prescribed to treat, and potential adverse reactions that may be experienced.

Completing the Medical Record Review

One important step that must occur during the preoperative assessment phase is for the nurse to review the patient's medical record to verify that all pertinent information is available. Reviewing the patient's medical record can also provide the nurse with important information needed to complete the preoperative assessment. Some facilities may still use paper records, while other facilities may have converted to electronic charting. However organizations document patient care, certain items are universally required:

- a signed **informed consent** that may include some or all of the following: surgical, anesthesia, blood products, photography, special laboratory testing, presence of additional people in the OR;
- a current history and physical examination performed by the admitting physician or his or her delegate; however, if this person is different from the person performing the procedure, there may be an additional note by the surgeon;

- a preanesthesia assessment;
- baseline admission vital signs;
- laboratory results;
- radiographic reports; and
- height and weight in kilograms because most emergency medications are administered based on weight.[3]

Another component of the medical record review that is very important for the perioperative nurse to review is the presence of an **advance directive** (ie, a legal document that allows the patient to provide instructions ahead of time on end-of-life care) or medical orders, if applicable to the patient (see sidebar Advance Directives and Medical Orders). This is especially important because the patient depends on the perioperative nurse to act on his or her behalf to ensure that all members of the perioperative team respect the patient's wishes, most particularly when the patient cannot speak for himself or herself when under the effects of anesthesia.

Performing Medication Reconciliation

Medication reconciliation is the process of comparing the medications that a patient is using at home currently with the medications that are ordered for him or her by the surgeon or the surgeon's delegate (eg, perioperative nurse practitioner, the surgeon's physician's assistant).[4] Medication reconciliation begins with the preoperative assessment. The preoperative nurse should collect from the patient a list of current home medications, to include dose, frequency, medications taken on an as-needed basis, and the last dose of each medication. The nurse must also collect information about alternative and herbal supplements, medical marijuana, alcohol use, and recreational drug use. This list may have been compiled by a preadmission nurse before the patient arrived in the surgical department, in which case the perioperative nurse should again review this list with the patient and his or her designated support person or legal guardian on arrival at the surgical department to determine whether any changes have been made. Participating in medication reconciliation helps promote safe patient outcomes.[3] During the process of medication reconciliation, the nurse should also review any patient medication allergies and possible interactions with expected medications.

Advance Directives and Medical Orders

Living will—a document designed to control certain future health care decisions only when a person becomes unable to make decisions and choices on his or her own

Durable power of attorney—a legal document in which a person names someone to be his or her proxy (ie, agent) to make all health care decisions if the person becomes unable to do so

DNR—do not resuscitate; written physician orders instructing health care providers not to perform cardiopulmonary resuscitation

AND—allow natural death; the provision of only comfort measures for the actively dying patient

POLST—physician orders for life-sustaining treatment

PSDA—the Patient Self-Determination Act, a federal law that requires most health care institutions to provide information on advance directives at the time of admission

FIGURE 1.2 Safety Checklist

Surgical Safety Checklist

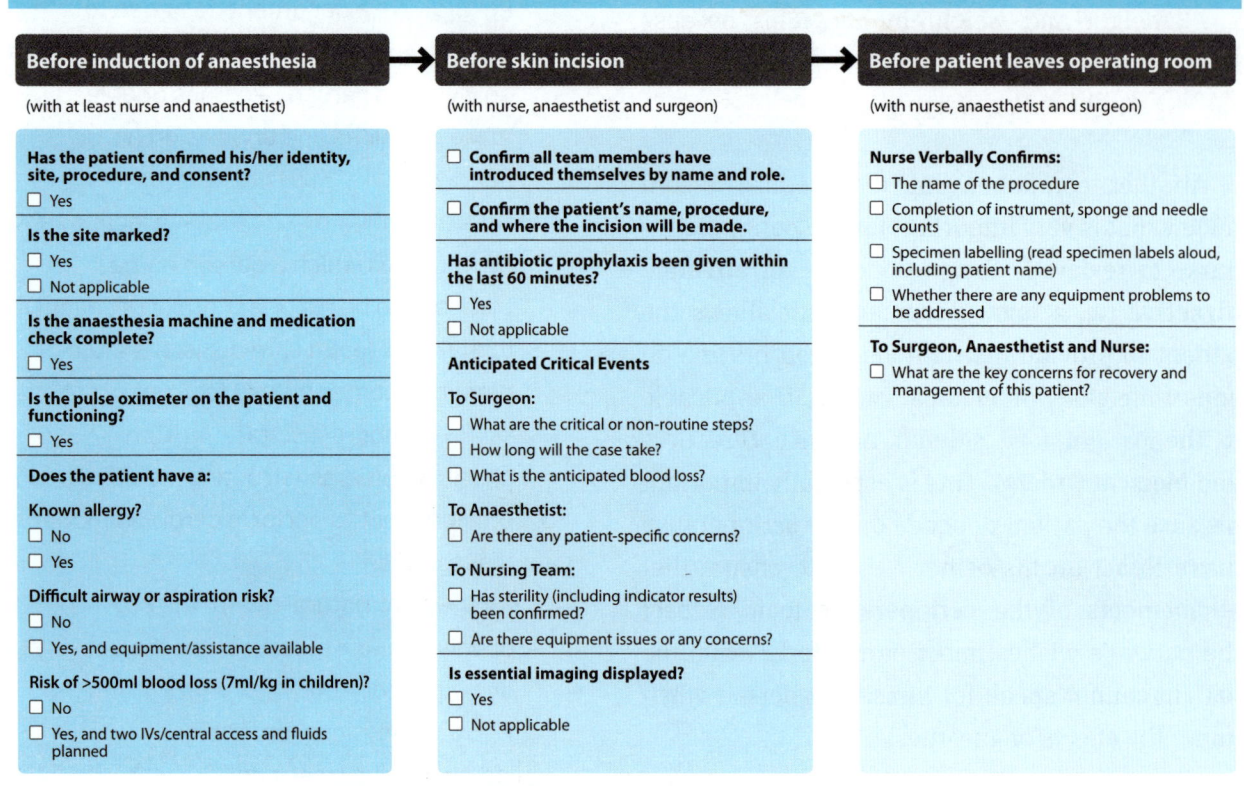

Before induction of anaesthesia → **Before skin incision** → **Before patient leaves operating room**

(with at least nurse and anaesthetist) | (with nurse, anaesthetist and surgeon) | (with nurse, anaesthetist and surgeon)

Before induction of anaesthesia

Has the patient confirmed his/her identity, site, procedure, and consent?
☐ Yes

Is the site marked?
☐ Yes
☐ Not applicable

Is the anaesthesia machine and medication check complete?
☐ Yes

Is the pulse oximeter on the patient and functioning?
☐ Yes

Does the patient have a:

Known allergy?
☐ No
☐ Yes

Difficult airway or aspiration risk?
☐ No
☐ Yes, and equipment/assistance available

Risk of >500ml blood loss (7ml/kg in children)?
☐ No
☐ Yes, and two IVs/central access and fluids planned

Before skin incision

☐ Confirm all team members have introduced themselves by name and role.

☐ Confirm the patient's name, procedure, and where the incision will be made.

Has antibiotic prophylaxis been given within the last 60 minutes?
☐ Yes
☐ Not applicable

Anticipated Critical Events

To Surgeon:
☐ What are the critical or non-routine steps?
☐ How long will the case take?
☐ What is the anticipated blood loss?

To Anaesthetist:
☐ Are there any patient-specific concerns?

To Nursing Team:
☐ Has sterility (including indicator results) been confirmed?
☐ Are there equipment issues or any concerns?

Is essential imaging displayed?
☐ Yes
☐ Not applicable

Before patient leaves operating room

Nurse Verbally Confirms:
☐ The name of the procedure
☐ Completion of instrument, sponge and needle counts
☐ Specimen labelling (read specimen labels aloud, including patient name)
☐ Whether there are any equipment problems to be addressed

To Surgeon, Anaesthetist and Nurse:
☐ What are the key concerns for recovery and management of this patient?

This checklist is not intended to be comprehensive. Additions and modifications to fit local practice are encouraged.

Based on the WHO Surgical Safety Checklist (http://www.who.int/patientsafety/safesurgery/en) © World Health Organization 2008. All rights reserved. Reproduced with permission of the World Health Organization.

Preprocedure Verifications: The Universal Protocol

Using a comprehensive surgical safety checklist (Figure 1.2), such as the one developed by the World Health Organization,[5] is part of The Joint Commission's (TJC) Universal Protocol.[6] Per the Universal Protocol, there are three components of verification: preprocedure verification, appropriate site marking, and the surgical time out prior to the start of the procedure.

CONFIRMING PATIENT IDENTITY

Proper identification requires the use of two identifiers.[2] Most organizations use a minimum of the patient's name and date of birth as these identifiers. In an ideal situation, this simply requires the perioperative nurse to introduce himself or herself to the patient and ask the patient to state his or her name and date of birth. This task becomes more difficult when the patient is unable to answer the questions. This inability could be a result of young age, serious illness, or incapacitated mental status, among other medical reasons. In this situation, the perioperative nurse can identify the patient with the help of a parent, legal guardian, or legal representative[2] or by matching the patient's name, date of birth, and medical record number on the chart with the information on the patient's identification band. Regardless of the method used, proper identification of the patient must be a priority during the preoperative assessment.

> **EXAM TIP**
>
> According to the WHO's surgical safety checklist, the perioperative nurse must first properly identify the patient before beginning any care.

VERIFYING THE SCHEDULED PROCEDURE/SITE MARKING

After identification of the patient, the next step in the assessment phase is verification of several items, including the procedure; informed consent (eg, surgical, anesthesia, blood, photography); the operative site; and side or site marking. Both AORN[7] and TJC[6] actively support the nursing practice of verifying at several stages throughout the patient's care to avoid surgical harm as a result of preventable medical errors (eg, wrong-patient, wrong-side, or wrong-site surgery). To verify the procedure, the perioperative nurse asks the patient or the patient's legal representative (eg, parent or guardian of an underage, unemancipated minor, person holding power of attorney for the patient) to tell him or her what procedure is being performed on the patient that day. This information is then compared with what was booked on the surgical schedule. Verification of consent is a similar process. The perioperative nurse examines the consent and compares it with what the patient or patient's legal representative states is the procedure that will be performed on him or her that day. The nurse should verify additional required consents such as consent for anesthesia, blood product administration, photography to be performed intraoperatively, and presence of ancillary people in the OR (eg, students, residents, product representatives). If the procedure is on a particular side of the body, the patient should be asked to point to the site.[2] Typically, the surgeon marks the operative site with his or her initials using indelible ink that will not be washed off or removed during the skin-prepping stage. Alternative methods to mark the surgical site may be used as long as the method is unambiguous and the facility policy regarding site marking is consistent across the health care organization. The role of the perioperative nurse is to verify that the surgical site has been marked and matches with the information both on the consent and what the patient states (Table 1.1).

TABLE 1.1 Steps to Procedure Verification

1	Confirm the patient's identity
2	Ask the patient (or designated support person) what procedure is being performed
3	Compare the patient's (or designated support person's) stated procedure with the informed surgical consent
4	Verify the surgical site (and side if applicable) with the patient (or designated support person)
5	Verify presence of site marking as performed by the surgeon

TIME OUT

Time out is another step of the Universal Protocol and the WHO's surgical safety checklist. Time out is the actual pause in care to review correct patient, procedure, and equipment. The time out occurs at several stages during the patient's surgical experience. In the preoperative phase, the time out is performed before any invasive procedures, such as line placement or blocks. A time out is also performed when the patient arrives in the OR or procedure room, before induction of anesthesia. Including this step allows the patient to have an active involvement in his or her surgical care. Another time out may be performed after surgical prep and drape, prior to the surgical incision (see Chapter 3). During the time out, it is expected that all activity and conversation cease and all surgical team members participate.

Identifying Applicable Nursing Diagnoses

The next step in the nursing process is identification of pertinent and **approved nursing diagnoses.** To identify appropriate nursing diagnoses, the perioperative nurse must review the collected patient data. Nursing diagnoses were first used in the 1950s.[1] They have evolved into a select list as delineated by **NANDA International**.[8] Each NANDA-I nursing diagnosis is broken down into several easier-to-manage pieces:

- diagnostic indicators (ie, the information gathered to make the diagnosis);
- defining characteristics (ie, the sign and symptoms experienced by the patient);
- related factors (ie, problems that are causing the diagnosis); and
- risk factors (ie, the situations that put the patient in the place that he or she may develop the diagnosis).[7]

For the majority of the nurse's patients in the surgical suite, an "at risk" diagnosis will be used. Most of the nursing interventions performed are aimed at preventing the problem from occurring. Examples of NANDA nursing diagnoses are presented in Table 1.2. A frequent at-risk diagnosis for a surgical patient is risk for infection. Examples of interventions that a perioperative nurse may take to aid in the prevention of infection would be to remove hair from the surgical site preoperatively using a clipper rather than a razor, performing appropriate skin preparation, and maintaining sterility throughout the surgical procedure.

The **Perioperative Nursing Data Set (PNDS)** is a set of perioperative-specific nursing diagnoses, interventions, and outcomes that was developed by AORN.[9] Facilities are not required to use the PNDS framework; however, many choose to use it to help nurses individualize nursing care plans for perioperative patients. Using the data collected from the medical history and physical examination allows the preoperative nurse to develop the nursing care plan using the PNDS to select applicable nursing diagnoses. Some examples of common nursing diagnoses specifically relevant to the perioperative environment include *risk for injury, risk for imbalanced body temperature, risk for impaired skin integrity,* and *risk for pain.* After nursing diagnosis selection, the preoperative nurse can plan appropriate nursing interventions and desired outcomes.

Documentation

Accurate documentation of the preoperative assessment and selection of nursing diagnoses are essential parts of perioperative nursing care. Documentation must be complete and accomplished in a timely manner. In many organizations, a different nurse may be assigned to care for the patient preoperatively than intraoperatively, which makes accurate and timely documentation imperative for continuation of care. Documentation should always be dated, timed, and signed, as is relevant with any legal medical

TABLE 1.2 Examples of Perioperative Nursing Diagnoses[1]

- Acute pain
- Anxiety
- Deficient knowledge
- Disturbed sleep pattern
- Dressing/grooming self-care deficit
- Excess fluid volume
- Hyperthermia
- Hypothermia
- Impaired urinary elimination
- Ineffective airway clearance
- Ineffective coping
- Ineffective health management
- Ineffective peripheral tissue perfusion
- Readiness for enhanced emancipated decision-making
- Risk for aspiration
- Risk for imbalanced body temperature
- Risk for impaired skin integrity
- Risk for infection
- Spiritual distress

1. NANDA International. *Nursing Diagnoses 2015-2017: Definitions and Classification*. 10th ed. Philadelphia, PA: Wiley-Blackwell; 2015.

documentation. Although not always thought of when speaking of documentation, hand overs (hand offs) are used by facilities to ensure that accurate and consistent care of patients continues during personnel changes. Based on recommendations and guidelines from TJC, AORN, and the WHO,[10-12] hand overs during the preoperative and postoperative phases of care should be a formalized process to prevent communication breakdowns. (See Chapters 4 and 5 in this guide for more in-depth discussions of communication and hand overs.)

Key Concepts and Review: Case Study

Nurse A is on call for the OR and receives word that she is needed for an emergency laparoscopic appendectomy. The shift supervisor informs Nurse A that the patient, CB, is a 15-year-old boy arriving from the emergency department. As she waits for the patient to arrive and begins to pull the necessary supplies with the scrub person, Nurse A starts to consider the variables for this surgical procedure. Not only will Nurse A and the scrub person need to pull the supplies specific to Surgeon X's preference card, Nurse A will also need to determine whether this 15-year-old patient is of pediatric size or adult size and adjust supply selection accordingly. Nurse A considers who will be with the patient—thus who will be able to sign parental consent for the surgical procedure. Nurse A starts planning for the developmental age of a 15-year-old and the age-appropriate assessment techniques that will be best for the preoperative assessment.

CB arrives in the preoperative holding area via stretcher; Nurse A notes that there are an adult man and woman with him. Nurse A receives a brief report from the emergency department nurse who explains that CB

- arrived in the emergency department a few hours ago complaining of right lower quadrant pain that he had been experiencing for the past 18 hours,
- has been running a fever for the past 48 hours, and
- had one episode of vomiting before arriving at the emergency department.

While in the emergency department, CB

- experienced another episode of vomiting for which he received ondansetron 4 mg IV and has not experienced any further episodes since being medicated,
- complained of pain for which he received hydromorphone 1 mg IV 45 minutes before being transferred to the OR, and
- underwent a computed tomography (CT) scan that confirmed the diagnosis of acute appendicitis.

The emergency department nurse finishes her report, stating that the man and woman with CB are his parents and the signed informed surgical consent is in the chart.

STOP AND THINK. Based on the report that Nurse A just received, what are some key assessment items that you may be concerned about for CB? The patient

- has been running a fever for the past 48 hours and may be dehydrated,
- recently received narcotics for complaints of pain, and
- recently received medication for vomiting.

Nurse A approaches CB's stretcher and introduces herself to both him and his parents. Nurse A verifies CB's identity by comparing his stated name and birth date with the information on his chart and on his identification bracelet. As an extra safety measure, Nurse A also confirms his identity with his parents. Nurse A notes that CB

- is a well-nourished male patient;
- is wearing a hospital gown, but otherwise appears clean and well groomed;
- is 5'11" and weighs 220 lb (100 kg);
- is awake but appears drowsy although he rouses easily and answers questions appropriately;
- is flushed and he grimaces with any movement; and
- complains of right lower quadrant pain, rating it 5 on a pain scale of 0 to 10.

His vital signs are temporal temperature 101.4°F, pulse 104, respirations 22, blood pressure 115/76, and pulse oximetry 97% on room air.

CB makes a conscious attempt to keep himself covered with the hospital gown and blanket. He states that his only current medication is cetirizine as needed for allergies, but adds that he goes to his doctor for allergy shots every other week. Nurse A notes that CB identified an allergy to amoxicillin/clavulanate and checks CB's chart and bracelet and confirms this with CB and his mother. When asked about past surgical experience, CB's mom states that he underwent an esophagogastroduodenoscopy and colonoscopy two years ago and had his left hip pinned three years ago for a slipped growth plate. Nurse A asks CB whether he has any other known medical problems, which both he and his parents deny.

Nurse A reviews the chart and finds the surgical consent. CB's father confirms that his son is "having his appendix removed with a small camera" and Nurse A verifies that the consent reads "laparoscopic appendectomy" and is properly signed and witnessed. Nurse A reviews CB's most recent laboratory results, noting that his white blood cell count is 11,500. Because of his age, there is no requirement for a current chest x-ray or electrocardiogram.

STOP AND THINK. Based on this newly obtained information, are there any potential changes to Nurse A's current perioperative plan?
- Adult-sized, 15-year-old boy—there is no need to consider pediatric equipment.
- Allergic to amoxicillin/clavulanate—avoid this medication as a preoperative antibiotic.
- Past history of left hip pinning—assess the patient's range of motion for any positioning issues.

During the preoperative assessment, Nurse A keeps in mind that CB is a 15-year-old boy and his current stage of development is identity versus role confusion. Nurse A provides privacy for CB during the assessment. Asking his parents to step out of the room helps create an environment that allows CB to speak more openly. Maintaining a professional demeanor allows CB a sense of self-image and fosters a good relationship.

Nurse A assesses CB's general appearance visually. She notes his flushed color and while watching his physical activity, notices his symmetrical movement and continued guarding of the right lower quadrant. As she assesses him, Nurse A pays close attention to his affect, noting that he makes good eye contact, has appropriate body language, and demonstrates behavior congruent with that of a 15-year-old boy.

Through touch, Nurse A notices that CB's skin is hot and dry but his skin turgor suggests that his hydration status is still adequate. Nurse A notices that CB does not retract from her touch. His speech is clear and coherent. When Nurse A asks when he ate last, CB says it has been 24 hours since he ate anything solid and six hours since last drinking. Nurse A assesses clear lung sounds and a regular heart rhythm and verifies that the vital signs collected immediately before his transport to the preoperative holding area are consistent with those just obtained. Nurse A confirms with CB his understanding of the scheduled procedure and asks if he has any questions. Nurse A then asks when was the last time he voided, and he states it was just before coming from the emergency department and denies the need to go at this time. Assessing for the presence of body piercing is an important safety measure, so Nurse A asks CB whether he has any piercing, including any piercings that are not visible, which he denies.

Key items of the preoperative assessment of CB are
- height 5' 11" and weight 100 kg;
- drowsy, but rouses easily and is oriented to person, place, and time;

- vital signs: temporal temperature 101.4°F, pulse 104, respirations 22, blood pressure 115/76, and pulse oximetry 97%;
- right lower quadrant pain that the patient rates as 5 on a 0-to-10 scale;
- currently takes cetirizin as needed and receives biweekly allergy shots;
- past surgical history includes an esophagogastroduodenoscopy and colonoscopy and left hip pinning;
- no other medical problems;
- flushed, hot, dry skin;
- has been NPO 6 hours for liquids and 24 hours for solids;
- has no body piercings; and
- chart review reveals:
  - white blood cell count of 11,500;
  - current history and physical assessment are present and consistent with the nurse's preoperative assessment; and
  - the informed surgical consent for "laparoscopic appendectomy" is signed and witnessed.

Nurse A notes that also included on the chart is the surgeon's handwritten history and physical examination, both of which confirm her preoperative assessment results.

Nurse A asks CB's parents to come back into the room to wait with him until it is time to go to the surgical suite. Nurse A asks if either CB or his parents have any remaining questions. CB's mother asks how long the procedure will take and where they should wait. Nurse A answers based on her knowledge of the surgeon, procedure, and facility practices.

After completing the preoperative assessment, Nurse A stops to see Surgeon X and Anesthesiologist Y to review any concerns or issues. Surgeon X requests that Nurse A insert an indwelling urinary catheter before the start of the procedure. Nurse A makes a note to obtain those additional supplies. Anesthesiologist Y states that he plans to premedicate CB before leaving the holding area. With no further discussion, Nurse A leaves to finalize room preparation and develop a care plan specific to CB based on the following possible nursing diagnoses:

- acute pain,
- nausea,
- risk for imbalanced body temperature,
- risk for imbalanced fluid volume,
- ineffective breathing pattern, and
- risk for infection.

References

1. Steelman VM. Foundations for practice. In: Rothrock JC, ed. *Alexander's Care of the Patient in Surgery*. 15th ed. St Louis, MO: Elsevier; 2015:1-15.
2. Phillips N. Foundations for perioperative practice. *Berry & Kohn's Operating Room Technique*. 13th ed. St Louis, MO: Elsevier; 2017:15-35.
3. Guideline for medication safety. In: *Guidelines for Perioperative Practice*. Denver, CO: AORN, Inc; 2017:295-333.
4. Derose R. Otorhinolaryngologic surgery. In: Rothrock JC, ed. *Alexander's Care of the Patient in Surgery*. 15th ed. St Louis, MO: Elsevier; 2015:626-678.
5. Surgical safety checklist. The World Health Organization. http://apps.who.int/iris/bitstream/10665/44186/2/9789241598590_eng_Checklist.pdf.
6. Universal protocol—wrong site surgery resources. The Joint Commission. http://www.jointcommission.org/standards_information/up.aspx.
7. Correct site surgery tool kit. AORN, Inc. http://www.aorn.org/guidelines/clinical-resources/tool-kits/correct-site-surgery-tool-kit.
8. Herdman TH, Kamitsuru S, eds. NANDA International Nursing Diagnoses: Definitions and Classification 2015-2017. 10th ed. Oxford, UK: Wiley Blackwell; 2014.
9. Petersen C, ed. *Perioperative Nursing Data Set*. 3rd ed. Denver, CO: AORN, Inc; 2011.
10. Transition of care (ToC) portal. Transitions of care: the need for collaboration across entire care continuum. The Joint Commission. September 2016. https://www.jointcommission.org/toc.aspx.
11. Guideline for transfer of patient care information. In: *Guidelines for Perioperative Practice*. Denver, CO: AORN, Inc; 2017:711-716.
12. Communication during patient hand-overs. The World Health Organization. http://www.who.int/patientsafety/solutions/patientsafety/PS-Solution3.pdf?ua=1.

Practice Exam Questions

1. Which patient population is more sensitive to dosage errors?
    A. Male patients ages 25 to 40
    B. Bariatric patients
    C. A patient with a history of polypharmacy
    D. Pediatric patients

2. The National Patient Safety Goals directed at improving staff communication review the need for
    A. ensuring important test results are communicated to the right person on time.
    B. transferring patients to the correct next level of care.
    C. completing perioperative charting prior to transfer to the postanesthesia care unit.
    D. conducting a daily huddle on the unit.

3. Which of the following is a potential contraindication to the use of a pneumatic tourniquet?
    A. The patient has undergone previous joint replacement surgery.
    B. The patient is older than 80 years.
    C. The patient has sickle cell anemia.
    D. The patient's operative extremity has been shaved.

4. Which of the following is part of the surgical safety checklist?
    A. When the patient last ate food or drank fluids.
    B. Whether any special equipment, devices, or implants will be needed.
    C. Whom the surgeon should talk to after surgery.
    D. What pharmacy the patient uses.

5. A patient taking ginger preoperatively is at risk for surgical complications that include bleeding, hypotension, and
    A. hypoglycemia.
    B. bradycardia.
    C. hypokalemia.
    D. liver dysfunction.

Aspirin

6. A patient is on long-term acetyl salicylic acid therapy. Preoperatively, the patient should be counselled to discontinue taking the medication _____ prior to surgery.
   - A. 1 week
   - B. 2 weeks
   - C. 3 weeks
   - D. 4 weeks

7. A patient-specific risk factor for venous thromboembolism (VTE) is
   - A. a previous history of stroke.
   - B. the duration of surgery.
   - C. the intraoperative position.
   - D. use of a pneumatic tourniquet.

8. Actively warming surgical patients with forced air to prevent hypothermia should begin
   - A. as soon as the patient enters the OR or procedure room.
   - B. in the recovery room.
   - C. in the preoperative holding area.
   - D. just before the surgeon makes the incision.

9. Which of the following indicators demonstrates a patient who is at increased risk of developing a pressure ulcer during a surgical procedure?
   - A. Aged 50 or older
   - B. History of recent gallbladder surgery
   - C. Female patient
   - D. Poor preoperative nutritional status

10. Based on data collected during the patient assessment, the perioperative RN
    - A. identifies an outcome.
    - B. formulates a nursing diagnosis.
    - C. develops a plan of care.
    - D. performs nursing interventions.

Answers with Supported Rationales

1. Answer D is correct. Pediatric patients are at higher risk of medication errors related to dosing for body size. Patient weight should always be recorded in kilograms for medication dosage calculations. Other populations at high risk include geriatric patients and those patients with impaired body systems. Reference: Phillips N. Surgical pharmacology: avoiding pharmaceutical error. In: *Berry & Kohn's Operating Room Technique*. 13th ed. St Louis, MO: Elsevier; 2017:125.

2. Answer A is correct. Test results are critical to maintaining patient safety and must be communicated in a timely manner to the appropriate personnel. Reference: The Joint Commission. Hospital: 2018 National Patient Safety Goals. https://www.jointcommission.org/assets/1/6/2018_HAP_NPSG_goals_final.pdf.

3. Answer C is correct. Some of the potential contraindications for tourniquet use include venous thromboembolism, impaired circulation or peripheral vascular compromise, previous revascularization of the extremity, extremities with dialysis access, acidosis, hemoglobinopathy (eg, sickle cell anemia), and extremity infection. Reference: Guideline for care of patients undergoing pneumatic tourniquet-assisted procedures. In: *Guidelines for Perioperative Practice*. Denver, CO: AORN, Inc; 2017:160.

4. Answer B is correct. The comprehensive surgical checklist is part of the Universal Protocol that is supported and endorsed by both the World Health Organization and The Joint Commission. Identifying if there are any special equipment, devices, or implants needed for the surgical procedure is part of the preoperative check-in. Reference: Phillips N. Foundations of perioperative patient care standards: Universal Protocol. In: *Berry & Kohn's Operating Room Technique*. 13th ed. St Louis, MO: Elsevier; 2017:20-21.

5. Answer B is correct. Ginger is often used as an antiemetic, digestive aid, cough suppressant, and to relieve menstrual cramp. Potential complications include bradycardia, bleeding, and hypotension. Reference: Phillips N. Preoperative preparation of the patient. In: *Berry & Kohn's Operating Room Technique*. 13th ed. St Louis, MO: Elsevier; 2017:373, Table 21-1.

6. Answer B is correct. Patients taking aspirin for prophylactic purposes may be asked to discontinue its use 2 weeks preoperatively. Reference: Phillips N. The patient: the reason for your existence. In: *Berry & Kohn's Operating Room Technique*. 13th ed. St Louis, MO: Elsevier; 2017:111.

7. Answer A is correct. A patient-specific risk factor for VTE is a previous history of VTE or stroke. The duration of surgery, the intraoperative position, and the use of a pneumatic tourniquet are procedure-specific risk factors. Reference: Guideline for prevention of venous thromboembolism. In: *Guidelines for Perioperative Practice*. Denver, CO: AORN, Inc; 2018:778.

8. Answer C is correct. Research has shown that, to be most effective, forced air warming should be initiated in the preoperative holding area and continued intraoperatively. Preoperatively warming the patient with forced air warming before induction of anesthesia minimizes heat loss more effectively than use of warmed cotton blankets alone. Reference: Steelman VM. Concepts basic to perioperative nursing. In: Rothrock, JC, ed. *Alexander's Care of the Patient in Surgery*. 15th ed. Philadelphia, PA: Elsevier; 2015:10.

9. Answer D is correct. The perioperative nurse should take additional precautions to decrease the risk of developing a pressure ulcer in patients who are older than 70 years of age; who require vascular procedures or any procedure lasting longer than four hours; who are thin, small in stature, or have poor preoperative nutritional status; who are diabetic or have vascular disease; or who have a preoperative Braden score that is less than 20. Reference: Guideline for positioning the patient. In: *Guidelines for Perioperative Practice*. Denver, CO: AORN, Inc; 2017:693.

10. Answer B is correct. Based on the data collected, recorded, and interpreted during patient assessment, the perioperative RN formulates a nursing diagnosis. Outcomes and a plan of care are derived from formulated nursing diagnoses. Interventions are performed after the plan of care has been developed. Reference: Steelman VM. Concepts basic to perioperative nursing. In: Rothrock JC, ed. *Alexander's Care of the Patient in Surgery*. 15th ed. St Louis, MO: Elsevier; 2015:3-6.

2 Plan of Care

✎ KEY TERMS

- Age-specific needs
- Behavioral responses
- Cultural diversity
- Disease processes
- Environmental hazards
- Interdisciplinary collaboration
- Legal and ethical responsibilities
- Patient education
- Patient outcomes
- Patient rights
- Patient-centered model
- Perioperative safety
- Physiological responses
- Preoperative patient preparation
- Standard precautions
- Surgical Care Improvement Project (SCIP)
- Transcultural nursing care
- Transmission-based precautions

✓ REQUIRED NURSING SKILLS

- Adherence to legal and ethical guidelines
- Developing a plan of care
  - Age-specific considerations
  - Anticipated physiological and behavioral responses
  - Cultural considerations
  - Special needs
  - Standard and transmission-based precautions
- Identifying desired patient outcomes
- Identifying nursing interventions to assist in the plan of care
- Patient education

The purpose of a plan of care is to identify nursing interventions that will help the patient meet desired outcomes. A patient-centered model requires the perioperative nurse to identify these outcomes early in the patient-nurse interaction so that the nurse can address individual variations related to responses to surgery, **age-specific needs** (ie, patient characteristics based on stages of growth and development), **cultural diversity** (ie, variances in beliefs, actions, customs, and values among racial, ethnic, religious, or social groups), legal and ethical issues, and any other special patient needs when developing the plan.

This chapter provides information on the key components of a plan of care based on desired patient outcomes. The perioperative registered nurse (RN) is primarily responsible for developing, executing, and evaluating the plan of care. Ensuring safe patient care is the goal for any plan of care, regardless of patient age, operative setting, or procedure being performed.

Identifying Desired Patient Outcomes

After assessing the patient, the perioperative nurse identifies the nursing diagnoses applicable to that particular patient. The perioperative nurse, patient, and other health care providers use these diagnoses to chart a course of action toward desired goals that will aim at returning the patient to an optimal state of wellness.[1] These goals are known as **patient outcomes** and the course of action becomes the plan of care. Nurses repeatedly evaluate the patient's progress toward achieving the outcome and revise the plan of care based on events experienced during the perioperative period (Figure 2.1). To be able to evaluate whether a desired patient goal has been met, the outcome must be specific and written in measurable terms. Those outcomes directly influenced by nursing interventions are known as nursing-sensitive or nursing-specific outcomes.[2] Measuring the effects of nursing interventions on patient outcomes is one way to identify best perioperative practices.

FIGURE 2.1 The Cyclical Nature of the Plan of Care

The arrows represent the repeated adjustments that may be made to the plan of care based on events occurring as nursing interventions are implemented to move the patient toward achieving the desired patient outcomes.

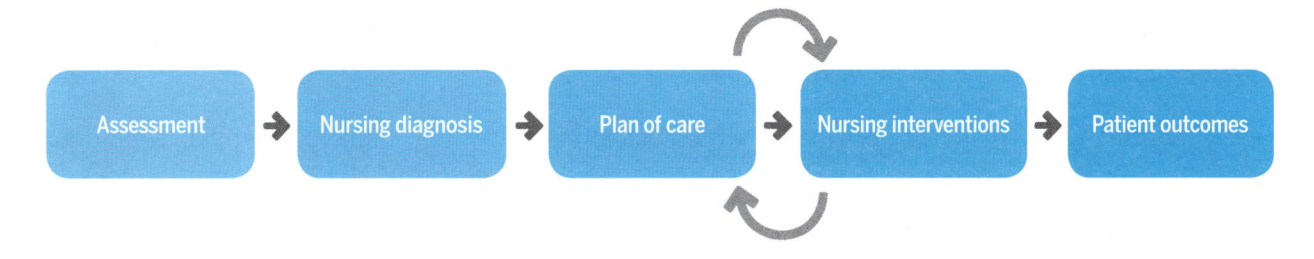

Assessment → Nursing diagnosis → Plan of care → Nursing interventions → Patient outcomes

Developing a Patient-Centered Perioperative Plan of Care

The patient is at the center of all nursing interventions; therefore, it only makes sense to include him or her in the plan of care. This active participation between the patient and the health care team is vital in meeting goals to achieve successful outcomes. AORN has designed a **patient-centered model** focused on outcomes (Figure 2.2).[3] This model moves the perioperative nurse from a role as a technician to one of serving as an integral partner with the patient and other caregivers in achieving positive outcomes during the perioperative experience. The three patient-centered quadrants—safety, physiological responses to surgery, and patient and family behavioral responses—serve as the framework for the development of a plan of care.

Every patient outcome may be influenced by the perioperative nurse's actions (eg, a lapse in monitoring aseptic technique may result in a surgical site infection). Therefore, the plan of care should be based on current best practices, professional organization standards, appropriate use of resources, and sound nursing judgment, all of which combine to reflect competent nursing practice. Every patient brings a unique set of health care needs and desired outcomes to the surgical experience. The perioperative nurse individualizes the plan of care to accommodate these variances. For example, for a patient with diabetes, the nurse understands that hyperglycemia increases the risk for infection. Not only will aseptic technique need to be strictly monitored, but the patient's blood glucose must also be checked at regular intervals and medications administered as necessary to ensure that blood glucose levels remain within normal limits.

One of the best ways to confirm completion of nursing interventions related to the plan of care is through use of a checklist (Figure 2.3). A checklist does not, however, take the place of thoughtful and thorough documentation. Regardless of the method of documentation (ie, electronic versus paper), the perioperative nurse should provide a description of nursing care delivered and the patient's response.

FIGURE 2.2 Perioperative Patient Focused Model

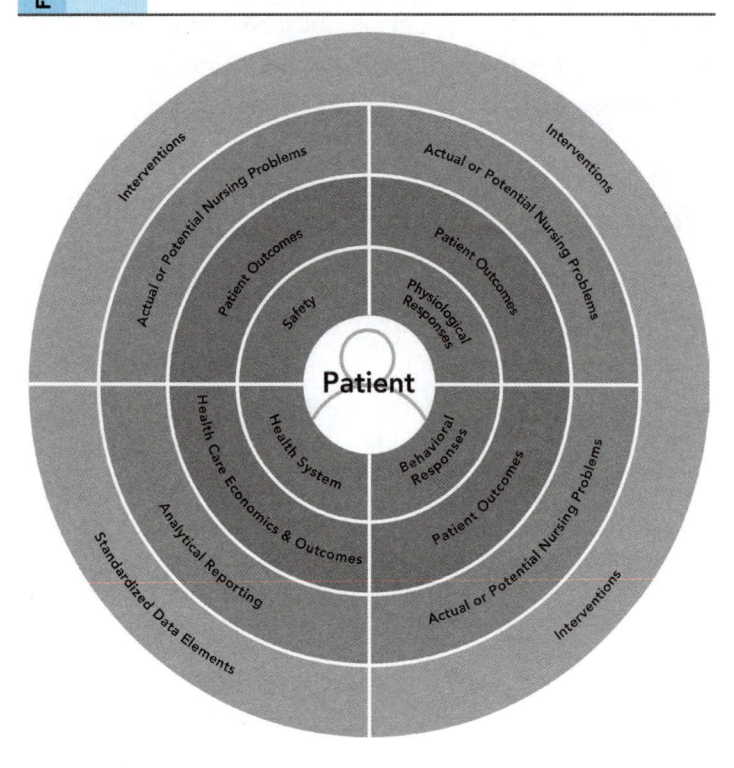

Guidelines for Perioperative Practice. Denver, CO: AORN, Inc; 2017:3. Reprinted with permission from AORN, Inc, Denver, CO.

Developing a patient-centered perioperative plan of care requires the nurse to look at the patient and the planned operative or other invasive procedure in a comprehensive and consistent manner. The nurse develops a plan of care that encompasses

- identifying the patient's anticipated physiological responses (eg, impaired thermal regulation, altered tissue perfusion),

- recognizing the patient's behavioral responses,
- determining infection prevention strategies (eg, prophylactic antibiotics, standard precautions, transmission-based precautions),
- managing patient medications (eg, prescription herbal supplements, over-the-counter medications, recreational illegal substances, analgesics), and
- ensuring perioperative safety (eg, environmental, chemical, and radiation hazards; fire risk; positioning injuries).

Throughout this process, the perioperative nurse must address any patient age-specific considerations, cultural considerations, and special needs, when applicable (as illustrated in the discussion below).

IDENTIFY ANTICIPATED PHYSIOLOGICAL RESPONSES

The human body responds to **disease processes** (eg, lung cancer) and the resultant trauma of surgery (eg, thoracotomy for lobectomy) in some predictable ways. Nursing interventions focus on anticipating and decreasing any adverse responses to the disease process and its required surgery. Any invasive procedure brings with it inherent risks, which may include impaired thermal regulation and altered tissue perfusion. These risks often influence each other and exacerbate their cumulative adverse effects.

Impaired Thermal Regulation

The temperature of the room, IV fluids and prep solutions, and exposure of the surgical site all contribute to heat loss. The perioperative nurse implements warming interventions based on patient risk factors and the type and anticipated length of surgery. For instance, the nurse employs interventions to prevent hypothermia for all patients, regardless of age, while under a general or regional block anesthetic for longer than one hour.[4] Interventions include prewarming the patient in the preoperative area; continuing this warming intraoperatively and postoperatively by applying active warming devices, monitoring the patient's temperature intraoperatively and postoperatively, and using warm fluids in all perioperative phases.[5]

Age-specific considerations. Infants, because of their increased body surface-to-weight ratio and thinner layer of subcutaneous fat, have difficulty maintaining a normal body temperature.[6] Simple physiological responses to hypothermia (ie, shivering, vasoconstriction) may tax an already compromised cardiovascular system in the elderly.[7]

> **EXAM TIP**
>
> Hypothermia increases the risk for a surgical site infection (SSI), causes discomfort, increases the risk for pressure ulcer development, and adversely affects the coagulation cascade, resulting in an increased risk for bleeding and delayed wound healing, which alters tissue perfusion and prolongs recovery time.[1]
>
> 1. Wagner VD. Patient safety chiller: unplanned perioperative hypothermia. *AORN J.* 2010;92(5):567-571.

> **EXAM TIP**
>
> In terms of temperature regulation, size does matter. The very young and the frail elderly are both at risk for hypothermia.

FIGURE 2.3 Sample Perioperative Plan of Care Checklist

PERIOPERATIVE PLAN OF CARE Page 1

Patient Name: _____

Age: _____ Proposed Procedure: _____ DNR Status: _____

Type of Anesthesia: General __ Spinal/Epidural __ Mac __ Moderate Sedation __ Regional Block __ Local __

Family History: Malignant Hyperthermia _____ Coagulopathy _____ Other _____

Temperature: _____ Blood Pressure: _____ Heart Rate: _____ Respiratory Rate: _____

Oxygen Saturation: _____ Pain Rating (Zero To 10): _____

Mobility Status: _____ Skin Integrity: _____ Cognition: _____

Transmission-Based Precautions: Contact __ Droplet __ Airborne __ N/A __

Nursing Diagnoses (at risk for): _____ _____ _____

Desired Patient Outcomes: _____ _____ _____

Current Medications (Include Over-the-Counter, Herbs, and Recreational)

NAME OF MEDICATION	REASON FOR TAKING	DOSE/FREQUENCY	LAST TAKEN

IV status: Site: _____ Needle: _____ ga Type of IV Fluid Hanging: _____

Laboratory or Diagnostic Results Outside Normal Limits: Y / N

  Communicated to Appropriate Team Members: _____ Time: _____

Allergies: _____ NPO since: _____

Mechanical Antithrombotic Devices Applied:

  Time: _____ Type: _____ Right: _____ Left: _____ Bilateral: _____ N/A

Warming Device Applied: Time: _____ Type: _____

Consent Signed: _____ Site Marked: _____ Laterality Verified: Right / Left N/A

Altered Tissue Perfusion

Adequate tissue perfusion relies on the adequacy of blood flow to a designated area of the body.[8] Therefore, any disruption in circulation or oxygenation may affect tissue viability. The perioperative plan of care includes interventions such as using supplemental oxygen, maintaining normothermia, and ensuring adequate volume replacement to support blood flow and oxygenation to potentially compromised tissue.[9]

Page 2

X-rays with Patient: Y / N / N/A

Hearing Aid/Glasses/Dentures Removed: Y / N / N/A Dispensation: _____

Loose/Chipped Teeth: Y / N Location: _____ Anesthesia Professional Notified: _____ Time: _____

Jewelry Removed: Y / N Dispensation: _____ Queried About Genital Piercings: Y / N

Preoperative Medications Administered

MEDICATION	DOSE	TIME	ADMINISTERED BY
Prophylactic Antibiotic			
Prophylactic Anticoagulant			

SPECIAL NEEDS

Instrumentation: _____ Available in Room: _____

Positioning Aids: _____ Available in Room: _____

Transfer Assistance/Aids: _____ Notified at: _____

Laser Type: _____ In Room and Checked: _____ Safety Aids in Place: _____

X-ray / Ultrasound / Pathology _____ Notified at: _____

Consult with: _____ Notified at: _____

PREOPERATIVE EDUCATION

Verbal: _____ Written: _____ Audio/Visual: _____

Family Member Present: _____ Special Needs: Interpreter _____ Literacy Level _____

Age-Specific: Y / N   Teach Back/Return Demonstration: Y / N

Comments: _____ Nurse Initials _____

POSTOPERATIVE EDUCATION

Verbal: _____ Written: _____

Caregiver Present: _____ Special Needs: Interpreter _____ Literacy Level _____

Age-Specific: Y / N   Teach Back/Return Demonstration: Y / N

Comments: _____ Nurse Initials _____

Discharge to: PACU Phase I ___ PACU Phase II ___ ICU ___ Home ___ Other ___

Age-specific considerations. Acute and chronic cardiovascular and respiratory conditions put the elderly at increased risk for altered tissue perfusion. One intervention that the RN circulator can employ is to pad bony prominences to decrease pressure and encourage adequate tissue perfusion.

Special needs. Patients with any condition that alters tissue perfusion (ie, vascular disease, diabetes mellitus, immobility, obesity) are at increased risk for impaired skin integrity. The RN circulator should

2 Plan of Care   27

identify these conditions during the preoperative interview and be prepared to implement appropriate interventions. Whenever possible, the RN circulator positions the patient before anesthesia is induced so that the patient can participate in positioning and identify problems.

> **EXAM TIP**
>
> Tissue that is not oxygenated is at increased risk for infection and delayed healing.

RECOGNIZE BEHAVIORAL RESPONSES

Anxiety and stress are two **behavioral responses** that have physiological and psychological ramifications that can influence surgical outcomes. Anxiety related to the surgical procedure is influenced by the physical, emotional, social, developmental, and cognitive status of the patient. The patient's and family's experiences with health care, including previous surgeries, can potentially influence the coping mechanisms used to respond to stressors related to the surgical experience.[10] Although it is normal to be anxious in response to a stressful situation, excessive anxiety

- triggers the fight-or-flight response (eg, increased heart rate, respiratory rate, and blood pressure);
- interferes with problem solving, which can affect judgment, concentration, and the ability to make sound decisions; and
- decreases the immune response.[10]

During the perioperative period, undertreated or unacknowledged anxiety may result in

- increased induction time for anesthesia,
- prolongation of the effects of medications,
- increased length of stay,
- increased pain with resulting increased need for analgesics, and
- increased rate of postoperative complications.[11]

The perioperative nurse should screen for a history of depression or anxiety disorders and review the patient's medications to aid in the development of an anxiety reduction plan of care that focuses on providing comfort to the patient through nonpharmacological and pharmacological means. Anxiety reduction techniques provide comfort, address the physiological signs and symptoms of the stress response, and improve patient outcomes. Nonpharmacological techniques include clear communication and distraction techniques (ie, humor, music), which are especially useful during the preoperative period and during procedures performed under local anesthesia. Humor in a culturally appropriate way has been found to decrease stress, increase pain tolerance, and increase mood.[11]

Age-specific considerations. Adolescents are more likely to undergo emergence delirium than children or adults.[10] Perioperative nurses should plan to provide extra measures to keep the patient safe during this vulnerable time. The geriatric population's normal aging processes, along with the presence of comorbidities, may inhibit the ability to react to signs and symptoms of stress (ie, elevated heart rate and blood pressure).[7] The perioperative nurse should endeavor to reduce the adverse physiological and behavioral effects of the stress response by incorporating appropriate pharmacological and comfort measures.

Family and caregiver patterns. One way to help manage a patient's anxiety is for the perioperative nurse to include family members, significant others, or the primary caregiver as part of the surgical decision-making team whenever possible.[12] A family member may be able to alert the nurse if the patient is hesitant to acknowledge his or her anxiety or to ask for assistance. The perioperative nurse should notify the appropriate medical provider if the patient prefers a preoperative anxiolytic such as a short-acting benzodiazepine instead of or in addition to nonpharmacological stress reduction techniques. In addition to serving as a patient satisfier, these interactions improve the quality of care and patient safety.

DETERMINE INFECTION PREVENTION STRATEGIES

The Surgical Care Improvement Project (SCIP) provides standardized, evidence-based interventions to improve the care received by patients undergoing operative and other invasive procedures.[13] The SCIP addresses common but avoidable complications such as SSIs. In addition to being important for safety, quality, and patient satisfaction reasons, compliance with meeting SCIP initiatives affects reimbursement by the Centers for Medicare & Medicaid Services (CMS). Hospitals are now being reimbursed based on the quality, rather than the quantity, of patient care provided. Known as value-based purchasing or pay-for-performance, this system provides perioperative nurses an opportunity to demonstrate their value on the surgical team by providing safe, quality, evidence-based patient care.[14]

Prophylactic Antibiotics

Administering prophylactic antibiotics is included in SCIP guidelines as one way to reduce the risk for acquiring an SSI. Surgical site infections are the most common and most costly health care–acquired infections. Perioperative nurses are key in implementing interventions to prevent SSIs.

The plan of care includes ensuring that the appropriate antibiotic is administered at the right time, in the correct dose, and by the recommended route.[15] The nurse must confirm any allergies to the medication before administering the medication. The nurse also should take into consideration the time frame required for antibiotic administration before using a tourniquet or any other device that interferes with circulation.

Special needs. Lengthy surgical procedures and patients with increased body mass indices may require additional or increased antibiotic dosing. Nursing interventions associated with administering prophylactic antibiotics are provided in Table 2.1.

Standard Precautions

The Centers for Disease Control and Prevention (CDC) developed standard precautions (ie, activities used in the care of all patients, regardless of known or suspected disease processes) as a frontline infection prevention strategy to be incorporated for all patients, regardless of known or suspected infectious status. Precautions to minimize the risk for transmission of infectious agents include

- washing hands frequently and correctly,
- using appropriate personal protective equipment (PPE) depending on the anticipated type of exposure,

TABLE 2.1 SCIP Initiatives: Antibiotic Prophylaxis[1,2]

ANTIBIOTIC PROPHYLAXIS	SPECIAL CONSIDERATIONS	NURSING INTERVENTIONS
Cefazolin 1 gm administered 60 minutes before the incision for patients < 79 kg.	Redose for surgeries longer than 3 hours.	• Verify two patient identifiers. • Verify allergies.
Cefazolin 2 gm administered 60 minutes before the incision for patients > 80 kg.	Redose for surgeries longer than 3 hours.	• Identify home remedies that may interact with the antibiotic.
Cefazolin 3 gm administered 60 minutes before the incision for patients > 120 kg.	Redose for surgeries longer than 3 hours.	• Administer the correct dose at the correct time via the correct route to the correct patient.
Vancomycin 15 mg/kg administered 2 hours before the incision for patients who have an allergy to penicillin or its derivatives.	Redose for surgeries longer than 8 hours; dependent on renal function.	• Evaluate the patient's response to the medication. • Document nursing interventions and patient outcomes.

SCIP, Surgical Care Improvement Project

1. Bratzler DW, Dellinger EP, Olsen KM, et al. Clinical practice guidelines for antimicrobial prophylaxis in surgery. *Am J Health-Syst Pharm.* 2013;70:602.
2. Petersen C, ed. Medication administration. In: *Perioperative Nursing Data Set*. 3rd ed. Denver, CO: AORN, Inc; 2011:208.

- implementing methods to safely handle sharps, and
- implementing procedures to clean the patient environment and equipment.

These precautions apply to contact with all blood, body fluids (with the exception of sweat), mucous membranes, and nonintact skin.[16] Blood does not have to be visible to institute standard precautions. Hand hygiene continues to be the most effective means to prevent the spread of infection. Depending on the anticipated type of exposure, use of PPE (ie, gloves, masks, eye protection, face shields, gowns) may be added. The goal of using PPE is to protect the health care worker, the environment, and the patient. The use of PPE does not take the place of handwashing, however, and nurses must pay special attention when removing PPE, especially gloves, to prevent contaminating their hands or clothes.

Transmission-Based Precautions

The CDC designed transmission-based precautions for patients with known or suspected infectious diseases and they are implemented in addition to standard precautions.[17] One method for the nurse to identify at-risk patients is by inquiring about recent foreign travel or contact with persons from countries with known outbreaks (eg, Ebola virus disease, tuberculosis). Patients who are known as or suspected of being infectious are transported in a manner that limits exposure to other patients, visitors, and facility personnel. Patients under droplet or airborne precautions must wear a mask during transport.

To choose the appropriate PPE, it is necessary to understand the route of transmission. It is important to realize that a pathogen may have multiple forms of transmission (ie, contact, airborne, and/or droplet). When in doubt on the transmission route, err on the side of caution when selecting PPE. Common pathogens and appropriate PPE are listed in Table 2.2.

Contact precautions. Contact precautions are used for pathogens that are spread through either direct or indirect patient contact. Direct transmission follows the passage of infectious organisms between two people; indirect transmission occurs after contact with contaminated surfaces (eg, OR bed, instruments, equipment). Single-use patient care items and thorough cleaning and disinfecting of nondisposable equipment will decrease the risk of indirect transmission of pathogens.[18]

Airborne precautions. Airborne precautions are instituted for pathogens that are small (ie, 5 micrometers or less) and therefore can stay suspended in the air. These pathogens are easily spread through sneezing, coughing, or talking. Place patients suspected of or diagnosed with an airborne disease in a negative-pressure room to prevent air circulation of the pathogen to other areas of the hospital.[1]

> **EXAM TIP**
>
> When to Perform Hand Hygiene[1]
> - Before and after every patient contact
> - After known or potential contact with the patient's bodily secretions or excretions
> - Before and after eating
> - After using a restroom
> - Before donning gloves and after removing gloves or other PPE
> - Anytime hands are visibly dirty or contaminated
>
> 1. Guideline for hand hygiene. In: *Guidelines for Perioperative Practice*. Denver, CO: AORN, Inc; 2017:36.

> **EXAM TIP**
>
> After a person with an airborne disease has been cared for in the OR, the OR should be closed and not cleaned until 99% of the airborne particles have been removed from the air (eg, 15 air exchanges/hour for 28 minutes).[1]
>
> 1. Guideline for prevention of transmissible infections. In: *Guidelines for Perioperative Practice*. Denver, CO: AORN, Inc; 2017:514.

Droplet precautions. Pathogens greater than 5 micrometers in size require droplet precautions.[18] Although also spread through sneezing, coughing, and talking, these larger microbes tend to settle to the ground within three feet of the patient source. Distance from the source, therefore, can be considered an additional PPE as a means of infection control.

MANAGE PATIENT MEDICATIONS

The nurse should identify any medications (eg, antihypertensives, anticoagulants, pain medications, insulin) that the patient is taking currently. Identifying comorbidities allows the nurse to gain valuable insight into conditions that may affect the plan of care and require additional nursing interventions. Patients with poorly managed hypertension or those who are on medications with anticoagulant properties may experience increased bleeding during the procedure. Patients with diabetes may require additional blood glucose monitoring to keep levels within the recommended range.

TABLE 2.2 Transmission-Based Precautions[1-4]

DISEASE	ROUTE OF TRANSMISSION	REQUIRED PERSONAL PROTECTIVE EQUIPMENT
• HIV • Hepatitis B • Hepatitis C • Staphylococcus aureus • Clostridium difficile	Contact	• Gown and gloves • Mask, and eye protection if there is risk of contact with eyes or mucous membranes
• Meningitis • Pneumonia • Mumps • Rubella • Pertussis	Droplet	• Surgical mask • Gloves, gown, and eye protection if there is risk of spray to eyes or mucous membranes
• Mycobacterium tuberculosis • Varicella • Rubeola	Airborne	• NIOSH N-95 fit-tested respirator • Gloves, gown, and eye protection if there is risk of spray to eyes or mucous membranes

1. Guideline for prevention of transmissible infections. In: *Guidelines for Perioperative Practice*. Denver, CO: AORN, Inc; 2017:507-542.
2. Benson SM, Novak DA, Ogg MJ. Proper use of surgical N95 respirators and surgical masks in the OR. *AORN J*. 2013;97(4):462.
3. Transmission-based precautions. Centers for Disease Control and Prevention. 2017. https://www.cdc.gov/infectioncontrol/basics/transmission-based-precautions.html.
4. Hart PD. Bloodborne pathogen violations: compliance is key to prevention. *AORN J*. 2011;94(5):483-484.

Herbal Supplements, Over-the-Counter Medications, and Illegal Substances

Unless specifically asked, patients may not mention that they use herbal supplements, over-the-counter medications, or illegal substances. Patients may be embarrassed or defensive about using them. Just as likely, patients may not consider these as medications or may not realize that the actions and side effects of these products may affect surgical and anesthetic outcomes. It is very important, therefore, for nurses to ask patients specifically about use of herbal supplements, over-the-counter medications, or illicit, illegal, and recreational drugs. Common herbs and their side effects are listed in Table 2.3.

Cultural and ethnic considerations. Self-care practices based on alternative therapies are more likely to include the use of herbs and homeopathic substances to treat illnesses. Many cultures, including Asian, Native American, Middle Eastern, and African ethnic groups, have their own traditional medical systems.[19] Competency in **transcultural nursing care** includes sensitivity to differences in self-care health practices in diverse patient populations. The most successful plan of care will incorporate the patient's own health promotion practices as much as possible.

Pain

Untreated or undertreated pain prolongs recovery, increases the risk for developing chronic pain, and is a huge patient dissatisfier.[20] The perioperative nurse should discuss the patient's desired pain management goals preoperatively and include them in the proposed surgical and anesthetic plans of care.

TABLE 2.3 Effects of Herbs on Surgery and Associated Nursing Implications[1]

EFFECT	HERB	NURSING IMPLICATIONS
May increase bleeding	• Feverfew • Garlic • Ginger • Gingko Biloba • Ginseng • Vitamin E	• Have hemostatic supplies on hand
May cause liver inflammation	• Echinacea • Kava	• Anticipate increased bleeding • Have hemostatic supplies on hand • Anticipate delayed induction and/or prolonged emergence
May elevate blood pressure	• Goldenseal • Licorice	• Anticipate increased bleeding • Have hemostatic supplies on hand
May prolong effects of anesthesia	• Kava • St John's Wort • Valerian	• Anticipate delayed emergence

1. Larner R. Integrative health practices: complementary and alternative therapies. In: Rothrock JC, ed. *Alexander's Care of the Patient in Surgery*. 15th ed. St Louis, MO: Elsevier; 2015:1171-1172.

Perioperative nurses provide interventions to address both the physiological and psychological effects of pain. A multimodal approach (eg, opioids, non-opioids, and regional blocks, combined with nonpharmacological and comfort measures) not only treats pain more effectively but decreases the adverse side effects related to the extensive use of opioids alone. Document and communicate the pain management plan, including the pain assessment, pain management goals, and outcomes, to the next health care provider in the transfer-of-care report to ensure seamless continuity of care.

Age-specific considerations. For infants and young children, use pain intensity and pain distress scales (eg, FACES, FLACC [Face, Legs, Activity, Cry, Consolability]) rather than the standard zero-to-10 numeric pain intensity scale.[21] The nurse should always include the primary caregiver in the pain assessment and management plan for children because typically primary caregivers are more knowledgeable than the health care provider about individual variations in the manifestation of pain by their children.

The nurse should assess the patient for chronic pain, especially the elderly who may suffer from arthritis, neuralgias, or ischemic disorders secondary to diabetes or cardiovascular disease.[7] Such normal

> **⊙ EXAM TIP**
>
> Nurses must remember that pain is always what the patient says it is, not a judgment made by the health care provider.

intraoperative activities as transfers and positioning can exacerbate any preexisting pain, even when these activities are accomplished while the patient is under general anesthesia.

Cultural considerations. The perception of painful or noxious stimuli is influenced by culture, gender, type of surgery, and responses to previous painful experiences. Nonverbal cues may be a more accurate means of assessing pain, especially in cultures that value a stoic response to pain.

ENSURE PERIOPERATIVE SAFETY

The perioperative environment brings a unique set of challenges in the provision of safe patient care. In no other area of health care is the patient so vulnerable. Virtually every piece of equipment used in the OR can cause harm to the patient, who is often unable to avoid injury because of an altered state of consciousness or mobility. By signing a consent for surgery, the patient is placing trust in the health care team to act in his or her best interests to safely provide quality care.

Environmental Hazards

In addition to providing a safe environment for the patient, the perioperative nurse expands the culture of safety to include all members of the health care team. Environmental risks and hazards to be addressed in the perioperative plan of care include chemical and radiation hazards, fire risk, and potential positioning injuries (see also Chapter 3).

Chemical Hazards

Chemical agents are used for a variety of purposes in the perioperative setting. Chemicals are used to disinfect rooms and instruments and process specimens as well as in the manufacture of medications and anesthetic agents.[22] Formalin and ethylene oxide are known carcinogens and require careful handling and disposal to prevent cumulative adverse effects for health care providers. Other substances, such as hydrogen peroxide and glutaraldehyde, can cause burns and eye damage. Employers are required to provide safety data sheets (formerly known as material safety data sheets [MSDSs]) for every chemical present in the workplace to employees who could be exposed to these substances. It is the employee's responsibility, however, to be aware of hazardous substances in the work setting and take necessary precautions to limit exposure, including appropriately using PPEs.

> **EXAM TIP**
>
> Occupational exposure limits are regulated by the Occupational Safety and Health Administration (OSHA), which also requires manufacturers to supply safety data sheets for all hazardous materials.

Radiation Hazards

Radiation safety is based on three tenets: time, distance, and shielding. The plan of care includes steps to minimize exposure to radiation and potential tissue damage for both the patient and the surgical team. The nurse begins by assessing the patient for previous radiation exposure and verifying the

> **EXAM TIP**
>
> Radiation safety is based on three tenets: time, distance, and shielding.[1]
>
> 1. Guideline for radiation safety. In: *Guidelines for Perioperative Practice.* Denver, CO: AORN, Inc; 2017:362.

correct surgery, site, and side. Managers are required to provide appropriate shielding devices to protect against potential tissue injury for both the patient and perioperative personnel based on the surgical procedure and site.[23] The nurse shares responsibility with the other surgical team members to coordinate care so that the amount of time tissue is exposed to radiation is limited.

Fire Risk

The risk of fire is inherent in any operative or invasive procedure where the three elements of the fire triangle are present: an ignition source (eg, electrosurgical unit, laser), oxygen, and fuel (eg, drapes, sponges).[24] The RN circulator should incorporate a fire risk assessment and risk reduction strategy into every patient's plan of care. Patient and surgical risk factors and prevention strategies are listed in Table 2.4.

Lasers. The type of laser used determines the appropriate safety devices to protect against unintentional hazards related to laser use.[25] For instance, the RN circulator should be prepared to

- provide protective eyewear for the patient and surgical team members,
- ensure that the anesthesia professional has fire-resistant endotracheal tubes available for procedures involving the upper respiratory tract,
- ensure that anodized instrumentation is used, and
- provide the scrub team with a smoke evacuator.

Surgical team members should follow fire prevention measures at all times and the RN circulator should control access to the OR by posting warning signs on all doors.

Positioning Injuries

Positioning the patient safely is based on the

- surgical procedure being performed,
- surgeon's preference,
- anesthesia professional's access to the patient's airway and IV lines, and
- patient's unique physiological condition.

The surgical team collaborates to position the patient to maximize respiratory excursion and to minimize bleeding secondary to venous congestion.[26]

Pressure ulcers are caused by inadequate tissue perfusion, usually over bony prominences. The RN circulator works to prevent injury by anticipating and procuring the appropriate positioning equipment, assistive devices, and aids. The surgical team is very conscientious in moving the patient carefully to prevent shearing of tissue. Using the appropriate transfer devices, positioning equipment, and padding materials is particularly helpful in preventing positioning injuries.

Age-specific considerations. Age may not be an accurate indication of the size of positioning devices needed for the procedure. Childhood obesity rates indicate that preadolescents may weigh as much as some adults, although developmentally they still function as children. The RN circulator must consider both developmental and age-related needs when developing a care plan for a patient in this age group. Patients older than 70 years of age are at increased risk for pressure ulcer development secondary to positioning. Special care should be taken when handling this patient population.

TABLE 2.4 Fire Risk and Prevention Strategies[1-3]

PATIENT AND SURGICAL RISK FACTORS	FIRE TRIANGLE COMPONENT	PREVENTION STRATEGIES
Use of electrosurgery	Ignition source	Store electrosurgical unit pencil in holster when not in use.[1]
Use of a laser	Ignition source	Place laser in standby mode when not in use.[1]
Fiber-optic light cable	Ignition source	Do not leave cable on drapes when light source is on.[2]
Head, neck, and upper chest procedures	Ignition source in close proximity to oxygen	Evaluate need for supplemental oxygen during local or moderate sedation procedures and titrate to patient needs.[2]
Drapes covering head	Concentration of oxygen	Prevent buildup of oxygen under drapes.[2]
Hair left at surgical site	Fuel	Tie or braid hair at surgical site when appropriate or use a water-soluble gel to coat hair.[2]
Flammable skin prep solutions	Fuel	Prevent pooling of prep solution and allow to dry completely.[3]

1. Guideline for safe use of energy-generating devices. In: *Guidelines for Perioperative Practice*. Denver, CO: AORN, Inc; 2017:129-155.
2. Guideline for a safe environment of care, part 1. In: *Guidelines for Perioperative Practice*. Denver, CO: AORN, Inc; 2017:243-268.
3. Guideline for preoperative patient skin antisepsis. In: *Guidelines for Perioperative Practice*. Denver, CO: AORN, Inc; 2017:51-74.

Special needs. Surgeries lasting longer than four hours may put patients at increased risk for pressure ulcer development. The RN circulator should assess the patient's alignment, tissue perfusion, and skin integrity on an ongoing basis whenever possible before, during, and after the procedure.

Preoperative Patient Preparation

The preoperative phase is a busy time for personnel and patient alike. This phase includes

- attaining IV access;
- removing jewelry; and
- preparing the surgical site, to include preoperative showering or bathing, selective hair removal, and marking the surgical site.

IV ACCESS

The preoperative nurse, the anesthesia professional, or the RN circulator may initiate IV access. Typically, analgesics, sedatives, antibiotics, anesthetic agents, and emergency medications are administered via the IV route. Placing the IV catheter in the nondominant hand, if possible, is an example of individualizing the plan of care. Regardless of when or by whom the IV catheter is placed, the RN circulator is responsible for ensuring patency of the IV line as part of the preoperative assessment before transferring the patient to the OR. Positioning the patient must take into account the anesthesia professional's need for IV access during the procedure.

REMOVAL OF JEWELRY

Jewelry, including all body piercings even if they are not contained within the surgical site, should be removed before positioning the patient to avoid the risk of pressure injuries, accidental removal, or alternative site electrosurgical burns.[26] Taping a wedding ring to a patient's finger is not an acceptable alternative to removal because taping does not eliminate the risk of an alternative site electrosurgical burn. Genital piercings should be removed for the same reason. All jewelry must be removed from the patient's operative limb to accommodate for swelling postoperatively. Tongue piercings should be removed to prevent the piercing from becoming dislodged and possibly aspirated.

> **EXAM TIP**
>
> Removing jewelry is a safety strategy to help ensure that valuables are not lost or cause injury to the patient in the OR.

SURGICAL SITE PREPARATION

Surgical site preparation is an interdisciplinary effort and is essential for the safe performance of surgery. The purpose of preoperative surgical site preparation is to reduce the risk for SSIs by removing soil and transient microorganisms while leaving the surface skin intact. The second part of surgical site preparation is to correctly identify the surgical site for the intraoperative team.

Preoperative Showering or Bathing

Patient skin antisepsis has moved beyond the preoperative and intraoperative preps performed by the RN circulator to include patient participation in showering or bathing the night before and/or the day of surgery. Showering or bathing before surgery helps reduce the number of microbes on the skin and may reduce the incidence of SSIs. The type of soap or antiseptic used and the frequency of preoperative bathing should be based on manufacturer's recommendations and surgeon preference.

Hair Removal

Hair is no longer routinely removed from the surgical site before surgery. Skin trauma from shaving increases the patient's risk for acquiring an SSI, which supports the best practice of leaving hair at the surgical site unless the hair will interfere with the procedure.[27] If hair must be removed, the preoperative nurse should use a depilatory or clip the hair immediately before the operative procedure in an area outside the OR. To assess for adverse reactions, the depilatory lotion should first be used on a small test area in a location away from the surgical site at least 24 hours before the procedure.

Cultural Considerations

Religious emblems, head coverings, and undergarments that have cultural or spiritual significance should remain with the patient, if at all possible. Gender preferences for surgical team members should be respected also, if possible.

SURGICAL SITE MARKING

As reviewed in Chapter 1, one component of the Universal Protocol used to prevent wrong-site surgery is surgical site marking. The person performing the procedure should perform the marking and if possible with assistance from the patient. An indelible marker should be used because the marking must remain visible after preoperative patient skin antisepsis and draping.[27]

Patient and Family Education

Patient education begins at the moment the patient agrees to the operative or invasive procedure and continues throughout the perioperative experience. Shortened lengths of stay in health care facilities and the increased use of outpatient surgical facilities mean that most of a patient's recovery occurs outside the health care setting. Providing instructions preoperatively has been found to decrease patient anxiety and length of stay, assist with pain management, and reduce the incidence and severity of complications.[28] Ways to enhance retention of and compliance with patient instructions are provided in the sidebar Tips for Maximizing the Patient Education Experience.

The success of the surgical procedure may depend on the education provided to the patient and family during the perioperative period. Therefore, it is imperative that patient instructions, including those necessary for informed consent, be provided in a manner that the patient can understand. This includes matching literacy level, language, and format delivery to the patient's needs and abilities. The most effective way to determine a patient's understanding of instructions is to have the patient or caregiver repeat back in his or her own words or to perform a return demonstration of the skill being taught,[29] which is referred to as the "teach-back" method of patient education.

Postoperatively, the patient is often recovering from the effects of anesthesia and the ability to remember instructions is limited. For this reason, education must be provided at the level of understanding of the person responsible for providing care after discharge. Instructions should be provided in both oral and written formats in the primary language of the patient.

CULTURAL CONSIDERATIONS

The nurse should consider the patient's culture, language preference, socioeconomic status, and religious background when developing a teaching plan. Health care providers should not use family members as interpreters between patients and health care team members. The family member may not be able to transfer the complexities of a surgical procedure into the correct medical terminology. Patient confidentiality may also be compromised if a family member is asked to interpret sensitive information.[30]

AGE-SPECIFIC CONSIDERATIONS

Perioperative nurses should address the unique needs of the patient in regard to his or her stage of development.[10] The nurse should talk with the patient about the proposed surgical procedure at the patient's developmental level.

Infants and toddlers. Infants and toddlers less than two years old have limited verbal ability and depend on others to meet their physical and emotional needs. Patient education and consent for the procedure will be directed to the primary caregiver. The principal stressor in this age group is separation from the primary caregiver.[31] Limit the amount of time the patient and caregiver are separated. If the caregiver accompanies the patient to the OR, provide basic instruction on principles of perioperative safety and a brief overview of what to expect as the infant or toddler undergoes induction.

Children. Perioperative nurses must incorporate the short attention span and limited vocabulary of children into the plan of care. Stories, videos, play activities, and a tour of the OR a day before the scheduled procedure are effective strategies to address this age group's magical thinking, fear of mutilation, and separation anxiety.[32] Limit the amount of information provided to children younger than age 7.

Adolescents. Of all the age groups, adolescents experience the most rapid cognitive growth. Adolescents are egocentric, have a need to establish their own identity and independence, are extremely reliant on peer support, and place high importance on physical appearance. These factors should be incorporated into the plan of care by providing privacy and plenty of opportunities to ask questions.[10] A safe environment should be provided when inquiring about sexual activity and drug use. Parents must still be included in patient education and are responsible for informed consent until the patient has reached legal age or is emancipated; however, the patient should be included in the decision-making process as much as possible and ideally should be allowed to give consent for the procedure if at all possible.

Adults. Education for adults should be based on what he or she needs to know, his or her readiness to learn, and what the patient already knows.[29] The nurse should supplement verbal instructions with written materials whenever possible. Patients who are highly anxious or in pain may not fully understand verbal instructions. Educational materials for this age group are widely available, but to accommodate reading and comprehension levels, nurses should ensure that the materials are written at the third to fifth grade reading level.[28]

Geriatric patients. Aging affects the ability to process information. Perioperative nurses should leave the patient's hearing and vision aids in place for as long as possible, and return them to the patient

---

Tips for Maximizing the Patient Education Experience[1]

- Arrange for a quiet, private, teaching environment as much as possible.
- Avoid medical terminology and jargon.
- Break down instructions into manageable steps.
- Arrange material in a logical sequence.
- Give reasons and benefits for activities.
- Make instruction relevant to the situation.
- Do not provide too much information at one time.
- Repeat, repeat, repeat.

1. Phillips N. Preoperative preparation of the patient. In: *Berry & Kohn's Operating Room Technique*. 13th ed. St Louis, MO: Elsevier; 2017:371.

early in the postoperative period. Nurses should speak slowly, clearly, and reduce background noise as much as possible, without appearing to be condescending. Perioperative managers should ensure that written materials are available in a large font. Nurses should include family members or other caregivers in patient education sessions as long as the patient approves, and allow them to remain with the patient as much as possible.[7]

Collaboration with Interdisciplinary Team Members

Collaboration with other health care team members provides resources and services to the patient that may extend beyond the scope of practice or expertise of the surgical team. Early notification of the need for assistance from ancillary departments (eg, radiation, ultrasound, pathology) maximizes efficient use of time in the OR, which translates into improved surgical outcomes and increased patient and staff member satisfaction.[33] In addition to providing direct patient care, **interdisciplinary team members** serve as a valuable source of education for the perioperative team.

Legal and Ethical Implications

Federal law requires health care providers to discuss patients' wishes for care at the time of admission. The Federal Patient Self Determination Act of 1990 includes **patient rights** related to informed consent, living will, power of attorney for health care, do-not-resuscitate (DNR) or allow-natural-death (AND) orders, and organ procurement (see also Chapter 1).[34]

PATIENT RIGHTS AND RESPONSIBILITIES

Every patient has the right to be informed of treatment options and to make independent decisions about the proposed plan of care, even if those decisions do not align with those of the health care provider team.[35] As the patient advocate, the perioperative nurse serves to explain unfamiliar terms and facilitate dialogue that will support positive outcomes.

Patients who present for surgery with DNR or AND orders may trigger an ethical dilemma for health care providers. The AND order is a physician-initiated directive that provides patients and families an opportunity to make proactive end-of-life decisions regarding what options are desired (eg, fluids, medications, nutrition). An AND order differs from a DNR order, which specifies the actions not to take (eg, CPR).[36] These orders do not mean that care or treatments are automatically withheld. Conversely, a DNR order should not be automatically suspended during the perianesthesia stage of care. A patient with a DNR order may seek surgical treatment to improve quality of life (eg, debulking a tumor for pain relief) but may not desire extension of life.

Perioperative nurses should document and clearly communicate instructions to refuse life-saving interventions early and often in the patient care experience.[37] Determining how to handle life-threatening events during an operative or invasive procedure requires an informed discussion among the patient, the surgeon, and the anesthesia professional. The goal of this conversation is to help the patient and surgical team find a balance between providing safe patient care and dealing with the moral and ethical consequences of respecting the patient's wishes. Advocacy involves informing patients of their rights, providing patients with the information they need to make an informed consent, and supporting patients in their decisions.[38] The perioperative nurse, as the patient's advocate, may need to initiate this discussion.

> ## Key Concepts and Review
>
> Managing the care of perioperative patients requires critical thinking, independent judgment in clinical decision-making, collaboration among all other health care team members, and adhering to an ethical code that guides practice. The patient is at the center of all care activities and should be involved in the decision-making process as an integral part of the health care team. The plan of care promotes safe patient care by involving the patient and primary caregiver in a culturally and age-appropriate manner. Perioperative nurses should employ additional resources as needed.
>
> The perioperative nurse determines applicable patient-centered outcomes related to the nursing diagnoses selected during the preoperative assessment. The nurse incorporates nursing interventions into the plan of care to address the patient's physiological and behavioral responses to surgery. Patient responses to interventions are compared with the desired outcomes to determine success in meeting the goals of the plan.
>
> Patient safety remains at the core of every nursing intervention. Employing evidence-based practices, using sound clinical judgment to drive decisions, and including the patient as an active member of the perioperative team are integral to meeting desired optimal patient outcomes.

References

1. Phillips N. Foundations of perioperative patient care standards. In: *Berry & Kohn's Operating Room Technique*. 13th ed. St Louis, MO: Elsevier; 2017:15-35.
2. Steelman VM. Concepts basic to perioperative practice. In: Rothrock JC, ed. *Alexander's Care of the Patient in Surgery*. 15th ed. St Louis, MO: Elsevier; 2015:1-15.
3. Introduction to the 2017 edition. *Guidelines for Perioperative Practice*. Denver, CO: AORN, Inc; 2017:3.
4. Guideline for prevention of unplanned hypothermia. In: *Guidelines for Perioperative Practice*. Denver, CO: AORN, Inc; 2017:567-590.
5. Wagner VD. Patient safety chiller: unplanned perioperative hypothermia. *AORN J*. 2010;92(5):567-571.
6. Mower J. Incorporating age-specific plans of care to achieve optimal perioperative outcomes. *AORN J*. 2015;102(4):370-385.
7. Bashaw M, Scott DN. Surgical risk factors in geriatric perioperative patients. *AORN J*. 2012;96(1):58-74.
8. Martin LL, Cheek DJ, Morris SE. Shock, multiple organ dysfunction syndrome, and burns in adults. In: McCance KL, Huether SE, eds. *Pathophysiology: The Biologic Basis of Disease in Adults and Children*. St Louis, MO: Elsevier; 2014:1668-1698.
9. Anderson DJ. Prevention of surgical site infection: beyond SCIP. *AORN J*. 2014;99(2):315-319.
10. Monahan JC. Using an age-specific nursing model to tailor care to the adolescent surgical patient. *AORN J*. 2014;99(6):733-749.
11. Davis-Evans C. Special needs populations: alleviating anxiety and preventing panic attacks in the surgical patient. *AORN J*. 2013;97(3):355-361.
12. Steelman V. Pursuing excellence through patient engagement. *AORN J*. 2014;100(2):119-122.
13. Fact sheet: summary of SCIP measure changes for 01/01/2014. Surgical Care Improvement Project. 2013. http://www.jointcommission.org/assets/1/6/SCIP-FactSheet_010114v4.3.pdf.

14. Finkler SA, Jones CB, Kovner, CT. The health environment. In: *Financial Management for Nurse Managers and Executives.* St Louis MO: Elsevier; 2013:9-39.
15. Wanzer L, Goeckner B, Hicks RW. Perioperative pharmacology: antibiotic administration. *AORN J.* 2011;93(3):340-351.
16. Healthcare-associated infections: IV. Standard precautions. Centers for Disease Control and Prevention. 2011. http://www.cdc.gov/HAI/settings/outpatient/basic-infection-control-prevention-plan-2011/standard-precautions.html.
17. Transmission-based precautions. Centers for Disease Control and Prevention. 2017. https://www.cdc.gov/infectioncontrol/basics/transmission-based-precautions.html.
18. Guideline for prevention of transmissible infections. In: *Guidelines for Perioperative Practice.* Denver, CO: AORN, Inc; 2017:507-539.
19. Larner R. Integrative health practices: complementary and alternative therapies. In: Rothrock JC, ed. *Alexander's Care of the Patient in Surgery.* 15th ed. St Louis, MO: Elsevier; 2015:1161-1174.
20. Hayes K, Gordon DB. Delivering quality pain management: the challenge for nurses. *AORN J.* 2015;101(3):327-337.
21. Odom-Forren J. Postoperative patient care and pain management. In: Rothrock JC, ed. *Alexander's Care of the Patient in Surgery.* 15th ed. St Louis, MO: Elsevier; 2015:270-294.
22. Patton R. Workplace issues and staff safety. In: Rothrock JC, ed. *Alexander's Care of the Patient in Surgery.* 15th ed. St Louis, MO: Elsevier; 2015:47-68.
23. Guideline for radiation safety. In: *Guidelines for Perioperative Practice.* Denver, CO: AORN, Inc; 2017:339-371.
24. Guglielmi CL, Flower J, Dagi TF, et al. Empowering providers to eliminate surgical fires. *AORN J.* 2014;100(4):412-428.
25. Guideline for safe use of energy-generating devices. In: *Guidelines for Perioperative Practice.* Denver, CO: AORN, Inc; 2017:129-155.
26. Guideline for positioning the patient. In: *Guidelines for Perioperative Practice.* Denver, CO: AORN, Inc; 2017:691-709.
27. Guideline for preoperative patient skin antisepsis. In: *Guidelines for Perioperative Practice.* Denver, CO: AORN, Inc; 2017:51-74.
28. Liebner LT. I can't read that! Improving perioperative literacy for ambulatory surgery patients. *AORN J.* 2015;101(4):416-427.
29. Phillips N. Preoperative preparation of the patient. In: *Berry & Kohn's Operating Room Technique.* 13th ed. St Louis, MO: Elsevier; 2017:364-378.
30. Weldon JM, Langan K, Miedema F, Myers J, Oakie A, Walter E. Overcoming language barriers for pediatric surgical patients and their family members. *AORN J.* 2014;99(5):616-632.
31. Harris TB, Sibley A, Rodriguez C, Brandt ML. Teaching the psychosocial aspects of pediatric surgery. *Semin Pediatr Surg.* 2013;22(3):161-166.
32. Macindo JRB, Macabuag KR, Macadangdaang CMP, et al. 3-D storybook: effects on surgical knowledge and anxiety among four- to six-year-old patients. *AORN J.* 2015;102(1):62.e1-e10.
33. Herlehy AM. Influencing safe perioperative practice through collaboration. *AORN J.* 2011;94(3):217-218.
34. Federal Patient Self Determination Act 1990. 42 U.S.C. 1395 cc (a): Section 4751. http://euthanasia.procon.org/sourcefiles/patient_selfdetermination_act.pdf.
35. Phillips N. Legal, regulatory, and ethical issues. In: *Berry & Kohn's Operating Room Technique.* 13th ed. St Louis, MO: Elsevier; 2017:36-52.
36. AORN Position Statement: perioperative care of patients with do-not-resuscitate or allow-natural-death orders. AORN, Inc; 2014. http://www.aorn.org/guidelines/clinical-resources/position-statements.
37. Zinn J. Do-not-resuscitate orders: providing safe care while honoring the patient's wishes. *AORN J.* 2012;96(1):90-94.
38. Guglielmi CL, Stratton M, Healy GB, et al. The growing role of patient engagement: relationship-based care in a changing health care system. *AORN J.* 2014;99(4):517-528.

Additional Resources

Age specific:

AORN Position statement on care of the older adult in perioperative settings. AORN, Inc; 2015. http://www.aorn.org/guidelines/clinical-resources/position-statements.

Law for older Americans: health care advanced directives. American Bar Association. https://www.americanbar.org/groups/public_education/resources/law_issues_for_consumers/directive_whatis.html.

Patient/family education:

Ask Me 3™. National Patient Safety Foundation. http://www.npsf.org/?page=askme3.

Regulatory agencies/guidelines:
- ECRI Institute: https://www.ecri.org/Pages/default.aspx
- Food and Drug Administration: http://www.fda.gov
- National Institute for Occupational Safety and Health: http://www.cdc.gov/niosh
- Occupational Safety and Health Administration: http://www.osha.gov

Safety is personal: partnering with patients and families for the safest care. National Patient Safety Foundation's Lucian Leap Institute. http://www.npsf.org/?page=safetyispersonal.

Infection control:

Boyce J, Pittet D. Guideline for Hand Hygiene in Health-Care Settings. Recommendations of the Healthcare Infection Control Practices Advisory Committee and the HICPAC/SHEA/APIC/IDSA Hand Hygiene Task Force. *MMWR Recomm Rep.* 2002;51(RR-16):1-45. http://www.cdc.gov/mmwr/PDF/rr/rr5116.pdf.

Hand hygiene in healthcare settings. Centers for Disease Control and Prevention. http://www.cdc.gov/handhygiene.

Occupational safety and health standards. Toxic and hazardous substances: bloodborne pathogens. 29 CFR §1010.1030 (2012). Occupational Safety and Health Administration. http:www.osha.gov/pls/oshaweb/owadisp.show_document?p_table=STANDARDS&p_id=10051.

Siegel J, Rhinehart E, Jackson M, Chiarello L; the Healthcare Infection Control Practices Advisory Committee. *Management of Multidrug-Resistant Organisms in Healthcare Settings.* Atlanta, GA: Centers for Disease Control and Prevention; 2006:1-74. https://www.cdc.gov/mrsa/pdf/mdroguideline2006.pdf.

Siegel J, Rhinehart J, Jackson M, Chiarello L. Health Care Infection Control Practices Advisory Committee. *Guidelines for Isolation Precautions: Preventing Transmission of Infectious Agents in Healthcare Settings.* Atlanta, GA: Centers for Disease Control and Prevention; 2007:1-218. https://www.cdc.gov/niosh/docket/archive/pdfs/NIOSH-219/0219-010107-siegel.pdf.

📖 Practice Exam Questions

1. A patient's life-threatening injuries prevent required hair removal before transfer to the OR. The best course of action for the perioperative nurse to follow is to
    A. leave the hair at the incision site and prep the patient.
    B. use a razor and 3" cloth tape to remove the hair.
    C. moisten the area to be prepped and use a disposable clipper.
    D. use a depilatory cream on the surgical site.

2. When prescribed, intermittent pneumatic compression devices should be applied and functioning
    A. after the administration of regional or general anesthesia.
    B. before the administration of regional or general anesthesia.
    C. before the patient arrives in the operating or procedure room.
    D. after the patient arrives in the operating or procedure room.

3. In planning for the transfer of an 18-pound child to the gurney after bilateral myringotomies with insertion of ear tubes, the perioperative nurse plans for which of the following patient transfer aids?
    A. A lateral transfer device, one caregiver, and the anesthesia professional
    B. A lateral transfer device, two caregivers, and the anesthesia professional
    C. A lateral transfer device, three caregivers, and the anesthesia professional
    D. A mechanical lift device, three caregivers, and the anesthesia professional

4. Lead shielding used to minimize the patient's exposure to ionizing radiation should be placed
    A. between the patient and the source of radiation, but not within the path of the beam that originates from the x-ray tube.
    B. between the patient and the source of radiation, and within the path of the beam that originates from the x-ray tube.
    C. between the patient and the image intensifier side of the fluoroscopic unit, but not within the path of the beam that originates from the x-ray tube.
    D. between the patient and the image intensifier side of the fluoroscopic unit, and within the path of the beam that originates from the x-ray tube.

5. An 18-year-old patient is hesitant to remove her acrylic tongue piercing before an exploratory laparoscopy for a possible ruptured ovarian cyst. The most appropriate verbal response for the perioperative RN to provide is
    A. "You can always get another piercing if the opening for this one closes."
    B. "If the piercing is dislodged while the breathing tube is put in, it could block your airway or be pushed into your lung."
    C. "It's our policy that all jewelry be removed prior to surgery."
    D. "Your tongue could be burned if your jewelry serves as an alternate ground for the electrocautery."

44 CNOR EXAM PREP

6. Which of the following statements reflects a female patient's accurate understanding of her scheduled total abdominal hysterectomy?
    A. "I'm having all my female parts removed."
    B. "I'm having a TAH."
    C. "I'm having my uterus removed."
    D. "I'm having my uterus removed through my vagina."

7. The plan of care for an obese patient in the supine position may include
    A. using two chest supports that extend from the clavicle to the iliac crest.
    B. placing an axillary roll under the patient's dependent thorax.
    C. elevating the patient's head 25 degrees.
    D. the use of foam heal padding.

8. Assessing the surgical patient's psychosocial state allows the perioperative RN to contribute to the plan of care by
    A. suggesting modifications to the patient's position.
    B. communicating effectively with other members of the perioperative team.
    C. ensuring the requisite supplies and equipment are readily available.
    D. providing explanation, comfort, and emotional support.

9. A patient scheduled for a bronchoscopy states he has had a persistent cough with blood-tinged sputum, night sweats, and a loss of appetite with significant weight loss over the past three months. Which action should be taken?
    A. Leave the portable HEPA filter unit "on" while the patient is intubated to supplement normal room air exchanges.
    B. Schedule the patient for the first procedure of the day, when the infection preventionist is available.
    C. Provide the patient with a NIOSH N-95 fit-tested respirator to wear during transport.
    D. Notify environmental services to delay cleaning the OR until the air exchange system has had time to remove 99% of airborne particles.

10. A 28-year-old Hispanic male is scheduled for repair of an incarcerated inguinal hernia. He does not speak English. The consent form is only available in English. The best way for the perioperative nurse to ensure informed consent for this patient is to
    A. witness the patient's signature on the consent form.
    B. arrange for a medical interpreter.
    C. allow a family member to interpret for the surgeon.
    D. arrange for a Spanish-speaking staff member to interpret for the surgeon.

Answers with Supported Rationales

1. Answer C is correct. Prevention of hair dispersal for hair removed in the OR may be accomplished by wet clipping. Reference: Guideline for preoperative patient skin antisepsis. In: *Guidelines for Perioperative Practice*. Denver, CO: AORN, Inc; 2017:56.

2. Answer B is correct. When prescribed, intermittent pneumatic compression devices should be functioning, and graduated compression stockings should be applied before the administration of regional or general anesthesia. Reference: Guideline for prevention of venous thromboembolism. In: *Guidelines for Perioperative Practice*. Denver, CO: AORN, Inc; 2018:777.

3. Answer A is correct. For patients up to 52 pounds, a lateral transfer device, one caregiver, and an anesthesia professional should be used for a supine-to-supine patient transfer. Reference: Guideline for positioning the patient. In: *Guidelines for Perioperative Practice*. Denver, CO: AORN, Inc; 2017:698.

4. Answer A is correct. Lead shielding used to minimize the patient's exposure to ionizing radiation should not be placed within the path of the beam that originates from the x-ray tube, and should not be placed between the patient and the image intensifier side of the fluoroscopic unit. Reference: Guideline for radiation safety. In: *Guidelines for Perioperative Practice*. Denver, CO: AORN, Inc; 2017:348.

5. Answer B is correct. A tongue piercing is an aspiration risk and should be removed if at all possible. Reference: Preoperative preparation of the patient. In: *Berry & Kohn's Operating Room Technique*. 13th ed. St Louis, MO: Elsevier; 2017:374.

6. Answer C is correct. A total abdominal hysterectomy involves removal of the uterus and cervix. Reference: Gynecologic and obstetric surgery. In: *Berry & Kohn's Operating Room Technique*. 13th ed. St Louis, MO: Elsevier; 2017:684.

7. Answer C is correct. Patients who are obese may have difficulty breathing in a recumbent position. Elevating the obese patient's head and neck helps establish a patent airway, ease intubation, decrease ventilator pressure, and prevent aspiration. Reference: Guideline for positioning the patient. In: *Guidelines for Perioperative Practice*. Denver, CO: AORN, Inc; 2018:723.

8. Answer D is correct. Planning requires knowledge of the patient's psychosocial state and feelings about the proposed operation so that the perioperative RN can provide explanation, comfort, and emotional support. Reference: Steelman VM. Concepts basic to perioperative nursing. In: Rothrock JC, ed. *Alexander's Care of the Patient in Surgery*. 15th ed. St Louis, MO: Elsevier; 2015:6.

9. Answer D is correct. Cleaning and disinfecting the procedural area should be delayed until 99% of airborne contaminants have been removed via the air exchange system. Reference: Guideline for prevention of transmissible infections. In: *Guidelines for Perioperative Practice*. Denver, CO: AORN, Inc; 2017:513-514.

10. Answer B is correct. The patient must be provided information related to his surgery in terms that he can understand by a medical interpreter. Reference: Clark-Cutaia MN. Hernia repair. In: Rothrock JC, ed. *Alexander's Care of the Patient in Surgery*. 15th ed. St Louis, MO: Elsevier; 2015:390.

3 Intraoperative Care

KEY TERMS

- As low as reasonably achievable (ALARA)
- Asepsis (aseptic technique)
- Blood and blood products
- Ergonomics
- Event-related sterility
- Friction
- Hand hygiene
- Hazardous materials
- Immediate-use steam sterilization (IUSS)
- Implants and explants
- Instructions for use (IFU)
- Malignant hyperthermia (MH)
- Medication management
- Nominal hazard zone
- Personal protective equipment (PPE)
- Positioning
- Sharps safety
- Shearing
- Skin antisepsis
- Smoke plume
- Sterile technique
- Surgical attire
- Surgical conscience
- Traffic patterns
- Wound classification
- Wound healing

REQUIRED NURSING SKILLS

- Adhering to the Universal Protocol
- Assisting with anesthesia management
- Confirming, presenting, and preparing implants
- Ensuring the sterility of surgical products and instrumentation
- Identifying and controlling environmental factors
- Implementing infection control interventions

continues >

47

✅ REQUIRED NURSING SKILLS, CONTINUED

- Maintaining a sterile field using aseptic technique
- Maintaining accurate patient records and documentation
- Maintaining the dignity, modesty, and privacy of the patient
- Maintaining the patient's normothermia
- Managing the patient's hemodynamic needs
- Monitoring and evaluating the effects of pharmacological and anesthetic agents
- Monitoring and maintaining patient and personnel safety
- Optimizing patient care based on behavioral and physiological responses
- Performing counts
- Preparing and labeling solutions, medications, and medication containers
- Preparing the surgical site
- Selecting procedure-specific protective materials, instruments, and supplies
- Testing and using equipment according to manufacturer's instructions for use
- Utilizing ergonomics and proper body mechanics
- Verifying specimens with surgical team
    > Preparing, labeling, and transporting specimens

Care of the patient during the intraoperative phase of the perioperative experience is one of the most complex nursing care processes. Perioperative nurses not only must be prepared to successfully and safely care for the patient, but they must also orchestrate all of the activities that occur in the OR suite. This includes meeting the needs of the surgeon, anesthesia professional, and scrubbed team members. Planning for intraoperative care takes place in stages long before the patient arrives at the facility. The perioperative nurse only has a brief time to get to know and assess the patient's needs before surgery. This short time frame contributes to the challenge of providing care intraoperatively. This chapter addresses only those responsibilities and tasks that start with greeting the patient just before the procedure and end with the procedure's completion.

Universal Protocol

The Universal Protocol for preventing wrong site, wrong procedure to include laterality, and wrong person surgery was developed by The Joint Commission (TJC).[1] This standardized process for patient safety was adopted by the World Health Organization in 2007 and has since become a key safety measure for many professional organizations that are associated with complex operative and invasive procedures.[2] Most recently, AORN has published a comprehensive surgical checklist[3] that incorporates statements from the World Health Organization and TJC and indicates, by color, when both organizations endorse the same strategy to keep patients safe. The American Society of Anesthesiologists also recognizes the importance of patient safety and endorses the sign-in portion of the checklist.[4] This allows the RN circulator and anesthesia professional the opportunity to ensure not only the right patient and procedure, but also the anesthetic approach and prophylactic antibiotic needs.

> **EXAM TIP**
>
> If all members of the surgical team are present when the patient enters the room, the sign-in and time-out processes may be performed together.

The perioperative nurse implements the preprocedure verification process of the Universal Protocol checklist with the patient and patient representative before entering the OR suite. This is a purposely repetitive process performed by multiple members of the health care team, but this redundancy helps to exclude human error or inadvertent omission by addressing all the elements of the checklist multiple times. The process is completed again at the sign-in, time out, and sign-out. Each phase encourages the entire surgical team to interact, which decreases the risk of patient injury. A comprehensive surgical checklist addresses all the activities related to the preoperative and intraoperative Universal Protocol (see also Chapter 1).

Patient and Personnel Safety

Creating a safe perioperative environment for patients and personnel is the responsibility of health care organization leaders (managers). Following established policies and procedures created to protect personnel and patients is the responsibility of the perioperative RN. Protecting the patient from injury is a team effort, with the nurse demonstrating nursing practice based on knowledge of what can potentially cause injury. Implementing interventions to prevent injury to personnel, patients, and visitors, to include hazards from chemicals, fire, smoke plume, radiation, lasers, surgical positioning, and ergonomics, is essential to the role of the perioperative RN.

CHEMICAL SAFETY

Safe handling and disposal of chemicals are guided by local, state, and federal regulations. Facility leaders are responsible for providing education and training related to the management of chemicals that personnel and patients may encounter. Chemicals that may be present in the perioperative environment include

- cleaning agents,
- formalin,
- high-level disinfectants,
- methyl methacrylate, and
- sterilants.

The Occupational Safety and Health Administration requires facility managers to ensure that safety data sheets (ie, formerly known as material safety data sheets [MSDSs]) are available to employees.[5] The safety data sheets (SDSs) contain the following information about each chemical in the workplace:

- physical properties,
- composition of ingredients and compound stability,
- toxicology information,
- specific hazard identification,
- instructions for use,
- proper handling including storage,
- required **personal protective equipment** (PPE),
- fire extinguishing details,
- recommendations for accidental spills,
- first aid for exposure, and
- proper disposal.

Nurses must adhere to the requirements defined by the facility in supporting safe handling of chemicals and need to know the location of

- PPE specific for each chemical;
- the emergency spill kit;
- respiratory protection appropriate to the chemical, to include respirators, local exhaust or hoods, or specific air exchanges; and
- emergency eyewash stations.

FIRE SAFETY

The potential for a fire in the perioperative setting is a risk to personnel, patients, and visitors. AORN has developed a Fire Safety Tool Kit available to the public with educational resources for personnel.[6] Perioperative team members must understand the elements that support the potential for fire as well as what actions and strategies can reduce the potential risk for surgical fires.

The RN circulator completes a fire risk assessment and communicates the results to the entire team before the start of each surgical procedure.

> **EXAM TIP**
>
> All three elements of the fire triangle (ie, fuel, ignition, oxidizers) are present in the perioperative setting.

The nurse then documents this assessment in the perioperative record. This assessment should include identifying

- fuel sources (eg, alcohol-based prep solutions, drapes, endotracheal tubes),
- ignition sources (eg, electrosurgical unit devices, fiber-optic light cords, lasers),
- oxidizers, and
- whether the surgical site will be above the xiphoid.

Strategies the nurse should implement and monitor to reduce the risk of a surgical fire include

- following manufacturer instructions for use (IFU) for all equipment and products;
- avoiding contact of ignition sources with combustible materials;
- preventing prep solutions from pooling on sheets, drapes, and patient hair;
- allowing skin antiseptics to dry before placing surgical drapes;
- protecting the patient's facial hair and eyes with water-soluble gel and eye lubricants during surgical procedures above the neck;
- ensuring that sterile water or normal saline is on the back table when ignition sources are used to help extinguish a fire rapidly;
- being aware of strategies to reduce airway fires; and
- implementing strategies when an airway fire occurs.

During head, face, neck, and upper chest surgery, stop supplemental oxygen at least one minute before and during use of electrocautery, electrosurgery, or laser use, if possible.[7]

Additional fire safety measures in the perioperative setting include ensuring that

- water-mist or carbon dioxide fire extinguishers are immediately available in the OR or procedure room;
- all personnel know the location of medical gas controls and know how to shut them off;
- equipment does not obstruct fire extinguishers, electrical panels, emergency egress pathways, or pull alarms;
- an 18-inch clearance from the ceiling is allowed for items on shelves to prevent obstruction of fire sprinklers; and
- evacuation routes are posted.[8]

SMOKE PLUME

Heat-generating devices such as electrosurgical units and lasers generate smoke or plume. Surgical smoke or plume is defined as the by-product of use of energy-generating devices.[9] Contaminants in **smoke plume** may include

- benzene,
- bio-aerosols,
- formaldehyde,
- hydrogen cyanide,
- living cells,
- toxic gases and vapors, and
- viruses.[9]

These contaminants can cause irritation to the eyes and upper respiratory tract. Steps to reduce exposure to these elements include use of evacuation systems with capture devices that use ultra-low particulate air (ULPA) or high-efficiency particulate air (HEPA).[9] When a central suction system is used for evacuation, use of an in-line filter between the suction canister and the wall connection should be considered.

RADIATION SAFETY

Using established safety strategies and limiting exposure to radiation used for diagnostic, interventional, and therapeutic procedures in the perioperative setting are critical for the safety of the perioperative team and the patient. Use of the principles of time, distance, and shielding supports the risk reduction strategy of **as low as reasonably achievable** (ALARA).[10] Managers are required to provide training related to the hazards of radiation and the strategies to reduce risk. Considerations related to radiation safety are outlined in Table 3.1.

> **EXAM TIP**
>
> Radiation safety is based on three tenets: time, distance, and shielding.[1]
>
> 1. Guideline for radiation safety. In: *Guidelines for Perioperative Practice*. Denver, CO: AORN, Inc; 2017:362.

LASER SAFETY

When establishing a laser safety program, facility managers must identify processes and safety measures to protect the perioperative team as well as the patient. Establishing a laser safety committee or assigning a laser safety officer who is responsible for monitoring compliance with established laser safety protocols supports best practice for laser safety. Managers should provide education and training for the perioperative team related to the safe use of lasers. Components of this education should include the following[11]:

- Only properly trained and qualified personnel should operate lasers. A dedicated laser operator should have no other responsibilities when the laser is being operated.
- The treatment area where lasers are used should be properly identified and access should be controlled.
- Patients and personnel should be protected from unintentional laser exposure (eg, use of anodized instruments, protection of exposed skin or tissue with moist sponges, proper handling of laser fibers).

TABLE 3.1 Radiation Safety Strategies[1]

PATIENT CONSIDERATIONS

- Collaborate with the surgical team to reduce the patient's exposure during procedures.
- Reduce the potential for skin injury to the patient by limiting the time fluoroscopic units are activated.
- Consider using lead shielding of body parts not intended to be included in the field.
- Shield the patient's gonads and ovaries when procedures requiring radiation are near the legs and hips.
- Shield the fetus when a pregnant patient is undergoing a procedure requiring radiation.

OCCUPATIONAL EXPOSURE CONSIDERATIONS

- Obtain applicable state and governmental regulations for occupational exposure guidance.
- Reduce exposure to the surgical team by reducing time the fluoroscopic beam is active.
- Keep patient close to the image intensifier side to reduce radiation scatter.
- Have personnel stand on the image intensifier side to reduce exposure.
- Use assistive devices rather than personnel to hold the patient to help reduce exposure to personnel.
- Use all available shielding options (eg, aprons, wraparound aprons, thyroid shields, lead eyewear where applicable).
- Ensure personnel and patients declare pregnancy or suspected pregnancy to allow for proper monitoring of mother and fetus.

PROTECTIVE DEVICES AND RADIATION MONITORING

- Test shielding devices for integrity before placing them in use and at least annually afterward.
- Handle lead aprons and thyroid shields properly, which includes hanging them vertically or storing them flat to avoid folding.
- Collaborate with radiation department personnel to test and maintain documentation related to testing of protective devices.
- Clean protective devices after use with facility-approved disinfectants.
- Ensure that the organization's radiation safety officer evaluates and determines which personnel will be monitored using dosimeters.

PROTECTION FROM EXPOSURE TO PATIENTS RECEIVING DIAGNOSTIC OR THERAPEUTIC RADIONUCLIDES

- Ensure that radiation safety officers oversee daily operations of the radiation safety program where therapeutic radionuclides are used, to include determining who is monitored as well as how occupational exposure is monitored and documented.
- Use the principle of time, distance, and shielding when caring for these patients.
- Handle patient body fluids and tissues according to government regulations and guidelines.

MANAGEMENT OF THERAPEUTIC RADIATION SOURCES

- Ensure that a radiation safety officer provides direct oversight of handling sources of radiation materials.
- Ensure that sources of sealed radiation materials, such as seeds and capsules, are handled with forceps.
- Ensure that radiation spills are managed with the assistance of a radiation safety officer.

1. Guideline for radiation safety. In: *Guidelines for Perioperative Practice*. Denver, CO: AORN, Inc; 2017:339-371.

- Approved eyewear specific to each laser used will be worn by the perioperative team in the **nominal hazard zone**, which is the space in which the level of direct, reflected, or scattered radiation used during normal laser operation exceeds the applicable maximum permissible exposure. This zone is usually defined as the space within the room where the laser procedure is performed.
- Patient's eyes will be protected from the laser beam using laser safety goggles or moistened eye pads.
- Plume generated from the laser will be removed using a smoke evacuation system.
- Considerations for basic electrical safety should be taken to prevent injury to personnel and patients. Manufacturer's instructions for use (IFU) should be followed. Liquids should not be placed on top of laser units.
- Risk of fire should be minimized by preventing pooling of surgical prep solutions and allowing surgical prep solutions to dry adequately. Drapes and sponges near where the laser is used should be kept moist. Sterile solution should be on the field to assist with extinguishing a fire.
- The patient's airway should be protected when the laser is used in the oral pharyngeal airway. A laser-resistant endotracheal tube with the balloon inflated with saline should be used. Use of a dye such as methylene blue with the saline can help with detection of a cuff puncture. The throat may be packed with moistened sponges.

Patient Positioning

Planning for **positioning** begins before the patient enters the OR suite. The RN circulator reviews the positioning preferences of the surgeon and compares these to the surgeon's history and physical examination and the nursing physical assessment. Positioning the patient is a team process involving the RN circulator, anesthesia professional, and surgeon. Patient factors that may lead to modification of typical positioning include the following:

- age (eg, pediatric, geriatric);
- weight, including assessment of tissue mass over bony prominences;
- height; and
- presence of comorbid conditions (eg, cardiovascular, respiratory, trauma, infection, limitations to range of motion, neurologic deficits).

Factors influencing positioning related to the surgical procedure may include the following:

- anticipated length of the procedure;
- availability of positioning devices;
- required surgical position;
- type of OR bed and mattress available;
- presence of a cold environment or exposure of large body surface area during procedure, which may contribute to inadvertent surgical hypothermia[12(p168)];

> **EXAM TIP**
>
> A patient weighing more than 157 pounds should be laterally transferred to the OR bed using a mechanical lifting device by three caregivers plus the anesthesia professional.[1]
>
> 1. Guideline for positioning the patient. In: *Guidelines for Perioperative Practice.* Denver, CO: AORN, Inc; 2017:698.

- moisture from pooling of prep solutions, which may lead to tissue maceration;
- potential for **shearing** (ie, sliding of skin and subcutaneous tissue over stationary muscle), which can occur in steep positions such as Trendelenburg;
- **friction** (ie, the act of rubbing one tissue over another tissue or surface), which can occur if the patient is dragged from one surface to another without using a friction-reducing transfer device (eg, using a draw sheet only with a heavy patient)[13(p706-707)];
- use of wound retractors for lengthy procedures;
- placement and location of safety straps; and
- use of compression devices.[12(p155)]

Surgical positions, potential complications, and related nursing interventions are listed in Table 3.2.

POSITIONING INJURIES

To prevent injury to personnel and the patient, the perioperative nurse assesses and plans for positioning needs based on the procedure being performed, the required position, and the individual needs of the patient. The perioperative RN uses concepts of **ergonomics** (ie, an applied science concerned with designing and arranging things people use so that the people and things interact most efficiently and safely[14]), body mechanics, ongoing assessment, and coordination with the perioperative team to reduce the patient's risk of positioning injury and to minimize the potential for complications.[13]

When positioning the patient, the perioperative nurse should

- anticipate and procure necessary equipment;
- initiate interventions to prevent development of pressure ulcers;
- optimize exposure for the surgical procedure, support patient comfort, and support optimal physiological responses related to the patient's circulatory and respiratory functions; and
- work collaboratively with the perioperative team using any necessary assistive devices to reduce injury to the patient or team members.

When securing the patient to the OR bed with a safety belt or other method, the perioperative RN should ensure that the device is applied with enough security to prevent the patient's position from changing inadvertently. The securing device should not be so tight as to restrict neurovascular function in the tissue directly in contact with it. The perioperative RN should ensure that there is a sheet or blanket between the patient's skin and the leg strap and that at least two fingers can be passed between the strap and patient.[15(p487)] The outcome of excellent surgical positioning is to place the patient in the best position for adequate surgical site exposure while

- ensuring the patient's modesty, dignity, and respect;
- maintaining optimal anatomic and physical function; and
- preventing harm to skin, muscle, and neurovasculature structures.

ERGONOMICS

The perioperative environment is known for having potential work-related injuries from patient transport and positioning, repetitive movements, and heavy lifting and holding. Transferring, lifting, and handling

TABLE 3.2 Surgical Positions and Potential Complications[1,2]

POSITION	POTENTIAL COMPLICATIONS	NURSING INTERVENTIONS
Supine with or without armboards	Pressure points › occiput › scapulae › olecranon › thoracic vertebrae › sacrum and coccyx › calcaneus	• Provide adequate padding of all bony prominences. • Ensure that hands are not touching any metal, especially if arms are tucked. • Pad adequately under the arms and elbows to prevent ulnar nerve pressure. • Consider using a pressure-reducing viscoelastic mattress, particularly if patient is obese or underweight. • Position arms on armboards no greater than 90-degree extension with the patient's palms up to prevent hyperextension and brachial nerve stretching. • Maintain head in midline position to prevent or minimize stretching of the patient's neck musculature.
Trendelenburg	• Supine pressure considerations • Potential increased intraocular and intracranial pressure • Increased blood pressure and cardiac output • Risk for tissue compromise as a result of shearing	• Monitor the needs of the anesthesia professional during long procedures. • Apply compression stockings and devices as ordered by surgeon.
Reverse Trendelenburg	• Similar to erect position • Supine pressure considerations • Venous circulation may be compromised in long procedures • Head and neck procedures may require rolled towel or pillow to produce hyperextension of the neck	• Monitor the needs of the anesthesia professional during long procedures. • Apply compression stockings and devices as ordered by the surgeon. • Use a padded footboard to help secure the patient in position.
Lithotomy • low • standard • high • exaggerated	• Risk of crushing the patient's digits • Potential for acute change in vasculature volume and cardiac exertion when positioning legs • Potential for undue strain on lumbar spine when positioning legs • Risk for hyperabduction of hips • Risk of decreased respiratory function and tidal volume in high and exaggerated positions because of increasing intra-abdominal pressure • Potential for compartment syndrome, which is more likely in high or exaggerated positions	• Prevent crushing the patient's digits in the table break. • Ensure proper alignment of lower extremities. • Raise legs simultaneously. • Lower legs slowly simultaneously. • Consult with surgeon and anesthesia professional to decrease the effect of cardiovascular and respiratory compromise in high and exaggerated positions. • Do not allow flexion of knees > 90 degrees. • Apply compression stockings and devices if surgery is anticipated to be longer than 2 hours.

POSITION	POTENTIAL COMPLICATIONS	NURSING INTERVENTIONS
Semi-Fowler/beach chair	• Neurovascular bundle strain • Slipping down on OR bed • Potential for decreased vascular return volume • Pressure points similar to supine position • Air embolism	• Maintain head in proper alignment. • Place pillow under knees to ease lumbar strain and relieve heel pressure. • Maintain nonoperative arm in anatomic position without strain on neurovascular bundle. • Be prepared to obtain special armboards and positioning to maintain nonoperative side arm for orthopedic procedure. • Use padded footboard to prevent patient from slipping down on the OR bed. • Apply compression devices per physician preference, particularly for procedures lasting longer than 30 minutes. • Prevent neck muscle strain. • Prevent undue strain on hips and knees. • Pad bony prominences. • Consider using pressure-reducing visco-elastic mattress for obese patients.
Sitting	• Same considerations as in semi-Fowler position • Intracranial pressure is reduced	• Ensure availability of a Doppler should the anesthesia professional require its use during neurological procedures. • Ensure availability of a bulb syringe for the scrub person to prevent air embolus.
Prone	• Pressure points include cheeks, eyes, ears, female breasts, male genitalia, knees and toes › Blindness may occur with prolonged pressure on the eyes • Assess range of motion of arms and cervical neck before induction of anesthesia and assess for any pain during range of motion • Respiratory volume is compromised because of limited anterolateral movement and potential limitation of diaphragmatic movements	• Assist the anesthesia professional in placement of proper pressure-reducing devices for the patient's head. • Provide positioning devices or special OR bed and padding according to surgeon preference. • Communicate any deficit in range of motion or pain before surgery to the anesthesia professional and surgeon. • Document any preprocedure deficits. • Ensure that the patient's abdomen is hanging freely between pelvis, hip, and chest supports. • Monitor for any kinking or dislodgement of endotracheal tubing when positioning patient for surgery and postoperatively.

1. Heizenroth PA. Positioning the patient for surgery. In: Rothrock JC, ed. *Alexander's Care of the Patient in Surgery*. 15th ed. St Louis, MO: Elsevier; 2015:173-184.
2. Guideline for positioning the patient. In: *Guidelines for Perioperative Practice*. Denver, CO: AORN, Inc; 2017:691-709.

patients are the most frequent precipitating triggers of back and shoulder problems in nurses. Some high-risk tasks specific to perioperative nurses include

- transferring patients on and off OR beds,
- repositioning patients in the OR bed,
- lifting and holding the patient's extremities,
- standing for long periods of time,
- holding retractors for long periods of time,
- lifting and moving equipment, and
- sustaining awkward positions.[16]

> **EXAM TIP**
>
> When placing the patient in steep Trendelenburg, ensure that the patient's knees are over the distal break in the table to allow for bending the knees to help secure the patient on the bed and protect from undue shear during the procedure.

The ergonomic tools in AORN's Safe Patient Handling Tool Kit provide perioperative nurses with a decision tree to plan and implement safe patient handling, safe lifting of patient's head and extremities, and tips for prolonged standing and retracting during procedures.[16] Employing these strategies in a particular setting requires working with an interdisciplinary team to assess, test, select, and implement mechanical devices and other strategies to limit injury as a result of incorrect ergonomic movement by perioperative team members and patients.

Procedure-Specific Protective Materials and Equipment

Based on the surgical procedure being performed, the nurse anticipates and plans for the necessary protective materials and equipment to support the safety of the patient as well as the surgical team. Requirements for the use of these items are dictated by state and national regulations. The responsibility of facility managers is to provide appropriate materials and equipment as well as initial and ongoing training to the individuals who use these items.

LEAD APRONS

Along with national and state regulations, the National Council on Radiation and Protection Measurements[17] and the US Nuclear Regulatory Commission[18] establish guidelines that facilities must incorporate into their radiation safety programs. When planning for procedures involving the use of radiographic equipment, both the patient and the surgical team need to be protected. Shielding in the form of lightweight lead aprons or wraparound skirts and vests should be available to all members of the surgical team. Additional types of shielding may include thyroid shields, gloves, and leaded safety glasses with side shields. Other types of shielding options are mobile rigid shields that can be wheeled into the necessary location. Types of shielding to protect patients come in the form of flexible gowns covering the area not being x-rayed, with particular attention to ovaries and gonads.

PERSONAL PROTECTIVE EQUIPMENT

Items selected as PPE are dependent on the activity being performed. It is the manager's responsibility to provide health care team members with appropriate PPE as well as to educate them on the proper use of the products. The following list identifies activities and the recommended type of PPE that would provide appropriate protection from exposure to blood and body fluids or potentially infectious materials.[19] Use of PPE is dictated by OSHA: "When engineering, work practice and administrative controls are not feasible or do not provide sufficient protection, employers must provide personal protective equipment (PPE) to their employees and ensure its use."[20(p4)] The required PPE may include

- gloves,
- fluid-resistant attire (eg, gowns),
- approved eye protection (eg, safety glasses, goggles, face mask),
- surgical masks approved for the perioperative setting, and
- approved N-95 masks or respirators for specific isolation needs.

The delineation of sterile versus unsterile is dictated by the activity being performed. If the activity is being performed within the established sterile field, certain items (eg, gloves, fluid-resistant attire) would need to be sterile items.

SAFETY GOGGLES

The use of safety goggles with side shields is required as part of PPE when there is a risk for exposure to splashing. This requirement includes the RN circulator when bagging sponges, when he or she is within close proximity to the sterile field, and any other risk of exposure from contaminants. As defined by the American National Standard for Safe Use of Lasers (ANSI), when lasers are used there are requirements for specific laser-approved goggles or eyewear based on the wavelength of the laser.[21] The surgical team must wear the specific goggle that is appropriate for the laser being used. Health care facility managers are required to provide the proper eye protection for surgical team members involved with those procedures.

SHARPS SAFETY

In addition to the above-mentioned PPE, strategies to reduce needle stick injuries should be employed. The AORN Sharps Safety Tool Kit provides many resources that can be implemented by facilities.[22] Following are some of the strategies to reduce the incidence of needle sticks:

- double gloving,
- no touch technique,
- use of a neutral zone,
- use of safety scalpels,
- use of a sharps/needle counter, and
- situational awareness and communication related to location of sharps.[21]

MANUFACTURER'S IFU

The perioperative nurse creates a safe environment for the patient undergoing surgical procedures that may involve the use of many types of equipment in accordance with the manufacturer's IFU. Managers are required to provide the necessary training for all surgical team members when equipment is purchased.

Collaboration between the manufacturer and the perioperative team is essential to learn the proper use and troubleshooting techniques to create a safe environment for the surgical team and patient. Education and training may include hands-on training, video-based training, and demonstration of initial competency followed by annual review. All of these steps help to reduce the potential for injury to the patient undergoing surgical procedures.

Environmental Factors

Perioperative nurses must understand the required environmental controls necessary to create a safe environment for the patient undergoing an operative or other invasive procedure. Knowing the established parameters and identifying any deviation are a critical task that helps decrease the risk of a patient developing a surgical site infection (SSI).

HUMIDITY, TEMPERATURE, AND VENTILATION

The nurse is responsible for understanding all aspects of the perioperative environment that must be monitored and controlled to decrease the risk of SSIs. This means that within the surgical environment, nurses must monitor humidity, temperature, and ventilation, including air exchanges. According to AORN, the following parameters for restricted areas in the OR are controlled by the facility's heating, ventilation, and air conditioning system (HVAC).[23]

- Ventilation:
    - Air should enter from ceiling or high vents.
    - Air should exit through vents low on the wall or near the floor.
    - Air pressure should be positive in relation to corridors and hallways.
    - A total of 20 air exchanges should occur per hour with a minimum of four exchanges coming from the outside.
- Humidity should be maintained between 20% and 60%.
- Temperature should be maintained between 68°F and 75°F (20°C and 24°C).

Doors to the OR should remain closed to maintain these ranges. In addition to the conditions that are recommended for the OR suites, other areas of the OR have specific parameters and airflow requirements.

TRAFFIC PATTERNS

Traffic patterns in the OR are designed to support movement of patients, personnel, equipment, and supplies. The areas of the OR are divided into three zones[23]:

- **Unrestricted**: In the unrestricted area there are no restrictions of dress attire; street clothes are permissible. Unrestricted areas may include locker rooms, lounge areas, and preoperative and postoperative areas with access to procedural rooms. Public access to these areas, however, may be restricted.
- **Semi-restricted**: This area contains the peripheral support areas, including storage for equipment and supplies. Hallways with access to the restricted areas and to the preoperative and postoperative areas are within this zone. Restrictions in this area include specifics related to dress attire. Personnel

in the semi-restricted area should wear surgical attire and cover all head and facial hair. This area has restricted access to those who are authorized to be in the area. This area has specific HVAC requirements.

- **Restricted:** This area includes the OR and other rooms where invasive procedures are performed. Specific attire is required, including a surgical face mask. Only authorized personnel are allowed in this area to support patient care.

To support and establish these defined areas of the perioperative environment, managers must provide proper signage, and all perioperative team members should ensure that doors are kept closed and help to monitor traffic flow.

NOISE

Noise and distractions from equipment, communication devices, and surgical equipment should be minimized in the OR. To support a healing environment for the patient, all noise should be reduced during the time of induction. Studies have shown that noise can affect the surgical team members, first and foremost, by causing communication difficulties, but noise also causes stress, increased work pressure, and fatigue.[23] Perioperative nurses should consider implementing strategies to manage noise-generating items:

- Turn off portable communication devices or set them to vibrate if needed.
- Set telephones, intercoms, and overhead paging to the lowest volume possible.
- Set music volume to a level that does not hinder communication among the surgical team.
- Set equipment alarms that have alarm volume control so that they are audible above environmental noise.

Managers should establish and enforce rules governing the use of personal hand-held devices (eg, mobile phone or tablet) in the surgical setting. These rules can be outlined in policies and procedures established at the organizational or departmental level.

Anesthesia Management

Perioperative RNs should have general knowledge of anesthesia management and the medications used by the anesthesia professional throughout the surgical procedure. The RN circulator provides support to all members of the surgical team and this role is crucial when the patient response to anesthetic medications is unexpected. The four levels of anesthesia vary according to the type of surgery being performed:

- minimal or light sedation (ie, anxiolysis),
- moderate sedation or analgesia,
- deep sedation or analgesia, and
- full anesthetic.[24]

Types of anesthesia may be characterized further by the following categories:

- local anesthesia;
- regional anesthesia, which includes

- nerve blocks and
- spinal or epidural blocks;
- managed anesthesia care (ie, MAC, MAC-IV); and
- general or balanced anesthesia.[24]

General anesthesia may be combined with any of the other types of anesthesia to limit inhalation anesthetics and provide analgesia postoperatively. The most commonly used general anesthetics are listed in Table 3.3. Other medications used to supplement general inhalation anesthetics include

- benzodiazepine reversal agent (eg, romazicon),
- benzodiazepines (eg, midazolam),
- muscle relaxant reversal agents (eg, cholinergics),
- muscle relaxants (ie, depolarizing versus non-depolarizing),
- narcotic reversal agent (eg, naloxone), and
- narcotics (eg, opioids, synthetic opioids).

The RN circulator assists the anesthesia professional with

- proper positioning of the patient,
- intubation by handing the prepared endotracheal tube or laryngeal mask airway when requested, and
- performing the Sellick maneuver (eg, cricoid pressure) as directed to prevent aspiration of stomach contents and aspiration in emergent intubation.

Cricoid pressure is performed by gently pressing the thyroid cartilage downward to close the upper esophagus, thus decreasing the possibility of regurgitated stomach contents from entering the airway during intubation.

> **EXAM TIP**
>
> The perioperative RN assists the anesthesia professional during intubation by performing the Sellick maneuver (ie, applying cricoid pressure) until the endotracheal tube balloon is inflated and the anesthesia professional instructs the nurse to release the cricoid pressure.

The RN circulator also helps provide support for the patient receiving spinal or epidural regional anesthesia. Proper positioning of the patient's spine in either the sitting or side-lying position allows the anesthesia professional to successfully access the spinal level most appropriate for the procedure.

The nurse should remain aware of all the anesthesia monitors and other cues from the anesthesia professional, since all methods of anesthesia affect the patient's cardiovascular and respiratory systems. Additionally, accurate monitoring of a patient's input and output is crucial to preventing hypervolemia or hypovolemia. If there is increased blood loss during the procedure, the RN circulator may be called on to retrieve volume expansion infusions or blood products. Scrub personnel are responsible for calculating the amount of irrigation fluid used throughout the procedure to assist with accurate blood loss volume totals. During hysterscopy and transurethral prostatectomy procedures, the RN circulator works cooperatively with the anesthesia professional to monitor intake and output to prevent fluid overload or electrolyte shifts.

TABLE 3.3 Sampling of Common Anesthetic Agents[1]

GENERIC NAME	USES	NURSING IMPLICATIONS
Nitrous oxide	• When rapid induction and recovery are desired • Short procedures when muscle relaxation is not important	• High levels of nitrous oxide can contribute to the support of a fire in the OR.
Desflurane	• Not used for induction with children • Can be used for maintenance in adults and children • When rapid elimination is desired	• Halogenated anesthetic agents are triggers for malignant hyperthermia.
Sevoflurane	• Used for adults and children • When rapid elimination is desired	• Halogenated anesthetic agents are triggers for malignant hyperthermia.
Propofol	• When rapid induction is desired • Short procedures alone • Prolonged anesthesia in combination with inhalation agents or opioids	• No known reversal agent • Not used for nurse administration of procedural sedation in most states.
Fentanyl	• High-dose narcotic anesthesia in combination with oxygen	• Reversal agent is naloxone.
Diazepam	• Premedication • Awake intubation • Induction	• Reversal agent is romazicon.
Midazolam	• Premedication • Moderate sedation • Induction in children	• Reversal agent is romazicon.

1. Phillps N. Anesthetic agents. In: *Berry & Kohn's Operating Room Technique*. 13th ed. St Louis, MO: Elsevier; 2017:426-427.

Hemodynamic Needs

From basic nursing education, the RN circulator should have an understanding of the principles of hemodynamics as they relate to **blood** circulation as well as the patient's medical history that could affect the patient undergoing a surgical procedure. With this knowledge and information gleaned from the preoperative assessment, the nurse works collaboratively with the surgical team to support the patient's hemodynamic status. Anticipation of potential blood loss as a result of the surgical procedure guides the nurse in providing necessary interventions specific to the patient's need. The surgical procedure and physician preference may determine the methods implemented to support anticipated blood loss. These measures may include autotransfusion or administration of blood products. Determining which method of blood administration to use may be dictated by the patient's religious beliefs (eg, Jehovah's Witness[25]) or emergent procedures with significant blood loss.

Intraoperatively, the RN circulator is responsible for collaborating with the anesthesia professional to monitor blood loss. This includes assisting with providing the anesthesia professional the ability to visually inspect the surgical sponges off the field or the suction devices used to collect fluids, including blood on the surgical field. If a more accurate calculation is necessary, a process to weigh the used sponges discarded from the surgical field can provide a more accurate means to determine blood loss. (See discussion of hemostasis later in this chapter.)

AUTOTRANSFUSION

Autotransfusion is the process of collecting the patient's blood intraoperatively and administering the blood back to the patient. Autotransfusion can be an acceptable method of preventing complications with bleeding in patients whose religion does not permit receiving blood transfusions if the circuit from collecting blood and returning units remains connected to the patient. The patient's own blood is captured through a suction tip and fed directly to a reservoir on a cell salvage unit. The blood is washed and reinfused back to the patient (see Chapter 7 for more discussion on blood salvaging). This process may be performed by a nurse who has been trained on the equipment or by other personnel in the perioperative setting. Proper labeling of all the units processed by a cell salvage unit is required and should include the

- patient name (ie, last name, first name),
- patient's hospital identification number,
- time of collection,
- time reinfusion started,
- time of expiration, and
- a label that specifically states "For Autologous Use Only."[26]

BLOOD PRODUCTS

Preoperative preparation includes identifying whether **blood products** are needed by confirming physician orders as well as completion of a type and screen or cross-match for such products. An important role of the nurse is to also confirm that the patient has given consent to the use of blood products. This consent may be an independent consent or part of the surgical consent obtained by the surgeon or anesthesia professional. Before the patient is anesthetized the nurse should confirm the availability of the prepared products.

> **EXAM TIP**
>
> Blood transport and storage are temperature based, not time based; therefore the RN circulator should maintain units of blood in the storage device from the blood bank until they are ready to transfuse. After a unit of blood is removed from storage, that unit of blood must be completely transfused within 4 hours.

The RN circulator will collaborate with the anesthesia professional if it is determined that blood or blood products need to be administered during the surgical procedure. Responsibilities may include

- obtaining the required products from the blood bank,
- maintaining the products while in the OR according to the American Association of Blood Banks guidelines for storage,
- confirming the correct patient and product type with the anesthesia professional,
- maintaining awareness of potential reactions to the products being administered, and
- anticipating the potential need for additional products.

The anesthesia professional may also employ methods to control bleeding (eg, induced hypothermia, hypotension).[24] (See Chapter 7 for discussion of adverse reactions to blood transfusions.)

Physiological Responses

The perioperative nurse is guided in the delivery of care to the surgical patient using the Perioperative Patient Focused Model (refer to Figure 2.2 in Chapter 2), which identifies three domains of nursing, with physiological response being the focus of this section.[27] Using this model, the nurse employs nursing diagnoses, nursing interventions, and patient outcomes when planning for patient care.

Understanding that different activities during the intraoperative phase can affect the patient's physiological responses is important so that the nurse can recognize and anticipate as the nurse works collaboratively with the surgical team. The perioperative RN has the responsibility to observe and anticipate the potential physiological responses to the anesthetic, positioning, and procedure being performed.

PATIENT'S TEMPERATURE CONTROL

The nurse's understanding of the effect of the surgical procedure being performed and the importance of maintaining normothermia for the patient is critical when planning for patient care. Prevention of hypothermia is critical for all patients with additional age-specific considerations. Unintentional hypothermia can result in discomfort to the patient but, more significantly, unintentional hypothermia can cause cardiac irregularities, bleeding issues, impaired wound healing, and delayed emergence from anesthesia. The nurse's role related to maintaining normothermia includes maintaining the room temperature at recommended levels. Additional interventions to be considered would include using patient warming devices, warm fluids for irrigation, and warmed IV fluids.

> **EXAM TIP**
>
> Your patient weighs 100 kg. During the procedure, the patient's ETCO$_2$ climbs to 51 mmHg. The anesthesia professional states that there may be an MH crisis. According to MHAUS, you know that the correct amount of dantrolene the patient requires initially is 250 mg (2.5 mg/kg x 100 kg = 250 mg). The concentration of the dantrolene that is available is 25 mg/vial; therefore, you direct the person mixing the dantrolene to prepare 10 vials.

Conversely, awareness of the development of hyperthermia is critical because this could indicate that the patient is developing **malignant hyperthermia** (MH). The Malignant Hyperthermia Association of the United States (MHAUS) provides an expansive resource for health care providers, including diagnosis, treatment, and training.[28] Malignant hyperthermia is a rare, life-threatening condition triggered by certain medications used in anesthesia (ie, inhaled anesthetics, succinylcholine). Increased temperature is a late sign of MH.

- Symptoms include hypercarbia, tachypnea, tachycardia, metabolic and respiratory acidosis, cardiac dysrhythmias, and temperature elevation.
- An early indicator can be rigidity of the jaw identified during intubation.
- Timely recognition and intervention using dantrolene sodium to treat the symptoms are critical.[29]

Dantrolene sodium is given intravenously through a large-bore IV at 2.5 mg/kg and repeated as needed until the patient responds with a decrease in end tidal carbon dioxide ($ETCO_2$), decreased muscle rigidity, and/or lowered heart rate. Large doses (> 10 mg/kg) may be required for patients with persistent contractures or rigidity.

INFECTION CONTROL

Preventing SSIs in the surgical patient is one of the primary responsibilities of perioperative nurses working collaboratively with the surgical team. Many strategies can be implemented to reduce the risk of a patient developing an SSI. These strategies are recognized by national organizations as well as national quality partnerships, which include TJC's Surgical Care Improvement Project[30] and the Centers for Medicare & Medicaid Services.[31] These agencies and initiatives include the use of hand hygiene guidelines established by the World Health Organization[32] and the Centers for Disease Control and Prevention.[33] Evidence-based practices related to management of antimicrobial prophylaxis and processes of hair removal and surgical skin preparation are examples of strategies the perioperative nurse must include when implementing interventions during surgical procedures.

TISSUE PERFUSION

Multiple factors affect the patient related to tissue perfusion. A thorough preoperative assessment by the perioperative nurse can determine underlying conditions (eg, history of cardiovascular disease, diabetes, or respiratory compromise), which can affect the patient's response to the planned surgical procedure. The perioperative nurse considers the type of surgical procedure being performed and implements appropriate interventions accordingly to help reduce the risk to the patient of poor perfusion. The perioperative nurse should consider the following interventions:

- Plan for anticipated blood loss and confirm need for blood replacement.
- Implement patient warming to support tissue perfusion.
- Implement positioning strategies to support the surgical procedure as well as tissue perfusion.
- Move the patient slowly when positioning and changing positions as required by the operative or other invasive procedure.

MEDICATION MANAGEMENT

The **management of medications** in the intraoperative setting is fraught with potential fail points that may place the surgical patient at risk. Fail points include, but are not limited to, the following problems:

- High-alert medications are available in multiple concentrations.
- Labeling of medications, both on and off the sterile field, is inconsistent.
- Look-alike, sound-alike medications are stored in close proximity to each other.
- Medication knowledge of allied health professionals in sterile attire is limited.
- Medications are prepared without pharmacist oversight.
- Medications are removed from original packaging for aseptic transfer to the sterile field.
- Methods for communicating physician orders (eg, verbal order, handwritten orders, standing surgeon preferences, electronic order transmission) are inconsistent.
- Multiple patient hand overs occur during long procedures or for breaks.
- Perioperative interventions often require rapid response.
- Workers are often fatigued and understaffed.[34]

> **EXAM TIP**
>
> The perioperative RN should implement safe medication practices by adhering to the seven rights of medication administration:
> 1. right patient,
> 2. right medication,
> 3. right time,
> 4. right dose,
> 5. right route,
> 6. right reason, and
> 7. right documentation.[1]
>
> 1. Guideline for medication safety. In: *Guidelines for Perioperative Practice*. Denver, CO: AORN, Inc; 2017:303.

TJC has retained medication safety in its 2017 National Patient Safety Goals.[35] According to NPSG.03.04.01, "Label each medication or solution as soon as it is prepared, unless it is immediately administered."[35(p3)] For example, medications in syringes, cups, and basins must be labeled, including normal saline and water. Do this in the location where medications and supplies are set up.[35]

The perioperative RN should use single-dose medications when possible to avoid cross-contamination between patients. Other safety concerns associated with the use of multiple-dose vials include

- the risk of administering too much medication,
- confusion in labeling and expiration dates with opened vials, and
- issues of proper disposal of unused pharmaceutical wastes.[34]

Agents used in the OR are not limited to only pharmaceutical agents. Dyes, adhesives, and radionuclides are also used in surgery. The perioperative RN needs to understand the mechanism of action of these agents and monitor the patient for any adverse reactions. To avoid error, the perioperative RN should double-check the medication against the order, focusing in on the name, dose, method of delivery, and expiration dates. This information should be compared with the patient's known allergies and current medication list. Errors with narcotic overdosing have occurred when fentanyl patches are not identified before initiation of anesthesia or postoperative narcotic pain management.[36] Similarly, undetected nitroglycerin patches may pose a risk perioperatively. Problematic medications identified most are

- anticoagulants,
- antibiotics, and
- steroidal compounds.[37]

The perioperative RN reviews medications before delivery to the field to avoid potential poor outcomes. Perioperative medication orders listed on preference cards are not considered standing orders and must be verified either with each patient before delivery of medications on the sterile field or by an annual review process with the professional provider (eg, surgeon) and pharmacist.[34]

The proper methods to deliver various forms of medication to the sterile field after the RN circulator verifies medication information with the scrubbed person are listed in Table 3.4. Immediately after receiving the medication from the RN circulator, the scrub person should label all medications on the field with the following information:

- medication name,
- strength or concentration,
- amount if not apparent by markings on the container (eg, syringe), and
- expiration date.

Discard any unmarked or unlabeled medication on the sterile field.

Pain Management

One of the most common concerns of patients, family, and friends is how well pain will be managed. The perioperative RN should document any existing pain by having the patient describe its location and quality and then rate the pain quantitatively. The nurse should also ask the patient if there is anything he or she does currently to decrease discomfort from existing pain. Some patients may use multiple strategies to manage their pain (eg, medication, heat, cold, distraction). Distraction strategies could include such things as listening to music and visual imagery. In addition to administering any ordered preoperative medications, the perioperative RN should allow the patient to express his or her concerns and then respond with compassion and caring responses that build toward a therapeutic and trusting relationship. Documentation of existing pain allows the postanesthesia care unit (PACU) nurse to compare the patient's postprocedural pain level to baseline and develop a more effective plan of care to manage the patient's pain.

ADMINISTRATION OF ANALGESICS

Opioid analgesic medications are used primarily during the operative and postoperative phases of care. Often, fentanyl is the medication of choice for sedation, monitored anesthesia care (MAC), and general anesthesia. Fentanyl citrate is the medication that is used most frequently for relief of pain perioperatively. Fentanyl binds with receptors at many sites in the central nervous system, increases the pain threshold, alters pain reception, and inhibits ascending pain pathways. Fentanyl administered by IV is a first-line medication of choice for treating acute pain in monitored settings because of its fast onset of pain relief.

Another common class of pain management medications used in operative and other invasive procedures is local anesthetics.[38] The most common local anesthetics are lidocaine (ie, 1%, 2%) and bupivacaine (ie, 0.25% to 2.0%). These medications may also be found in combination with concentrations of epinephrine, which is used to extend the anesthetizing effect by vasoconstriction of nearby

TABLE 3.4 Aseptic Medication Delivery Methods[1]

MEDICATION PACKAGING	DELIVERY METHOD	KEY POINTS
Solutions	• Remove the cap and deliver entire contents without splashing into a sterile receptacle on the sterile field.	• Do not splash or create an aerosol. 　› Aerosolation may cause anaphylaxis in susceptible people. • Do not recap unused solution for use later. 　› Lip of container is considered contaminated.
	• Deliver IV solutions via a bag decanter.	• Same principles above apply to unused solutions in IV bags.
Medications in vials	• Withdraw medications using a needle and syringe. • Dispense medication directly from the syringe after removing the needle. • Use a sterile transfer jet to dispense liquid medication into labeled container on sterile field.	• The needle entering the vial is considered contaminated. • Popping off the cap and removing the stopper contaminates the lip of the vial and introduces glass particles into the solution.
Glass ampule	• Use a filter needle to remove the medication. • Remove filter needle before dispensing medication into a sterile medicine cup.	• Filter needles are designed to capture small glass fragments; injecting the medication with filter needle attached may result in shards of glass being injected into patient. • Dispensing the medication with a needle may produce an aerosol and cause anaphylaxis in susceptible people.
Ointments and creams	• Use unit dose (ie, single-use) medications if possible. • If multidose tubes are used, discard half an inch of ointment or cream into the trash before dispensing onto the sterile field.	• Sterility of multidose tubes is questionable.

1. Phillips N. Surgical pharmacology. In: *Berry & Kohn's Operating Room Technique*. 13th ed. St Louis, MO: Elsevier; 2017:407-409.

venules. Local anesthetics are classified as either aminoamide or aminoester formulations. The aminoamide medications (eg, lidocaine, bupivacaine) are metabolized by the liver, have a longer duration of effect, and may accumulate after repeated doses in patients with hepatic insufficiency. The ester formulations (eg, procaine, tetracaine) are hydrolyzed rapidly by plasma cholinesterase and have short half-lives.

LOCAL ANESTHETIC SYSTEMIC TOXICITY (LAST)

When brain levels exceed a certain threshold of local anesthetic, systemic toxicity occurs. Toxic levels can be achieved with a single large subcutaneous injection, with rapid IV injection of a smaller dose, or by accumulation of repeated doses.[38] Constant monitoring of patients receiving local anesthetics helps to detect the subtle signs that may indicate that the patient is experiencing LAST. At a minimum, the perioperative RN should monitor the patient's

- pulse,
- blood pressure,
- respiratory rate,
- peripheral capillary oxygen saturation (SpO$_2$) by pulse oximetry,
- pain level,
- anxiety level, and
- level of consciousness.[38]

> **EXAM TIP**
>
> The cardiovascular and respiratory symptoms of patients with methemoglobinemia are generally unresponsive to oxygen supplementation. The pulse oximetry reading may indicate excellent saturation despite the obvious air hunger exhibited by the patient. In severe cases, blood samples may appear brown in color. Methemoglobin levels greater than 70% are life-threatening.

LAST occurs rarely, but when it does, the perioperative RN must be able to quickly identify it and inform the surgical team. This condition is treated by an infusion of 20% lipid emulsion.[38] Local anesthetic systemic toxicity is characterized by both central nervous system and cardiovascular system effects, and these can be further subdivided into three phases. The signs and symptoms of LAST by system and phase are presented in Table 3.5.

Other complications from local anesthetics include

- prolonged anesthesia;
- allergic responses (eg, bronchospasm, hives, shock); and
- methemoglobinemia after exposure to benzocaine, prilocaine, or lidocaine.

Methemoglobin results from the presence of iron in the ferric form instead of the usual ferrous form.[39] This results in a decreased availability of oxygen to the tissues. Methemoglobinemia may present with cyanosis, headache, dizziness, and tachypnea. Treatment with methylene blue should be considered in patients with

- significant symptoms,
- elevated methemoglobin levels (ie, 1.5 g/dL or 15% of total hemoglobin), or
- comorbid conditions that compromise oxygen delivery.

Behavioral Responses

Establishing a therapeutic relationship with the patient and his or her family members and understanding any concerns they have about the procedure help the perioperative nurse determine what additional information and education may be needed before transferring the patient to the OR suite. The interview also allows the perioperative nurse to assess whether or not additional safety equipment or instruments are

TABLE 3.5 Signs and Symptoms of Local Anesthetic Systemic Toxicity (LAST)[1]

CARDIOVASCULAR SYSTEM	CENTRAL NERVOUS SYSTEM
Initial Phase	**Initial Phase**
• Hypertension • Tachycardia	• An abnormal (eg, metallic) taste • Confusion • Dizziness • Drowsiness • Light-headedness • Numbness and tingling of the lips and tongue • Tinnitus
Intermediate Phase	**Excitation Phase**
• Decreased cardiac output • Mild to moderate hypertension • Myocardial depression	• Tonic-clonic convulsions may occur
Terminal Phase	**Depression Phase**
• Hypotension • Conduction defects • Peripheral vasodilation • Sinus bradycardia • Ventricular dysrhythmias, followed by cardiovascular collapse and death	• Unconsciousness • Central nervous system depression • Respiratory arrest

1. Guideline for care of the patient receiving local anesthesia. In: *Guidelines for Perioperative Practice*. Denver, CO: AORN, Inc; 2017:622-625.

needed to ensure patient safety. For instance, assessing the patient's physique and presence of any physical limitations allows the perioperative nurse to determine whether additional positioning or padding devices will be necessary to keep the patient safe. Assessing the patient's emotional status during the interview will inform the nurse on specific comfort measures to decrease anxiety that can be individualized to each patient. Most patients are reassured to know that their nurse will be dedicated to their care alone and will be at their side for induction of anesthesia. The presence of the perioperative nurse during the entire procedure is also a comfort for family members or significant others. Communicating to family members and friends during the procedure, with the patient's permission, may also decrease the anxiety that family members may experience.

COMFORT

The perioperative nurse should implement the following comfort measures and nonpharmacological methods to reduce anxiety on the patient's behalf:

- Introduce the patient to team members upon arrival in the OR suite.
- Provide for patient privacy by

- keeping the patient covered, unless access to the patient is needed (eg, performing venipuncture; applying blood pressure cuff, pulse oximetry probe, electrocardiogram leads; performing a nerve block or regional anesthesia);
- closing window shades, especially for surgery exposing sensitive areas;
- restricting access to the OR suite to only those personnel actively caring for the patient; and
- providing auditory privacy for patient and personnel to converse about the patient and his or her surgery.[40]

- Offer comfort and reassurance by
  - providing warm blankets,
  - staying at the bedside from induction to final positioning,
  - administering any anxiolytic medication according to physician order,
  - distracting the patient with conversation that focuses on the patient, and
  - explaining what processes the patient can expect as he or she comes out of anesthesia.
- Encourage the use of complementary care interventions such as
  - music therapy,
  - aromatherapy and essential oils,
  - hypnosis by a trained individual or self-hypnosis,
  - Reiki therapy,
  - guided imagery, and
  - relaxation tapes.[40]

ANXIETY

Anxiolytic medications belong to a benzodiazepine class of medications.[41] Of this class, there is only one medication that is routinely used as a preoperative anxiolytic, midazolam. It is used for induction of general anesthesia, preoperative sedation, moderate sedation, and to supplement nitrous oxide and oxygen for short surgical procedures.

Midazolam has a dose-dependent effect. Its onset of action occurs within one to three minutes when given intravenously. The perioperative RN should titrate the dose carefully and be mindful that the elderly may achieve anxiolytic effects of the medication with only half of the ordered dose. Midazolam also has an amnesic effect on most patients; this property contributes to an overall increase in satisfaction with operative procedures because often the patient cannot recall some of the perceived unpleasant activities associated with operative procedures.

In pediatric populations, midazolam may be given orally in a syrup formulation. Dosing in children is more difficult because the child may develop respiratory depression and arrest. Dosing of children should be in a controlled area that is equipped with pediatric emergency respiratory and cardiac support and an anesthesia professional readily available.

Cultural, Spiritual, or Ethical Patient Beliefs

Perioperative nurses should assess and accommodate the patient's cultural and spiritual beliefs as much as feasible during the intraoperative phase of care. Some of the most common cultural and spiritual beliefs held by groups living in the United States that may need to be addressed by the perioperative RN are presented in Table 3.6.[42] For instance, patients of Jewish and Muslim faiths require that amputated body parts be retained in the laboratory and returned to the patient or family members for burial in the patient's future gravesite. Similarly, Hmong believe that placentas should be buried at home so that, after death, the spirit may return. Some Vietnamese patients may be fearful of operative or other invasive procedures involving blood loss, and they may refuse to have blood drawn or body parts removed because they believe this may affect the ability to replace tissue that is needed in the afterlife.[42]

Cultural preferences can affect management of autologous and allograft tissue. People from some cultures (eg, Jehovah's Witnesses) may refuse to be exposed to blood or blood products from a donor (ie, allograft). These patients may refuse to have their own blood that is salvaged reinfused, unless it is in constant connection with them during collection and reinfusion. They believe, "Both the Old and New Testaments clearly command us to abstain from blood. . . . So we avoid taking blood not only in obedience to God but also out of respect for him as the Giver of life."[43] Interestingly, techniques for avoiding blood transfusions that were developed specifically for this group may have led to the increase of "bloodless surgery" that is now more common. Jehovah's Witnesses will accept colloid or crystalloid replacement fluids and infusion of hetastarch as volume expanders. Techniques of hypotensive anesthesia and hypothermia may also curtail blood loss during surgery.[44] Communication of a patient's cultural and spiritual beliefs should be incorporated in the surgical safety checklist to ensure that all team members are aware of and adapt to these special considerations.

AORN's Perioperative Explications for the American Nurses Association (ANA) *Code of Ethics for Nurses with Interpretive Statements*[45] provides perioperative nurses with guidance on how to address ethical concerns that arise when providing perioperative care. Nurses must be able to identify their own ethical dilemmas, as well as their patients' concerns, to adequately advocate for both sides of an ethical situation. The explications are intended to to help perioperative nurses relate the Code to their own areas

> **Ethical Case Question**
>
> MJ is a 53-year-old woman with advanced breast cancer. She has undergone several surgeries because of the spread of her cancer. She is comatose. She is experiencing difficulty breathing and the pulmonologist wants to schedule her for a bronchoscopy in the OR with anesthesia. The patient's husband gives consent. The perioperative RN is feeling uncomfortable with the scheduled procedure. Which of the following is the most appropriate response for the perioperative RN to take?
> - Call in another RN to scrub or circulate the procedure.
> - Tell the pulmonologist and refuse to do the procedure.
> - Call her immediate supervisor and ask for an ethics consult.
> - Tell the husband that his wife is not going to benefit from the procedure.
>
> The most appropriate response from the perioperative RN is to call her immediate supervisor and ask for an ethics consult. The patient's disease history and current status indicate that the surgery would not be beneficial and would possibly create more pain and suffering. The perioperative RN would effectively act as a patient advocate by consulting experts in ethics to evaluate the situation.

TABLE 3.6 Cultural and Spiritual Beliefs by Select Populations in the United States[1]

POPULATION	BELIEFS	PRACTICES AND NURSING IMPLICATIONS
Amish	Conservative Christian group	- Modern Western medical interventions directly conflict with beliefs. - Folk medical practices are more prevalent.

Chinese American	Includes Taoism, Buddhism, Islam, and Christianity	- Excessive eye contact is considered rude.
		- May nod or shake head to indicate yes or no responses.
		- Family oriented: patient may put family before personal concerns.
		  › Incorporate family members into plan of care.
		- Language barriers may exist.
		  › Provide interpreter services and written information in primary or preferred language.
		- May incorporate herbal treatments and over-the-counter medications with prescribed medications.
		  › Ask patient if he or she uses any herbal or over-the-counter preparations and provide appropriate precautionary education.
		  › Inform anesthesia professional and surgeon if patient uses herbal preparations that may affect care.
		- Believe in yin and yang: may incorporate traditional practices such as acupuncture and herbal treatments to restore balance; may eat certain foods to restore balance.
		  › Provide education on potential interactions with medications.

East Indian	Hindu	- Father is regarded as head of family and is the primary spokesperson.
		- Men may view eye contact by women as offensive.
		  › Female health care providers should try to avoid eye contact with male patients and family members.
		- Women avoid eye contact as a sign of respect.
		- Wife will not participate in health care teaching.
		  › Information should be directed to the husband.
		- Certain animals are viewed as sacred.
		  › May refuse bovine or porcine implants.

Haitian American	Includes Voodoo, Christianity	- May view illness as a hex or curse. - May rely on readers who predict future through card or palm readings and provide cures through the voodoo spirit. › Provide a safe environment to accommodate spiritual ministry.

3.6 Cultural and Spiritual Beliefs by Select Populations in the United States[1]

POPULATION	BELIEFS	PRACTICES AND NURSING IMPLICATIONS
Japanese American	Combination of Zen Buddhism, Confucianism, and Shintoism	- Tend to adopt religion predominant in culture. - Family plays significant role. - May provide bedside vigils for the patient. - Men may expect their wives or daughters to serve in the caretaker role in order to not bother the nurse. - Confidentiality and respect are highly important. › Patient information should not be shared with extended family members, even those close to the patient.

Jehovah's Witness	A restorationist Christian denomination with nontrinitarian beliefs distinct from mainstream Christianity	- Believe that personal experience and commitment are more important than the family.
		- Opposed to homologous blood transfusion but may agree to certain types of autologous transfusions.
		- May allow blood expanders.
		- Patients may refuse surgical and medical interventions for self and family members.
		- In the United States, consensus is that an adult patient has the right to refuse treatment, but treatment cannot be withheld from a minor.
		  › Careful review of surgical consent must be performed.
		  › If blood loss is expected in procedure, document what measures will be accepted.
		  › Inform surgical team of patient's wishes.

Jewish American	Includes Judaism, Orthodox Judaism	- Family involvement is very important.
		- Generally, seeks multiple medical opinions before deciding on treatment.
		  › Provide education to the satisfaction of the patient.
		  › May need extensive explanations.
		- May require a kosher diet.
		  › If patient maintains a kosher diet, do not administer or implant any tissues or medications that are of porcine derivative.
		- May require any tissue, organs, or limbs to be buried after laboratory examination is complete.
		  › If patient requests any tissue returned, work with surgeon and laboratory personnel to facilitate retrieval of specimens for burial by patient or family members.
		- Consider excess touching, particularly from members of the opposite sex, offensive, especially with Orthodox Jews.
		  › Use touch sparingly.

TABLE 3.6 Cultural and Spiritual Beliefs by Select Populations in the United States[1] CONTINUED

POPULATION	BELIEFS	PRACTICES AND NURSING IMPLICATIONS

Latter-day Saint	Mormon	• Believe obedience to the health laws enhances physical, mental, and spiritual well-being.
		• God mandates striving to achieve and maintain optimum health.
		• May request two priests to bless patient by laying on of hands and anointing with consecrated olive oil preoperatively.
		• Receiving or donating blood is individual choice.
		  › Careful review of surgical consent must be performed.
		  › If blood loss is expected in procedure, document what measures will be accepted.
		  › Inform surgical team of patient's wishes.
		• Organ donation and transplantation are individual decisions.
		• May reject pain medications.
		  › Supplement pain management plan with alternative interventions, if needed.

Mexican American	Predominantly Roman Catholic	• Spiritual healing and prayer are very common.
		• May have a Mexican folk healer visit (ie, Curandero) who relieves people of their sins, thereby allowing healing.
		• Eye behavior is important; for instance, admiring a child without touching the child is interpreted as giving the child the evil eye.
		  › Be aware of eye contact when assessing a child.
		• Patients may wear amulets to protect against evil spirits.
		  › Incorporate spiritual practices into plan of care.
		  › Ensure any amulet or rosary beads that remain with the patient are secured and away from the surgical site and will not interfere with proper positioning.

POPULATION	BELIEFS	PRACTICES AND NURSING IMPLICATIONS

Muslim	Islam	• Quran prohibits eating pork, the meat of dead animals, blood, and intoxicants.
		  › May refuse porcine or bovine implants.
		  › Do not administer or implant any tissues or medications that are of porcine derivative if patient maintains a halal diet.
		  › Clarify consent with patient for blood or blood component administration.
		• May require any tissue, organs, or limbs to be buried after laboratory examination is complete.
		  › If patient requests any tissue returned, work with surgeon and laboratory personnel to facilitate retrieval of specimens for burial by patient or family members.
		• Must fast for one month/year (ie, Ramadan).
		• Autopsy is not permitted.
		• Uses prayer and patience to deal with illness.
		• Considers illness an atonement for sins
		• Considers death part of the journey toward Allah.
		• May request clergy (ie, imam) to visit.
		• Will not always consent to autopsy or organ donation.
		• Modesty is paramount.
		  › Plan for modesty concerns.
		  › Provide limited exposure of body.
		  › Provide same-sex health care team if requested.
		  › Allow women to keep head covering if it will not interfere with procedure; may need to provide alternative to traditional head covering using surgical bouffant.
		  › If patient is married female, may need to incorporate husband in all aspects of care before transport to the OR.

Vietnamese American	Combination of three religions: Buddhism, Confucianism, and Taoism	• Avoidance of eye contact is a sign of respect. • The head is considered sacred; it is not polite to pat the head. • An upturned palm is offensive in communication. • Priest or monk may be present preoperatively; in a hospital situation, this visit may be misinterpreted or perceived that the patient may be facing a grave situation. • Include family in the plan of care. • If death is imminent, the parents or head of family are informed first.

1. Quinn DMD. How religion, language and ethnicity impact perioperative nursing care. *Nurs Clin N Am*. 2006;41(2):231-218.

of practice, especially when dealing with ethical issues in the context of health care.[45] Ethical issues may arise when the perioperative nurse

- has personal beliefs that are not in agreement with patient desires, so the nurse may need to arrange for another nurse to care for patient;
- is uncomfortable with the patient's cultural beliefs, so the nurse may need to gain further education;
- must advocate for the patient to protect him/her from incompetent, unethical, or illegal practices;
- questions care that appears inappropriate or substandard; or
- follows chain of command in reporting concerns when observing substandard care or behavioral, verbal, or physical abuse.[45]

Perioperative Asepsis

Perioperative **asepsis** (ie, **aseptic/sterile technique**) is a combination of techniques and protocols employed to prevent microorganisms from entering an open surgical wound or contaminating a sterile field during surgery. Components of perioperative asepsis include

- performing surgical skin antisepsis,
- wearing correct surgical attire,
- performing hand hygiene and the surgical hand scrub,
- gowning and gloving correctly, and
- maintaining the sterile field using aseptic technique:
  › preparing the sterile field,
  › draping the surgical field, and
- moving within the sterile field.

PERFORMING SURGICAL SKIN ANTISEPSIS

The goal of perioperative **skin antisepsis** is to reduce the risk of the patient developing an SSI by removing soil and transient microorganisms at the surgical site.[46] Reducing the amount of bacteria on the skin near the surgical incision lowers the risk of contaminating the surgical incision site. As part of preparing the skin for antisepsis, preoperative bathing and hair management at the surgical site contribute to a reduction of microorganisms on the skin.[46] A preoperative bath with either a soap or antiseptic agent, such as chlorhexidine gluconate, may help to reduce transient skin microbes. This practice contributes to the overall reduction of skin contaminates (eg, oils, dead skin, transient flora) before the surgical skin prep is performed.

Hair removal, if required because of location of the surgical site, should be performed outside of the OR suite to limit the amount of bacteria shed in the OR. An electric or battery-operated clipper or a depilatory should be used to remove hair near the surgical site.[46] Using a depilatory requires a pretest on a site removed from the surgical site to ensure that the patient does not have a skin reaction to the agent.[47] Hair removal with clippers should be performed with care to avoid nicking or cutting the underlying skin. Cuts or nicks in the skin may allow cutaneous bacteria to proliferate and contribute to a possible SSI.[47]

TABLE 3.7 Potential Harm from Povidone-Iodine Antiseptics[1]

TYPE OF PATIENT	RATIONALE	REACTION
Patient with a burn	Repeated application leads to iodine absorption and possibly iodism.	• Induced hyperthyroidism • Metabolic acidosis
Patient with a thyroid disorder undergoing thyroidectomy	Even a single application can result in iodism in patients with cancer or goiter.	• Interference with radioactive iodine therapy • Thyroid dysfunction

Neonates	Neonates and premature neonates have increased skin permeability of iodine.	• Iodism that leads to either
		  › hypothyroidism or
		  › transient hypothyroidism

Women who are pregnant	Iodine crosses the placenta.	• Higher cord blood concentrations of iodine
Women who are lactating	Retained iodine on the skin of the breast.	• Transient hypothyroidism in nursing newborn

1. Guideline for preoperative patient skin antisepsis. In: *Guidelines for Perioperative Practice*. Denver, CO: AORN, Inc; 2017:62-63.

Surgeon preference determines the solution and techniques to be used for skin antisepsis. The perioperative nurse should evaluate that preference with patient-reported allergies and with the location of the surgical site. The perioperative nurse must also follow the antiseptic manufacturer's instructions for use and must consider any contraindications of using a particular agent for his or her patient. There are some special (and sometimes conflicting) considerations that the perioperative nurse should keep in mind before using a surgical antiseptic agent:

- "There are currently no FDA-approved antiseptic alternatives on the market for use in the vaginal vault when povidone-iodine is contraindicated (eg, by patient allergy). Two alternatives to vaginal povidone-iodine [are] sterile saline and baby shampoo."[47(p51)]
- Chlorhexidine gluconate with low alcohol content (eg, 4%) is recommended as safe by the American Congress of Obstetricians and Gynecologists.[48(p720)]
- Povidone-iodine preparations should be used with caution or not at all in select patients, such as those who are susceptible to iodism (Table 3.7).
- Fish or seafood allergies do not necessarily mean that a patient would have an allergic reaction to topical iodine preparations.[47]
- Do not use iodine/iodophors, chlorhexidine gluconate, or alcohol internally; they are intended for external use only.[47]
- Preoperative antisepsis of the vagina with a povidone-iodine agent is effective for prevention of endometritis and SSIs for patients undergoing a cesarean delivery.[47]

TABLE 3.8 Surgical Attire[1]

Surgical scrubs	• Scrubs donned daily should be clean and freshly laundered in a health care–approved laundry facility. • Scrubs should be changed if soiled. • Tops should be tucked in or fit closely. • Non-scrubbed personnel should wear a long-sleeved scrub top or jacket. • Jackets should be buttoned or snapped. • Personal clothing that cannot be contained within the scrub attire should not be worn or should be laundered by a health care–approved laundry facility. • Personnel should change into street clothes when leaving the building.
Shoes	• Shoes should be clean and dedicated for the perioperative area. • Shoes should be close-toed and have heels as identified by Occupational Safety and Health Administration. • Shoes should not have holes or openings. • Single-use shoe covers or boots may be worn when the potential for contamination from fluids exists. • Shoe covers should be removed after use.
Masks	• Masks should be worn in conjunction with eye protection when there is a potential for exposure to fluids. • Masks should fit snugly and cover the mouth and nose. • Masks are single-use and should be changed for each new procedure. • Masks should be replaced and discarded when soiled. • Masks should not be allowed to dangle around the neck.
Jewelry, stethoscopes, and personal identification	• Jewelry that cannot be entirely confined by the surgical scrub attire should not be worn. • Stethoscopes should not be worn around the neck and should be cleaned after each use. • Fabric covers are not recommended for stethoscopes; if used, fabric covers should be laundered daily by a health care–approved laundry facility. • Identification badges should be secured to scrub top and should be cleaned on a regular basis. • Lanyards are not recommended for use with identification badges in the perioperative area.
Hair and facial covering	• A clean surgical head cover or hood should confine all hair and cover the ears, scalp, sideburns, and nape of the neck. • Bouffant-style covering does provide coverage of the hair and ears. • Skull-style caps do not provide coverage of the nape of the neck or the ears. • Single-use coverings should be discarded at the end of the shift or when soiled. • Reusable head coverings should be laundered daily by a health care–approved laundry facility.

TABLE 3.8 Surgical Attire[1] CONTINUED

Personal items	• Backpacks, briefcases, and other items should be cleaned with a low-level disinfectant before entering the semi-restricted or restricted areas. • If brought in, these items should not be placed on the floor. • Cell phones and other devices should be cleaned according to manufacturer's recommendations.
Cover apparel	• If worn, lab coats should be clean and for single use. • Evidence does not support the use of cover apparel to be worn to protect surgical scrubs.

1. Guideline for surgical attire. In: *Guidelines for Perioperative Practice.* Denver, CO: AORN, Inc; 2017:105-127.

A nonscrubbed perioperative team member may perform surgical skin antisepsis using sterile technique, including sterile gloves donned by the open-glove method. All surgical skin agents should be applied in a fashion that reduces pooling of solutions under the patient to prevent skin maceration and decrease the risk of fire. The individual performing the prep should apply the agent according to manufacturer's recommendations, which includes correct dwell time, pattern of use, and dry time. He or she should allow any alcohol-based skin agent to dry completely before draping the patient to avoid trapping fumes under the drape. If alcohol fumes are trapped under the drape, the potential for inadvertent fire increases, especially if alcohol is used in the head and neck area. The person performing the prep should carefully remove and dispose of any towels or pads used to absorb excess surgical prep agents to avoid contaminating the prepped site.[47]

Some surgical sites are more complex to prep than others. Sites containing areas considered contaminated (eg, umbilicus, stomas, draining sinuses, skin ulcers, perineum), as well as traumatic wounds or foreign substances, require preventive efforts to avoid overall contamination of the entire surgical site. Additionally, care needs to be taken not to expose mucous membranes, wounds, or burns to agents containing alcohol. Some anatomic areas (eg, shoulder, limbs, head, neck) require a second, nonscrubbed person to provide assistance during surgical skin antisepsis. For surgeries that include prepping the perineum and abdomen, the perineum should be prepped first to avoid splashing contaminants onto the abdomen. After the individual performing the prep changes into new sterile gloves, the abdomen should be prepped using a separate prep set.[15]

WEARING CORRECT SURGICAL ATTIRE

Recommendations for the selection of **surgical attire** are based on research, evidence, and regulatory requirements. The overall goal when establishing expectations for surgical attire is to reduce the potential risk of infection for the patient undergoing a surgical procedure. This discussion will not include guidelines for the use of PPE. A summary of appropriate attire in the semi-restricted and restricted areas of the OR is provided in Table 3.8.[49]

PERFORMING HAND HYGIENE AND THE SURGICAL HAND SCRUB

"Hand hygiene has been recognized as a primary method of decreasing health care–associated infections."[50(p29)] With this knowledge, the perioperative nurse must diligently adhere to the recommended practices related to hand hygiene. The three primary methods of **hand hygiene** are washing with soap and water, performing a surgical hand scrub, and using surgical hand rubs.

All health care personnel should perform hand hygiene

- upon arrival at and before leaving the health care facility,
- before and after having patient care contact,
- before donning and after removing gloves,
- before and after eating,
- before and after going to the rest room, and
- anytime the hands are contaminated.

The following list describes additional steps that decrease the likelihood for transmission of bacteria from the caregiver's hands to the patient:

- Fingernails should be short and well groomed.
- Chipped nail polish should be removed.
- Artificial nails or any nail enhancement should not be worn.
- Rings and arm jewelry should not be worn in the perioperative area.
- Health care providers should have intact skin when providing direct patient care.

> **EXAM TIP**
>
> Hand washing with soap and water is the only way to prevent the transfer of *Clostridium difficile*. Surgical hand rubs are not effective for killing *C. difficile* spores.

The surgical hand preparation should be performed by all scrubbed personnel before donning surgical attire. "The goal of surgical hand antisepsis is to remove soil and transient microorganisms from the hands and arms."[50(p29)] As with all processes, manufacturers' instructions should be followed when using products. Initial steps for either the brushless or brush method of surgical hand preparation are similar:

- Remove jewelry.
- Don a surgical mask.
- Wash hands and arms with soap and water if visible soil is present.
- Clean under the fingernails.

Surgical Hand Preparation Using the Brush Method

The traditional or timed method includes using a soft brush or sponge, which may or may not have approved surgical hand scrub product contained in the packaging, and performing the following steps:

- To prevent dermatitis, the surgical hand scrub should not be performed using a scrub brush.
- Wash for three to five minutes to allow for adequate coverage of the hands and arms with the product selected.
- Wash with an anatomical approach to cover all four sides of each finger and both hands and arms.
- Rinse hands and arms thoroughly by holding hands higher than elbows to prevent contamination from water dripping from less clean areas to cleaner areas.
- Dry hands before gowning and gloving with a sterile towel.[50]

Surgical Hand Preparation Using the Brushless Method

- Dispense the manufacturer's recommended amount of the product.
- Apply the product to the hands and forearms according to the manufacturer's written instructions.
- Rub hands thoroughly until completely dry.
- Don sterile gown and gloves.[50]

Do not use the brushless method if hands are visibly soiled or if the patient is diagnosed with or suspected of having *C. difficile*.

GOWNING AND GLOVING CORRECTLY

Selection of surgical gowns and gloves should be based on several factors that include evaluation for efficacy and cost, as well as procedure-specific requirements, end-user requirements, environmental considerations, and regulatory requirements.[51] Numerous regulatory agencies, including the US Food and Drug Administration, Occupational Safety and Health Administration, American National Standards Institute, and Association for the Advancement of Medical Instrumentation, provide strict guidelines for surgical gowns and drapes.[51] Gowns and gloves are considered PPE and are used to protect the perioperative team from blood and body fluids. The use of sterile gowns and gloves also supports establishing a sterile field for invasive procedures. Using sterile technique to create and maintain the sterile field directly influences positive patient outcomes.[51]

Following are several considerations for gowning and gloving of which perioperative nurses should be aware[15,51]:

- **Sterile technique** is used when donning sterile gowns and gloves.
- Gowns and gloves should be donned from a surface away from the instrument table.
- Closed gloving should be performed by the scrubbed person, keeping hands inside the sleeve of the gown until gloves have covered the gown cuff.
- Closed-assisted gloving is the preferred method when gloving team members during initial gowning and gloving.
- Double-gloving is recommended.

Following are several considerations related to sterile parameters of the surgical gown of which perioperative nurses should be aware[51]:

- The front of the gown is considered sterile from the chest to the level of the sterile field.
- The neckline, shoulders, and axilla should be considered contaminated.
- The back of the gown should be considered contaminated.

- Sleeves of the gown from two inches above the elbow to the cuff circumferentially are considered sterile.
- Sleeve cuffs are not considered sterile since they are permeable.

MAINTAINING THE STERILE FIELD

Creating, maintaining, and monitoring a sterile field are a critical responsibility of the perioperative RN. The actions to support this intervention have a direct effect on patient outcomes. Development of a **surgical conscience** is a vital step for any perioperative nurse or team member. The nurse monitors the sterile field for any breaks in technique, speaks up, and corrects any identified compromises. A surgical environment that is supported by a culture of safety helps the nurse and the team to provide positive outcomes for the patient.

Preparing the Sterile Field

The sterile field should be prepared as close to the time of the procedure as possible in the location in which the procedure will be performed; only the sterile field(s) for one patient should be prepared.[51] After the sterile field has been established, the field should be constantly monitored until the procedure is completed.[51] It is not acceptable to tape or secure doors in any fashion as a means to monitor the field.

For an unanticipated delay, or during times of inactivity, the sterile field may be covered with a sterile drape. Managers are responsible for establishing a defined process and providing personnel with a detailed description of this process (eg, policy). The OR manager should collaborate with infection control personnel when establishing criteria for delineating under which circumstances this process should be established.[51]

When surgical procedures involve both the abdominal and perineal areas, caution should be taken to maintain separate setups to reduce the chance of transferring microorganisms from the perineal area to the abdominal area. When performing bowel surgery, nurses should establish a standardized technique known as isolation technique. This process should include the following steps:

- Instruments and equipment that have contacted the inside of the bowel should not be used after the lumen of the bowel has been closed.
- Clean instruments should be used for closure.
- Contaminated instruments should be removed or covered so the surgical team does not touch them after closure begins, but remain visible for completing instrument counts.

According to the National Healthcare Safety Network, infections of the urinary tract as a result of passing transurethral instruments and catheters during gynecologic laparoscopic procedure are the most common type of health care–associated infections.[52]

Draping the Sterile Field

Sterile drapes are used to establish a barrier and minimize the passage of microorganisms from the unsterile to the sterile area. This process of establishing a sterile field is used for all invasive surgical procedures. Additionally, the Centers for Disease Control and Prevention has determined that full barrier precautions

TABLE 3.9 Movement Within the Sterile Field[1]

Scrubbed personnel	• Wear appropriate protective devices (eg, lead aprons) to allow scrubbed personnel to remain at the sterile field. • Do not leave the sterile field to retrieve items from an autoclave. • Ensure that hands and arms remain above waist level. • Avoid changing levels during the procedure. • Sit only when the entire surgical team is seated for a procedure.
Changing positions	• Scrubbed personnel should move back-to-back or front-to-front. • Nonscrubbed personnel should always face the sterile field and maintain a minimum of 12 inches from the sterile field.
General considerations	• Limit talking at the surgical field. • Keep number of personnel to a minimum. • Use methods of communication to reduce entering and departing the room when a procedure is under way. • Limit the number of door openings for breaks and retrieving supplies.

1. Guideline for sterile technique. In: *Guidelines for Perioperative Practice*. Denver, CO: AORN, Inc; 2017:93-95.

should be taken for the insertion of central venous catheters and peripherally inserted central catheters.[53] Perioperative nurses should consider the following concepts related to the use of sterile drapes:

- Unsterile equipment or furniture in or adjacent to the intended sterile field should be covered with a sterile drape.
- Gloved hands should be protected by using a cuff when placing the sterile drape.
- Drapes are placed from the surgical site out peripherally.
- Items falling below the level of the sterile field are not considered sterile.

Moving Within the Sterile Field

One method to prevent contamination of the established sterile field is to control and reduce the amount of movement in and around the sterile field. Scrubbed personnel should remain close to the sterile field and not leave the room where the procedure is being performed. Specific movements by the surgical team should be considered as outlined in Table 3.9.

Ensure the Sterility of Surgical Products and Instrumentation

Any item introduced to the sterile field must be sterile. Items can be sterilized at the health care facility or purchased from companies that provide the products already sterilized. Before being presented to the sterile field, perioperative personnel should inspect each item to ascertain that

- the item has been exposed to sterilization;
- the packaging remains intact and has not been compromised; and
- if there is an expiration date, the item is not expired.

It is important to understand that sterility is event related, not time related. In other words, an item is considered sterile if

- the item has been exposed to the parameters of sterilization,
- the integrity of the package remains intact, and
- the item packaging has not been compromised by excessive handling or unreliable conditions.

Event-related sterility is a term used to describe a sterile item that will remain sterile regardless of time but sterility may be compromised if the item is exposed to events such as excessive handling, humidity, or temperature.[51]

METHODS OF STERILIZATION

The nurse demonstrates knowledge of the various forms of sterilization and how to identify the method of sterilization of the product being presented to the sterile field (see also Chapter 6). Often, items sterilized at the health care facility are sterilized using steam under pressure or a form of plasma using hydrogen peroxide. Each of these processes uses a chemical indicator or integrator that will change color when exposed to the parameters of sterilization. Perioperative personnel must visually inspect these indicators before presenting the item to the field.

Forms of sterilization used by companies can include ethylene oxide or irradiation. Manufacturers are required to label their packaging with the method of sterilization as well as with the phrase "sterile unless damaged or opened." Before presenting these items to the field, perioperative personnel must confirm the presence of this labeling.

PACKAGE INTEGRITY

Before presenting a sterile item to the surgical field, the nurse must check the integrity of the package. There are a variety of methods of packaging, including wraps, peel packs, and rigid containers. Each method has specific considerations related to package integrity. To verify sterile integrity, perioperative nurses should

- inspect all packaging for any compromise caused by moisture, tearing, or other rough handling;
- ensure that the sterile contents of a wrapped package do not come in contact with the edges of the wrapper or peel pack before placing them on the sterile field; and
- verify the presence of external locks, filters, or valves when opening items in rigid containers, and ensure that all are intact and free of moisture before opening and placing them on the sterile field.[51]

EXPIRATION DATES

Sterility is event related and depends on maintenance of the integrity of the package.[51] Items may have an expiration date if there is the possibility of the product declining over a period of time (eg, medications that biodegrade over time). When expiration dates are present, the person opening the item should confirm the date before presenting the item to the sterile field. Items should not be used if the date of expiration has passed.

Specimen Management

Specimen management is an essential component of the perioperative RN's scope of practice. It is the responsibility of the surgical team to identify, document, and properly care for all surgical specimens.[54] Errors in specimen management can lead to incorrect diagnoses and medical management; therefore, communication is essential, from the initial acquisition of the specimen by the surgeon, as it passes to the scrub person, and finally as it is passed to the RN circulator. Specimens can be sent to pathology in multiple ways (eg, frozen, fresh, permanent, cultures). During the preoperative assessment, the RN circulator confirms the site or side from which the surgeon plans to obtain specimens. Most specimen management policies include the following steps:

- notifying applicable personnel (eg, pathologist for frozen),
- specifying the requirements for specimen collection and handling,
- identifying the correct method of transfer and transport needs,
- delineating the requirements for containment,
- verifying the method of preservation,
- clarifying correct disposition of the specimen, and
- documenting all of these specifics in the intraoperative record.[54]

Specimens cannot all be handled in exactly the same fashion and most importantly must be "collected and handled in a manner that protects and preserves the integrity of the specimen,"[54(p451)] to include when they are transferred off the sterile field. For instance, forensic specimens may require unique handling to preserve the chain of custody.[54] The collection and disposition of forensic specimens can occur at any facility; therefore policies and procedures must be outlined by the facility because of the possibility that the specimen may be used in litigation. Special care must be taken when collecting forensic specimens so that they are not altered in any way before analysis. Such considerations include placing them in dry plastic containers, not allowing them to come in contact with metallic basins if they contain metal, and handling them as little as possible.[55]

Perioperative personnel must become familiar with facility policies for handling other specimens (eg, breast tissue specimens, amputated digits for reimplantation, radioactive specimens, explanted medical devices) to eliminate errors. If specimens have markers (eg, suture, paint), the RN circulator must annotate those markers on the label and requisition form for orientation for pathology so appropriate diagnoses may be made. The RN circulator is then responsible for containing, preserving, and transporting the specimen in such a way that the specimen and the confidentiality of protected patient information are secured. During this entire process, the RN circulator must ensure that health care personnel are protected from exposure to blood, body fluids, or other potentially infectious material.

Finally, the RN circulator must label the specimen containers to communicate patient, specimen, preservative, and biohazard information. Each specimen must be labeled with the following information:

- the patient's name, identification number, and date of birth;
- the origin of the specimen and laterality, if applicable;
- the date and time the specimen was obtained and placed in preservative, if applicable;

- the surgeon's name;
- preservative and biohazard information; and
- any other information required by the facility.

Perioperative managers and RNs work closely with multiple agencies to ensure that policies are in place and adhered to for the collection, transfer, and final disposition of specimens within a given facility.[54]

IMPLANTS AND EXPLANTS

Perioperative nurses are responsible for complying with tracking regulations for implantable materials and devices and must use meticulous aseptic technique with minimal handling.[55] Perioperative nurses are required to provide accurate and complete documentation on all implantable devices for tracking purposes. All implantable material is subject to recall for various reasons. Nevertheless, patients have the right to refuse tracking of their medical device. It is up to the team to educate the patient on why the devices are tracked.[55] Although some facilities may require more documentation, the minimum documentation should include

- device identification,
- date of manufacturer,
- patient information,
- location of implantation, and
- surgeon information.

Furthermore, if the item was sterilized in the facility, documentation should include assurance that all parameters for sterilization were met. **Immediate-use steam sterilization** (IUSS) is a sterilization process for unwrapped items that are intended to be used immediately and are not intended to be stored and used later. Immediate-use steam sterilization is not recommended for any implantable device.[55] Implantable materials include biologic and synthetic materials. When items are explanted, most are sent to the pathology laboratory for evaluation.

AUTOLOGOUS TISSUE

Autologous tissue is tissue (eg, avulsed teeth, cranial bone flaps, parathyroid glands, skin, veins) that is harvested and then preserved for later reimplantation into the donor's own body. AORN cites variations in practice settings, but provides basic guidelines for the handling of autologous tissues.[56] Each type of autologous tissue harvested has individual guidelines for preservation:

- Avulsed teeth should be placed in a storage medium that provides physiological osmolality.
- Cranial bone flaps may be frozen or cryopreserved.
- Parathyroid gland tissue may be cryopreserved.
- Skin may be refrigerated and stored in a storage medium or normal saline, or may be cryopreserved.
- Veins may be refrigerated and stored in normal saline, Lactated Ringer's, or a storage medium.

Regardless of the type of autologous tissue being harvested for later use, perioperative nurses must be familiar with their facility's policies and procedures for transfer, storage method, and/or transfer to storage facilities. For autologous tissue reimplantation, it is essential that perioperative nurses follow the directions for preparing the autologous tissue for reimplantation. It is crucial that sterile practices and procedures are adhered to in both the collection and redistribution of the autologous tissue.

Perioperative nurses are responsible for complying with tracking regulations from the Food and Drug Administration (FDA) for implantable materials and devices, and must use meticulous aseptic technique with minimal handling.[57] The FDA tracks certain implantable devices to facilitate a recall as a result of potential complications with the device.[58]

Surgical Counts

Accountability of surgical items is paramount to safe patient care. Retained surgical items (RSIs) are a safety risk to patients undergoing surgical procedures. Surgical counts must be conducted consistently for every operative or invasive procedure according to the facility's policy and procedure.[59] The RN circulator and scrub person should perform the counts audibly, visibly or visually, and concurrently.[59] If it is possible for an item to be left behind in the patient, it must be counted. This includes fragments or pieces of instruments and any other countable items. Although all surgical team members play a role in preventing RSIs, documenting the count is the responsibility of the RN circulator.[59] All RSIs are "never events" that are reportable to TJC.

Counted items include surgical soft goods (eg, radiopaque sponges, laparotomy sponges, electrosurgical unit [ESU] scratch pads), sharps (eg, surgical needles, blades, hypodermic needles, ESU tips), and instruments. Counts should be standardized and simplified to allow for a smooth flow in the OR with as little interruption as possible. The scrub person and the RN circulator count all items consecutively in a standardized routine, from the sterile field to the Mayo stand, to the back table, and then off the field.[59] Times when the count process should be performed include

1. at the time of instrument assembly for sterilization,
2. before the procedure begins to establish the baseline,
3. when new items are added to the field,
4. at the time of permanent relief of either the scrub person or the RN circulator,
5. before closure of a cavity within a cavity (eg, uterus or bladder),
6. when a cavity closure begins, and
7. when final closure begins.[59]

If the count is not correct at any point, the following steps should be taken to investigate and reconcile any discrepancies[59]:

1. The RN circulator or scrub person informs the surgeon immediately.
2. The RN circulator or scrub person repeats the entire count procedure.
3. The RN circulator searches the trash, under furniture, on the floor, in the laundry, and any other receptacle in the room.
4. The scrub person searches the sterile field.
5. The surgeon searches the wound.
6. The RN circulator notifies the supervisor.

7. The surgical team follows the facility's policy for x-rays to be taken before the patient leaves the OR if all search options have been exhausted and the discrepancy has not been resolved.
8. The RN circulator documents the incorrect counts and all actions taken in the record.
9. The RN circulator completes and submits an incident report as soon as possible after turning care over to the PACU nurse. There should be no mention of the incident report being filed in the patient's chart, but any interventions performed, such as intraoperative x-ray and results, should be documented.[60]

The perioperative manager is responsible for developing and periodically reviewing and revising the policies and procedures for performing counts and the prevention of RSIs. Additionally, managers should conduct a review of policies concerning the processes in place to deal with unretrieved device fragments and the use of adjunct technologies that supplement the manual count procedures.[59] The perioperative manager is also responsible for ensuring that all surgical personnel are educated and trained on these policies and procedures initially and for ensuring ongoing competency evaluation. As part of this process, the perioperative manager is responsible for promoting ongoing quality improvement of the count process anywhere that operative or other invasive procedures are performed to prevent the occurrence of RSIs and improve outcomes for surgical patients.[59]

Perioperative Documentation

According to the adage, "If it was not documented, it was not done." Many facilities today use electronic health records for documentation. It is essential for perioperative documentation to include a standardized plan of care. "Documentation should require little time to complete, be specific to the perioperative setting, and provide continuity across various areas in surgery."[61(p8)] "Proper perioperative nursing documentation describes assessment, planning, and implementation of the perioperative patient care reflecting individualization of care and evaluation of patient outcomes."[7(p25)] Perioperative documentation should include

- the patient's preoperative pertinent medical and surgical history;
- patient identification and verification;
- significant intraoperative times;
- the patient's condition on transfer;
- the patient's level of consciousness or anxiety;
- the intraoperative position and supportive supplies to prevent injury;
- disposition of the patient's personal property;
- the patient's skin condition before and after surgery;
- condition of the IV site during a local procedure;
- medications administered and any adverse reactions;
- use of a tourniquet cuff, to include location, padding, the person who placed the tourniquet, and total tourniquet time during which it was employed;
- counts of sponges, sharps, and instruments performed and their status;
- surgical procedure performed;
- equipment used and biomedical numbers in case of a patient injury;
- specimens and cultures obtained and their disposition;

FIGURE 3.1 Accurately Identifying Surgical Wounds[1]

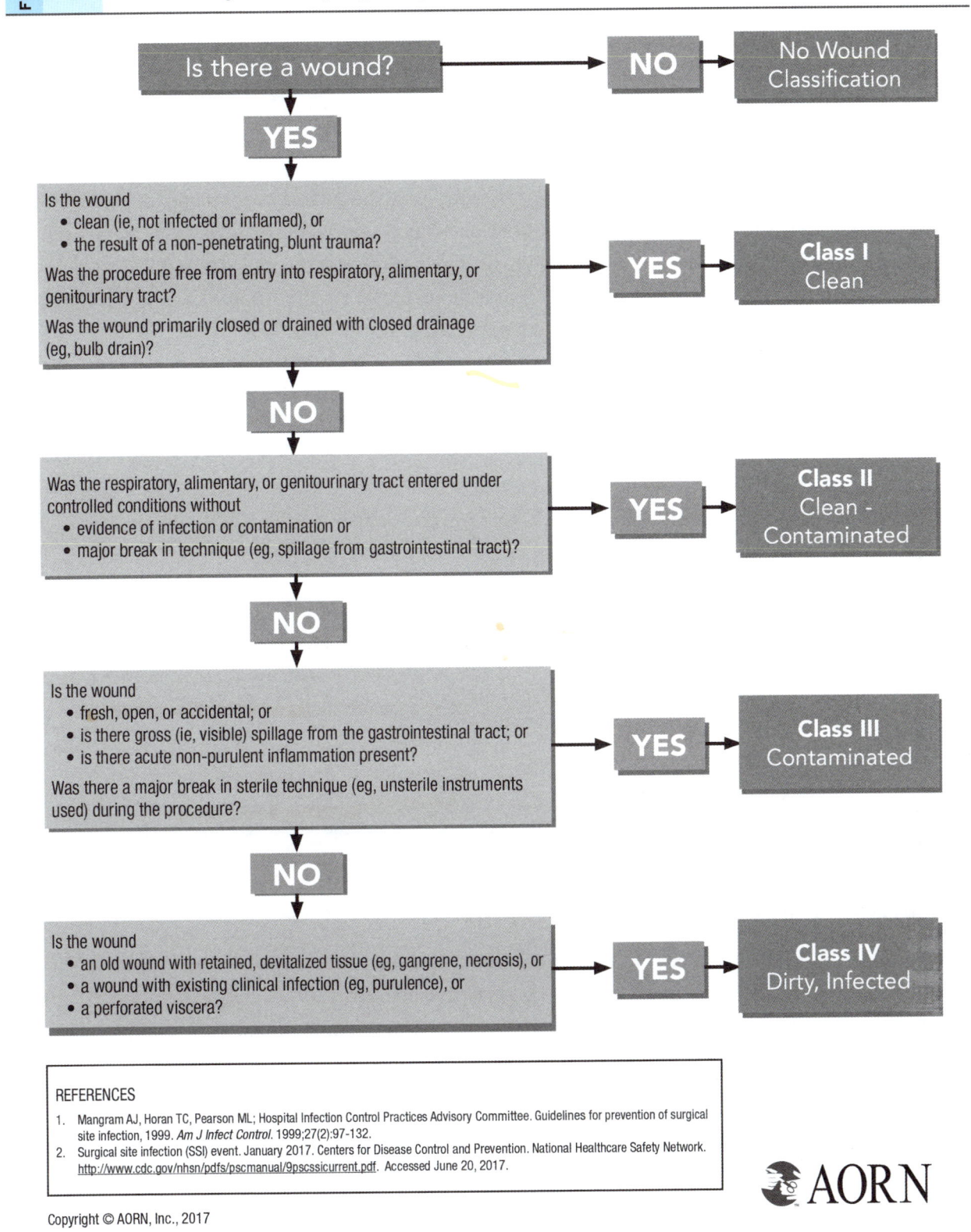

Is there a wound? → **NO** → No Wound Classification

↓ **YES**

Is the wound
- clean (ie, not infected or inflamed), or
- the result of a non-penetrating, blunt trauma?

Was the procedure free from entry into respiratory, alimentary, or genitourinary tract?

Was the wound primarily closed or drained with closed drainage (eg, bulb drain)?

→ **YES** → **Class I** Clean

↓ **NO**

Was the respiratory, alimentary, or genitourinary tract entered under controlled conditions without
- evidence of infection or contamination or
- major break in technique (eg, spillage from gastrointestinal tract)?

→ **YES** → **Class II** Clean - Contaminated

↓ **NO**

Is the wound
- fresh, open, or accidental; or
- is there gross (ie, visible) spillage from the gastrointestinal tract; or
- is there acute non-purulent inflammation present?

Was there a major break in sterile technique (eg, unsterile instruments used) during the procedure?

→ **YES** → **Class III** Contaminated

↓ **NO**

Is the wound
- an old wound with retained, devitalized tissue (eg, gangrene, necrosis), or
- a wound with existing clinical infection (eg, purulence), or
- a perforated viscera?

→ **YES** → **Class IV** Dirty, Infected

REFERENCES
1. Mangram AJ, Horan TC, Pearson ML; Hospital Infection Control Practices Advisory Committee. Guidelines for prevention of surgical site infection, 1999. *Am J Infect Control.* 1999;27(2):97-132.
2. Surgical site infection (SSI) event. January 2017. Centers for Disease Control and Prevention. National Healthcare Safety Network. http://www.cdc.gov/nhsn/pdfs/pscmanual/9pscssicurrent.pdf. Accessed June 20, 2017.

Copyright © AORN, Inc., 2017

AORN

---

1. Guideline for prevention of transmissible infections. In: *Guidelines for Perioperative Practice.* Denver, CO: AORN, Inc; 2017:529 (figure). Reprinted with permission from AORN, Inc, Denver, CO.

- drains placed;
- wound classification;
- dressings applied;
- all personnel in the room during surgery, to include product representatives and students; and
- any complications that occurred and actions performed in response.

WOUND CLASSIFICATION

Wound classifications are determined by the probability that the patient will sustain a postoperative infection based on predetermined criteria. AORN has developed a decision tree to assist surgical teams in determining which wound classification to document for surgical procedures (Figure 3.1). This decision tree is based on the Centers for Disease Control and Prevention's classification of surgical wounds.[62,63] There are four types of wound classifications with expected infection rates:

1. Clean wounds (ie, expected infection rate 1% to 5%) (eg, knee arthoscopy)
2. Clean-contaminated wounds (ie, expected infection rate 8% to 11%) (eg, laryngoscopy)
3. Contaminated wounds (ie, expected infection rate 15% to 20%) (eg, laparoscopic appendectomy for appendicitis)
4. Dirty or infected wounds (ie, expected infection rate 27% to 40%) (eg, amputation of gangrenous extremity)

The RN circulator, in cooperation with the surgeon, is responsible for documenting the wound classification at the end of the procedure being performed. It is important to verify the wound classification at the end of the procedure in the event that during the procedure there was a break in technique or process that changed the planned wound classification.

> **EXAM TIP**
>
> When a Penrose drain is placed, there is a fresh, open wound, so Class III/Contaminated is the correct classification; however, if the drainage from the wound is purulent, then it is a Class IV/Dirty-Infected wound.

Hemostasis and Wound Management

Hemostasis is the arrest or stoppage of blood flow. Hemostasis can be achieved by the individual's physiology via the coagulation cascade, or it can be accomplished surgically. Surgical hemostasis can be achieved by external means (eg, the application of a tourniquet to an extremity, manual pressure [eg, holding pressure with packing laparotomy sponges]) or by chemical or internal mechanical agents that assist the body in the arrest of active bleeding. Two types of bleeding are encountered in surgery:

- active bleeding from arteries and/or veins, and
- venous oozing from cut surfaces.

Complete hemostasis, without the formation of a hematoma, and the elimination of dead space are crucial factors in successful closure of a wound.[63] Hemostats or other clamping instruments, ties, or electrosurgery are employed by the surgical team to stop obvious bleeding. This is the most common

TABLE 3.10 Chemical Hemostatic Agents[1]

AGENT	MATERIAL AND ACTION	NURSING CONSIDERATIONS
Absorbable gelatin	• Powder or compressed pad from porcine gelatin • Provides framework for fibrin deposition and clot formation on areas of capillary bleeding	• Not soluble and swells to up to 40 times its own weight • Sponge or pad form may be used dry or with warm saline solution, epinephrine, or thrombin (ie, human or bovine) • Powder form is mixed with saline to create a paste, which is then applied to bleeding source • Should not be used in presence of infection or in small closed spaces, such as the spinal canal
Absorbable collagen	• Sponges made from bovine collagen • Applied dry to oozing or bleeding sites • Activates the coagulation cascade, especially platelet aggregation	• Must be kept dry • Scrubbed team members should handle it with dry gloves and dry instruments because it has an affinity for wet surfaces • Keep away from the skin incision, as it will form a barrier to wound healing
Microfibrillar collagen	• Available in loose form or in a nonwoven pad • Made from bovine corium collagen • Activates the coagulation cascade, especially platelet aggregation • Applied dry to bleeding surface with firm pressure, then any excess material is removed	• May swell up to 20% its volume within 10 minutes • Considerations same as for absorbable collagen
Oxidized cellulose	• Made from oxidized cotton cellulose or oxidized regenerated cellulose (rayon) • Available as a pad or in a knitted fabric that is either low-density or high-density • Applied dry and may even be sutured in place • Creates a gel when in contact with blood, forming a clot rapidly • Not recommended for use on bone	• Absorbs 10 times its own weight • Has some bacteriocidal properties • Use only minimum amount needed • Inactivated in the presence of thrombin
Thrombin	• Enzyme extracted from human or bovine blood • Promotes coagulation of blood and controls capillary bleeding by activating the coagulation cascade • Used as a topical hemostatic agent along with other agents or alone • Topical thrombin may be sprayed on areas that are hard to access with other methods	• Contraindicated for use in active bleeding • Contraindicated for patients with bovine allergies • Human recombinant product may contain viral or prion contamination

CONTINUES

TABLE 3.10 Chemical Hemostatic Agents[1] CONTINUED

AGENT	MATERIAL AND ACTION	NURSING CONSIDERATIONS
Oxytocin	• Pituitary hormone used to initiate or augment uterine contraction after the baby is born • Used commonly in cesarean deliveries • Controls uterine hemorrhage, although it can be used to induce labor for vaginal birth • Ergnovine maleate can also be used to treat uterine bleeding after childbirth or abortion after the placenta is delivered	• Synthetic oxytocin is prepared as an injection and can be delivered either intravenously or injected directly into the uterine muscle • Ergnovine has demonstrated cases of sustained contractions lasting more than 3 hours • Ergnovine is contraindicated if the patient has pre-eclampsia or eclampsia causing seizures
Phenol and alcohol	• Cauterizes tissue by coagulating proteins • Used on a cotton swab to cauterize tissue	• Used in some podiatric surgeries • Is neutralized by 70% alcohol • Caution: it can cause severe burns
Epinephrine	• Adrenal hormone that causes vasoconstriction • Is used along with local anesthetics to prolong the anesthetic effect by increasing the time for the anesthetic to be cleared from the surgical area • Can be used with gelatin sponges to increase hemostatic process	• Excess epinephrine can be absorbed systemically, causing rapid heart rate
Silver nitrate	• Packaged as applicator sticks with molded silver nitrate in 20% to 50% silver chloride solution • Used to treat burns or other moist wounds • Also used to seal areas of previous surgical incisions that are left open to heal by secondary intention	• Should not be used on the face because it may cause discoloration of the skin • Staining darkens to black in the presence of light

1. Phillips N. Wound healing and hemostasis. In: *Berry & Kohn's Operating Room Technique*. 13th ed. St Louis, MO: Mosby; 2017:565-568.

type of internal mechanical hemostasis. Other types of mechanical hemostasis include thermal agents, such as cryosurgery, diathermy, handheld electrocautery, argon beam coagulator, hemostatic scalpel, ultrasonic-harmonic scalpel, and laser photocoagulation.

Other mechanical means of achieving hemostasis include using external pressure to occlude or create a barrier to the flow of blood. Examples of this type include pneumatic/simple tourniquets. Medical antishock trousers (MAST) are an extreme compression device that has been used for trauma victims to prevent shock. The garment is deflated only after the victim is in the OR and anesthesia is induced.[63]

Chemical agents that are used in hemostasis are described in Table 3.10. These agents are designed to work with various points of the clotting cascade to form a clot. Some are absorbed during the wound healing process while others are more permanent. The perioperative nurse should know the benefits and limitations of each type of chemical agent. Use of porcine- or bovine-sourced agents may be contraindicated by the patient's faith or by allergy to porcine or bovine derivatives. Hemostatic materials should not be packed into closed spaces where they could cause undue pressure on nerves or other tissues, such as in the spinal canal.[63]

DRAINS

Drains may be placed near an incision via a separate stab wound to promote wound healing when the surgeon anticipates excess drainage of air and fluids. Drains are used to promote the evacuation of fluids such as serum, blood, lymph, intestinal secretions, bile, and pus.[64] Larger drains may be placed when copious amounts of fluids are expected. Chest tubes, common bile duct, and bladder tubes (ie, indwelling urinary retention catheters) allow fluids to be captured in a closed container for accurate measurement. Some drains promote the wicking of fluid away from the surgical site by capillary action and gravity. Some drains may be fenestrated, while others are just one long tube, as in the Penrose drain. Open drains deposit collected fluid directly into a dressing, while closed drains collect fluid into a reservoir.

DRESSINGS

Dressings come in a wide variety of materials and properties. The surgeon will prefer to choose a dressing based on the type of wound, type of protective properties he or she desires for the patient, and what is available and cost-effective to promote initial wound healing.

Primary dressings are placed directly on the surgical wound. They should be made of an absorbent material that will wick drainage from the wound and move it toward the periphery. Cotton or synthetic materials may be used as primary dressings. These dressings can also contain antimicrobial properties and can be made of nonadherent material, if no debridement is desired.

Secondary dressings are placed directly over the primary dressing to absorb additional drainage. They serve to add a layer of protection of the wound to decrease likelihood of further trauma. Pads with cotton filling are often used for this purpose.

Most dressings are secured to the patient's surrounding skin by some type of tape or a transparent dressing. Choices are many and depend on surgeon preference, patient needs, and avoiding any allergic skin reaction, such as with a latex material or tape allergy. Typically, the perioperative RN is responsible for securing the dressing at the end of the procedure. Consideration must be given to the patient's skin condition at the time the dressing is applied. The perioperative RN should understand how frequently the dressing will be changed postoperatively to determine which type of tape to use.

Other specialty dressings may be needed depending on the type of wound. For instance, a wound that cannot be closed by primary intention may be dressed with a negative pressure dressing that serves to promote granulation of tissue and remove excess secretions simultaneously. This negative pressure wound therapy dressing is applied in the OR by placing a sponge dressing within the wound and securing it with a transparent dressing that contains a tubing connected to a reservoir in the vacuum unit. Contraindications for this type of dressing include

- exposure of vital organs within the wound,
- inadequately debrided wounds (ie, granulation tissue will not form over devitalized/necrotic tissue),
- untreated osteomyelitis or sepsis within the vicinity of the wound,
- presence of untreated coagulopathy,
- necrotic tissue with eschar,
- malignancy in the wound, and
- allergy to any component of the dressing.[64]

WOUND HEALING

Wound healing is the body's response to repair tissue disruption that has occurred through surgical intent, traumatic events, or a chronic condition that occurs over time. There are three primary phases of wound healing: inflammatory, proliferative, and remodeling. Numerous factors affect the body's ability to heal wounds, to include environmental factors, one's own skin flora or fauna, and surgical technique.[64] Wounds are closed in a number of ways:

- Primary intention, which occurs when wounds are created with aseptic technique and then are closed as soon as possible with suture, staples, tape, or surgical adhesives.[64]
- Secondary intention or granulation and contraction, for wounds with tissue loss and the inability to proximate edges. The wounds of secondary intention are typically left open so they can heal from inside out. Dressing changes are normally required for this type of wound healing.[64]
- Delayed primary closure or third intention, which frequently includes wounds that require debridement first and then later require primary or secondary closure.[64]

SUTURE

Suture is defined as "a generic term for all materials used to repair and re-approximate incised or torn tissue."[65(p186)] Suture materials have three properties:

- physical characteristics (eg, tensile strength, memory),
- handling characteristics (eg, pliability), and
- tissue-reaction characteristics (eg, absorption).[65]

Suture is composed of two main categories: absorbable and nonabsorbable. Examples of absorbable suture include surgical gut, collagen sutures used in eye surgeries, and synthetic absorbable suture often used in laparotomies.[65] Nonabsorbable sutures are divided into three classes:

- Class I: silk and synthetic fibers
- Class II: cotton or linen fibers
- Class III: sutures with composition of monofilament or multifilament metal wire

Examples of nonabsorbable suture include

- silk (ie, should not be used if infection is present),
- cotton (eg, umbilical tape),
- nylon (ie, used in ophthalmology),
- polyester fiber (ie, used as general closure of fascia),
- polypropylene (ie, often used in the presence of infection),
- barbed suture (ie, used extensively in plastic surgery), and
- stainless steel.[65]

Surgical needles have three basic components: the eye, the body, and the point or tip. "Needle selection is determined by the type of tissue, suture material, and action to be performed."[65(p191)] Needle types are further broken down into the type of point or tip. Examples are

- taper point (ie, most soft tissues below the skin's surface);
- penetrating point (ie, ligaments and tendons);
- blunt point (ie, friable tissues);
- protect point (ie, primarily for fascia);
- reverse cutting (ie, skin closures);
- cutting taper (ie, microsurgery);
- spatula side cutting (ie, eye surgery); and
- regular cutting, which is used for general skin closures.[65]

Suture packaging is color coded and is universal across companies.[65]

Key Concepts and Review: Case Study

Ms V is a 26-year-old woman who is scheduled for an umbilical hernia repair that was diagnosed earlier this month. According to her history and physical examination performed by her primary care physician, Ms V has the following comorbidities:
- elevated blood pressure without a diagnosis of hypertension, and
- obesity (BMI 30).

Her preoperative EKG results show a mild sinus bradycardia, and her chest x-ray is normal.

Ms V is admitted to the ambulatory surgery center of a hospital accompanied by her mother. Ms V is oriented to person, place, and time, and her vital signs upon admission are
- heart rate: 90,
- respiratory rate: 16,
- blood pressure: 161/70,
- oxygen saturation on room air: 100%, and
- tympanic temperature: 98.1°F (36.7°C).

The RN circulator scrub person have prepared the OR suite. They have completed the initial instrument, sharp, sponge, and miscellaneous counts, which the RN circulator has recorded. The OR bed has been set up for a supine position with the patient's arms extended on armboards. The RN circulator has deemed that no special positioning accessories are needed. The RN circulator expects the procedure to last no longer than 1 hour based on the surgeon's history.

The RN circulator greets the patient in the day surgery bay and identifies her with two methods of identification. The patient confirms that she is having an umbilical hernia repair with mesh by the correct physician. The RN circulator detects that the patient is nervous and offers reassurance that she will be with the patient throughout the procedure and will communicate to the patient's mother as the surgery proceeds. The patient expresses relief that her mother will be informed. The patient further confirms that she has had no adverse reaction to anesthesia and she is not allergic to any medications or food. The RN circulator then assesses the patient's IV site to ensure patency and notes that there is a 1 gm cefazolin antibiotic infusing into the IV for surgical prophylaxis. However, the patient is not wearing any sequential compression sleeves as ordered by the surgeon. The RN circulator receives the hand-over report from the day surgery RN, and after placing compression sleeves on the patient and initiating compression by starting the generator, the RN circulator takes the patient to the OR suite on a gurney.

As the RN circulator enters the OR suite with Ms V, she introduces the patient to the anesthesia professional and scrub person. The anesthesia professional and RN circulator jointly verify the patient's identity, procedure, antibiotic, and allergies during the sign-in.

Ms V is able to move slowly to the OR bed while the scrub person and RN circulator each stand on opposite sides of the bed to ensure safety. When Ms V is safely in the middle of the OR bed, the RN circulator secures her with a safety belt, ensuring enough gap to place at least two fingers between the patient's thighs and the lap belt. The patient is instructed to place her arms on both armboards, and the RN circulator confirms that the armboards are level with the OR bed and extended at less than a 90-degree angle and that Ms V feels comfortable. The anesthesia professional and RN circulator place a forced-air warming blanket over Ms V's upper body to prevent unintended hypothermia.

The surgeon comes into the OR with her assistant and the RN circulator conducts the time out with the patient participating by confirming the procedure; the RN circulator confirms that all mesh implant sizes are available. The anesthesia professional induces general anesthesia using a 7.0 endotracheal tube to secure the airway. The RN circulator provides assistance as requested by the anesthesia professional by performing the Sellick maneuver during intubation.

The RN circulator places the electrosurgical unit's dispersal pad on the patient's left upper thigh; the skin is intact and warm. The RN circulator prepares the surgical site using the surgeon's preferred surgical skin antiseptic product of chlorhexidine gluconate and alcohol. The RN circulator knows that alcohol-containing skin antiseptic agents increase the risk of surgical fire. The RN circulator ensures that no excess skin prep fluid has pooled under the patient during the prep.

The surgical team then drapes the patient and the surgeon makes the initial incision. The procedure progresses smoothly. The RN circulator telephones the patient's mother in the surgical waiting area at the time the mesh is being inserted to inform her that all is going well. The RN circulator notes all times of the procedure, personnel involved and their roles, and all equipment being used in the electronic health record. The RN circulator denotes the type of mesh used for the hernia repair, its lot number, and expiration date. The entire mesh is used during the surgery, so the size of mesh is the same as on the package. When the mesh is in place and the surgeon begins closing the wound, the scrub person and RN circulator conduct the sponge, sharp, and miscellaneous counts.

The RN circulator confirms that the surgeon did not encounter any infection or other inflammation during the procedure and marks the wound classification as class I (ie, clean) because the gastrointestinal tract was not entered. The RN circulator notifies the PACU RN that Ms V will be coming out shortly and the anesthesia professional indicates that the patient will have no significant needs in the PACU. As the incision is closed, the RN circulator initiates the sign-out with all surgical team members. There have been no unanticipated complications and the surgeon states that the patient will require routine PACU care and will be discharged home later that same day. The RN circulator confirms with the surgeon during the postoperative debriefing that there is no specimen. The RN circulator calls the OR charge RN to ask for additional personnel to help transfer the patient to the gurney from the OR bed. Because of her weight, four people will be needed along with a transfer device to safely transfer Ms V to the gurney. The RN circulator provides the scrub person with the surgical dressing. The RN circulator removes the electrosurgical unit dispersive pad and notes that the site is intact, warm, and dry. When the patient is extubated, the team transfers her to the gurney using a transfer device and raises the side rails on both sides of the gurney. The RN circulator accompanies the anesthesia professional with the patient to the PACU and gives the PACU RN a full report.

This case study may be of a typical general surgery patient without any major complications, but it is a good example of the complexities of perioperative nursing, which requires knowledge of physiological, psychosocial, and procedural content in concert with the ability to perform the necessary tasks to keep the patient safe.

References

1. Universal Protocol. The Joint Commission. http://www.jointcommission.org/standards_information/up.aspx.
2. Safe Surgery Saves Lives Frequently Asked Questions. World Health Organization. http://www.who.int/patientsafety/safesurgery/faq_introduction/en/.
3. Comprehensive surgical checklist. AORN, Inc. http://www.aorn.org/aorn-org/guidelines/clinical-resources/tool-kits/correct-site-surgery-tool-kit/aorn-comprehensive-surgical-checklist.
4. Global Support for Safe Surgery Saves Lives. The World Health Organization. http://www.who.int/patientsafety/safesurgery/endorsements_received/en.
5. OSHA Brief. Hazard communication standard: safety data sheets. Occupational Safety and Health Administration. https://www.osha.gov/Publications/OSHA3514.html.
6. Fire Safety Tool Kit. AORN, Inc. http://www.aorn.org/aorn-org/guidelines/clinical-resources/tool-kits/fire-safety-tool-kit.
7. Patient safety and risk management. In: Rothrock JC, ed. *Alexander's Care of the Patient in Surgery.* 15th ed. St Louis, MO: Elsevier; 2015:34.
8. Koffel WE. Complying with Fire Safety Codes. *Health Facilities Management.* July 1, 2015. http://www.hfmmagazine.com/articles/1614-complying-with-fire-safety-codes.
9. Guideline for surgical smoke safety. In: *Guidelines for Perioperative Practice.* Denver, CO: AORN, Inc; 2017:477-505.

10. Guideline for radiation safety. In: *Guidelines for Perioperative Practice*. Denver, CO: AORN, Inc; 2017:339-371.
11. Guideline for safe use of energy-generating devices. In: *Guidelines for Perioperative Practice*. Denver, CO: AORN, Inc; 2017:129-155.
12. Positioning the patient for surgery. In: Rothrock JC, ed. *Alexander's Care of the Patient in Surgery*. 15th ed. St Louis, MO: Elsevier; 2015:155-185.
13. Guideline for positioning the patient. In: *Guidelines for Perioperative Practice*. Denver, CO: AORN, Inc; 2017:691-709.
14. Ergonomics. Merriam-Webster.com. http://www.merriam-webster.com/dictionary/ergonomics.
15. Phillips N. Positioning, prepping, and draping the patient. In: *Berry & Kohn's Operating Room Technique*. 13th ed. St Louis, MO: Elsevier; 2017:479-513.
16. Safe Patient Handling Tool Kit. AORN, Inc. https://www.aorn.org/guidelines/clinical-resources/tool-kits/safe-patient-handling-tool-kit.
17. National Council on Radiation and Protection Measurements. http://ncrponline.org.
18. US Nuclear Regulatory Commission. http://www.nrc.gov.
19. Guideline for prevention of transmissible infections. In: *Guidelines for Perioperative Practice*. Denver, CO: AORN, Inc; 2017:471-503.
20. Personal protective equipment. Occupational Safety and Health Administration. https://www.osha.gov/Publications/osha3151.html.
21. Laser Institute of America. American National Standard for Safe Use of Lasers, ANSI Z136.1. Orlando, FL: Laser Institute of America; 2014.
22. Sharps safety tool kit. AORN, Inc. https://www.aorn.org/guidelines/clinical-resources/tool-kits.
23. Guideline for a safe environment of care, part 2. In: *Guidelines for Perioperative Practice*. Denver, CO: AORN, Inc; 2017:269-293.
24. Phillips N. Anesthesia: techniques and agents. In: *Berry & Kohn's Operating Room Technique*. 13th ed. St Louis, MO: Elsevier; 2017:414-446.
25. Management of patients who refuse blood transfusion. *Indian J Anaesth*. 2014;58(5):658-664. https://www.ncbi.nlm.nih.gov/pmc/articles/PMC4260316/.
26. American Association of Blood Banks. *Standards for Perioperative Autologous Blood Collection and Administration*. 6th ed. Bethesda, MD: American Association of Blood Banks; 2014.
27. Introduction to the AORN Guidelines for Perioperative Practice. *Guidelines for Perioperative Practice*. Denver, CO: AORN, Inc; 2017:1-4.
28. About MHAUS. Malignant Hyperthermia Association of the United States. https://www.mhaus.org/about/.
29. Managing an MH crisis. Malignant Hyperthermia Association of the United States. http://www.mhaus.org/healthcare-professionals/managing-a-crisis.
30. Surgical Care Improvement Project. The Joint Commission. https://www.jointcommission.org/surgical_care_improvement_project_scip_measure_information_form_version_21c/.
31. Surgical site infections. Centers for Medicare and Medicaid Services. https://partnershipforpatients.cms.gov/p4p_resources/tsp-surgicalsiteinfections/toolsurgicalsiteinfections.html.
32. WHO Guidelines on hand hygiene in health care. The World Health Organization. 2009. http://www.who.int/infection-prevention/publications/hand-hygiene-2009/en/.
33. Hand hygiene in health care settings. Centers for Disease Control and Prevention. https://www.cdc.gov/handhygiene/index.html.
34. Guideline for medication safety. In: *Guidelines for Perioperative Practice*. Denver, CO: AORN, Inc; 2017:289-327.
35. National Patient Safety Goals effective January 2017-Hospital Accreditation Program. The Joint Commission. https://www.jointcommission.org/assets/1/6/NPSG_Chapter_HAP_Jan2017.pdf.
36. Safe use of opioids. The Joint Commission Sentinel Event Alert. 2012;49:1-5. http://www.jointcommission.org/assets/1/18/SEA_49_opioids_8_2_12_final.pdf.

37. Phillips N. Surgical pharmacology. In: *Berry & Kohn's Operating Room Technique*. 13th ed. St Louis, MO: Elsevier; 2017:403-413.
38. Guideline for care of the patient receiving local anesthesia. In: *Guidelines for Perioperative Practice*. Denver, CO: AORN, Inc; 2017:617-628.
39. Methemoglobinemia. MedlinePlus. https://medlineplus.gov/ency/article/000562.htm.
40. Guideline for complementary care interventions. In: *Guidelines for Perioperative Practice*. Denver, CO: AORN, Inc; 2017:543-555.
41. Benowitz NL. Benzodiazepines. In: Olson KR, Kent R, eds. *Poisoning & Medication Overdose*. 6th ed. New York, NY: McGraw-Hill; 2012:454-457.
42. Quinn DMD. How religion, language and ethnicity impact perioperative nursing care. *Nurs Clin N Am*. 2006;41(2):231-218.
43. Why don't Jehovah's Witnesses accept blood transfusions? Jehovah's Witnesses.org. https://www.jw.org/en/jehovahs-witnesses/faq/jehovahs-witnesses-why-no-blood-transfusions/.
44. Lawson T, Ralph C. Perioperative Jehovah's Witnesses: a review. *Br J Anaesth*. 2015;115(5):676-687.
45. AORN's Perioperative Explications for the ANA *Code of Ethics for Nurses with Interpretive Statements*. 2017. https://www.aorn.org/guidelines/clinical-resources/code-of-ethics [member access only].
46. Guideline for preoperative patient skin antisepsis. In: *Guidelines for Perioperative Practice*. Denver, CO: AORN, Inc; 2017:51-74.
47. Spry C. Infection prevention and control. In: Rothrock JC, ed. *Alexander's Care of the Patient in Surgery*. 15th ed. St Louis, MO: Elsevier; 2015:69-123.
48. American College of Obstetricians and Gynecologists Women's Health Care Physicians; Committee on Gynecologic Practice. Committee Opinion No. 571: Solutions for surgical preparation of the vagina. *Obstet Gynecol*. 2013 Sep;122(3):718-720.
49. Guideline for surgical attire. In: *Guidelines for Perioperative Practice*. Denver, CO: AORN, Inc; 2017:105-127.
50. Guideline for hand hygiene. In: *Guidelines for Perioperative Practice*. Denver, CO: AORN, Inc; 2017:29-50.
51. Guideline for sterile technique. In: *Guidelines for Perioperative Practice*. Denver, CO: AORN, Inc; 2017:75-103.
52. Healthcare-Associated Infections (HAIs). Catheter-Associated Urinary Tract Infections (CAUTI). Centers for Disease Control and Prevention. http://www.cdc.gov/HAI/ca_uti/uti.html.
53. O'Grady NP, Alexander M, Burns LA, et al; Health-care Infection Control Practices Advisory Committee (HICPAC). *Guidelines for the Prevention of Intravascular Catheter-Related Infections*. Atlanta, GA: Centers for Disease Control and Prevention; 2011.
54. Guideline for specimen management. In: *Guidelines for Perioperative Practice*. Denver, CO: AORN, Inc; 2017:447-476.
55. Phillips N. Diagnostics, specimens, and oncologic considerations. In: *Berry & Kohn's Operating Room Technique*. 13th ed. St Louis, MO: Elsevier; 2017:379-402.
56. Guideline for autologous tissue management. In: *Guidelines for Perioperative Practice*. Denver, CO: AORN, Inc; 2017:191-241.
57. Guideline for sterilization. In: *Guidelines for Perioperative Practice*. Denver, CO: AORN, Inc; 2017:865-892.
58. Medical Device Tracking—Guidance for Industry and Food and Drug Administration Staff. US Food and Drug Administration. https://www.fda.gov/MedicalDevices/ucm071756.htm.
59. Guideline for prevention of retained surgical items. In: *Guidelines for Perioperative Practice*. Denver, CO: AORN, Inc; 2017:375-420.
60. Documentation and confidentiality. In: Guido GW. *Legal and Ethical Issues in Nursing*. 4th ed. Prentiss Hall, NJ: Pearson; 2005:193.
61. Steelman VM. Concepts basic to perioperative nursing. In: Rothrock JC, ed. *Alexander's Care of the Patient in Surgery*. 15th ed. St Louis, MO: Elsevier; 2015:1-16.

62. Surgical Site Infection (SSI) Event. 2017. Centers for Disease Control and Prevention. https://www.cdc.gov/nhsn/pdfs/pscmanual/9pscssicurrent.pdf.
63. Phillips N. Wound healing and hemostasis. In: *Berry & Kohn's Operating Room Technique.* 13th ed. St Louis, MO: Elsevier; 2017:559-584.
64. Bak JR. Wound healing, dressings, and drains. In: Rothrock JC, ed. *Alexander's Care of the Patient in Surgery.* 15th ed. St Louis, MO: Elsevier; 2015:253-269.
65. McCarthy J. Sutures, needles, and instruments. In: Rothrock JC, ed. *Alexander's Care of the Patient in Surgery.* 15th ed. St Louis, MO: Elsevier; 2015:186-210.

Practice Exam Questions

1. When performing preoperative patient skin antisepsis, the perioperative RN should
   A. shave the area to be prepped immediately before applying the antiseptic.
   B. apply the antiseptic in concentric circles moving from the outer perimeter toward the incision site.
   C. clean the area to be prepped with 70% isopropyl alcohol before applying the antiseptic.
   D. allow the antiseptic solution to dry for the full time recommended in the manufacturer's instructions for use before surgical drapes are applied.

2. A _____ must be used to remove waste anesthesia gases from operating rooms.
   A. ventilation system
   B. anesthesia delivery system
   C. scavenging system
   D. air sampling system

3. Local anesthetic systemic toxicity is treated by administering
   A. 10% lipid emulsion.
   B. 15% hetastarch.
   C. 20% lipid emulsion.
   D. 25% hetastarch.

4. Placing the patient on the OR bed in the supine position with arms extended on armboards at greater than 90 degrees may cause injury to the
   A. axillary nerve.
   B. brachial plexus.
   C. median nerve.
   D. radial nerve.

5. The correct time to label containers designated for medications or solutions is
   A. when setting up the sterile field but before the medications are delivered to the field.
   B. when there are more than two medications being used on the sterile field.
   C. at the time the medication is delivered to the sterile field.
   D. just before using the medication on the patient.

6. A perioperative nurse is preparing to perform a skin prep for a patient scheduled for a right breast biopsy with needle localization. When the perioperative nurse removes the patient's gown, she discovers a wire inserted into the left breast. What is the appropriate action?
   A. Leave the wire in place and prep the left breast.
   B. Remove the wire and prep the right breast.
   C. Call the radiologist and tell him of the error.
   D. Postpone prepping until the discrepancy is resolved.

7. Potential harm from the use of povidone-iodine antiseptics includes
    A. deafness.
    B. thyroid dysfunction.
    C. neurotoxicity.
    D. allergic response to iodine.

8. A specific directive, written by a physician, about end-of-life decisions is a/an
    A. do-not-resuscitate order.
    B. allow-natural-death order.
    C. advance directive.
    D. required reconsideration.

9. Patients placed in the steep Trendelenburg position may be at risk for
    A. increased tidal volume.
    B. decreased tidal volume.
    C. decreased intracranial pressure.
    D. increased stroke volume.

10. When performing preoperative patient skin antisepsis, the perioperative RN should
    A. perform a surgical hand scrub and wear a sterile gown.
    B. perform a surgical hand scrub and wear short-sleeved scrub attire.
    C. perform hand hygiene and wear a sterile gown.
    D. perform hand hygiene and wear long-sleeved scrub attire.

11. The type of fire extinguisher to be used for an electrical fire is
    A. pressurized water.
    B. carbon dioxide.
    C. dry chemical.
    D. halon.

12. When risk for exposure to blood and body fluids exists, the following types of personal protective equipment (PPE) should be worn
    A. gloves, warm-up jackets, hair protection, and shoe covers.
    B. gloves, fluid-resistant gowns or aprons, and surgical masks.
    C. gloves, surgical masks, fluid-resistant gowns, and eye protection.
    D. lab coats, gloves, eye protection, and shoe covers.

13. Which of the following airflow pressures and total air exchanges per hour is most appropriate for sterile storage areas?
    A. negative airflow pressure with a minimum of 4 total air changes per hour.
    B. positive airflow pressure with a minimum of 4 total air changes per hour.
    C. negative airflow pressure with a minimum of 10 total air changes per hour.
    D. positive airflow pressure with a minimum of 10 total air changes per hour.

14. What incision should be used for C-section of a baby in the breech position?
    A. Kerr
    B. Kronig
    C. Low transverse
    D. Classic uterine incision

15. A sterile field has been prepared for a vaginal hysterectomy. The surgeon has been called away for an emergency C-section, delaying the scheduled case by at least one hour. The appropriate method for maintaining the sterile field for the delayed case is to
    A. tape the door closed.
    B. cover the sterile field with a sterile drape and leave the room.
    C. cover the sterile field with a sterile drape and remain in the room.
    D. wait for an hour and then tear down the back table.

16. A patient has lost 750 mL of blood intraoperatively. Vital signs are within normal limits. Which of the following interventions should the circulating nurse anticipate?
    A. Send a blood specimen for a stat type and cross-match.
    B. Set up an autologous blood transfusion unit.
    C. Send an order for two units of O-negative blood.
    D. Obtain additional crystalloids.

17. The RN circulator completing the final count for a knee arthroscopy discovers that an atraumatic needle is missing. After an exhaustive search, an x-ray is ordered. The results are negative and the surgeon closes the wound. How does the RN circulator document this incident?
    A. Document that the count was incorrect or unreconciled and describe the steps that were taken to rectify the count.
    B. Document that the count was correct because the x-ray was negative.
    C. Notify the supervisor and document what he or she instructs according to facility policy.
    D. Inform the patient that a needle may have been left in the wound.

18. A patient is scheduled for a total knee replacement. During the time out, the scrub nurse discovers that the incorrect implant is on the back table. The correct implant is available, but unsterile. The surgeon would like to continue with the case. What is the best course of action?
    A. Notify the surgeon that the correct implant may be sterilized via the immediate-use steam sterilization (IUSS) method if biological and class V indicators are placed in the load.
    B. Notify the surgeon that the correct implant may be sterilized via the ethylene oxide method if the aeration period is aborted.
    C. Notify the surgeon that a root cause analysis will be initiated.
    D. Cancel and reschedule the procedure.

19. An 18-year-old patient is scheduled for surgery to have cochlear implants placed. The patient refuses to have the implants tracked even after the team has informed her of the possible implications of a recall or adverse event. What is the next course of action?
    A. Cancel the procedure and have the procedure rescheduled at a different facility.
    B. Notify the surgeon and let him or her decide what to do.
    C. Proceed with the surgery and document in the perioperative notes that the patient has refused to allow tracking of the medical device.
    D. Report the incident to the US Food and Drug Administration.

20. When should the scrub person transfer specimens from the sterile field to the RN circulator?
    A. At the end of the procedure.
    B. When it is convenient for the scrub person.
    C. As soon as possible.
    D. Never, because specimens should not be passed off the sterile field.

Answers with Supported Rationales

1. Answer D is correct. Allowing the skin antiseptic to dry completely according to the manufacturer's instructions for use improves the safety and efficacy of preoperative patient skin antisepsis. Reference: Guideline for preoperative patient skin antisepsis. In: *Guidelines for Perioperative Practice*. Denver, CO: AORN, Inc; 2017:55, 64-66.

2. Answer C is correct. The use of scavenging systems to remove waste anesthesia gases is a regulatory requirement. Reference: Guideline for a safe environment of care, part 1. In: *Guidelines for Perioperative Practice*. Denver, CO: AORN, Inc; 2017:255.

3. Answer C is correct. The only medication that helps to reverse the effects of systemic local anesthetic toxicity is 20% lipid emulsion. Reference: Guideline for care of the patient receiving local anesthesia. In: *Guidelines for Perioperative Practice*. Denver, CO: AORN, Inc; 2017:623-624.

4. Answer B is correct. The brachial plexus is a group of nerves that run between the clavicle and the first rib. Hyperextension of the arm can press the clavicle and first rib together, applying excessive pressure on the brachial plexus. Reference: Heizenroth PA. Positioning the patient for surgery. In: Rothrock JC, ed. *Alexander's Care of the Patient in Surgery*. 15th ed. St Louis, MO: Elsevier; 2015:160-161.

5. Answer C is correct. Immediately upon receipt of the medication at the sterile field, the scrub person receiving the medication should label the medication container and all devices (eg, syringes) used to deliver or administer the medication. Reference: Guideline for medication safety. In: *Guidelines for Perioperative Practice*. Denver, CO: AORN, Inc; 2017:311.

6. Answer D is correct. Discrepancies in wrong-site surgery are addressed before starting the procedure. Reference: National Patient Safety Goals: Hospital Accreditation Program, Conduct a preprocedure verification process. UP.01.01.01. The Joint Commission; 2017. https://www.jointcommission.org/assets/1/6/2017_NPSG_HAP_ER.pdf.

7. Answer B is correct. Iodine may interfere with thyroid function in burn patients, patients undergoing thyroidectomy, neonates and premature neonates, and pregnant or lactating women. Answers A and C are harmful effects of chlorhexidine gluconate antiseptic solutions. An allergic response to an iodine-based antiseptic is not related to the iodine. Reference: Guideline for preoperative patient skin antisepsis. In: *Guidelines for Perioperative Practice*. Denver, CO: AORN, Inc; 2017:62-63.

8. Answer B is correct. An allow-natural-death order is a specific directive, written by a physician about end-of-life decisions in proactive terminology providing clarity about the intent of the care that will be provided to the patient. Reference: AORN Position Statement on Perioperative Care of Patients with Do-Not-Resuscitate or Allow-Natural-Death Orders. Denver CO: AORN, Inc; 2014.

9. Answer B is correct. Patients in the steep Trendelenburg experience decreased tidal volume caused by the pressure of abdominal contents against the diaphragm. Reference: Phillips N. Positioning, prepping, and draping the patient. In: *Berry & Kohn's Operating Room Technique*. 13th ed. St Louis, MO: Elsevier; 2017:493.

10. Answer D is correct. The perioperative team member should wear surgical attire that covers his or her arms while performing preoperative patient skin antisepsis. A sterile gown is not required. Reference: Guideline for preoperative patient skin antisepsis. In: *Guidelines for Perioperative Practice*. Denver, CO: AORN, Inc; 2017:65.

11. Answer D is correct. A halon fire extinguisher will smother an electrical fire without leaving a residue on the equipment. Reference: Phillips N. Potential sources of injury to the caregiver and the patient. In: *Berry & Kohn's Operating Room Technique*. 13th ed. St Louis, MO: Elsevier; 2017:220.

12. Answer C is correct: The use of appropriate PPE protects the health care provider's mucous membranes, skin, airway, and clothing from coming into contact with blood or body fluids that may contain infectious materials. Reference: Guideline for transmissible infections. In: *Guidelines for Perioperative Practice*. Denver, CO: AORN, Inc; 2017:514.

13. Answer B is correct. Sterile storage areas should have positive airflow pressure with a minimum of 4 total air changes per hour. Reference: Guideline for a safe environment of care, part 2. In: *Guidelines for Perioperative Practice*. Denver, CO: AORN, Inc; 2017:278.

14. Answer B is correct. An 8-cm vertical incision, Kronig, is made in the lower uterine segment after the bladder is separated and retracted away. This incision is used when the fetus is small, preterm, and in the breech position. Reference: Phillips N. Gynecologic and obstetric surgery. In: *Berry & Kohn's Operating Room Technique*. 13th ed. St Louis, MO: Elsevier; 2017:692.

15. Answer C is correct. After a sterile field has been established, it should not be left unattended. It is also appropriate to cover the sterile field with a sterile drape. Covering the field does not negate the need to provide continual observance in the room. The sterility of the back table is not time related. Reference: Guideline for sterile technique. In: *Guidelines for Perioperative Practice*. Denver, CO: AORN, Inc; 2017:91.

16. Answer D is correct. For patients with an estimated blood loss of less than 1,000 mL, crystalloids are the recommended fluid replacement. Reference: Gawronski DP. Trauma surgery. In: Rothrock JC, ed. *Alexander's Care of the Patient in Surgery*. 15th ed. St Louis, MO: Elsevier; 2015:1117.

17. Answer A is correct. If the x-ray is negative, the count is recorded as incorrect or unreconciled and the x-ray results are noted on the patient's intraoperative record, as well as a description of the search process. Reference: Patient safety and risk management. In: Rothrock JC, ed. *Alexander's Care of the Patient in Surgery*. 15th ed. St Louis, MO: Elsevier; 2015:32.

18. Answer A is correct. IUSS is reserved for those instances in which there is insufficient time to process by the preferred wrapped or container method. Biological and class V indicators must be run in the load with the implant. Reference: Guideline for sterilization. In: *Guidelines for Perioperative Practice*. Denver, CO: AORN, Inc; 2017:871-872.

19. Answer C is correct. Patients have the right to refuse tracking of their medical devices. If a patient refuses to have the device tracked, the nurse should document the refusal along with the required product information and report this information to the manufacturer, but should not include the patient-specific information. Reference: Fink T, Blumm RM. Reconstructive and aesthetic plastic surgery. In: Rothrock JC, ed. *Alexander's Care of the Patient in Surgery*. 15th ed. St Louis, MO: Elsevier; 2014:830.

20. Answer C is correct. Specimens should be passed off the sterile field as soon as possible. Passing the specimen off the sterile field as soon as possible reduces the potential for the integrity of the specimen to be compromised or for the specimen to be lost or misplaced. Reference: Guideline for specimen management. In: *Guidelines for Perioperative Practice*. Denver, CO: AORN, Inc; 2017:459.

4 Communication

KEY TERMS

- Assertive communication
- Authenticity
- Candor
- Communication techniques
- Critical/crucial conversations
- Cultural literacy
- Culture of safety
- Effective communication
- Emotional intelligence
- Hand overs (ie, hand offs)
- Health Insurance Portability and Accountability Act (HIPAA)
- Health literacy
- Information technology
- Jargon
- Nonverbal communication
- Speaking up
- Systems engineering
- Teach-back method

REQUIRED NURSING SKILLS

- Communicating effectively with patient and family members
- Communicating patient status and changes to the interdisciplinary health care providers
- Identifying barriers to communications
    - Participating in the implementation of effective solutions for such barriers
- Providing and documenting perioperative education
- Providing relevant information and preparing the patient for discharge
- Utilizing hand-over communication for continuity of patient care

In preparing to deliver safe and effective patient care, perioperative registered nurses (RNs) most often focus on the technical competencies required to achieve desired outcomes and too often fail to give specific consideration to the role of competent communication. The Joint Commission has identified effective communication as an important patient safety issue.[1] Health care itself is largely communication dependent. When critical information is missing, misunderstood, or poorly communicated, the decisions that nurses make can lead to both minor and major unintended outcomes (Table 4.1).

Communication is the exchange of information between two or more people. Effective communication implies the adage, "You say it; they get it!" Effective communication influences and motivates others to perform actions that further common goals and lead to desired outcomes.[2] The process of making that happen in the perioperative setting, however, requires strong communication skills by all members of the surgical team. Communicating effectively requires that team members convey clear, concise, and complete information at the right time to the right person in a respectful manner appropriate for the recipient. Each health care provider and each patient is a unique individual influenced by his or her background, education, and experience. It follows that communication styles for both the delivery and the receipt of information will vary among individuals. **Effective communication** requires mastery of communication techniques, knowledge of factors that influence communication, and the ability to apply principle to practice. It also requires that effective processes for communicating patient care information be incorporated into the overall perioperative plan of care.[3]

Simply put, effective communication is saying the right thing, in the right way, to the right person, at the right time. This might sound simple, but the number of adverse events related to failed communication indicates that there are significant challenges associated with communicating effectively. This chapter presents delivery styles and techniques, listening skills, influences on interpreting what is said

TABLE 4.1 Possible Sequelae to Ineffective Communication

- Adverse events
- Avoidable readmissions
- Delays
- Inappropriate treatment
- Increased costs
- Increased hospital length of stay
- Inefficiency from rework
- Omission of care
- Other negative patient experiences

and acting upon it, and assertive communication that will help you move forward when the receiver of the communication does not comprehend the message. Scenarios are used to illustrate key concepts.

Factors That Influence Effective Communication

Many factors influence effective communication. Perioperative nurses should be aware of and prepared to deal with these factors, to include nonverbal communication, listening, assertiveness, authenticity, emotional intelligence, communication tools, and a culture of safety. The environment in which communication takes place, and the characteristics of the individuals involved, have a significant effect on the quality of communication. Effective **communication techniques** include paying attention, listening carefully, and speaking assertively, which can be very difficult in the time-sensitive environment where many things are going on at the same time. It is very easy to become distracted, and distractions interfere with effective communication. Managing the environment is as important as developing good communication skills. Communicating effectively is a skill that can be developed and improved with practice and commitment.

No one is born with good communication skills. People learn from role models and from experiences. Those who have good role models and are self-confident become effective communicators more quickly. Others have to learn what is involved in communicating effectively and practice until they are successful.

Nonverbal Communication

The look on a person's face, the position of his or her arms, the person's posture, and the tone of voice used all help reflect what the person is feeling. These are examples of **nonverbal communication**. Much of communication is nonverbal, requiring no words. Tapping the foot and drumming fingers on a table are clear indications that the person is impatient or irritated. Leaning forward and listening intently are indications that the person is trying to understand what is being communicated.

There is a prevalence of barriers to nonverbal communication in the OR setting. For example, masks hide facial cues among team members in the OR and threaten to potentially mislead communication among surgical team members and the patient. The two responsibilities associated with nonverbal communication are, first, to manage it proactively, and second, to be sure that it aligns with your verbal message. The first can be challenging because emotions and bodily reactions to emotions are not always easily controlled. Control of nonverbal communication is one of the skills that effective communicators must master. Using body language that aligns with the message is a bit easier, but still requires consideration and control. Members of the surgical team must remember to remove the surgical mask when speaking to the patient in the preoperative and postoperative areas so that the patient can see the person speaking and pick up on the nonverbal cues that humans unconsciously display. Furthermore, many people unknowingly rely on watching the person's mouth to augment their ability to hear.

LISTENING

There is a difference between listening and hearing. Listening is active; listening is accomplished with purpose. Hearing is what the ears can decipher from the environment. Effective communication requires that the listener get complete and accurate information. That means listening carefully to what the speaker is saying. Hearing clearly what people are saying in a loud and chaotic environment can be challenging, especially when masks hide facial cues that are usually very helpful in interpreting communication. In such a challenging environment, there is a high probability of miscommunication. Validating communication sometimes requires asking an individual to repeat what's been said.

Distractions are also common in the hectic environment of the OR. Listening carefully and consciously can help a person focus on what needs to be heard while ignoring sounds that interfere with concentration. It takes practice and commitment to distinguish between sounds that are normal (eg, electrosurgical unit being activated) and sounds that require attention (eg, electrocardiogram monitor alarming). Listening requires paying attention, validating what is heard, and managing distractions.

Listening also includes the ability to take in more than the words that are heard. Effective listening includes picking up on information to better understand the circumstances surrounding the conversation, such as the emotions associated with the conversation and nonverbal communication cues. For the patient, the stress of facing a surgical procedure can be distracting, making listening intently and retaining information difficult. The nurse must take special care to validate that the patient understands important information that has been communicated.

> **EXAM TIP**
>
> Distractions and roadblocks are not acceptable excuses for poor communication; failure to speak up makes the nurse complicit in any related adverse patient outcome.

Assertiveness

Assertiveness is the ability to speak up when it is necessary.[4] It is an essential skill required for effective communication in the perioperative arena—a skill that every nurse can and must master. **Assertive communication**, or **speaking up**, requires self-assurance and confidence, essential elements of a competent nurse. When a nurse knows that sharing information is crucial to patient safety, it becomes that nurse's responsibility to ensure that the information is communicated effectively, which means that the information is not only sent but also received. That is not always easy when a colleague is busy, focused, has a personal agenda, or has a very strong personality. Every nurse must make the personal commitment to develop the ability to communicate assertively and to engage in a crucial conversation when the situation demands one.

Nurses are not necessarily born assertive; they master the skill by attaining the knowledge necessary to make patient care decisions, understanding their obligation to provide the best environment for the patient, and committing to doing everything that is necessary to ensure that the patient receives safe and effective care. Assertiveness is a commitment that requires practice. Nurses learn the skill from accomplished colleagues and from their own experiences.

Each time a nurse speaks up, holds his or her ground, and demands that the best interests of the patient be recognized, the nurse gains confidence and competence in the role of patient advocate. Adverse outcomes related to lack of assertive communication can be learning experiences as well.

Authenticity

Authenticity implies that an individual is genuine and trustworthy and that he or she is consistently open and truthful. Authentic individuals are self-aware and comfortable with who they are; they are confident.[2] Confidence comes with a solid knowledge base, an understanding of the dynamics of the situation. **Candor** implies honesty and an ability to deliver information in a way that limits the potential for misunderstanding and ill will.[5] Verbal and nonverbal communication should align with each other.

Authentic individuals commit enthusiastically to the goals of the team. They are consistent and energetic in pursuit of those goals. Authentic individuals are comfortable with assertive communication when important issues like patient safety are at risk.

Emotional Intelligence

Emotionally intelligent nurses understand that feelings have an effect on behavior and communication and know that people have difficulty separating feelings from actions. **Emotional intelligence** is the ability to recognize and interpret emotions and use them as a resource for crafting effective communication, including the ability to reflect on the situation before reacting to it. For

> **EXAM TIP**
>
> Emotional intelligence alerts the nurse to the level of anxiety of the patient and family. Providing information tailored to the needs of the patient increases patient confidence and reduces anxiety level.

example, staying calm when emotions (either of the patient, team members, or both) are high allows nurses to manage their emotions and those of others. Emotional intelligence empowers nurses to tailor communication to enhance patient-centered care. For example, showing empathy toward patients can help them respond more positively to the care they receive.

Communication Tools

Systems, protocols, and tools are recognized as drivers of positive patient outcomes.[6] Written tools are a component of **systems engineering**, the process of organizing the environment and providing tools that promote desired outcomes and decrease the likelihood of human error. An example of systems engineering is written tools designed to ensure that all pertinent information has been identified, collected, and communicated among health care team members. When each individual involved in the transfer of patient information follows the same process, communication is consistently complete and comprehensive, without error.

Several popular communication tools that can be used as templates are presented in Table 4.2. They each identify essential categories of information and promote logical progression of thought. All of the popular tools represent standardized organization of pertinent material. The tools are an adjunct to critical thinking. Any of them can help nurses remember all of the pertinent information that will enable their colleagues to provide safe and effective patient care. The best communication documents to use in a particular facility, however, have been customized by that facility's multidisciplinary team of caregivers who have a stake in the communication process.

TABLE 4.2 Frequently Used Communication Methods in the Perioperative Setting[1,2]

METHOD	DESCRIPTION
SBAR	Situation, Background, Assessment, Recommendation
I PASS the BATON	Introduction, Patient, Assessment, Situation, Safety concerns, Background, Actions, Timing, Ownership, Next
PACE for health care	Patient/Problem, Assessment/Actions, Continuing Intentions/Changes, Evaluation
Five Ps	Patient, Plan, Problem, Precautions, Physician
SHARQ	Situation, History, Assessment, Recommendations, Questions
5Ws, 1H	Who, What, When, Where, Why, and How

1. Guideline for team communication. In: *Guidelines for Perioperative Practice*. Denver, CO: AORN, Inc; 2018:752.
2. Chard R, Makary MA. Transfer-of-care communication: nursing best practices. *AORN J.* 2015;102(4):335.

Culture of Safety

Communication takes place most effectively in a **culture of safety** in which everyone is encouraged to speak up when there are opportunities for improvement or to ensure patient safety.[7] No professional likes to hear bad news, but leaders need to hear about problems or they cannot solve them.[8] In such an environment, errors are analyzed for ways in which they can be prevented in the future and blame is only assessed when errors are the result of negligence or willful behavior. This is an ideal environment for **crucial conversations**, those conversations that must take place regardless of the difficulty of engaging in them, because patient safety is involved. Even in a culture of safety, however, personalities and relationships have a significant effect on one's ability to communicate assertively.

Barriers to Effective Communication

Clear communication requires attention to the task at hand. Multitasking, especially for the RN circulator, is a common phenomenon in the OR. Each of the other team members has a specific focus, but the RN circulator must maintain an awareness of everything that is going on and be responsive to any indication that something specific requires attention. It is very difficult to isolate a single activity, but there are many times when that is necessary, such as performing a surgical count, taking a verbal order, or identifying a specimen for pathology. Perioperative personnel should be cognizant of the effects of barriers to communication (eg, distractions, health literacy, age, cultural influences).

> ### SCENARIO
>
> **Consider the following scenario and the quality of communication by the nurse.**
> Surgeon: What's taking so long?
> RN circulator: I'm working as fast as I can. I can't help it if someone else is using the laser you want and the scrub person is at lunch. This slow turnover isn't my fault! (Mumbles)
>
> **Consider the scenario again, this time with the nurse demonstrating emotional intelligence in her response.**
> Surgeon: What's taking so long?
> RN circulator: Dr M, I know that you are in a hurry. We'll have access to the laser in just a few minutes. In the meantime, I'll have the room ready when the scrub person gets back from lunch. There will be no delays in getting the procedure set up. Dr E (ie, the anesthesia professional) is assessing the patient right now. If you could assess and consent her now, I'll be in the preoperative area in just a few minutes to bring her back to the room.
>
> **The lesson.** As seen in Scenario 2, the emotionally intelligent nurse assesses the situation to determine whether the impatience the surgeon is exhibiting is related to something the nurse can address or to a prior situation. In either case, the emotionally intelligent nurse will determine whether something productive can be done to fix the problem. By interpreting emotions and addressing the facts of the situation, nurses can engage in productive communication to promote team collaboration.

Distractions. Managing distractions by setting priorities and making it very clear to the team that attention must be focused on a specific activity is essential to effective circulating. For instance, investigations of most instances of a retained surgical item have determined that the count was documented as correct. The team must be advised and reminded that the count process requires the full attention of the scrub person and RN circulator. Some distractions, such as answering phone calls and leaving the room for supplies, can be managed by facility policy or increased efficiency; however, other distractions must be managed by establishing priorities and communicating clearly with the team.

Disrespect, or the perception of disrespect, is a common distraction that diverts attention from the message of the conversation. When one individual **belittles** another, feelings supersede thinking and the clarity of the message can be lost. Fear and anxiety also interfere with clear communication. For the patient, fear and anxiety make concentrating difficult. For the nurse, anxiety and self-doubt may interfere with the ability or the willingness to be assertive and to engage in crucial conversations.

In addition to distractions, which present a barrier to concentration and clear communication, other barriers must be acknowledged and addressed. Language, including **jargon** (ie, language unique to a particular group) and slang, can interfere with an individual's ability to interpret what he or she hears. For many patients, English is not their primary language; some patients do not speak English at all. The

> ### SCENARIO
>
> **Consider a scenario in which a patient was harmed. How could it have happened? Which practice errors are preventable?**
>
> The perioperative team feels pressured to get the procedure started quickly. The scrub person is hastily setting up the back table and the RN circulator is attending to the patient. The surgeon is not in the room. The anesthesia professional is preparing to perform a lower leg nerve block. Two surgical technologists are available to help the RN circulator, but neither knows where to find some things that the scrub person needs, so the RN circulator runs to obtain the items. She returns to discover that the anesthesia professional has begun the block. She asks whether a time out was performed before he began the block; it had not been done. The anesthesia professional placed the block in the wrong leg, which is a reportable event, one that could have been avoided.
>
> Review the scenario. The environment in which the event occurred is not uncommon. Although the patient and the procedure are the team's only priority, the RN circulator sought to provide the needed equipment. Perioperative personnel can be in situations where they are hurried or trying to help. For example, staffing shortfalls are possible in the OR, and it is possible to have new employees who are not yet experienced in the OR. Although it may seem easier to adopt the mentality of "I'll just do it myself," rather than take the time to explain in detail or negotiate for help, this scenario demonstrates that it is important to avoid that temptation.
>
> How should the perioperative team have protected that patient from harm? The nurse had choices. She could have asked for help or established better priorities, staying with the patient while sending one of the technologists to the front desk for help in finding the supplies. If she had remained in the room, she could have been assertive about implementing the time out, which would have prevented the adverse event from occurring. Most adverse events are the result of failing to speak up, failing to be assertive, and failing to ensure the best environment for safe patient care.
>
> The lesson. Each patient and each procedure are the most important things to the perioperative team members are doing now. Each patient deserves the perioperative team's highest level of communication and decision-making on his or her behalf.

preoperative interview and patient teaching rely on clear communication, so language barriers must be addressed with a translator or sufficient validation of understanding to assure the nurse that communication has been effective. Because medical terminology is involved, and the accuracy of information shared during assessment and education is so important, translation should be performed by a professional translator, even when family members who speak English are present. This is particularly important because even though the family member may speak English, he or she may not be able to translate complicated medical terms. Furthermore, requiring a family member to act as the translator may compromise patient confidentiality. Typically, facilities have a protocol in place for requesting a translator.

Another barrier related to language is a strong accent that can make it difficult to understand words that are clearly spoken by someone who speaks English very well. In surgery, words spoken through a mask can be muffled and easy to misinterpret. It is the nurse's responsibility to ensure that communication has been effective.

Health literacy. Communication must be appropriate to the individual's health literacy. This means taking the person's academic and intellectual preparation, as well as his or her knowledge of health care and health care terminology, into consideration, particularly in regard to patients and families. Historically, materials prepared for documentation, marketing, and training have been written at an eighth grade reading level. Today, this is considered too advanced for many patients. When a nurse speaks with a patient, especially when the patient is a low-literacy learner, the nurse should say things in the simplest and most direct manner possible.

> **EXAM TIP**
>
> The elements of clear communication are simplicity, clarity, and brevity.

Medical terminology and jargon can be a significant barrier to communication with patients and families. Words that clinicians use every day (eg, lap chole, induction, vital signs) may be unknown to them. Acronyms (eg, PACU, BP, SCD) can be completely indecipherable. When there is any doubt whatsoever, validate your patient's understanding of what you have said. Solutions to these barriers in communication include using the **teach-back method** (ie, asking the patient to repeat instructions using his or her own words) and finding different words to convey your message. An important clue when assessing understanding is noting whether that patient's emotional response and nonverbal communication are consistent with the message received.

Compounding the ability of patients and family to assimilate information is the stressful environment in which the communication takes place. Fear and apprehension interfere with concentration and recollection, so communication must accommodate these barriers. Both repetition and validation of comprehension are important. Nurses should take the time to develop communication techniques that provide two-way communication (ie, Socratic communication versus didactic [one-way] communication]) and to elicit feedback in the patient's own words to ensure that the patient not only heard patient-care instructions but understood the information as well.

Cultural influences. People from every country, religion, and ethnic background live in and visit the United States, any of whom might become a patient in a health care facility. It is a challenge to attain **cultural literacy** (ie, awareness of the influences of language, culture, race, and ethnicity on health care and health care decision-making) for every culture; however, it is essential to become knowledgeable of the predominant cultures receiving care in your facility. Cultural awareness is most important with elderly patients because they are more likely to follow their traditions, as well as with pediatric patients cared for by older family members.

Characteristics unique to a culture include the following:

- use of language,
- role of family,
- significance of religion or spirituality,
- definitions of illness,
- use of healing or treatment practices in health provision,

- behaviors relative to the health care experience, and
- methods of making health care decisions.

For instance, in the Hispanic culture, *familismo* (the belief that the needs of the family take precedence over the needs of any single family member) has a significant effect on health care decisions, particularly if pursuing medical help will prove a hardship to the family. For Muslims, a man's facial hair may have either cultural or religious significance. Should a surgical procedure require trimming of beard or mustache, a conversation with the patient is essential to ensure that important patient and family psychosocial needs are met.

Communicating in the Perioperative Area

The perioperative area presents significant challenges to effective communication; therefore, strong communication skills are an essential competency for perioperative nurses. Communication competency includes recognizing opportunities to share essential information with the patient and his or her family members, demonstrating knowledge of the information required for safe patient care, and demonstrating the ability to send and receive information in a timely fashion, including soliciting feedback to validate the effectiveness of the communication.

As the patient travels through the phases of the surgical experience, **hand overs** involve communicating information from health care provider to health care or home caregiver to ensure the continuity and safety of the patient's care. The quality of that information has a direct effect on patient safety and optimal patient outcomes.[3]

PREOPERATIVE COMMUNICATION

Gathering the information needed to provide safe patient care requires both knowledge and skill. The preoperative interview is just one step in the complex process of managing a surgical procedure. With experience and good communication tools, the preoperative interview leaves the patient with realistic expectations and the nurse with pertinent information that enables the surgical team to customize care to meet the patient's specific needs.

> **SCENARIO**
>
> **Consider this interchange in an emergency department.**
>
> A patient was transported to the emergency department by ambulance while experiencing a myocardial infarction. He did not survive the team's resuscitative efforts. The emergency department physician approaches the patient's wife and says, "Our resuscitation efforts were unsuccessful. Is there anyone we can call for you?" She shakes her head. Several hours later, she sees the physician enter the waiting room and approaches him to ask, "Is my husband well enough for me to take him home now?" The absence of distress when the physician gave her the sad news should have been a clue that the patient either misunderstood or misinterpreted the word "resuscitation." The physician should have validated the patient's response to ensure that he or she had communicated effectively. Although communication is described as a two-way street, in the health care environment the clinician must assume more than half of the responsibility for ensuring that communication is successful.

In the ambulatory arena, patient education and discharge planning must be done before the day of the procedure. During the preoperative phase, the nurse validates and reinforces the information the patient has already received. It is less than ideal to wait until the day of surgery to initiate education because the patient's level of stress and anxiety interferes with his or her ability to learn and retain information.

Hand-over communication, information shared among professionals as they pass responsibility for patient care from one to another, is especially significant in the surgical area. Some of the assessment data that the RN circulator needs to customize care for the patient may have been gathered or supplied by other health care professionals during the preoperative period of care. The quantity and quality of information available to the RN circulator have a significant effect on the patient's surgical experience. If important information is missing from the chart, patient care might be compromised or the procedure might be delayed.

> **EXAM TIP**
>
> Sometimes assertiveness is necessary on the part of the nurse to emphasize the importance of information, such as a patient's lack of knowledge, when other team members do not realize its significance.

The RN circulator's preoperative assessment can also identify conditions that may have significant implications for patient safety, such as a potential latex allergy, risk for malignant hyperthermia, or a preexisting infection. The patient may not understand the procedure or may have unrealistic expectations that must be addressed before surgery. The most important thing about this information is that it be communicated to the appropriate individuals and that it be acted on to prevent an adverse patient experience.

INTRAOPERATIVE COMMUNICATION

Surgery is a team activity and all team members should be involved in communication related to the patient. There are many structured communication activities during a procedure. Those surgical team members not directly involved in the conversation should listen carefully to the interchange and support the communication in any way possible. For instance, during the surgical count, every team member should be vigilant, careful not to interfere with the count process, and ready to help look for any item that might be missing. The greatest opportunities for error occur during the time out, specimen identification, surgical counts, medication management, verbal order validation, change of shift or personnel, and personnel debrief.

Time out. One very important team communication is the time-out procedure in which each member of the team is introduced and participates actively in the conversation. The team validates that essential information (eg, patient's vital statistics, allergies) is available, required documents (eg, informed consent, history, and physical examination) are present and completed correctly, necessary equipment and supplies (eg, implants) are immediately available, and required interventions (eg, antibiotic administration, application of sequential compression devices) have occurred. Team members verify that they are about to perform the correct procedure on the right patient, on the right side, at the right level. Performing the time out addresses other potential risks as well (eg, increased fire risk for a procedure performed on the upper chest, neck, or head). Each team member describes how he or she is prepared to prevent or address that risk. By the end of the time out and before the initial incision is made, all of the known elements that place the patient at risk should have been discussed and resolved.

Getting everyone's attention to begin the time out is not always an easy task. It can require the nurse to use assertive communication and display emotional intelligence to help others avoid feeling pressured to hurry or skip this step.

Specimen identification. Accurate identification of a specimen for analysis by the pathology department is a critical activity. The patient's diagnosis and treatment often depend on the pathologist's interpretation of specimen tissue, and the pathologist's diagnosis is specifically related to the information that accompanies the specimen. The RN circulator verifies with the surgeon the name of the tissue and the surgeon's intention for analysis. Other team members should listen closely and should not cause distractions during the interchange among the surgeon, nurse, and scrub person.

The RN circulator must be positive that he or she hears and documents the surgeon's instructions accurately. Often, specimens are labeled so that their orientation to the surgical site is clear; the RN circulator must clearly communicate this orientation to the pathologist. Whether a specimen comes from the right or the left, upper or lower can be significant. An error in describing a specimen or in communicating the surgeon's instructions to the pathologist can have serious consequences for the patient.

Surgical counts. Intraoperative surgical counts can be challenging because both the RN circulator and scrub person have other responsibilities potentially interfering with their concentration. The Joint Commission has identified that not having a policy that clearly defines the count process or not implementing the policy is the primary culprit in cases of retained surgical items. This is an opportunity for assertive communication.[9] If the count is complicated, involving large numbers of instruments, sharps, or sponges, the scrub person should make the instruments and supplies that will be needed during the count available to the rest of the scrub team, and the RN circulator should request support so that the count can proceed uninterrupted.

Medication management. Medication errors are among the most common threats to patient safety. Many of the fluids and medications used in surgery are clear and indistinguishable from one another. Most facilities have detailed policies and procedures regarding labeling of all fluids and medications not in their original containers and reading labels aloud when preparing medications or when transferring medications or fluids to the sterile field. With changes of personnel during a procedure, it is especially important that all fluids and medications be easily identified; assuming that irrigation in an unmarked basin is normal saline when it is, in fact, sterile water can have devastating consequences for the patient. If the scrub person does not know whether the fluid in which gelfoam is soaking is saline or thrombin, it must be discarded and replaced—a very expensive and preventable error.[10]

Verbal order validation. In an environment like the OR with many distractions and the potential for muffled speech through a mask, validating verbal orders is especially important. Did the surgeon order *pitressin* or *pitocin*? It is essential to validate medication orders both verbally and in writing. If necessary, spell out the name of the medication to prevent misunderstanding. The nurse should use the read-back method to ensure accuracy when receiving verbal orders from another health care provider.

Documenting orders in the health record is also important. Facility policy will dictate whether a verbal order from a physician's assistant or RNFA employed by a physician must be validated with the physician. In all cases, clear and validated communication is essential for patient safety.

Change of shift or relief of personnel. Knowledge is essential for making the right decisions. Any individual charged with care of a patient, regardless of how short a time he or she will have that responsibility, must have all of the information required to make safe and appropriate decisions.

> ### SCENARIO
>
> **Consider a scenario in which there is a personnel change during a procedure.**
> Scrub person 2 has relieved scrub person 1 on an exploratory laparotomy following a motor vehicle accident. The surgeon tells scrub person 2 to prepare several liters of normal saline to irrigate the abdominal cavity. The scrub person places a sterile basin at the edge of the table and asks the RN circulator for 2 liters of sterile saline. The RN circulator points out that during her hand-over report, RN circulator 1 said she had poured sterile saline into the basin sitting in the ring stand. Scrub person 2 glances at the basin; she had assumed that solution was for cleaning instruments because it was not labeled. Scrub person 1 had not mentioned before leaving to eat lunch that it was irrigation fluid. Scrub person 2 looks again for a label to verify that it is normal saline but does not find one. She asks the RN circulator again to fill the basin on the table with sterile saline. The RN circulator insists that scrub person 2 should use the saline in the ring stand.
>
> **Assessment.** A crucial conversation is needed here. From a practical standpoint, it is easy to assume that the ring stand basin holds sterile saline, even though it is not labeled. RN circulator 2 says that RN circulator 1 told her that she had poured the sterile saline shortly before being relieved for lunch. There is no other fluid commonly used in large quantities during an exploratory laparotomy, but the fluid is not labeled and the empty bottles were not saved to support the RN circulator's assertion. If it were not sterile saline, it could be something that might do the patient significant harm.
>
> **The lesson.** Should scrub person 2 take that chance, or should she follow protocol about not using unlabeled medications or fluids and ensure that she is providing for the best possible outcome for her patient? This is not a difficult decision to make. As the patient advocate, the scrub person should dispose of the fluid in the basin on the ring stand and insist on new saline; she should then label the basin accordingly.

Clear, concise, and complete communication is essential to ensure the continuity of safe patient care. Relieving personnel for breaks, lunch, or shift changes occurs every day in every type of surgical setting. Whoever is left caring for the patient must know what is important, especially when the information is not something the nurse saw directly. The nurse being relieved must give the oncoming nurse a hand-over report that focuses on

- the progress of the surgical procedure, to include any plans that might require instruments or supplies not currently available;
- the status of the count;
- what specimens have been collected or are expected; and
- what medications or irrigation solutions the scrub person has on the field.

Personnel debrief. Perioperative managers should provide surgical team members an opportunity to express feelings and concerns and to make suggestions for improvement. Providing a debriefing opportunity is especially important when an incident or situation occurs that either has an emotional effect on surgical team members or has the potential for helping to avoid injury to the patient. Involvement in a situation in which a patient is harmed, or could have been harmed, may have a significant emotional effect. A debrief is an opportunity for personnel to express feelings and to examine the situation for opportunities to prevent a recurrence.

When a mistake has been made, nurses speak up so that real or potential patient consequences can be addressed in a timely fashion, or a process can be improved to prevent a recurrence. A debrief is also an opportunity for perioperative managers to reinforce their commitment to a safety culture and to encourage personnel to continue being proactive, speaking up, and protecting patients by preventing errors.

> **EXAM TIP**
>
> In a culture of safety, employees are encouraged to speak up whenever there is an opportunity to prevent an error.

POSTOPERATIVE COMMUNICATION

Communication after a surgical procedure begins with the transfer to the postanesthesia care unit (PACU) and includes preparation for discharge and reinforcement of patient teaching. Just as with handing care of the patient to another clinician during the procedure, a comprehensive report to the PACU nurse is essential.

Meeting the patient's needs postoperatively, to include maintaining stability of body systems, pain control, and level of consciousness, requires an understanding of the patient's experiences during surgery. While the PACU nurse has access to the medical record, he or she can only understand the patient's surgical experience if the RN circulator tells him or her about it during the hand-over report (see Chapter 5 for a more in-depth discussion of transfer-of-care communication). This is an excellent opportunity to implement the SBAR thought process by sharing information related to

- the patient's surgical experience,
- any background information that will affect decision-making,
- a clear assessment of the patient's current status, and
- recommendations for intervention.

In the ambulatory environment, postoperative communication may be more condensed because the patient will be discharged from the facility rather than into the care of another clinician. Emphasis is on reinforcing information given to the patient before the day of the procedure and providing discharge information to the patient and his or her responsible party after surgery.

Health Care–Information Management in the Perioperative Setting

The documentation, storage, and retrieval of patient health information (PHI) has evolved to reflect technological advances in communication. Most health care facilities use information technology to store at least part of their PHI in an electronic format, either as an electronic medical record (EMR) or electronic health records (EHR). The terms EMR and EHR are not interchangeable. The EMR is similar to traditional paper patient charts and is used to track sets of patient information and document patient responses to interventions. Drawbacks of the EMR include that it is typically site-specific, making it difficult to transfer information from one health care setting to another.[11] To address limitations of the EMR, the EHR was specifically designed to share information among health care providers in a variety of settings, as well as between providers and patients. Rather than capture a patient-care experience at one point in time, the EHR chronicles a patient's medical information throughout the person's lifetime.[12]

Both types of electronic PHI management serve to increase the quality of services and treatments provided by

- facilitating communication among providers,
- decreasing errors associated with handwritten orders, and
- reducing health care costs by
    > improving patient outcomes and
    > avoiding duplication of costly treatments and tests.

Because of these perceived benefits, hospitals participating in Medicare and Medicaid programs are provided with financial incentives to move PHI to electronic (ie, EHR or EMR) format.[11]

Use of EMR or EHR requires maintaining the privacy and security of information, in accordance with the Health Insurance Portability and Accountability Act (HIPAA) but allowing health care providers and insurance companies access to patient health care information while maintaining patient confidentiality. Title II of HIPAA gives patients the right to access their own medical records, correct errors, and to be informed of who accesses their PHI and how that information is used.[13]

Perioperative nurses should be aware of the following HIPAA privacy regulations when communicating patient care activities:

- If PHI can identify a patient (eg, name, date of birth, social security number, telephone numbers, driver's license number, postal or e-mail addresses, health insurance identification numbers, medical record numbers, full-face photographs), it should never be sent to a non-secure source that could be distributed and viewed by multiple people. This includes any form of media, including electronic, paper, or verbal.
- Perioperative nurses should ensure that PHI is shared only with authorized persons. Except in certain circumstances, patients have the right to determine who receives their PHI. This has implications for the perioperative nurse who provides updates on the progress of a surgical procedure to family members or significant others.

Operationalizing HIPAA regulations in the perioperative setting requires limiting access to PHI to authorized users. Perioperative nurses should not share their computer passwords or leave open computer screens unattended. Perioperative nurses should also be familiar with the backup plan when electronic documentation platforms are disrupted by technology failures or routine updates to avoid loss of data and interruptions in patient care.[13]

The HIPAA privacy rules require that employees and volunteers are provided with training on

- the organization's policies and procedures regarding patient privacy and confidentiality,
- reporting standards for infractions, and
- consequences for employees who violate organizational or HIPAA privacy rules.[14]

It is the responsibility of the perioperative nurse to maintain initial and continuing competency to ensure that documentation and transfer of PHI meet federal and organizational standards.

Perioperative nurses have an ethical obligation to protect their patients' privacy, including protecting the confidentiality of PHI.[15] Nursing actions that compromise HIPAA regulations can jeopardize the patient's trust in the professional relationship with the nurse. Additionally, persons who knowingly obtain or disclose identifiable patient information face fines of $50,000 to $250,000 and up to 10 years of imprisonment based on the severity of the wrongful conduct.[15]

Key Concepts and Review: Case Study

The delivery of safe patient care is based on caregivers having the information they need to make appropriate decisions. The effective transfer of patient information requires that caregivers be skilled communicators and use tools that promote the transfer of complete and accurate information. Effective communication takes practice, and each individual caring for patients in the perioperative arena is responsible for developing and using the communication skills and tools necessary to ensure patient safety. Remember that important components of patient safety are listening carefully, giving concise and accurate information, being emotionally intelligent and authentic, using the communication tools embraced by the facility, and above all, speaking up about any concern.

CASE STUDY

According to the surgery schedule, Mr Davidson is scheduled for a right total knee replacement at 7:30 AM.

1. The RN circulator, Judy Evans, is interviewing Mr Davidson, a 68-year-old man with early-onset dementia. Mr Davidson lives with his son and daughter. Mr Davidson's son is with him in the preoperative holding area. Judy speaks slowly and clearly so that Mr Davidson can follow the conversation. Mr Davidson's surgical consent has been signed for a right total knee replacement, but the operative site is not marked. The x-rays are in the OR on the x-ray monitor. Because Judy spent extra time interviewing Mr Davidson and validating information with his son, there is pressure from the surgical team to bring the patient to the room and get the procedure started.

   Think about what Judy knows about her patient. Is there anything she should be communicating to other members of the team?

2. While Judy is with the patient in the preoperative holding area, the scrub person and anesthesia professional are setting up for a left knee replacement according to the x-rays on the x-ray monitor. Judy brings the patient into the room and while she is helping him move to the OR bed, both the scrub person and the anesthesia professional ask her for supplies.

   What is Judy's primary responsibility as the RN circulator? What should she be doing at this point?

3. As soon as Mr. Davidson is positioned comfortably on the OR bed and the safety strap is securely in place, Judy leaves the room to collect the supplies for her teammates. While Judy is out, the surgeon comes and tells the anesthesia professional to get started. The surgeon talks to the anesthesia professional as he begins his anesthesia routine. When Judy returns, the patient is asleep and the surgeon is looking at the x-rays. The surgeon looks at Judy and says, "Get some help so we can position and prep." Judy and the surgeon begin the positioning process and Judy is concentrating on getting some additional help for the prep.

Judy has been running since she brought the patient to the room. What do you think might be an effective way to handle Judy's situation?

4. The patient is prepped and draped. The surgeon is again looking at the x-rays. He asks the scrub person for the scalpel.

What is the next thing that should happen?

ANSWERS TO CASE STUDY

1. A thorough assessment followed by appropriate management of the information gathered is the primary responsibility of the RN circulator at this point. Although everything seems in order, The Joint Commission's Universal Protocol for Preventing Wrong Site, Wrong Procedure and Wrong Person Surgery requires preprocedure verification and site marking. Although the procedure has been verified with the son and the surgical consent, Judy should call the surgeon to the preoperative holding area to mark the right knee.

2. Quite often the perioperative nurse has several things to do at the same time. Using critical thinking to prioritize tasks is an essential component of perioperative nursing. Although the supplies needed by the scrub person and the anesthesia professional are important, the RN circulator's first responsibility is to the patient. Judy should be at the patient's side during intubation. She could defer getting the supplies until it was safe to leave the patient, or arrange for someone else to get them. There is always a mechanism in place for calling for help.

3. At this point, Judy has been so busy since bringing the patient to the room that she has not taken time to assess what is going on around her. Setting priorities and concentrating on what is most important to ensure safe care for the patient would prevent this chaotic situation.

4. There has been no conversation with the team about the procedure. Judy is concentrating on one task at a time while losing sight of the big picture. While she and the surgeon are positioning the patient, Judy is thinking about getting someone in to hold the leg for the prep. Although everyone on the surgical team is responsible for participating in the time out, it usually falls to the RN circulator to ensure that the time out is initiated before the surgeon takes possession of the scalpel. When everyone is forced to stop what they are doing and assess their responsibilities related to the procedure, it should become evident very quickly that there is a discrepancy between the operative report and the preparations for a left knee replacement. The operative report was verified by the RN circulator during the preoperative assessment. A careful look at the x-rays determined that they were placed incorrectly on the x-ray monitor.

The lesson. The time out prevented a wrong-site surgery, but the need for reprepping and redraping increased the patient's time under anesthesia, the time the OR was in use, the costs associated with the procedure, and disruption of the flow of the OR schedule and the surgeon's schedule. Setting priorities and communicating effectively with team members promote an environment that is calm and purposeful with focus on managing the patient's care safely. Conversely, when incidents occur, team members become rushed, harried, and disgruntled with themselves and with each other, a situation that does not facilitate patient safety.

References

1. Take 5 with The Joint Commission: why patient-centered communication matters. 2013. The Joint Commission. http://hwcdn.libsyn.com/p/2/1/6/2167cdf30f13173a/Take_5_TCordero_pt_ctr_comm_FINAL.mp3?c_id=5827788&expiration=1444061617&hwt=e6edce7de0163b7e873329519e96630b.
2. Daft RL. Traits, behaviors, and relationships. In: *The Leadership Experience*. 6th ed. Stamford, CT: South-Western College Publications; 2014:34-63.
3. Guideline for transfer of patient care information. In: *Guidelines for Perioperative Practice*. Denver, CO: AORN, Inc; 2017:711-716.
4. Boynton B. Assertiveness. In: *Successful Nurse Communication*. Philadelphia, PA: FA Davis Company; 2015:43-56.
5. Daft R. What does it mean to be a leader? In: *The Leadership Experience*. Stamford, CT: Cengage Learning; 2015:2-32.
6. Chard R, Makary MA. Transfer-of-care communication: nursing best practices. *AORN J*. 2015;102(4):329-339.
7. Boynton B. Understanding organization culture. In: *Successful Nurse Communication*. Philadelphia, PA: FA Davis Company; 2016:122-129.
8. Daft R. Leadership communication. In: *The Leadership Experience*. 6th ed. Stamford, CT: Cengage Learning; 2015:258-289.
9. The Joint Commission. Preventing unintended retained foreign objects. *Sentinel Event Alert* (issue 51). October 17, 2013. https://www.jointcommission.org/assets/1/6/SEA_51_URFOs_10_17_13_FINAL.pdf.
10. Guideline for medication safety. In: *Guidelines for Perioperative Practice*. Denver, CO: AORN, Inc; 2017:295-333.
11. McMullen PC, Howie WO, Philipsen N, et al. Electronic medical records and electronic health records: overview for nurse practitioners. J Nurse Pract. 2014;10(9):660-665.
12. Gummadi S, Housri N, Zimmers TA, Koniaris LG. Electronic medical record: a balancing act of patient safety, privacy, and health care delivery. *Am J Med Sci*. 2014;348(3):238-243.
13. Summary of the HIPAA Privacy Rule. US Department of Health and Human Services Office for Civil Rights. May 2003. http://www.hhs.gov/sites/default/files/privacysummary.pdf.
14. Guideline for health care information management. In: *Guidelines for Perioperative Practice*. Denver, CO: AORN, Inc; 2017:591-616.
15. AORN's Perioperative Explications for the ANA *Code of Ethics for Nurses with Interpretive Statements*. 2017. https://www.aorn.org/guidelines/clinical-resources/code-of-ethics [member access only].

Additional Resource

Patient hand-off/over tool kit. AORN, Inc. http://www.aorn.org/guidelines/clinical-resources/tool-kits.

Practice Exam Questions

1. Which of the following is a common root cause of sentinel events?
   a. Failure to use written communication tools
   b. Breakdown in communication
   c. Absence of or failure to follow policies and procedures
   d. Fear of reprisal for speaking up

2. When communicating patient information to other team members, perioperative RNs should
   a. speak loudly and slowly.
   b. avoid using body language.
   c. use the read-back method.
   d. provide the information in writing.

3. What is the greatest value of a standardized process for transferring patient information?
   a. Improves the accuracy, reliability, and quality of information.
   b. Shortens the time it takes to transfer information from one caregiver to another.
   c. Ensures that the same information is transferred for every patient.
   d. Ensures that the transfer process adheres to facility policy.

4. Structure and processes for transfer of patient information should be developed
   a. according to The Joint Commission and Centers for Medicare & Medicaid Services guidelines.
   b. by a multidisciplinary team comprising caregivers who participate in the transfer of patient information.
   c. by the health care facility's Risk Management Department.
   d. using the SBAR format.

5. During an intraoperative hand over (ie, hand off) between scrub persons before a change in personnel using the SBAR format, the information under Situation includes pertinent procedural information, name of the procedure, and
   a. patient allergies.
   b. name of the patient.
   c. names of the surgical team.
   d. medications on the back table.

6. Postoperative teaching for a male patient after inguinal hernia repair should include the application of ice packs 3 to 4 times a day to the scrotal area to prevent edema for the first
   a. 2 days.
   b. 4 days.
   c. 6 days.
   d. 7 days.

7. There should be a process in place to _____ the efficacy of standardized formats.
    A. identify
    B. determine
    C. evaluate
    D. share

8. Effective communication skills are best demonstrated when the caregiver's body language is
    A. consistent with the spoken word.
    B. viewed as more important than the spoken word.
    C. kept to a minimum or avoided.
    D. animated.

9. If corrections are made to the medical record, the correction should
    A. be initialed.
    B. start over on a new page.
    C. be covered with correction fluid.
    D. include date, time, and initials.

10. The Health Information Technology for Economic and Clinical Health (HITECH) Act
    A. guarantees the privacy of individuals receiving health services and the confidentiality of identifiable health information.
    B. addresses the use of electronic health information technology to improve health care quality.
    C. enhances the ability of the United States government to monitor and detect activities that indicate support for terrorism.
    D. gives citizens some control over the information collected about them by the federal government and its agencies.

Answers with Supported Rationales

1. Answer B is correct. Including briefings and debriefings before and after surgery, respectively, allows for improved communication among team members. The goal of effective communication is to ensure that all team members are aware of key safety strategies and prepared for the surgical procedure. Reference: Steelman VM. Concepts basic to perioperative nursing. In: Rothrock JC, ed. *Alexander's Care of the Patient in Surgery*. 15th ed. Philadelphia, PA: Elsevier; 2015:7.

2. Answer C is correct. Perioperative team members should use the read-back method when communicating patient information to other team members. Reference: Guideline for team communication. In: *Guidelines for Perioperative Practice*. Denver, CO: AORN, Inc; 2018:752.

3. Answer A is correct. Using a standardized format promotes optimal communication by all perioperative team members during transfer of patient care information. Reference: Guideline for team communication. In: *Guidelines for Perioperative Practice*. Denver, CO: AORN, Inc; 2017:751.

4. Answer B is correct. All members of the team should be encouraged to participate and recommend information requirements for the standardized process of sharing patient information. Patient safety is improved when all members of the team contribute to communication standards. Reference: Guideline for team communication. In: *Guidelines for Perioperative Practice*. Denver, CO: AORN, Inc; 2017:751.

5. Answer B is correct. The patient name is included in the Situation part of SBAR hand overs. The other options are all part of the background format. Reference: Murphy EK. Patient safety and risk management. In: Rothrock JC, ed. *Alexander's Care of the Patient in Surgery*. 15th ed. St Louis, MO: Elsevier; 2015:28.

6. Answer A is correct. Apply and demonstrate to the male patient scrotal support or ice packs to decrease scrotal edema and discomfort. Ice is usually left on for 15–20 minutes, 3 or 4 times per day for the first 2 days. Reference: Clark-Cutaia MN. Hernia repair. In: Rothrock JC, ed. *Alexander's Care of the Patient in Surgery*. 15th ed. St Louis, MO: Elsevier; 2015:390.

7. Answer C is correct. Evaluation of documentation is an essential process not only to identify areas for improvement but also to implement any changes deemed necessary. Any compromise of patient safety from deficient data transfer must be addressed. Reference: Guideline for patient information management. In: *Guidelines for Perioperative Practice*. Denver, CO: AORN, Inc; 2017:606.

8. Answer A is correct. A key element in effective communication is to demonstrate appropriate body language that matches the spoken word. Reference: Phillips N. Perioperative education. In: *Berry & Kohn's Operating Room Technique*. 13th ed. St Louis, MO: Elsevier; 2017:11.

9. Answer D is correct. Including date, time, and initials of the person making the correction is necessary for legal documentation. If a new page is needed, the original page should be included in the record. Correction fluid should never be used. Reference: Phillips N. Legal, regulatory, and ethical issues. In: *Berry & Kohn's Operating Room Technique*. 13th ed. St Louis, MO: Elsevier; 2017:45.

10. Answer B is correct. The HITECH Act is a component of the American Recovery and Reinvestment Act that addresses the use of electronic health information technology to improve health care quality, coordination of care, and health information privacy and security. Reference: Guideline for patient information management. In: *Guidelines for Perioperative Practice*. Denver, CO: AORN, Inc; 2017:608.

5 Transfer of Care

✎ KEY TERMS

- Care coordination
- Discharge follow-up
- Hand overs
- Interdisciplinary services
- Phases of care (preoperative, intraoperative, postoperative)
- Regulatory guidelines for discharge planning
- Transfer-of-care criteria

☑ REQUIRED NURSING SKILLS

- Collaborating with interdisciplinary services
- Documentation in the health record
- Evaluating patient status
- Facilitating transfer of patient care to the next level of patient care
- Transfer-of-care communication

The practice settings for perioperative registered nurses (RNs) include traditional ORs, ambulatory surgery centers, physicians' offices, cardiac catheterization laboratories, endoscopy suites, interventional radiology suites, and any other area where operative or other invasive procedures may be performed. Whatever the practice setting, the perioperative RN is one member of an interdisciplinary team whose common goal is for all patients to have safe, coordinated transfers of care throughout the perioperative continuum.

In January 2015, The Joint Commission (TJC) recommended in their Hospital National Patient Safety Goal 2, "Improve the effectiveness of communication among caregivers."[1] As reported in *Quick Safety* in November 2015, sentinel event data compiled by TJC from January 2014 to October 2015 identified 197 sentinel events, for which the root causes included failures in patient communication in 127 incidents, patient education in 26, and patient rights in 44.[2] Such occurrences of communication breakdowns can be reduced. Perioperative nurses can be leaders in the transfer of care information. Perioperative nurses want their patients to transition smoothly and successfully through the perioperative continuum. According to Chard and Makary, "Understanding best practices in transfer-of-care communication begins with a foundation of strong communication skills."[3(p331)] Optimal communication in the perioperative setting should include all members of the perioperative team: "When health care professionals are not communicating effectively, patient safety is at risk for several reasons: lack of critical information, misinterpretation of information, unclear orders over the telephone, and overlooked changes in status."[4]

> **EXAM TIP**
>
> A face-to-face interaction during hand overs allows for a greater range of communication methods, facilitates nonverbal communication, and helps to ensure accurate information has been received.

Optimal communication incorporates both verbal and written components, and includes a face-to-face interaction.[5] **Hand overs** (ie, hand offs) are interactive, two-way communications that occur between the giver of information and the receiver of information. The giver of the information should provide information about

- current and timely relevant patient assessments, including the patient's sociocultural, religious, or personal beliefs;
- any procedures or treatments that the perioperative patient underwent;
- any unplanned or adverse events that might have occurred during the perioperative phases;
- special or medical equipment needs the patient may have; and
- any provider orders that will be carried forward in the patient's continuum of care.

The receiver of the information should

- engage in a verification process of the information he or she received using a read-back or repeat-back method,

- actively listen and connect with the giver during the discussion,
- synthesize the patient's current information and formulate an appropriate plan of care, and
- incorporate a distinct time when the receiver will ask the giver any questions needing further clarification to confirm understanding of the information received.

Incorporation of a hand-over tool uses scientific research, which is evidence based and includes best practices.

The OR setting is a dynamic and complex environment presenting many challenges for effective communication among health care providers, patients, and families.[6] It is reported that some nursing units may "transfer or discharge 40% to 70% of their patients every day,"[7(p36)] which demonstrates not only the frequency of hand overs occurring daily in the perioperative setting but also the possible communication breaches at each transfer of care. Realizing that every perioperative patient undergoes multiple transfers of care, the high risk for errors increases. Interruptions of the nurse's workflow during transfers of care can increase the likelihood of errors, including information loss or miscommunication.

> **EXAM TIP**
>
> To communicate effectively during care transfers, the perioperative RN should
> - use a standardized language set;
> - provide current, timely, relevant, accurate patient assessment information;
> - address the patient's sociocultural, religious, or personal beliefs; and
> - help move the perioperative patient along the continuum of care safely and effectively.

AORN and the US Department of Defense Patient Safety Program collaboratively developed a web-based tool kit with resources to guide perioperative team members during transfers of care.[8] Included in AORN's Patient Hand-off/over Tool Kit are several examples of hand-over tools for perioperative team members to incorporate into their processes.[8] Three examples are

- I PASS THE BATON (Introduction, Patient, Assessment, Situation, Safety Concerns, Background, Actions, Timing, Ownership, Next),
- I-SBAR (Introduction, Situation, Background, Assessment, Recommendation), and
- the Five Ps (Patient, Plan, Purpose, Problem, Precautions).

AORN does not endorse or advocate one tool or strategy over another. (See Chapter 4 for a more in-depth discussion of communication tools.)

Perioperative nursing care encompasses three **phases of care: preoperative phase, intraoperative phase,** and **postoperative phase.** A transfer of care occurs as the patient undergoing an operative or other invasive procedure transitions through a continuum of these phases (Figure 5.1). Additional transfers of care may occur for personnel shift changes or relief breaks. Much like the telephone game played during childhood, the risk of inaccurate or forgotten information increases during each episode of transferred care from one team member to another.

Transfer-of-care communication is the nurse's responsibility. The nurse should ensure the accuracy of the information, provide clear and concise information, and prevent interruptions. It is not uncommon during the perioperative phases of care for a patient to be unable to communicate. Therefore, it is imperative for the perioperative nurse to act as the patient's advocate to ensure that the patient's needs are met.

FIGURE 5.1 Transfers of Care by Phase

Perioperative patients undergo multiple transfers of care.

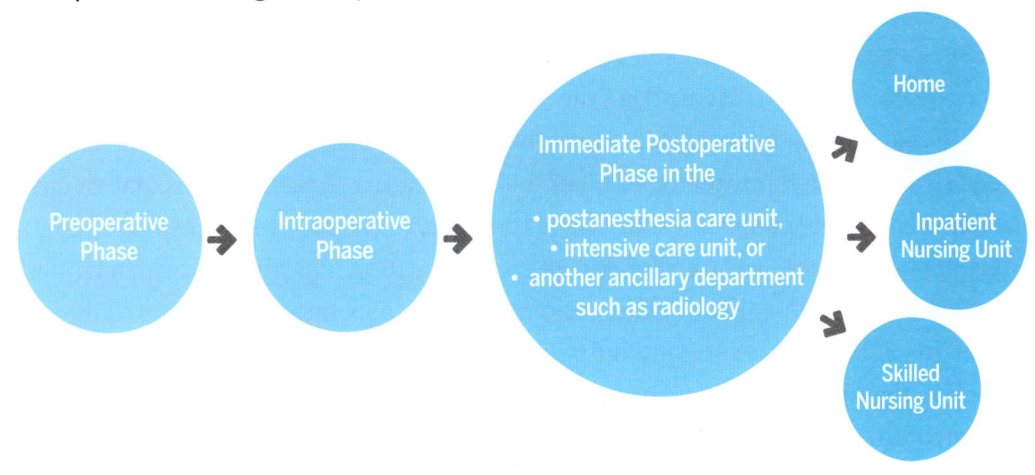

Preoperative Phase → Intraoperative Phase → Immediate Postoperative Phase in the
- postanesthesia care unit,
- intensive care unit, or
- another ancillary department such as radiology

→ Home
→ Inpatient Nursing Unit
→ Skilled Nursing Unit

Perioperative Transfers of Care

Typically, there are four transfers of care during the perioperative continuum of care. These care transfers have specific **transfer-of-care criteria** and are based on the perioperative phases of care:

1. preoperative evaluation provider to preoperative nurse,
2. preoperative nurse to intraoperative nurse,
3. intraoperative nurse to postoperative nurse, and
4. postoperative nurse to patient and his or her family member or home care provider or to the next level of in-hospital care.[5,9]

PREOPERATIVE EVALUATION PROVIDER TO PREOPERATIVE NURSE

Preoperative evaluation providers are instrumental in preparing the patient for surgery or invasive procedures. Ideally, a patient should be evaluated approximately two weeks but no more than 30 days before the scheduled procedure. At this appointment, the provider performs a complete head-to-toe physical assessment, which includes all body systems. The preoperative evaluation provider should obtain and document the patient's past and current medical conditions and previous surgical procedures, and also the significant medical and surgical histories of the patient's family members. This assessment should discuss the patient's social history, including use of alcohol, tobacco, or other recreational drugs. The provider should ask the patient for a complete current medication list with dosing information, including any herbal supplements or over-the-counter products. The provider should explain to the patient the NPO instructions for the evening before and on the day of surgery. Included in NPO instructions, the nurse should also explain specifically to the patient which of his or her current medications should be taken with a sip of water on the morning of surgery, which medications should be held until after surgery, and which if any medications the patient should bring to the health care facility on the day of surgery (eg, emergency inhalers). The provider should determine whether the patient has any piercings, including any that are not readily visible, and should instruct the patient to remove the piercings and all jewelry before arriving at the hospital. If the patient is resistant to removing jewelry or piercings, the nurse should explain the danger of burns if electrosurgery is used during the procedure and also accidental removal should they be caught on equipment. The nurse should also instruct the patient to remove nail polish and artificial nails on the surgical extremity, explaining the increased risk of fungal growth under artificial nail coverings.

The preoperative evaluation provider uses all of this information to perform a risk factor assessment to determine whether additional preoperative testing (eg, cardiac, respiratory, blood testing, x-rays) is required before the upcoming procedure. The transfer-of-care communication typically occurs in a written format.

A transfer of care occurs from the provider performing the preoperative evaluation to the preoperative nurse. Many facilities, however, especially outpatient surgery centers, do not have a preoperative evaluation provider. In this situation, the preoperative nurses at that facility often perform the preoperative evaluations (except for the actual physical examination and ordering additional preoperative tests) by telephone, which includes providing preoperative education. This telephonic evaluation typically occurs a day or two before surgery. The nurse takes written notes (eg, electronic or hard copy) about this telephonic interview and passes on the information gleaned to the preoperative nurse(s) who will be caring for the patient on the day of surgery in the form of a written transfer-of-care communication.

PREOPERATIVE NURSE TO INTRAOPERATIVE NURSE

On the day of surgery, when the patient arrives in the preoperative unit, the preoperative nurse conducts a preoperative nursing assessment. The preoperative nurse reviews the written communication from the preoperative evaluation provider or any subsequent evaluation. The preoperative nurse then performs a physical assessment of the patient. The nurse uses the findings from the preoperative evaluation, the results of any testing, and the current patient status to formulate a nursing care plan specific to that patient.

The nursing process (ie, assessment, diagnosis, planning, implementation, evaluation) allows the preoperative nurse to develop a nursing care plan with nursing diagnoses that helps ensure that the patient's discharge planning is thorough and individualized to his or her needs (as discussed in Chapter 1). Creating a nursing care plan with nursing diagnoses, either actual or potential, provides a fluid and dynamic method to provide guidance as the patient progresses through the continuum of the perioperative experience (see Chapter 2).

To prepare the patient for the transfer of care from the preoperative phase to the intraoperative phase, the preoperative and intraoperative nurses must perform many steps. Surgical and procedural areas have a variety of evidence-based checklists from which they may choose that can be incorporated into their practices. Whichever checklist a facility chooses to use can be easily adapted and modified to fit into individual surgical and procedural practices.

Nursing care provided in the preoperative area, for the most part, consists of care delivered by an individual nurse or nurses. Although hand overs occur between the preoperative nurse and the intraoperative nurse, the intraoperative nurse will not be the sole provider of care during the procedure. The intraoperative nurse is a member of a surgical team rendering care during the intraoperative phase. The number of team members differs and depends on the type of procedure being performed. Typically, surgical teams consist of the surgeon, the anesthesia professional (eg, anesthesiologist, certified registered nurse anesthetist [CRNA]), RN circulator, and scrub person (ie, nurse or surgical technician).

The RN circulator receives the patient who is scheduled to undergo an operative or other invasive procedure from the preoperative nurse. The preoperative nurse and RN circulator participate in hand-over communication that is multifaceted (Table 5.1).

> **EXAM TIP**
>
> Patients may feel more comfortable sharing sensitive health information with a nurse. The nurse functioning on a team delivering surgical care must prioritize the patient's care and share information as needed with other team members.

When the patient has arrived in the surgical or invasive procedural suite, the RN circulator employs TJC's Universal Protocol.[10] This protocol serves as a guide to help health care providers prevent wrong-person, wrong-procedure, or wrong-site (or -side) surgery. As the receiver of the patient, the RN circulator conducts a preprocedure verification process. The purpose of this verification process is to address any missing information or discrepancies before starting the procedure. The RN circulator verifies the correct patient using two unique identifiers: the correct procedure and the correct site or side. If possible, the nurse includes the patient in this verification process.

After verifying the correct patient, correct procedure, and correct site or side, the RN circulator verifies the following:

- the provider performing the procedure;
- the presence of a completed and current, signed, and dated history and physical examination;
- the presence of a preanesthesia assessment;
- the type of anesthesia planned;
- the signed informed consents (eg, surgical, anesthetic, blood products as appropriate);
- the presence of any advance directives;
- the presence of diagnostic and radiological testing results as ordered;
- the availability of blood products as ordered;
- the availability of implants, devices, or special equipment as requested;
- medications, including the date and time of the last dose;
- medication or food allergies;
- the need for applicable venous thromboembolism prophylaxis;
- the need for quality measure interventions for beta-blocker therapy;
- Surgical Care Improvement Project measures (eg, prophylactic antibiotic administration);
- the need for standard precautions (eg, respiratory, contact isolation);
- the presence of catheters or other invasive lines; and
- the presence of site marking by the licensed independent practitioner who will perform the procedure according to the organization's written policy.

Occasionally during the course of a procedure, the need for a personnel change occurs because of relief breaks or personnel shift constraints. Based on the facility's policy, a pared-down iteration of patient transfer information occurs. Interruptions may occur by the surgical team during verbal communication

TABLE 5.1 The Transfer from Preoperative to Intraoperative Care

- Confirm the patient's correct identity using two unique identifiers (eg, full name and date of birth).
- Confirm the planned surgical procedure.
- Confirm the procedural site, including laterality if appropriate.
- Confirm the medical diagnosis.
- Confirm the provider performing the procedure.
- Identify the presence of required legal documents.
- Identify the presence of any advance directives documents.
- Confirm that an updated history and physical examination is present, signed, and dated.
- Confirm that diagnostic and radiological testing results are present.
- Verify the availability of blood products if ordered.
- Specify precautions required (eg, respiratory or contact isolation).
- Verify the presence of requested prostheses or implants.
- Verify NPO status.
- Review the patient's current list and dosages of medications, including date and time of last dose taken.
- Identify any known medication or food allergies.
- Provide current vital signs.
- Discuss pain assessment and pain management goals.
- Discuss the presence of any unremoved jewelry or piercings.
- Identify any unremoved artificial nail coverings.
- Specify the patient's current height (ie, pounds and kilograms), weight, and body mass index.
- Discuss applicable age-related, sociocultural, spiritual, educational, or physical needs.
- Verify whether venous thromboembolism prophylaxis is needed.
- Verify whether quality measure interventions for beta-blocker therapy are needed.
- Identify Surgical Care Improvement Project measures (eg, prophylactic antibiotic administration) that may be needed.

---

hand overs, risking the accuracy or completeness of information. Recognizing that errors, miscommunication, or lack of communication may occur during these personnel changes, many facilities attempt to assign personnel to procedures based on their scheduled work hours to decrease the potential number of transfers of care.

When the surgical procedure is complete and before the patient is transferred from the procedural room, a debriefing may be performed. An example of a simple debriefing tool is answering in the following questions:

1. What went well?
2. What needs improvement (eg, systems, supplies, staffing, communication issues)?
3. How can these problems be resolved and prevented in the future?

When transferring care of the patient, the RN circulator provides a hand-over report to the nurse who will assume the patient's care during the immediate postoperative phase.

INTRAOPERATIVE NURSE TO POSTOPERATIVE NURSE

During the final minutes of the procedure and at a point when intraoperative care will not be compromised, the RN circulator provides a report to the nurse from the receiving unit, typically the postanesthesia care unit. Providing advanced notice allows the receiving nurse the opportunity to prepare for the patient's arrival. This report includes information about the patient's preoperative and intraoperative care, and relays any pertinent needs for the patient's postoperative recovery. The receiving postoperative nurse should use a hand-over communication tool to record the patient's information that was communicated. Use of a hand-over tool facilitates a process intended to reduce errors and omissions of pertinent information. The RN circulator should follow the headings set forth in the tool to help eliminate confusion and redundancy in information relayed. The overarching goal of the hand-over tool is to hardwire the hand-over process, which increases the effectiveness of care-transfer communication, decreases miscommunication or failed communication, and provides for a safe patient exchange.

Nurse-to-nurse hand overs of the postprocedural patient to the postoperative care unit should include

- the patient's personal identifying information;
- the procedure the patient underwent, including any deviations or additional procedures incurred;
- the type of anesthesia received and the patient's current state of emergence and airway status;
- the patient's hemodynamic status and current vital signs;
- estimated blood loss, and blood products received intraoperatively and available for postoperative care;
- medications received intraoperatively, including antibiotics, pain medications, and antiemetics;
- current laboratory values, if known;
- allergies;
- any untoward events that may have occurred intraoperatively; and
- any potential issues that might occur postoperatively.

Also included in the transfer of care should be

- any types of drainage tubes or invasive lines placed and their locations;
- any special needs (eg, patient who is hard of hearing or deaf, is blind, or does not speak English; patient who requires hearing aids, dentures, or glasses);
- any preoperative physical limitations or findings (eg, paraplegia, quadriplegia, facial paralysis, previous eye surgery, preoperative level of consciousness, skin breakdowns or bruising); and
- any equipment needs postoperatively (eg, continuous passive motion machine, cryotherapy ice machine, mechanical ventilator).

POSTOPERATIVE NURSE TO PATIENT AND HOME CARE PROVIDER

Postoperative care consists of care provided in phases, including phase I, phase II, intensive care or other inpatient unit, or an extended care unit if needed. The American Society of PeriAnesthesia Nurses (ASPAN) defines phase I as the level of care typically provided in a postanesthesia care unit (PACU) or if needed in an intensive care unit, in which close monitoring is required, including airway and ventilatory support, progression toward hemodynamic stability, pain management, fluid management, and other acute aspects of patient care. After the patient has progressed beyond these elements of care, the patient can progress to phase II level of care. The nursing roles in phase I focus on providing postanesthesia nursing in the immediate postanesthesia period, then transitioning to phase II, the inpatient setting, or an intensive care setting for continued care. Basic life-sustaining needs should be of the highest priority. Frequent monitoring is required during this phase.[11(p7,30-42)]

ASPAN defines phase II as the level of care in which plans and care are provided to progress the patient home. The nursing roles in this phase focus on preparation for care in the home or an extended care environment. This may be in the same location as phase I care. Many PACUs provide blended levels of care, in which all levels of care are provided in the same location. Often, this is done for staffing reasons or for continuity of care. So if a patient is ready to go to the bathroom and is awake and stable enough, he or she is not necessarily a phase I patient anymore. Instead, the patient has progressed to phase II level of care, even if the patient is in the same location. The same goes for discharging a patient home from phase I. If a patient is ready to go home, then the patient has progressed beyond phase I level of care to phase II level of care, and may go home if he or she has met discharge criteria. These phases are levels of nursing care and should not be mistaken for locations of care.[11(p7,30-42)]

The perioperative patient's transition from phase I to phase II level of care is based on the nurse's assessment of the patient's postoperative status. This assessment confirms stable vital signs, which include a normothermic temperature, blood pressure measurements within 20 mmHg of preprocedural measurements, respiratory rate, heart rate and rhythm, and oxygen saturation levels ≥ 90%. Depending on facility policy, some PACU nurses use a postanesthesia scoring system (eg, Aldrete scoring) to determine whether the patient has met defined discharge criteria. The patient's pain should be well controlled, and the patient's airway should be stable and secure. The PACU nurse manages the patient's pain to the patient's satisfaction, alleviates discomfort, strives to prevent postoperative complications, implements steps to initiate appropriate wound healing, ensures adequate fluid and nutritional intake, verifies acceptable urinary and bowel elimination, and assesses the patient's psychosocial and neurological status.

Patient-Centered Transfer of Care Through Discharge Planning

Ideally, discharge planning starts when the decision for surgery is made. Sometimes a patient may be hospitalized for an extended period of time allowing many opportunities for discharge planning. Frequently, however, the patient's stay at the health care facility is very short, so the sooner discharge planning is started the more time the team has to prepare. The postoperative care nurse is an essential member of the patient's discharge planning team. The discharge planning team consists of the patient and/or a family member or home care provider, the surgeon or physician, nurses from all phases of the surgical experience (eg, a perioperative nurse, medical-surgical unit nurse), plus a variety of other health care providers depending on the patient's needs. For instance, other members of the team may include a pharmacist, physical therapist, respiratory therapist, social worker, case manager, nutritionist, or wound/ostomy nurse. The discharge planning team

> **EXAM TIP**
>
> A well-coordinated discharge process is essential for preventing unplanned readmissions that will trigger financial disincentives from third-party payers.

oversees discharge of the patient or transfer of patient care from the inpatient or ambulatory surgical unit to the home or to an extended care facility. Before being discharged, the patient undergoes evaluations to determine where he or she should be placed after discharge.

Depending on the patient's personal plan of care, the patient may be discharged to his or her home or the home of a family member where he or she will not require any additional services. The patient may be discharged to his or her home or the home of a family member where he or she will require additional support from a family member, a caregiver, or a home health care agency. If the patient is not ready to be discharged to his or her own home or the home of a family member because of ongoing medical needs, he or she may be transferred to a rehabilitation facility, a short-term rehabilitation facility, or an extended care facility for long-term nursing care.

Coordination of the patient's care includes personnel from several **interdisciplinary services** who collaborate as a team. Physical therapists work with the patient to determine whether he or she is able to walk without assistance from an assistive device such as a walker or cane or will require the assistance of a medical care provider (eg, home health nurse, medical aide). Respiratory therapists evaluate the patient to determine whether he or she will require the use of home oxygen continuously, during periods of rest, or not at all. The social worker or case manager explores home health or visiting nurse agencies for continued in-home care or transfer to a long-term care facility after discharge.

If the patient is discharged to his or her own home or to the home of a family member, additional equipment and supplies may be needed for continuing care. These may include a hospital bed, a shower chair, a bedside commode, oxygen supplies, assistive walking

Postoperative Phases of Care: True or False FAQs[1]

Q: True or false? Phase I is the time when the postoperative patient is nearing discharge and requires the least amount of nursing care.

A: False. According to ASPAN, phase I is when the postoperative patient requires close monitoring, airway and ventilatory support, hemodynamic stability, pain management, and other factors related to acute patient care. Constant vigilance is required during this phase, as well as a 1:1 nurse-to-patient ratio that should be respected when considering staffing needs.

Q: True or false? According to ASPAN guidelines, postoperative nursing care can be provided in the same physical location for phase I patients as the care being provided for phase II patients.

A: True. Phases signify the level of care provided by the nurse, and not an actual physical location. Many facilities have designed their PACUs to incorporate blended levels of patient care provided by the nurse. This may include equipping the PACU with patient bathrooms, so when the patient is awake and stable enough, he or she can ambulate to the bathroom with assistance; or equipping the PACU with patient dressing rooms, so when the patient has met discharge criteria and is ready for discharge, he or she may discharge from the PACU phase II area. Incorporating these features into a PACU allows the facility to decrease costs by eliminating the need for a different unit or location for phase II patients, which in turn reduces staffing needs.

1. Frequently Asked Questions. ASPAN. http://www.aspan.org/Clinical-Practice/FAQs.

devices, or personal hygiene supplies (eg, diapers, disposable gloves, specialized skin care items, ostomy products, wound care supplies, sterile dressings). Coordination amongst the services ensures that the discharge care plan remains patient centered.

Regulatory Guidelines for Discharge Planning

Discharging patients is a multifaceted process that involves collaboration with multiple disciplines and services, complex **care coordination**, and precise communication. Ongoing communication, both oral and written, is a key component of a smooth transfer of care from the procedural facility to the home or extended care facility. Many inpatient facilities use a "huddle," during which the interdisciplinary discharge planning team discusses the ongoing discharge planning for a patient. Topics covered in a face-to-face huddle include anticipated date of discharge, discharge destination (eg, home, extended care facility), medical services or supplies needed after discharge, and the list of medications.

Updated and ongoing planning efforts should be recorded in the patient's electronic medical record for all team members to review. Social workers or case managers should provide information regarding the patient's discharge destination. This includes home or extended care facility, name of the company that will provide needed durable medical equipment, and name of home health or visiting nurse agency that will provide in-home care to the patient. The pharmacist should provide any updates regarding medications the patient will be receiving after discharge. The physician should provide notation regarding the planned date of discharge. The physical therapist should include notes regarding the patient's ability to perform activities of daily living with or without assistance.

Patient education and teaching are a critical component of reducing patient readmissions. Nurses use the teach-back technique (ie, repeat-back, read-back, return demonstration) when asking the patient to explain to the nurse in the patient's own words any recently taught material. Use of the teach-back technique allows the nurse to immediately identify and correct any mistakes that the patient may have made. The nurse must document any patient teaching or education in the patient's medical record or electronic health record.

The nurse should review and have the patient sign a printed patient discharge instruction sheet and then give the patient or other responsible adult a copy of the sheet at the time of discharge. Included on this sheet are any follow-up provider appointments; any follow up laboratory or radiological tests; any postoperative restrictions (eg, limit of weight to lift; physical restrictions like no walking up or down stairs); and any wound care, dressing changes, or drain care required. The nurse should ensure that pertinent contact

> **EXAM TIP**
>
> Tasks to Include in the Discharge Checklist[1]
> - Patient education
> - Teach-back techniques taught
> - Medication reconciliation
> - Follow-up provider appointments
> - Follow-up testing appointments
> - Provider contact information
> - Supplies provided
> - Contact information for durable medical equipment companies
> - Postdischarge follow-up telephone call information
>
> 1. Checklist for post-discharge follow-up phone calls. Agency for Healthcare Research and Quality. http://archive.ahrq.gov/professionals/systems/hospital/red/checklist.html.

TABLE 5.2	Example Talking Points During the Postoperative Follow-up Phone Call

- The patient's comprehension of any education or teaching that was provided
- Questions related to medications prescribed, dosing, or side effects
- Questions related to upcoming provider appointments or testing appointments
- Questions regarding wound care (eg, condition of the wound, excessive bleeding)
- Questions regarding the patient's current status (eg, pain, nausea, vomiting, and symptoms of infection)
- The patient's overall perception of care received

information regarding telephone numbers for the patient's physician or when to call 911 is clearly noted on the discharge instruction sheet.

Additionally, the pharmacist or nurse should provide a copy of the patient's discharge medication reconciliation sheet to the patient or responsible adult after reviewing it for medication dosages, administration times, side effects, or drug-to-drug interactions. This process is intended to reduce the number of adverse drug events that may lead to an emergency department visit or a readmission.[12]

A follow-up telephone call within 48 to 72 hours of the patient's discharge is a valuable tool. During this call, the nurse identifies and addresses any unmet or unclear needs the patient may have encountered (Table 5.2).[13]

Many health records use a discharge checklist to help reduce discharge errors. The use of a checklist helps the nurse ensure that all components of the discharge process are completed according to **regulatory guidelines** (see Regulatory Guidelines for Discharge Planning sidebar), which is especially helpful when multiple discharge team members are coordinating the patient's **discharge follow-up.** A checklist is a helpful tool for internal chart audits as well as for complying with chart audits by regulatory agencies.

Documentation of Transfer of Care

Every action, process, and transfer of patient care occurring throughout the perioperative experience must be documented. Proper perioperative documentation is the collection of data related to whether patient goals have been met and patient outcomes have been achieved. Perioperative documentation should include patient information, physical and psychosocial assessments, nursing diagnoses, nursing interventions, patient goals, patient outcomes, patient education, and discharge planning. Documentation should be comprehensive and meticulous and serve as a means of communication as the patient progresses through the perioperative experience. All perioperative team members should maintain strict confidentiality. To ensure compliance with the Health Insurance Portability and Accountability Act (HIPAA), only those health care team members directly involved in a patient's care should view, hear, read, or discuss the patient's information.[14] This includes any hand-over materials, patient education materials, take-home medication instructions, and discharge instructions. Only family members or other

Meeting Regulatory Guidelines for Discharge Planning

The goals of discharge planning are to
- ensure that patients are discharged in a timely manner,
- decrease the incidence of postoperative complications,
- lessen the likelihood of hospital readmissions, and
- increase patient satisfaction.

The quality of discharge planning can have a direct influence on patient outcomes. The Centers for Medicare & Medicaid Services (CMS) have established regulations to be included as part of the postoperative care pathway. All hospitals that receive Medicare and Medicaid funding must include
- an evaluation conducted by a registered nurse or other qualified personnel,
- identification of an adequate discharge plan for patients likely to suffer adverse health events after discharge,
- inclusion of post-hospital care services which, when possible, respect patient and family preferences, and
- documentation of the discharge plan in the patient's record.[1]

The CMS imposes a financial penalty on facilities whose readmission rates are above the national average. As of 2015, penalties have increased to 3% on all Medicare payments if the facility's readmission rate is above the national average.[2] As part of the development of an individualized plan of care, perioperative nurses should identify those patients at increased risk for readmission or postoperative complications and include nursing interventions to address those risks. The perioperative nurse should communicate the assessment findings to those health care providers involved in discharge planning. Risk factors include
- increased age,
- comorbidities and/or chronic illness,
- extensive or lengthy surgical procedures,
- polypharmacy, and
- social and economic factors affecting home care.[2]

The Joint Commission evaluates the effectiveness of discharge planning as one of their requirements for hospital accreditation. The discharge planning process is traced from the point the patient is admitted until after discharge. Information obtained during a survey tracer include who is involved with discharge planning and when, types of patient education and communication practices that help ensure patient and caregiver understanding, and methods for transferring information to other providers of care. In addition, the competency of personnel involved in patient discharge is evaluated through a review of personnel records and files.[3]

1. Revision to State Operations Manual (SOM), hospital appendix A to read interpretive guidelines for 42 CFR §482.43, discharge planning. Department of Health and Human Services. Centers for Medicare & Medicaid. https://www.cms.gov/Medicare/Provider-Enrollment-and-Certification/SurveyCertificationGenInfo/Downloads/Survey-and-Cert-Letter-13-32.pdf.
2. Prabhakar AM, Harvey HB, Oklu R. Thirty-day hospital re-admissions: a metric that matters. *J Vasc Interv Radiol*. 2013;24(10):1509-1511.
3. Tracer methodology 101: effective discharge planning. *The Source*. 2013;11(2):6-7, 19. https://www.jcrinc.com/assets/1/7/SS12dl.pdf.

caregivers who have been granted permission by the patient or who have been granted access through legal measures should receive any verbal instructions or written take-home materials.

Transitions of Care: Engaging Patients and Families

TJC has developed a Transitions of Care Portal, which focuses on the movement of patients between various health care settings.[15] Patient-centered care is a partnership among health care team members and their patients. This dynamic respects and encourages patients' participation in their own care. Patient-centered discharge planning after a surgical procedure that involves an interdisciplinary team, the patient, and his or her family helps to decrease errors, omissions, and readmissions and increases patient adherence, patient engagement, and patient satisfaction in complex care coordination.

Key Concepts and Review

Patients having operative or other invasive procedures typically undergo multiple transfers of care during the perioperative continuum of care. Each exchange involves facilitation from the transferring nurse to the receiving nurse. Beginning in the preoperative nursing unit where the patient is admitted, he or she will undergo a detailed physical assessment by an individual preoperative nurse. The nurse gathers, records, assesses, and evaluates the data. The preoperative nurse and intraoperative nurse (ie, RN circulator) will perform a transfer of care. The RN circulator is a member of a surgical team, which includes a surgeon, an anesthesia professional, and a scrub person (eg, RN or surgical technician). After the procedure is completed, the RN circulator transfers the care of the patient to the postoperative nurse. Postoperative care is delivered to the patient in phases: Phase I is the immediate postanesthesia phase. During phase I, the patient undergoes various assessments to confirm that the patient is able to independently maintain an open airway and is hemodynamically stable with vital signs that have returned to the preprocedural baseline. The phase I nurse transfers the patient to phase II, during which nurses provide care in the second phase area of the postanesthesia care unit, an ambulatory surgical unit, a medical/surgical unit in the hospital, or at home. During this phase the patient's body is reestablishing its physiological balance and level of homeostasis.

Preparing the patient for discharge involves a team approach. This planning team consists of the patient and/or a family member or home care provider, the surgeon or physician, nurses from all phases of the surgical experience (eg, perioperative nurse, medical-surgical unit nurse), plus a variety of other health care providers (eg, pharmacist, physical therapist, respiratory therapist, social worker, case manager, nutritionist, wound/ostomy nurse) depending on the patient's needs. Care of the perioperative patient who is transferring from the hospital or ambulatory surgical unit is a multifaceted process that involves collaboration with multiple disciplines and services, complex care coordination, and precise communication.

Communication is the key factor in successful transfers of patient care. In an effort to prevent communication breakdowns, hand-over tools are used so the giver of information provides the receiver of information with the necessary and pertinent patient information in a verbal (ie, oral and written) format. Equally important is written communication in the form of documentation in the patient's medical record, whether it is a hard copy chart or an electronic health record. Timely, comprehensive, and meticulous entries in the patient's record allows members of the discharge planning team to review the patient's discharge instruction sheet. Use of a discharge instruction sheet, which is reviewed, signed, and provided to the patient or responsible adult by the nurse at the time of the patient's discharge, helps to reduce discharge errors and provides documentation related to patient education, any teach-back techniques taught, medication reconciliation, follow-up provider appointments, follow-up testing appointments, and provider contact information.

According to TJC, "All health care providers want their patients to have a smooth transition to their next care setting or provider, or to their home. But this doesn't always happen. While many aspects of transitions of care depend on the efforts and actions of health care providers to make for a smooth and successful transition, the involvement of the patient and his or her family also is critical."[2] Perioperative nurses are in a key position to keep perioperative transfers of care patient-centered, so that errors, omissions, and readmissions are decreased, and patient compliance, engagement, and satisfaction are increased.

References

1. National Patient Safety Goals effective January 1, 2015. The Joint Commission. http://www.jointcommission.org/assets/1/6/2015_NPSG_HAP.pdf.
2. Transitions of care: engaging patients and families. *Quick Safety.* The Joint Commission; November 2015, issue 18. http://www.jointcommission.org/assets/1/23/Quick_Safety_Issue_18_November_20151.PDF.
3. Chard R, Makary MA. Transfer-of-care communication: nursing best practices. *AORN J.* 2015;102(4):329-339.
4. O'Daniel M, Rosenstein AH. Chapter 33: professional communication and team collaboration. In: Hughes RG, ed. *Patient Safety and Quality: An Evidence-Based Handbook for Nurses.* Rockville, MD: Agency for Healthcare Research and Quality; April 2008. http://www.ncbi.nlm.nih.gov/books/NBK2637/.
5. Guideline for transfer of patient care information. In: *Guidelines for Perioperative Practice.* Denver, CO: AORN, Inc; 2017:711-716.
6. Friesen MA, White SV, Byers JF. Handoff: implications for nurses. In: Hughes RG, ed. *Patient Safety and Quality: An Evidence-Based Handbook for Nurses.* Rockville, MD: Agency for Healthcare Research and Quality; 2008:285-332.
7. Hendrich AL, Fay J, Sorrells AK. Effects of acuity-adaptable rooms on flow of patients and delivery of care. *Am J Crit Care.* 2004;13(1):35-45.
8. Patient Hand-off/over Tool Kit. AORN, Inc. http://www.aorn.org/search#q=hand-off%20tool%20kit.
9. Seifert PC. Implementing AORN recommended practices for transfer of patient care information. *AORN J.* 2012;96(5):475-493.
10. Universal Protocol. The Joint Commission. http://www.jointcommission.org/standards_information/up.aspx.
11. American Society of PeriAnesthesia Nurses. *2012-2014 Perianesthesia Nursing Standards, Practice Recommendations and Interpretive Statements.* Cherry Hill, NJ: ASPAN; 2012:7, 30-42.
12. Budnitz DS, Shehab N, Kegler SR, Richards CL. Medication use leading to emergency department visits for adverse drug events in older adults. *Ann Intern Med.* 2007;147(11):755-765.
13. Checklist for post-discharge follow-up phone calls. Agency for Healthcare Research and Quality. https://archive.ahrq.gov/professionals/systems/hospital/red/checklist.html.
14. Summary of the HIPAA Privacy Rule. US Department of Health and Human Services. https://www.hhs.gov/sites/default/files/privacysummary.pdf.
15. Transitions of Care Portal. The Joint Commission. https://www.jointcommission.org/toc.aspx.

Practice Exam Questions

1. A multidisciplinary team has been convened to review several recent incidents where the wrong patient has been brought from the medical-surgical unit to the preoperative holding area. Which of the following actions would prevent this incident from occurring in the future?
   A. Requiring an RN to accompany the patient to the preoperative holding area.
   B. Reviewing with transport personnel the process for confirming the correct patient's identity.
   C. Ensuring that the OR charge nurse calls the unit before transport of the patient.
   D. Posting the surgical schedule at the nurse's station on the medical-surgical unit.

2. The importance of educating patients and family members about prevention of wound infections postoperatively is part of the
   A. National Patient Safety Goals.
   B. Surgical Care Improvement Project.
   C. AORN *Guidelines for Perioperative Practice*.
   D. Centers for Disease Control and Prevention.

3. Documentation of transfer-of-care communication should be
   A. done by each member of the perioperative team participating in the hand over.
   B. presented in SBAR format to ensure the consistency of hand-over documentation.
   C. approved by all personnel involved in the hand over.
   D. done using a standardized documentation format.

4. Policies and procedures related to transfer of patient information should be
   A. reviewed annually.
   B. available in the practice setting.
   C. written by a registered nurse.
   D. written using the SBAR format.

5. The perioperative patient's transition from phase I to phase II level of care is based on
   A. the length of time the patient has been in phase I.
   B. the nurse's assessment of the patient.
   C. the patient's blood pressure measurement.
   D. the patient's oxygen saturation.

6. The goal to "improve the effectiveness of communication among caregivers" is proposed by
   A. the Centers for Medicare & Medicaid Services.
   B. the Occupational Safety and Health Administration.
   C. the United States Department of Health and Human Services.
   D. The Joint Commission's National Patient Safety Goals.

7. Discharge education should include adverse effects of opioid pain medications, including constipation, vomiting, and
    A. respiratory depression.
    B. hypotension.
    C. hypertension.
    D. diarrhea.

8. The goal of performing a follow-up telephone call within 48 to 72 hours of the patient's discharge is to
    A. monitor the patient's heart rhythm.
    B. confirm patient's understanding of and compliance with instructions.
    C. finalize paperwork for submission to the patient's insurance provider.
    D. schedule follow-up appointments.

9. Which teaching method has been shown to improve communication and teamwork?
    A. Role-playing
    B. Case studies
    C. Online modules
    D. Simulation

10. What can compromise the accuracy of the nurse's transfer of patient care?
    A. Interruptions
    B. Patient acuity
    C. Patient diagnosis
    D. Paper charting

Answers with Supported Rationales

1. Answer B is correct. The patient is accurately identified before transport to the OR. Reference: Phillips N. Preoperative preparation of the patient. In: *Berry & Kohn's Operating Room Technique*. 13th ed. St Louis, MO: Elsevier; 2017:376.

2. Answer A is correct. NPSG #7 discusses the importance of preventing hospital-associated infections. It is required that education for prevention of SSI be documented in the patient's medical record. Reference: Spry C. Infection prevention and control. In: Rothrock JC, ed. *Alexander's Care of the Patient in Surgery*. 15th ed. St Louis, MO: Elsevier; 2015:81.

3. Answer D is correct. Clear and timely communication is the goal of documentation related to patient care. Use of a standardized format allows for the provision of consistent and reliable communication. Reference: Guideline for team communication. In: *Guidelines for Perioperative Practice*. Denver, CO: AORN, Inc; 2017:751.

4. Answer B is correct. Health care staff must have access to policies and procedures related to the transfer of patient care information readily available for reference. Policies should be written by an interdisciplinary team. Reference: Guideline for transfer of patient care information. In: *Guidelines for Perioperative Practice*. Denver, CO: AORN, Inc; 2017:714.

5. Answer B is correct. There is no length of time requirement for the patient's stay in phase I. The length of time is dependent on the nurse's assessment of the patient's status. Although blood pressure measurement and oxygen saturation are both components of a patient assessment, the patient assessment contains blood pressure measurement, oxygen saturation, minimal pain, absent or controlled nausea and vomiting, uncompromised cardiopulmonary status, stable vital signs, urine output of ≥ 30 mL per hour, and the ability to maintain open airway. Reference: Odom-Forom J. Postoperative patient care and pain management. In: Rothrock JC, ed. *Alexander's Care of the Patient in Surgery*. 15th ed. St Louis, MO: Elsevier; 2015:286.

6. Answer D is correct. In January 2015, The Joint Commission mandated its Hospital National Patient Safety Goal 2, "Improve the effectiveness of communication among caregivers." The other answers are examples of federal regulatory agencies that mandate compliance issues. Reference: National Patient Safety Goals. Effective January 1, 2015. The Joint Commission. http://www.jointcommission.org/assets/1/6/2015_NPSG_HAP.pdf; p 15.

7. Answer A is correct. Respiratory and central nervous depression are possible side effects of opioid pain medications. Reference: Odom-Forom J. Postoperative patient care and pain management. In: Rothrock JC, ed. *Alexander's Care of the Patient in Surgery*. 15th ed. St Louis, MO: Elsevier; 2015:287.

8. Answer B is correct. Instructions are reviewed and printed for the patient prior to discharge. A phone call will clarify whether the patient understood the directions and is continuing to be compliant. Reference: Ball KA. Surgical modalities. In: *Alexander's Care of the Patient in Surgery*. 15th ed. St Louis, MO: Elsevier; 2015:249.

9. Answer D is correct. Preventing communication errors when transferring patient care information is essential to safe patient care. Simulation has demonstrated the most improvements to communication and teamwork skills. Reference: Guideline for team communication. In: *Guidelines for Perioperative Practice*. Denver, CO: AORN, Inc; 2018:752.

10. Answer A is correct. Interruptions and distractions can lead to errors and a failure to give a complete report, affecting patient safety. Reference: Guideline for team communication. In: *Guidelines for Perioperative Practice*. Denver, CO: AORN, Inc; 2017:749.

6 Instrument Processing and Supply Management

KEY TERMS

- Bioburden
- Biofilm
- Biological indicator
- Chemical indicator
- Creutzfeldt-Jakob disease
- Decontamination
- Decontamination area
- Dynamic air-removal sterilization
- Gravity displacement sterilization
- Packaging integrity
- Physical monitor
- Prevacuum sterilization
- Qualification sterilizer testing
- Reverse osmosis
- Wet packs

REQUIRED NURSING SKILLS

- Documenting disinfection procedures
- Ensuring applicable environmental conditions of sterilization and storage areas
- Handling and disposing of hazardous and biohazard materials
- Managing materials and instruments provided by external sources
- Meeting regulatory requirements for tracking of equipment, instruments, and supplies provided by external source
- Performing disinfection procedures and cleaning techniques
- Performing sterilization evaluation techniques, including biological and chemical monitoring
- Selecting appropriate methods (cleaning, disinfecting, packaging, sterilizing, transportation, storage) and products for processing

This chapter focuses on cleaning, disinfecting, packaging, sterilizing, and transporting surgical instruments and supplies. Application of principles and practices related to instrument processing and supply management will help perioperative registered nurses (RNs) assess patients' health and safeguard them from and reduce the risk of acquiring surgical site and other infections. The perioperative area is unique in that all members of the team wear specific personal protective equipment (PPE) at various times. Understanding the parameters for contamination and maintaining a sterile field is critical in identifying and balancing the technical aspects of perioperative nursing with consistent use of aseptic technique, instrument processing, and supply management. A multidisciplinary approach to patient care in the perioperative setting is necessary, as each member of the perioperative team brings his or her area of expertise to providing care. Knowledge and integration of all areas of expertise allows the perioperative nurse to understand the importance and influence of the combined team, which can improve patient outcomes.

Perioperative Infection Prevention and Control Principles

The infectious process is a series of complex interrelationships of agent, host, and environment. Understanding health care–associated infections (HAIs) will help perioperative nurses identify opportunities to prevent and control diseases by accurate cleaning, packaging, transporting, sterilizing, and storing instruments and supplies.[1] Multidrug-resistant organisms (MDROs) are microorganisms, mostly bacteria, that are resistant to one or more classes of antimicrobial drugs (Table 6.1). Dealing appropriately with MDROs, by adhering to strict cleaning, disinfection, and sterilizing practices, is every perioperative team member's responsibility regardless of the type of health care facility or setting.[2]

Cleaning and Disinfecting Instruments, Equipment, and Endoscopes

Instruments and devices sold in the United States should have US Federal Drug Administration (FDA) clearance for use in surgery with written manufacturer-validated cleaning and decontamination guidelines. The perioperative nurse is part of the designated team who will use a product. Perioperative nurses are also involved in the evaluation and recommendation process to determine if products fit the facility's needs. Cleaning, decontamination, and sterilization capacities of the setting are part of the evaluation process. New, repaired, refurbished, or loaned instruments need to be cleaned, decontaminated, inspected, and sterilized before being placed into use.[3,4] This is a guiding concept regarding surgical instrumentation and assists the perioperative nurse in setting priorities. A lack of planning in instrument processing is not a sufficient reason to default to immediate-use steam sterilization (IUSS).

During the surgical procedure, the scrub person should keep instruments as free of debris as possible to prevent corrosion, rusting, and pitting.[4] The scrub person should flush lumens between uses with

TABLE 6.1 Drug-Resistant Pathogens[1]

(Listed in order of most resistant to least resistant to medications)
- Prions (eg, Creutzfeldt-Jakob disease)
- Bacterial spores (eg, *Clostridium difficile*)
- Protozoa (eg, *Cryptosporidium parvum*)
- Helmith eggs (eg, *Ascaris lumbricoides*)
- Mycobacteria (eg, *Mycobacterium tuberculosis*)
- Small, non-enveloped viruses (eg, *Norovirus*)
- Protozoal cysts (eg, *iardia*)
- Fungal species (eg, *Aspergillus fumigatus*)
- Gram-negative bacilli (eg, *Acinetobacter baumannii, Enterobacteriace*)
- Vegetative fungi and algae (eg, *Candida albicans*)
- Large, non-enveloped[a] viruses (eg, *Adenovirus*)
- Gram-positive bacteria (eg, *Staphylococcus*)
- Enveloped[b] virus (eg, herpesviruses, poxviruses)

a Non-enveloped viruses do not have an outer lipid membrane; these viruses are virulent; are resistant to heat, acids, and drying; and cause host cells to lysis.

b Enveloped viruses are surrounded by an outer lipid membrane; these viruses are less virulent, are sensitive to heat, acids, and drying; and rarely cause host cells to lysis.

1. Siegel J, Rhinehart E, Jackson M, Chiarello L; Healthcare Infection Control Practices Advisory Committee. *Management of Multidrug-Resistant Organisms in Healthcare Settings.* Atlanta, GA: Centers for Disease Control and Prevention; 2006:1-74.

sterile water that is kept in a sterile labeled ring stand away from the field.[5] This will remove debris and decrease the risk of the formation of **biofilm** (ie, cells that may collect on instruments and may protect microorganisms from disinfectants).

All instruments that have been on the sterile field during the procedure must be cleaned whether they have been used or not.[6] The scrub person should separate instruments with multiple parts, if possible, and should open all instruments that have clamps to allow thorough cleaning.[6] The scrub person should place delicate instruments, to include fiber-optic cords, rigid endoscopes, and microsurgical instruments, in a separate area to protect them.[5] The scrub person should also separate sharp instruments (eg, scissors, towel clips) that could injure sterile-processing personnel.[5] The scrub person must discard liquids that are used to decontaminate instruments at the point of use before being transported to the **decontamination area** (ie, area for collection, retention, and cleaning of soiled and/or contaminated items) or placed in leakproof containers such as suction containers with lids.[5]

> **EXAM TIP**
>
> The process of decontamination is an essential part of the sterilization process. The importance of carefully following the manufacturer's recommendations for decontamination procedures cannot be overemphasized.

TABLE 6.2 The Basics of Decontamination Area Cleaning Products[1,2]

Cleaning products used in the decontamination area should be
- Nonabrasive, low foaming, easy to remove during rinsing, and biodegradable
- Effective for removing soil
- Nontoxic in the correct dilution
- Able to test for concentration levels
- Cost-effective and have a long shelf life

Items that are needed in the decontamination area for cleaning instruments include
- Brushes
- Enzymatic and non-enzymatic cleaners
- Soft, low-linting cloths
- Testing equipment
- 70% to 90% isopropyl alcohol
- A thermometer
- Measuring devices

---

1. Guideline for cleaning and care of surgical instruments. In: *Guidelines for Perioperative Practice*. Denver, CO: AORN, Inc; 2017:822, 825.
2. ANSI/AAMI ST79: *Comprehensive Guide to Steam Sterilization and Sterility Assurance in Health Care Facilities*. Arlington, VA: Association for the Advancement of Medical Instrumentation; 2017.

Preparation for cleaning and decontamination (ie, removal of contaminants using a manual or automated process with disinfectants that will render blood and body fluids harmless) should occur as soon as possible after conclusion of the surgical procedure.[3,4] The decontamination area should have

- automated equipment to clean all types of instruments in use;
- adaptors and accessories to connect to cleaning equipment;
- a filtered, medical-grade air supply (ie, compressed air); and
- water for rinsing instruments (eg, water deionized or processed via reverse osmosis [ie, a water-purifying process to eliminate impurities]).[5]

The decontamination area also must have an eyewash station as well as a sink for personnel to wash their hands.[6,7]

Personnel working in the decontamination area must wear a hair covering and PPE, including an impervious gown with sleeves, gloves extending over the cuff, a mask and eye protection or eye shield, and shoe covers or boots. Personnel should perform hand hygiene after PPE removal.[4-7] Cleaning products that should be used in the decontamination area and items that are needed for cleaning are listed in Table 6.2. Personnel should follow the manufacturer's cleaning product written instructions for use (IFU), to include water quality, hardness, temperature, and pH; correct concentration and dilution of the product; adequate contact time; and proper storage, shelf life, and use life. Managers must ensure that decontamination policies and procedures describe effective removal of bioburden and that this occurs before sterilization.[4,6] **Bioburden** (ie, microbial load) is the amount of microbial contamination on an instrument; efforts to decrease or remove bioburden improve the ability to achieve sterilization.[4,6]

Ultrasonic cleaners can be used to remove some hard-to-reach areas if the IFU is followed. Personnel should remove gross debris from instruments before placing the instruments into the ultrasonic cleaner.[6] Instruments with similar metals should be placed in the ultrasonic together unless otherwise stated in the IFU for that specific ultrasonic cleaner.[5] Stainless steel instruments should not be mixed in the ultrasonic washer with instruments made of metals (eg, brass, copper, aluminum, chrome).[5] Mixing metals may result in electroplating (ie, ion transfer from one instrument to another), which could cause etching or pitting of the instruments, allowing microorganisms to stick to the surface imperfections. Personnel should completely submerge all instruments, especially instruments with lumens, followed by a thorough rinsing.[4] After ultrasonic cleaning, personnel should place surgical instruments and containment devices (eg, instrument pans) in the washer disinfectors/decontaminators, according to the IFU, to allow all surfaces to come in contact with the cleaning solution.[8]

> **EXAM TIP**
>
> Knowledge of and the consistent application of IFUs are a frequently cited deficiency in accreditation processes.

After cleaning, personnel should inspect the instruments for thoroughness of the process. This includes checking all powered equipment for on and off function and using lighted magnification to check hard-to-clean areas.[4] Personnel should inspect the internal channels of reusable shavers with an endoscopic camera or borescope.[9] Personnel should check electrode insulation to identify cracks and worn spots to prevent future failure.[5] Moisture should be removed at the end of the washer-sterilizer cycle or before sterilization using alcohol in instruments with lumens.[5] This promotes drying as well as inhibits microbial growth and prevents biofilm formation.[5]

Special Processes Related to Cleaning and Disinfection

Certain situations require special cleaning and sterilization processes. Some of these instances include dealing with intraocular ophthalmic instruments, laryngoscope blades and handles, and prions.

Intraocular ophthalmic instruments have been linked with toxic anterior segment syndrome (TASS), an acute inflammation of the anterior segment of the eye. This postoperative complication after eye surgery causes toxic damage to intraocular tissues, resulting in vision loss. Decontamination and sterilization practices have been found culpable in causing TASS (Table 6.3); therefore, personnel must follow manufacturers' IFU to prevent this serious postoperative complication.[6,8]

Laryngoscope blades and handles are considered semi-critical and should be cleaned and high-level disinfected or sterilized according to manufacturers' IFU after every use. Semicritical items come in contact with nonintact skin or mucous membranes. Cleaning followed by high-level disinfection minimizes the risk of pathogen transmission. Personnel must remove the batteries from the laryngoscope handles before cleaning and disinfecting them according to the manufacturers' IFU. Personnel should then insert the batteries into the laryngoscope handles and place the handles and blades in separate packages, stored correctly to prevent contamination.[6]

TABLE 6.3 Causes of Toxic Anterior Segment Syndrome (TASS)[1]

- Inadequately flushing phacoemulsification and irrigation/aspiration hand pieces
- Using enzymatic cleaners
- Using an incorrect concentration of the detergent
- Using contaminated ultrasonic fluids
- Adding antibiotics to balanced salt solutions
- Using epinephrine with preservatives
- Using powdered gloves
- Reusing single-use products
- Failing to maintain instruments correctly

1. Cutler Peck CM, Clouser S, Danford C, Edelhauser HE, Mamilis N. Toxic anterior syndrome: common causes. *J Cataract Refract Surg.* 2010:36(7):1073-1080.

Prions cause transmissible spongiform encephalopathy (eg, Creutzfeldt-Jakob disease), and instruments contaminated with prions must be handled with special precautions. Perioperative personnel must use single-use gowns, gloves, drapes, and supplies and should wear protective eyewear.[6,8] (A more in-depth discussion of single-use processing is provided later in this chapter.) If reusable instruments are used on high-risk patients, these instruments should be easy to clean and should tolerate an extended steam sterilization cycle.[10] Single-use brain biopsy sets designed for high-risk patients are preferable.[8]

Stainless steel has a high attraction to prion absorption[11]; therefore, instruments contaminated with prions should not be allowed to dry before the prions are removed.[11,12] Instruments should be kept moist with a wet towel or submersed in water.[8] Managers should ensure that cleaning chemicals with prionicidal activity that are compatible with the instruments are used.[8] According to the Society for Hospital Epidemiology of America (SHEA), after instruments that have been exposed to prions have been decontaminated, they should undergo

- immersion in 1 N sodium hydroxide (ie, 1NaOH is a solution of 40 g in 1 L of water) for 60 minutes, then removed, rinsed with water, and sterilized using one of the cycles described below[12]; and
  - **prevacuum sterilization** (ie, a steam sterilization cycle in which air is removed at the beginning of the cycle from the chamber, which depends on one or more pressure and vacuum excursions) at 273°F (134°C) for 18 minutes; or
  - **gravity displacement sterilization** (ie, a steam sterilization cycle in which incoming air displaces residual air in the sterilizer through a port or drain near the bottom of the sterilizer chamber) at 270°F (132°C) for 60 minutes.

Immediate-use steam sterilization should not be used on instruments exposed to high-risk tissue.[8,12] Operating room personnel should notify personnel in the decontamination and sterile processing areas that instruments are contaminated or potentially contaminated with prions so that they are prepared to use the special prion processing procedure.[5]

TABLE 6.4 Requirements for Documentation of Instrument Cleaning and Disinfection

- Date and time of cleaning and disinfection
- Identification of instruments
- Method and verification of cleaning
- Audit results
- Identifier of mechanical instrument washer efficacy results
- Name of person performing the cleaning and decontamination
- Lot numbers of cleaning agents
- Testing results for insulated instruments
- Disposal of defective equipment
- Maintenance of cleaning equipment

Managers should ensure that personnel are correctly documenting the cleaning and disinfection processes. Records will be maintained based on the requirements of local, state, and federal regulations (Table 6.4). Personnel who clean and care for instruments should receive basic and ongoing education.

Cleaning, disinfecting, and sterilizing endoscopes properly are critical in the prevention of serious and life-threatening infections. The US Food and Drug Administration (FDA) found that routine cleaning of endoscopes used for retrograde cholangiopancreatography (ERCP) recommended by the manufacturer may not remove all of the debris.[13] In April 2015, the FDA received 75 reports of Carbapenem-resistant enterobacteriaceae (CRE) infections linked to reprocessed duodenoscopes that had occurred from January 2013 to December 2014. The FDA issued an alert in February 2015 regarding the difficulty of cleaning duodenoscopes because of their complex design.[13-15]

There are three main reasons why the medical community considers CRE epidemiologically important:

1. Often, these organisms are resistant to multiple classes of antibiotics, which significantly limits treatment options.
2. Infections caused by these organisms are associated with high mortality rates, up to 50% in some studies.
3. Many CREs possess carbapenemases, which can be transmitted from one Enterobacteriaceae to another, potentially facilitating transmission of resistance.[16]

Enterobacteriaceae are a common cause of infections in both community and health care settings; therefore, carbapenem resistance among these organisms could have a far-reaching effect.[16,17]

The design of the duodenoscopes may prevent thorough cleaning and disinfection. Personnel must pay scrupulous attention before performing high-level disinfection by inspecting and manually cleaning the duodenoscope elevator mechanism located at the distal tip of the duodenoscope.[15] Using a magnifying glass may help ensure that debris is removed from the elevator mechanism. Personnel should flush the channel with alcohol if this is compatible with the manufacturer's instructions. The channels of the duodenoscope and elevator mechanism should be thoroughly dried with forced air before placement in storage.[17]

Staff training and competency should be completed with verification for processing procedures. Sterile processing managers should assess the competence of all personnel at orientation and at least annually as well as anytime a break in technique is identified. Sterile processing managers should maintain documentation of all training and competency verification.[15]

Sterile processing and perioperative managers may consider implementing at least one of the following enhanced methods for reprocessing duodenoscopes that have been suggested by the Centers for Disease Control and Prevention (CDC) and the FDA to improve the process. Enhanced methods for processing flexible duodenoscopes may include implementing HLD followed by

- endoscope quarantine until the duodenoscope is culture-negative,
- a liquid chemical sterilant processing system,
- a second HLD,
- ethylene oxide sterilization, or
- FDA-cleared low-temperature sterilization.[18]

Nonculture testing with adenosine triphosphate or bioluminescence assays have been used to assess duodenoscope reprocessing by detecting residual organic material after cleaning. This does not correlate with bacterial concentrations but may determine the presence of debris remaining after cleaning.[15]

Packaging

Perioperative nurses must have knowledge of packaging methods used in their facility. Before purchasing packaging materials, perioperative nurses must participate in a thorough evaluation of available types of packaging for different sterilization methods.[8,19,20] Perioperative nurses may participate in identifying a few of the requirements in determining the best products, including FDA clearance for the selected types and sizes of packaging materials. These requirements specify that packaging materials must

- be in compliance with the manufacturer's IFU,
- be free of toxins,
- have tamper-free seals,
- provide identification of contents before opening,
- maintain sterility,
- be suitable for items being sterilized,
- allow for removal of sterilant and air, and
- be resistant to tears/punctures.[6,8,19,20]

Personnel should ensure that an external chemical indicator (CI; device used to monitor exposures to sterilization parameters) is available, and that storage requirements are specified (see later discussion in this chapter of chemical and biological indicators). A 25-lb weight limit for instrument pans is important because heavier containers may affect the drying time as well as be an ergonomic risk for personnel handling the devices.[6,19,20] The ability to present the item to the sterile field aseptically is important as well for safety. Nurses may be asked to participate in testing of the product, which includes correct placement of biological indicators in the packages.[6,19,20]

6 Instrument Processing and Supply Management **163**

Packaging materials should match the different types of sterilization methods, which include steam, ethylene oxide, low-temperature hydrogen peroxide gas plasma, and ozone sterilization.[20] (Types of sterilization are discussed in depth later in this chapter.) Perioperative nurses must handle packaging materials in a way that prevents contamination. Shelf life is event related (ie, amount of handling, exposure to humidity) rather than related to the length of time the package is on the shelf or the date it was sterilized.[8,19] Packages with broken seals, loss of **package integrity** (ie, undamaged condition of a sterilized package), moisture penetration, or exposure to airborne contaminants, compromising the sterility of the package, should not be used.[8,19]

> **EXAM TIP**
>
> Packaging materials are specific to the sterilization method used. Perioperative nurses must be knowledgeable of these requirements.

Personnel should inspect all items to be sterilized for cleanliness, function, and to determine whether the items can be packaged to support sterilization. Correct packaging allows for appropriate sterilization.[8,19,20] Instruments with multiple parts should be separated if possible, and in the unlocked position. Sequential wrapping with two single wraps, or a single wrap with two layers, is used to prevent microbial migration. Paper and toner inks on count sheets may pose a concern in an instrument container for patients who may be sensitive to either the paper or ink.[19,20]

Personnel should use peel pouches according to the manufacturer's IFU. Peel pouches should not be used inside wrapped or container sets because it may not be possible to place them in the container in a manner that allows adequate exposure to meet sterilization parameters. Only use two pouches, one inside the other, if IFU approved. Personnel should place peel pouches paper side to paper side and pouches should be properly spaced and positioned on edge to allow sterilant contact and drying during sterilization.[6,19,20]

Personnel should follow the manufacturer's IFU when using rigid containers for sterilizing. Personnel should evaluate the container before and after sterilization and drying for signs of humidity, tears in packaging, and presence of appropriate indicators. Personnel should also follow the manufacturer's IFU when placing cassettes or trays in a rigid container. Inspection of the rigid container after each use should include all the working parts of the container. Personnel should secure the filters and valve system before sterilization and should clean rigid containers after each use. When opening the rigid container for use, OR personnel should check the filters for defects and determine whether the valve is functional, there is no humidity, and the indicator has turned before placing the container contents on the sterile field. Wrapped items should be checked for perforations and humidity and whether the indicator has turned. Personnel should not use towels in the container unless required to do so by the manufacturer's IFU.[6,19,20]

> **EXAM TIP**
>
> Basic knowledge regarding the use of peel pouches is essential for perioperative nurses.

When a pack or container is identified as wet, perioperative nurses and the sterile processing department personnel must work cooperatively to identify and resolve the problem. **Wet packs** (ie, moisture is present in a pack or container and should not be used) may need to involve the infection preventionist as well as the facility manager if there is a possibility that the steam delivery to the sterilizer is malfunctioning; if so, the load should be quarantined according to lot number, surgeons should be notified, and the sterilizer should be repaired if needed. Perioperative nurses should participate in quality assurance and performance improvement regarding measures that need to be taken to prevent internal or external moisture, which indicates steam sterilization problems.[6,8,19,20]

Documentation on the package label includes

- sterilizer identifier,
- cycle or load number,
- date of sterilization,
- description of contents, and
- assembler identification.

Package labels should be visible and secured so they are not dislodged during processing, storage, and movement to point of use.[6,19,20]

Sterilization of Instruments and Supplies

Items used for patient care that are categorized as critical require sterilization. Critical items include any objects that enter sterile tissue or the vascular system, such as surgical instruments, cardiac and urinary catheters, implants, and ultrasound probes, and these items must be sterile to prevent any microbial contamination that could transmit disease.[8]

SINGLE-USE ITEMS

Single-use means that personnel must use that item only one time unless the health care facility has an FDA-approved program for sterilization of single-use items in place. The facility must follow the FDA requirements if single-use, in-house processing is used. The FDA requirements include policies, procedures, competencies, and education specific to reprocessing single-use devices, all of which should be developed by the facility. This process must meet the FDA-published requirements for reprocessing single-use devices. Single-use items can only be reused if the manufacturer's reuse directions are included in the packaging. A single-use item that does not have additional use information is not covered by the manufacturer and cannot be resterilized. Single-use items that are resterilized may not function appropriately and put the patient at risk for injury.[8,20]

Considerations for controlled environments (eg, soiled/decontamination area, sterilizer equipment access, environmental services) include negative airflow. Areas requiring positive airflow are sterilizer loading and unloading, preparation and packaging, textile packaging room, and clean/sterile storage. Sterile processing and perioperative managers should ensure that monitoring of environmental controls is completed regularly according to facility policies, and that results are documented.[20,21]

STERILIZATION TYPES, USES, AND MONITORING REQUIREMENTS

Perioperative nurses should be able to identify the functions of the different sterilization methods used in their facility and what instruments and supplies can be sterilized with each type of sterilization process. During orientation at a new facility, the perioperative manager or educator ensures that the perioperative nurse is able to identify the monitoring requirements for each type of sterilization process.

Saturated steam under pressure can be used to sterilize heat- and moisture-stable items. The critical step in steam sterilization is removal of air from the chamber. Pressure, temperature, time, and moisture are four parameters of steam sterilization.[6,8,19] Both terminal sterilization and IUSS follow the manufacturer's written guidelines for required cycles for different device times and load configurations. Examples of items that can be sterilized with saturated steam are stainless steel instruments, glass, and towels. Some powered instruments, specialty orthopedic instruments and devices, and neurosurgery devices may use saturated steam but may require longer exposure or drying times.[8,20]

Immediate-use steam sterilization should not be used frequently because it may be a related risk of infection; IUSS should only be used if there is not enough time for a full cycle.[6,8,20,22,23] Implants should not be sterilized by IUSS. Physical monitors (ie, printouts, digital readings, graphs, or gauges that monitor sterilization parameters) must be done for IUSS as well. If IUSS is required, biological and chemical indicators should be used to monitor the cycle. A class V chemical integrating indicator or a class VI emulating indicator should be used in the sterilization container. Cycle-specific class VI indicators should only be used on specific cycles for which they are labeled.[19,20] Follow the manufacturer's IFU. Records for IUSS should include

- the item sterilized and the patient IUSS is used for;
- the type of cycle (eg, gravity displacement, dynamic air removal);
- the cycle parameters (eg, temperature and duration of cycle);
- monitoring results;
- date and time cycle was run, cycle operator; and
- reason for IUSS.[6,8,20]

Follow-up audits of IUSS records will provide a monitoring system for quality assurance in the use of this cycle and should be done on an ongoing basis. An example of an item that may require IUSS is a one-of-a-kind instrument that was dropped on the floor and is required for a particular surgery. Another situation would be an emergent procedure that requires a specialized set of instruments that are clean but have not been sterilized and time is of the essence. In any situation, personnel must follow manufacturers' IFU when processing instruments and supplies with IUSS. Low inventory is not an acceptable reason for routine use of IUSS.

Ethylene oxide (EO) sterilization is low-temperature sterilization used for moisture- and heat-sensitive items. Personnel should adhere strictly to the manufacturer's guidelines when using EO sterilization. Ethylene oxide kills microbes by replacing a hydrogen atom in a molecule in the organism with an alkyl group. Key molecules that EO disrupts are proteins and DNA. Correct loading of the baskets or cart is imperative because it allows for circulation and penetration of the EO and moisture vapors. Packages penetrated by EO should be aerated in a mechanical aerator to remove the EO at the end of the cycle. Butyl rubber, nitrile, or neoprene gloves should be worn to handle unaerated EO-sterilized articles. Sterilized articles must be completely aerated because EO is a known carcinogen.[6,8,20,24,25] Personnel must pay attention to the

- article composition and size,
- article preparation and packaging,

- density of the load,
- type of EO sterilizer/aerator used,
- manufacturers' IFU, and
- temperature penetration pattern of the aerator's chamber.[8,20,25]

Instruments with lumens and instruments that may not tolerate steam sterilization may be processed with EO sterilization. Follow the manufacturer's IFU.[20]

Low-temperature hydrogen peroxide gas plasma can be used to sterilize moisture- and heat-sensitive items according to the device manufacturer's IFU. Hydrogen peroxide vapor and low-temperature hydrogen gas plasma sterilization are used in combination. An electrical field is created by a radio frequency that is applied to the chamber to create a gas plasma. Microbial free radicals (eg, hydroxyl and hydroperoxyl) are generated in the plasma.[8] Hydrogen peroxide is a strong oxidizing agent. The hydroxyl free-radical agent in hydrogen peroxide kills microbes. This process does not require aeration. The manufacturer's IFU should be followed for devices requiring low-temperature hydrogen gas plasma sterilization.[8,20]

Acceptable lumen diameter and the length of the device should be evaluated. The placement of devices in the chamber should include correct contact with the sterilant. Both packaging and containers should be cleared by the FDA (liquid and cellulose-based paper are not appropriate). Trays, mats, and containers are designed and designated for this type of sterilization.[20] Some plastics, electrical devices, and corrosion-susceptible metal alloys that cannot tolerate high temperatures and humidity can require this method of sterilization.[20]

Low-temperature hydrogen peroxide vapor can be used to sterilize moisture- and heat-sensitive items according to manufacturers' guidelines. The hydrogen peroxide vapor oxidative process inactivates the microbes. Items sterilized in this way do not require aeration. Acceptable lumen diameter and length should be evaluated. Correct placement of devices will assist contact of the sterilant in the chamber. Personnel should ensure that all devices are clean, dry, and packaged in FDA-approved packaging for a low-temperature hydrogen peroxide vapor system. Liquid and cellulose-based paper are not appropriate. Trays, mats, and containers are designed and designated for this type of sterilization.[20]

Ozone sterilization should be used to sterilize moisture- and heat-sensitive items according to device manufacturers' IFU. The FDA approved ozone sterilization for use with metal and plastic surgical instruments. Ozone sterilization uses only oxygen and water in the sterilizer chamber. At the end of the process, a catalytic converter reverts raw materials back into oxygen and water. Personnel should first determine whether lumen diameter and length are acceptable before using ozone sterilization. Items should be packaged in FDA-approved rigid containers and nonwoven packages; cellulose-based paper is not appropriate. Correct placement of devices will assist with contact of the sterilant in the chamber.[8,20]

Dry heat sterilization is used for materials that are impermeable to moist heat and could be damaged by steam. Dental instruments, oils, and heat-stable powders are example of items that can tolerate high, dry heat. Dry heat coagulates the proteins in the microbe's cells. Heat energy transfers to items and sterilizes them.[8,20] Personnel should follow the manufacturer's IFU when selecting packaging and containers for use with dry heat sterilization. Small containers should be used when possible to allow for as low a package density as possible. Correct placement of devices will assist with contact of the sterilant in the chamber. The operator should use appropriate PPE (eg, insulated gloves, transfer handles) to prevent burns. At the end of the cycle, personnel should not touch the sterilizer chamber or items in the chamber. Allow packages to cool before handling.[8,20]

Peracetic acid liquid is a low-temperature sterilant that should be used for devices that are heat sensitive, can be immersed, are approved for this process, and cannot be sterilized using terminal sterilization methods. Peracetic acid is acetic acid plus an extra oxygen atom. It is effective even when organic matter is present and reacts with cellular components, causing cellular death. Only manufacturer-validated devices should be sterilized with this method. Critical items processed by the use of peracetic acid should be used immediately and not stored for later use. Personnel should transport the items to the point of use and use them immediately.[8,20]

High-Level Disinfectant: Glutaraldehyde is a saturated dialdehyde, which is used as a high-level disinfectant or chemical sterilant. The addition of an alkylating agent to the aqueous solution of glutaraldehyde makes it sporicidal. The solution then has a shelf life of 14 days. The advantage of glutaraldehyde is that it has biocidal properties (ie, activity in the presence of organic matter) and noncorrosive action on endoscopic equipment, thermometers, rubber, anesthesia, respiratory equipment, or plastic equipment. Its use may cause personnel to experience respiratory irritation from the vapor as well as allergic contact dermatitis. The glutaraldehyde bath should be placed in a well-ventilated area that has seven to 15 air exchanges per hour.[21] A tight-fitting lid should be kept on the container. Personnel should wear personal protective eye wear and nitrile or butyl gloves whenever working with glutaraldehyde. Another disadvantage of glutaraldehyde is its propensity for coagulating blood and adhering tissue to surfaces.[8,20]

Physical Monitors for Sterilization

Perioperative nurses should identify the need for documentation of monitoring results, and the documentation should be kept and easily retrievable. This provides verification that the recommended parameters are met, retained, and available for steam sterilization.

Personnel should place a **chemical indicator** (CI) on the outside and inside of the package; however, if the indicator is visible in the package, use only the inside indicator.

- Class I CIs (ie, process indicators) show whether the item has been exposed to the sterilization process and should be placed externally (eg, tape).
- Class II CIs (ie, specialty indicators) test for the presence of air in the sterilizer chamber (eg, Bowie-Dick air removal test sheets and pack).
- Class III CIs (ie, single-parameter indicators) react to one of the critical process parameters (eg, time, pressure).
- Class IV CIs (ie, multiparameter indicators) are more accurate than class III CIs because they react to two or more of the critical process parameters.
- Class V CIs (ie, integrating indicators) react to all critical parameters of sterilization and should be placed internally. Multilayered trays may require more than one indicator.
- Class VI CIs (ie, emulating indicators) react to all the critical parameters of a specialized sterilization cycle.[6,19,20]

Personnel should place CIs in the package area that offers the most challenge for air removal and sterilant contact. Personnel should follow the manufacturer's IFU for placement of CIs.[6,19,20]

> **EXAM TIP**
>
> Perioperative nurses should understand the types of chemical indicators and their appropriate usage.

Examples of methods to evaluate a steam sterilization quality-control monitoring program include printouts, digital readings, graphs, and gauges. Class I chemical indicators are placed on the outside of the package, class V or class VI on the inside of the package. A class III or IV may be used to monitor internal requirements, and **biological indicators** (a spore strip with a defined population of highly resistant spores that is used to test a specific sterilization method; see Table 6.5) are used to ensure that conditions are met for steam sterilization.[6,8,20]

Dynamic air-removal sterilization (ie, mechanically assisted air removal from a sterilization chamber). A Bowie-Dick air-removal test should be run in an empty chamber at the beginning of each day that the sterilizer is used. The Bowie-Dick tests whether all the air was removed from the chamber and whether residual air is present in the chamber during the cycle. Personnel should remove contents at the completion of a steam sterilization cycle from the sterilizer and allow the items to cool without touching for 30 minutes to two hours.[6,8,20]

Ethylene oxide. Personnel should monitor loads sterilized by EO for quality, which includes physical, chemical, and biological monitors. Managers must inform personnel of the health risks of EO exposure when they are assigned to operate or unload an EO sterilizer. Personnel should wear badges if there is a potential for exposure. The Occupational Safety and Health Administration requires that documentation be maintained. If an employee has inhaled concentrated EO gas, he or she must be moved into a fresh-air area immediately, be given oxygen if needed, and receive pulmonary resuscitation if needed.[6,8,20]

The manager should document the event in the employee's record and ensure that follow-up pulmonary function testing be performed for the time of exposure plus 30 years after termination of employment.[20]

Low-temperature hydrogen peroxide gas plasma. Quality monitoring includes printouts, digital readings, graphs, or gauges. Physical monitors include pressure and time. Personnel should perform biological monitoring to ensure sterilization (Table 6.5). Class I chemical indicators should be used on the outside of each package unless an internal indicator is visible. An FDA-cleared chemical indicator should be placed in the package to be sterilized.[8,20]

Low-temperature hydrogen peroxide vapor. Quality monitoring includes use of printouts, digital readings, graphs, or gauges. Physical monitors include pressure and time. Biological monitoring should be performed to ensure sterilization. Class I chemical indicators should be used on the outside of each package unless the internal indicator is visible. An FDA-cleared chemical indicator should be placed in the package to be sterilized.[20]

Ozone. Quality monitoring includes use of printouts, digital readings, graphs, or gauges. An FDA-cleared chemical indicator should be placed in the package to be sterilized. Physical monitors include pressure and time for each cycle. Class I chemical indicators should be used outside of each package unless the internal indicator is visible.[8,20]

Dry heat. Quality monitoring includes use of printouts, digital readings, graphs, or gauges. A class I chemical indicator should be used on the outside of each package unless the internal indicator is visible.

An FDA-cleared chemical indicator should be placed in the package to be sterilized.[8,20] Physical monitors include pressure and time for each cycle.[8,20,26]

Peracetic acid liquid. Quality monitoring includes the use of physical printouts, digital readings, graphs, gauges, and CIs to ensure that sterilization conditions have been met; if these conditions are not met, it can indicate a failure to achieve parameters. As of the printing of this book, there are no FDA-cleared biological indicators for peracetic acid liquid sterilizaton.[8,20] Quality assurance and improvement processes should be used to monitor patient, process, and system outcomes.[19]

Transporting Contaminated Instruments

Before transporting from the point of use (eg, OR), perioperative personnel should segregate the sharp instruments from the remainder of the instruments to prevent injuries to personnel. Personnel should ensure that disposable sharps (eg, scalpel blades, suture needles) are disposed of in a sharps container. Personnel should contain used or contaminated instruments to decrease exposure to personnel in movement from the point of use to the decontamination area as soon as possible after completion of the procedure. The container should be leakproof, puncture resistant, of sufficient capacity, and labeled with a biohazard sign.[7] Contaminated containers should be cleaned and disinfected properly for reuse.[5,7] Clean and sterile supplies should be physically separated from the decontamination area.[5,21]

Using wet towels to cover instruments or a manufacturer's approved instrument cleaner, personnel should keep instruments moist until they are cleaned. Water may be used; however, saline should not be used, because saline causes pitting of instruments.[7] Covered or enclosed carts with solid bottoms should be used for transporting sterile items to prevent contamination during transport.[5,20] Personnel should clean reusable covers and the cart after each use.[20]

Conditions for Storing Sterilized Instruments and Supplies

Controlling moisture, dust, lighting, and temperature and humidity extremes protects the sterilized items from becoming contaminated. Sterile storage areas should

- not exceed 75°F (24°C),
- have four total air exchanges per hour, and
- maintain a relative humidity of between 20% and 60% but no higher than 70%.[6]

Perioperative managers should limit access to sterile supply areas by trained personnel only. Managers should ensure that

- storage areas (eg, shelves, racks, bins, containers) are in compliance with fire codes and kept clean and dry[27];
- air circulation is not blocked by stored supplies[21];
- sterile supplies are kept 8 to 10 inches from the floor, two inches from outside walls, and 18 inches from the ceiling and sprinkler heads[5,27]; and
- sterile items are stored in closed cabinets or carts, not under sinks because of the possibility of moisture accumulation.[5,20,21]

Commercial Instruments and Supplies Provided by Industry Representatives

A health care facility plan for receiving and using loaned instrumentation is necessary to track and maintain quality controls and procedures to decrease loss. The plan must be well defined, the result of multidisciplinary efforts, and describe appropriate decontamination and sterilization processes. Perioperative nurses must understand these processes and be able to discuss them as well as be actively involved with this team. The plan should include details about

- how to acquire instruments and implants;
- written manufacturer's instructions for cleaning, assembly, and sterilization; and
- requirements to limit instrument set weight to no more than 25 pounds.[5,6,20]

Sterile processing personnel at the receiving facility should clean, decontaminate, and sterilize the loaned instruments before sending them to the point of use (eg, OR, cardiac catheterization laboratory). After use, personnel at the point of use should properly prepare the items before returning them to the sterile processing department for cleaning, decontamination, processing, and inventory. The instruments can then be returned to the industry representative. The sterile processing manager should maintain documentation of loaned transactions in a central location and give a copy to the industry representative.[20,28]

PROCESS FOR USE OF LOANED INSTRUMENTS

Requests for loaned instruments should be done in a timely manner to allow sufficient time for processing and inventory of the sets. Requests should include quantities, time of use, return, and restocking to prevent the need for IUSS. Loaned instruments arriving at the facility presterilized must be reprocessed to ensure sterility and prevent cross-contamination from another facility or during transport to the receiving facility.[28,29]

Sterile processing personnel should remove external shipping containers before transporting the items to the sterile processing area. Personnel should inspect rigid instrument containers upon receipt, and then clean and decontaminate the containers. Personnel should inventory the instruments and implants. Sterile processing personnel should use a class V integrating indicator during sterilization of implantable devices. At the completion of the procedure, sterile processing personnel should clean, decontaminate, inventory, and inspect the instruments before returning them to the industry representative.[5,30]

HAZARDOUS WASTE AND BIOHAZARDOUS MATERIALS

Perioperative nurses should be involved in establishing guidelines for bloodborne pathogen waste, hazardous medications, radioactive materials, and hazardous chemicals. Perioperative nurses understand that PPE (eg, impervious protective gown, gloves, a mask with a face shield, eye protection)[31] should be worn when handling items that are contaminated with blood, body fluids, tissues, or other potentially infectious materials in a liquid or semi-liquid state. OSHA describes this contamination as a large enough quantity that when a person squeezes the item, blood, body fluids, or other potentially infectious materials can be forced out of the item.[7] If squeezing the item does not release any fluid, then OSHA does not consider this hazardous waste.

TABLE 6.5 Biological Monitoring of Sterilizers[1-7]

TYPE OF STERILIZER	BIOLOGICAL TESTING DEVICE	TIMING OF TESTING	FURTHER MONITORING PERFORMED FOR THREE CONSECUTIVE CYCLES
Steam sterilizer	*Geobacillus stearothermophilus*	At least weekly, preferably daily	Further monitoring should be performed with a biological indicator (BI) process challenge device (PCD; an item that is designed to simulate a product to be sterilized and to constitute a defined challenge to the sterilization process, used to assess the effective performance of the process) for three consecutive cycles for *qualification sterilizer testing* (ie, a steam sterilization cycle in which air is removed at the beginning of the cycle from the chamber, which depends on one or more pressure and vacuum excursions) if the sterilizer • is moved, • has malfunctioned, or • requires a major repair to be performed.
Ethylene oxide	*Bacillus atrophaeus*	Every load	Further monitoring should be performed with a BI PCD for three consecutive cycles for qualification sterilizer testing if the sterilizer • is moved, • has malfunctioned, or • requires a major repair to be performed.
Low-temperature hydrogen peroxide plasma	*Geobacillus stearothermophilus*	At least daily	Further monitoring should be performed with a BI PCD for three consecutive cycles for qualification sterilizer testing if the sterilizer • is moved, • has malfunctioned, or • requires a major repair to be performed.
Low-peroxide hydrogen vapor	*Geobacillus stearothermophilus*	At least daily	Further monitoring should be performed with a BI PCD for three consecutive cycles for qualification sterilizer testing if the sterilizer • is moved, • has malfunctioned, or • requires a major repair to be performed.
Ozone	*Geobacillus stearothermophilus*	At least daily	Further monitoring should be performed with a BI PCD for three consecutive cycles for qualification sterilizer testing if the sterilizer • is moved, • has malfunctioned, or • requires a major repair to be performed.

TYPE OF STERILIZER	BIOLOGICAL TESTING DEVICE	TIMING OF TESTING	FURTHER MONITORING PERFORMED FOR THREE CONSECUTIVE CYCLES
Dry Heat	*Bacillus atrophaeus*	At least daily	Further monitoring should be performed with a BI PCD for three consecutive cycles for qualification sterilizer testing if the sterilizer • is moved, • has malfunctioned, or • requires a major repair to be performed.
Peracetic acid liquid	No FDA biological indicator available	NA	Use quality assurance to monitor patient, process, and system outcomes.

1. Rutala WA, Weber DJ; Healthcare Infection Control Practices Advisory Committee (HICPAC). *Guideline for Disinfection and Sterilization in Healthcare Facilities*. Atlanta, GA: Centers for Disease Control and Prevention; 2008:1-158. https://www.cdc.gov/infectioncontrol/guidelines/disinfection/index.html.
2. Guideline for sterilization. In: *Guidelines for Perioperative Practice*. Denver, CO: AORN, Inc; 2017:865-892.
3. Association for the Advancement of Medical Instrumentation, Accreditation Association for Ambulatory Health Care, AORN, et al. Immediate-use sterilization statement. http:/www.aami.org/publications/standards/ST79_Immediate_Use_Statement.pdf.
4. Association for the Advancement of Medical Instrumentation. ANSI/AAMI ST41: Ethylene oxide sterilization in health care facilities: safety and effectiveness. Arlington, VA: Association for the Advancement of Medical Instrumentation; 2012.
5. ANSI/AAMI ST40: Table top dry-heat (heated air) sterilization and sterility assurance in health care facilities. Arlington, VA: Association for the Advancement of Medical Instrumentation; 2004.
6. Mangram AJ, Horan TC, Pearson ML, Silver LC, Jarvis WR; Hospital Infection Control Practices Advisory Committee. Guideline for prevention of surgical site infection, 1999. *Infect Control Hosp Epidemiol*. 1999:20(4)250-78.
7. Occupational safety and health standards. Toxic and hazardous substances: ethylene oxide. 29 CFR §1910.1047. https://www.osha.gov/pls/oshaweb/owadisp.show_document?p_table=standards&p_id=10070.

Bloodborne pathogen waste. Personnel must place items that are caked with dried blood, body fluids, or other potentially infectious materials in closable, leakproof containers or bags that are color coded, labeled, or tagged for easy identification as biohazardous waste. This helps prevent personnel exposure to potentially infectious materials and prevents contamination of the environment.[7]

Hazardous materials. A list of hazardous materials should be posted in the department. Materials should be handled in compliance with OSHA standards. Use of current Safety Data Sheets helps perioperative nurses identify these medications. Perioperative managers should ensure that hazardous materials or solutions are stored in an area that is secured and that each item is clearly labeled with name, use, and warnings. Transporting hazardous materials or solutions must be done in a sealed container that is leakproof and nonbreakable and has a label that identifies the contents. Managers should ensure that spill kits and disposal containers are available and used to transport waste from the point of use to the disposal area. A label should be placed on the outside of the container to identify the waste contents. Extra care must be taken with cytotoxic agents that may leave a residue on instruments and subsequently require specific cleaning of these instruments.[31-33]

Radioactive materials. Perioperative nurses who collect and handle radioactive specimens must understand and follow facility policy and local, state, and federal regulations. Occupational doses of radiation should have a level as low as is reasonably achievable. The per year maximum radiation exposure limit for radiation workers is 5,000 millirem (mrem) per year (eg, a chest x-ray is 4 mrem).[34] Personnel should adhere to standard precautions when processing instruments used for handling radiation seeds.[35] Personnel should use forceps to handle radioactive specimens that were removed from a patient and place them into a container to protect personnel from exposure.[35]

Hazardous chemicals. Working with hazardous chemicals such as glutaraldehyde requires the perioperative nurse to know how to wear protective attire, which may include chemical-resistant gloves, protective eyewear, an impervious gown, a jumpsuit, or an apron. Managers should ensure that a well-ventilated area is available to further protect personnel. Personnel should use covered containers with tight-fitting lids to contain disinfectants. Hydrogen peroxide, glutaraldehyde, and orthopthaldehyde are other high-level disinfectants that require care in their usage to prevent personnel injury, especially allergic reactions, skin irritation, and serious eye injury.[6,8,20,31]

Key Concepts and Review

The role of the perioperative nurse requires knowledge of instrument processing and supply management. In delivering patient care the perioperative nurse collaborates with team members while serving as a resource. Personnel should maintain ongoing awareness of infection prevention and control principles and practices by using proper PPE and following standard and transmission-based precautions when cleaning and disinfecting contaminated instruments and supplies. Following the manufacturers' IFU helps provide a safe system for protecting instruments. Documentation of the steps taken in cleaning, disinfecting, packaging, sterilizing, transporting, and storing instruments and supplies protects patients and provides a record of the process.

References

1. Siegel J, Rhinehart J, Jackson M, Chiarello L. Health Care Infection Control Practices Advisory Committee. 2007 *Guidelines for Isolation Precautions: Preventing Transmission of Infectious Agents in Healthcare Settings*. Atlanta, GA: Centers for Disease Control and Prevention; 2007:1-218.
2. Siegel J, Rhinehart J, Jackson M, Chiarello L. Health Care Infection Control Practices Advisory Committee. *Management of Multidrug-Resistant Organisms in Healthcare Settings*. Atlanta, GA: Centers for Disease Control and Prevention; 2006:1-74.
3. ANSI/AAMI TIR30 2011: *A Compendium of Processes, Materials, Test Methods, and Acceptance Criteria for Cleaning Reusable Medical Devices*. Arlington, VA: Association for the Advancement of Medical Instrumentation; 2011.
4. AAMI TIR12: *Designing, Testing, and Labeling Reusable Medical Devices for Reprocessing in Health Care Facilities. A Guide for Medical Device Manufacturers*. Arlington, VA; 2010.
5. Guideline for cleaning and care of surgical instruments. In: *Guidelines for Perioperative Practice*. Denver, CO: AORN, Inc; 2017:815-849.
6. ANSI/AAMI ST79: *Comprehensive Guide to Steam Sterilization and Sterility Assurance in Health Care Facilities*. Arlington, VA: Association for the Advancement of Medical Instrumentation; 2017.
7. Toxic and Hazardous Waste Substances: Bloodborne Pathogens. 29 CFR §1910.1030 (2012). Occupational Safety and Health Administration. https://www.osha.gov/pls/oshaweb/owadisp.show_document?p_id=10051&p_table=STANDARDS.

8. Rutala WA, Weber DJ; Healthcare Infection Control Practices Advisory Committee (HICPAC). *Guideline for Disinfection and Sterilization in Healthcare Facilities*. Atlanta, GA: Centers for Disease Control and Prevention; 2008:1-158. https://www.cdc.gov/infectioncontrol/guidelines/disinfection/index.html.
9. Ongoing safety review of arthroscopic shavers. US Food and Drug Administration. http://www.fda.gov/MedicalDevices/Safety/AlertsandNotices/ucm170639.htm.
10. McDonnell G, Dehen C, Perrin A, et al. Cleaning disinfection and sterilization of surface prion contamination. *J Hosp Infect*. 2013;85(4):268-273.
11. Secker TJ, Herve R, Keevil CW. Adsorption of prion and tissue proteins to surgical stainless steel surfaces and the efficacy of decontamination following dry wet conditions. *J Hosp Infect*. 2011;78(4):251-255.
12. Rutala WA, Weber DJ; Society for Healthcare Epidemiology of America. Guideline for disinfection and sterilization of prion-contaminated medical instruments. *Infect Control Hosp Epidemiol*. 2010;31(2):107-117.
13. Endoscopic Retrograde Cholangiopancreatography (ERCP) Duodenoscopes: FDA Safety Communication—Design May Impede Effective Cleaning. FDA Safety Communication. US Food and Drug Administration. https://www.fda.gov/safety/medwatch/safetyinformation/safetyalertsforhumanmedicalproducts/ucm434922.htm.
14. Duodenoscope reprocessing: FDA safety communication—supplemental measures to enhance reprocessing. US Food and Drug Administration. http://www.fda.gov/safety/medwatch/safetyinformation/safetyalertsforhumanmedicalproducts/ucm457132.htm.
15. Interim protocol for healthcare facilities regarding surveillance for bacterial contamination of duodenoscopes after reprocessing. Centers for Disease Control and Prevention. http://www.cdc.gov/hai/pdfs/cre/interim-duodenoscope-surveillance-Protocol.pdf.
16. Healthcare-associated infections (HAIs). Carbapenem-resistant Enterobacteriaceae (CRE) infection: clinician FAQs. Centers for Disease Control and Prevention. http://www.cdc.gov/hai/organisms/cre/cre-clinicianFAQ.html.
17. Facility guidance for control of carbapenem-resistant enterobacteriaceae (CRRE)-November 2015 update CRRE toolkit. Centers for Disease Control and Prevention. https://www.cdc.gov/hai/organisms/cre/cre-toolkit/index.html.
18. Rutala RA, Weber DJ. ERCP scopes: what can we do to prevent infections? *Infect Control Hosp Epidemiol*. 2015;36(6):643-648.
19. Guideline for selection and use of packaging systems for sterilization. In: *Guidelines for Perioperative Practice*. Denver, CO: AORN, Inc; 2016:809-821.
20. Guideline for sterilization. In: *Guidelines for Perioperative Practice*. Denver, CO: AORN, Inc; 2016:823-850.
21. Facility Guidelines Institute. American Society for Healthcare Engineering. *Guidelines for Design and Construction of Hospitals and Outpatient Facilities*. Chicago, IL: American Society for Healthcare Engineering; 2014.
22. Association for the Advancement of Medical Instrumentation, Accreditation Association for Ambulatory Health Care, AORN, et al. Immediate-use sterilization statement. http://www.aami.org/publications/standards/ST79_Immediate_Use_Statement.pdf.
23. Mangram AJ, Horan TC, Pearson ML, Silver LC, Jarvis WR; Hospital Infection Control Practices Advisory Committee. Guideline for prevention of surgical site infection, 1999. *Infect Control Hosp Epidemiol*. 1999:20(4)250-278.
24. ANSI/AAMI ST41: *Ethylene Oxide Sterilization in Health Care Facilities: Safety and Effectiveness*. Arlington, VA: Association for the Advancement of Medical Instrumentation; 2012.
25. Occupational safety and health standards. Toxic and hazardous substances: ethylene oxide. 29 CFR §1910.1047. https://www.osha.gov/pls/oshaweb/owadisp.show_document?p_table=standards&p_id=10070.
26. ANSI/AAMI ST40: *Tabletop Dry-Heat (Heated Air) Sterilization and Sterility Assurance in Health Care Facilities*. Arlington, VA: Association for the Advancement of Medical Instrumentation; 2004.
27. Standard pendant and upright sprinklers. In: NFPA 13: *Standard for Installation of Sprinklers*. 2010 ed. Quincy, MA: National Fire Protection Association; 2010:51-58.
28. Duro M. New IAHCSMM loaner paper and policy template. *AORN J*. 2011;94(3):287-289.
29. IAHCSMM Position paper on the management of loaner instrumentation. International Association of Healthcare Central Service Materiel Management. https://www.iahcsmm.org/images/Resources/Loaner_Instrument/Position-Paper.pdf.

30. Hunter-Kunish GG. Processing loaner instruments in an ambulatory surgery center. *AORN J.* 2009;89(5):861-866.
31. Guideline for environment of care, part 1. In: *Guidelines for Perioperative Practice.* Denver, CO: AORN, Inc; 2017:243-267.
32. Preventing occupational exposures to antineoplastic and other hazardous drugs in health care settings. NIOSH Alert (Pub no. 20040165). National Institute for Occupational Safety and Health. https://www.cdc.gov/niosh/docs/2004-165/default.html.
33. Guideline for medication safety. In: *Guidelines for Perioperative Practice.* Denver, CO: AORN, Inc; 2017:295-333.
34. 10 CFR 20: Standards for Protection Against Radiation. 2013. United States Nuclear Regulatory Commission. https://www.gpo.gov/fdsys/pkg/CFR-2013-title10-vol1/pdf/CFR-2013-title10-vol1-part20.pdf.
35. Guideline for radiation safety. In: *Guidelines for Perioperative Practice.* Denver, CO: AORN, Inc; 2017:339-371.

Practice Exam Questions

1. The minimum distance between ceiling-mounted sprinkler heads and sterile stored items is _____ inches.
    A. 6
    B. 12
    C. 18
    D. 24

2. Which biologic indicator is validated for use with liquid peracetic acid sterilization?
    A. *Geobacillus stearothermophilus*
    B. Self-contained biologic indicator (SCBI)
    C. *Bacillus atrophaeus*
    D. No indicator is validated for use with peracetic acid sterilization.

3. Orthopedic instrument sets and implants have arrived at the sterile processing department to be sterilized prior to scheduled cases for the following day. The sets each weigh 32 pounds. The sterile processing technician should
    A. sterilize the sets as delivered.
    B. request that the perioperative nurse assigned to the case process the instruments using immediate-use steam sterilization (IUSS).
    C. use additional containers to separate the contents so that each set weighs 28 pounds per container.
    D. use additional containers to separate the contents so that each set weighs 25 pounds per container.

4. A package containing chemical sterilant is inadvertently punctured and splashes onto the hands of the perioperative nurse as she prepares an endoscope for sterilization. Information on how to handle the spill is best obtained from
    A. the facility pharmacist.
    B. a poison control center.
    C. the perioperative manager.
    D. the appropriate Safety Data Sheet (SDS).

5. When placing one peel pouch inside another
    A. the inner pouch should be placed with its plastic side facing the plastic side of the outer pouch.
    B. the inner pouch should be placed with the plastic side facing the paper side of the outer pouch.
    C. the inner pouch should be folded over to fit inside the outer pouch.
    D. the outer pouch should be labeled on the paper side.

6. Instruments undergoing high-level disinfection should be rinsed after the required exposure time with
    A. tap water.
    B. sterile water.
    C. sterile saline.
    D. sodium hypochlorite.

7. A surgeon requests the perioperative nurse retrieve a laparoscopy lens that has not completed its aeration cycle after being sterilized via ethylene oxide (EO). The most appropriate response to this request is
    A. "Instruments that have not completed the aeration cycle can cause burns to staff and patients."
    B. "There is an increased risk for cancer from instruments that have not been appropriately processed."
    C. "Materials that have not been appropriately aerated are a fire risk."
    D. "Our policy states that instruments must complete an eight-hour aeration cycle before they can be released for use."

8. The Bowie-Dick process indicator is used to
    A. demonstrate that an item has been exposed to the sterilization process.
    B. demonstrate that the conditions for sterilization have been met.
    C. detect air leaks in dynamic air-removal sterilizer chambers.
    D. set short-term exposure limits to toxic sterilants.

9. During morning report, the charge nurse relays that a positive biological indicator has been reported by sterile processing personnel for a load processed the day before. The perioperative nurse's first action is to
    A. notify surgeons whose patients may have been exposed to improperly sterilized instruments.
    B. include this information in postoperative calls to patients so that they can follow up with their surgeons.
    C. remove from use all instrument trays with the suspect load control numbers.
    D. notify the infection control nurse of a potential increase in surgical site infections.

10. An abdominal retractor is very difficult to assemble, and the surgical technologists have asked that it be sterilized assembled in the position in which it will be used. The most appropriate response to this request is
    A. "Our policy states that all equipment must be disassembled prior to sterilization."
    B. "As long as all the parts are accounted for during counts, this practice would be acceptable."
    C. "Let's ask the manufacturer's representative to come in and do an in-service on the correct way to assemble the retractor."
    D. "If the steam cannot reach all areas of the instrument, those areas are considered contaminated."

Answers and Supported Rationales

1. Answer C is correct. Fire code regulations specify that clearance from the top of stored items to the ceiling be 18 inches to allow for sprinkler systems to be effective. Reference: Guideline for sterilization. In: *Guidelines for Perioperative Practice*. Denver, CO: AORN, Inc; 2017:881.

2. Answer D is correct. There is no biological indicator available that has been validated for use with liquid peracetic acid sterilant systems. Reference: Guideline for sterilization. In: *Guidelines for Perioperative Practice*. Denver, CO: AORN, Inc; 2017:879.

3. Answer D is correct. Weight of instrument pans should not exceed 25 pounds. Reference: Guideline for cleaning and care of surgical instruments. In: *Guidelines for Perioperative Practice*. Denver, CO: AORN, Inc; 2016:812.

4. Answer D is correct. A current SDS should be readily available for all hazardous materials used in the perioperative suite. Reference: Guideline for processing flexible endoscopes. In: *Guidelines for Perioperative Practice*. Denver, CO: AORN, Inc; 2017:755.

5. Answer A is correct. The inner pouch should fit inside the outer pouch without folding it, and face in the same direction as the outer pouch (eg, plastic faces plastic) to allow for sterilant to pass through both pouches. Reference: Guideline for selection and use of packaging systems. In: *Guidelines for Perioperative Practice*. Denver, CO: AORN, Inc; 2017:856-857.

6. Answer B is correct. Rinsing with sterile water prevents recontamination of the instrument. Saline and sodium hypochlorite can corrode the finish of the instrument. Reference: Guideline for manual chemical high-level disinfection. In: *Guidelines for Perioperative Practice*. Denver, CO: AORN, Inc; 2018:894.

7. Answer A is correct. Insufficiently aerated items can cause skin irritation and tissue burns. Reference: Spry C. Infection prevention and control. In: Rothrock JC, ed. *Alexander's Care of the Patient in Surgery*. 15th ed. Philadelphia, PA: Elsevier; 2015:98.

8. Answer C is correct. The Bowie-Dick process indicator is used to detect air leaks and ineffective air removal in dynamic air-removal sterilizers. Reference: Guideline for sterilization. In: *Guidelines for Perioperative Practice*. Denver, CO: AORN, Inc; 2017:886,889.

9. Answer C is correct. Retrievable items should be immediately recalled to prevent harm to patients. Reference: Guideline for sterilization. In: *Guidelines for Perioperative Practice*. Denver, CO: AORN, Inc; 2017:883-884.

10. Answer D is correct. Sterilant (in this case steam) must be able to reach all surfaces in order to completely eliminate all organisms. Reference: Spry C. Infection prevention and control. In: Rothrock JC, ed. *Alexander's Care of the Patient in Surgery*. 15th ed. Philadelphia, PA: Elsevier; 2015:90-91.

7 Emergency Situations

KEY TERMS

- Air embolism
- American Society of Anesthesiologists (ASA)
- Anaphylaxis
- Autotransfusion
- Bronchospasm and laryngospasm
- Compartment syndrome
- Computed tomography (CT)
- Diagnostic peritoneal lavage (DPL)
- Fire
- Focused assessment with sonography (FAST)
- Glasgow Coma Scale (GCS)
- Golden hour
- Hemorrhagic shock
- Iatrogenic injury
- Malignant hyperthermia (MH)
- Mechanism of injury (MOI)
- Natural disaster
- Organ procurement
- Pulmonary embolism (PE)
- Rapid-sequence induction (RSI)
- Surgical classifications: elective, urgent, emergent
- Thermal injury
- Traumatic brain injury (TBI)
- Triage

REQUIRED NURSING SKILLS

- Coordinating members of the interdisciplinary health care team during emergency situations
- Performing appropriate nursing interventions for malignant hyperthermia, anaphylaxis, cardiac arrest, trauma, and terrorism
- Preparation for and management of medical emergencies, environmental hazards, natural disasters, and terrorist situations
- Protecting patient and resources from environmental hazards during disasters

No two surgeries are alike. Complications can occur at any moment during the surgical experience.[1] Perioperative registered nurses (RNs) must be educated in, and ever attentive to, the presentation of evolving emergency situations in the OR. Perioperative professionals who engage in multidisciplinary teamwork, maintain diligent awareness of potential emergent situations, and ensure accurate preparation for corrective actions can help influence positive outcomes of all surgical patients. This chapter provides an overview of intraoperative crises, to include medical emergencies (eg, air embolism, anaphylaxis, hemorrhage, cardiac instability, malignant hyperthermia, trauma), environmental hazards, natural disasters (eg, fire, toxic fumes, natural disasters, extreme weather), and terrorist situations (eg, active shooters).

Perioperative Crises

Perioperative nurses are the patient's primary advocate. Nurses are the eyes and ears of, and a champion for the best interest of, each patient during every procedure. Ensuring a patient's safety and security and promoting positive outcomes require vigilance, with continual assessment of changes in a patient's personal or environmental conditions that can result in adverse outcomes. Preventing wrong-patient, wrong-site, wrong-procedure events and ensuring accurate surgical counts, thus avoiding retained objects, are just a few of the issues that factor into maintaining a safe surgical environment. The highest-priority safety issues[2] in the surgical setting are presented in Figure 7.1.

Even the most basic of surgical procedures can threaten loss of life or limb for the patient if any of a variety of emergencies occur. Knowledge, situational awareness, and communication with team members during emerging crises can mean the difference between major and minor events in the perioperative environment. These include air embolism, anaphylaxis, hemorrhage, cardiovascular instability, malignant hyperthermia, and fire.

AIR EMBOLISM

An **air embolism** is when an air embolus (ie, air bubble) enters a vein or artery. It can enter the body through an opening (eg, traumatic limb amputation exposing arterial vessels, traumatic chest injury resulting in a pneumothorax), an IV, exposure of a blood vessel through bodily injury, or surgery. As an embolus travels through the venous or arterial circulatory system, it can potentially wedge in an area like the heart, lungs, or brain, where it can obstruct flow and cause a heart attack, stroke, or respiratory failure. Locating the source of air entry and returning the patient to a stable hemodynamic state are the primary goals of the health care team. Achieving this goal requires restoration of a normal oxygen level and prevention of further air entry into the vascular system,[3] which is accomplished by covering the surgical field immediately with saline-soaked dressing, tilting the OR bed, maintaining the patient's systemic arterial pressure, aspirating air from the right atrium, and providing hyperbaric oxygen therapy when possible.

FIGURE 7.1 Highest-Priority Safety Issues

A study by Steelman, Graling, and Perkhounkova[1] identified the top patient safety issues as reported by perioperative RNs. Of the 3,137 surveys received, the majority of respondents (nearly 70%) reported preventing wrong-site, -procedure, or -patient surgery as the top safety issue.

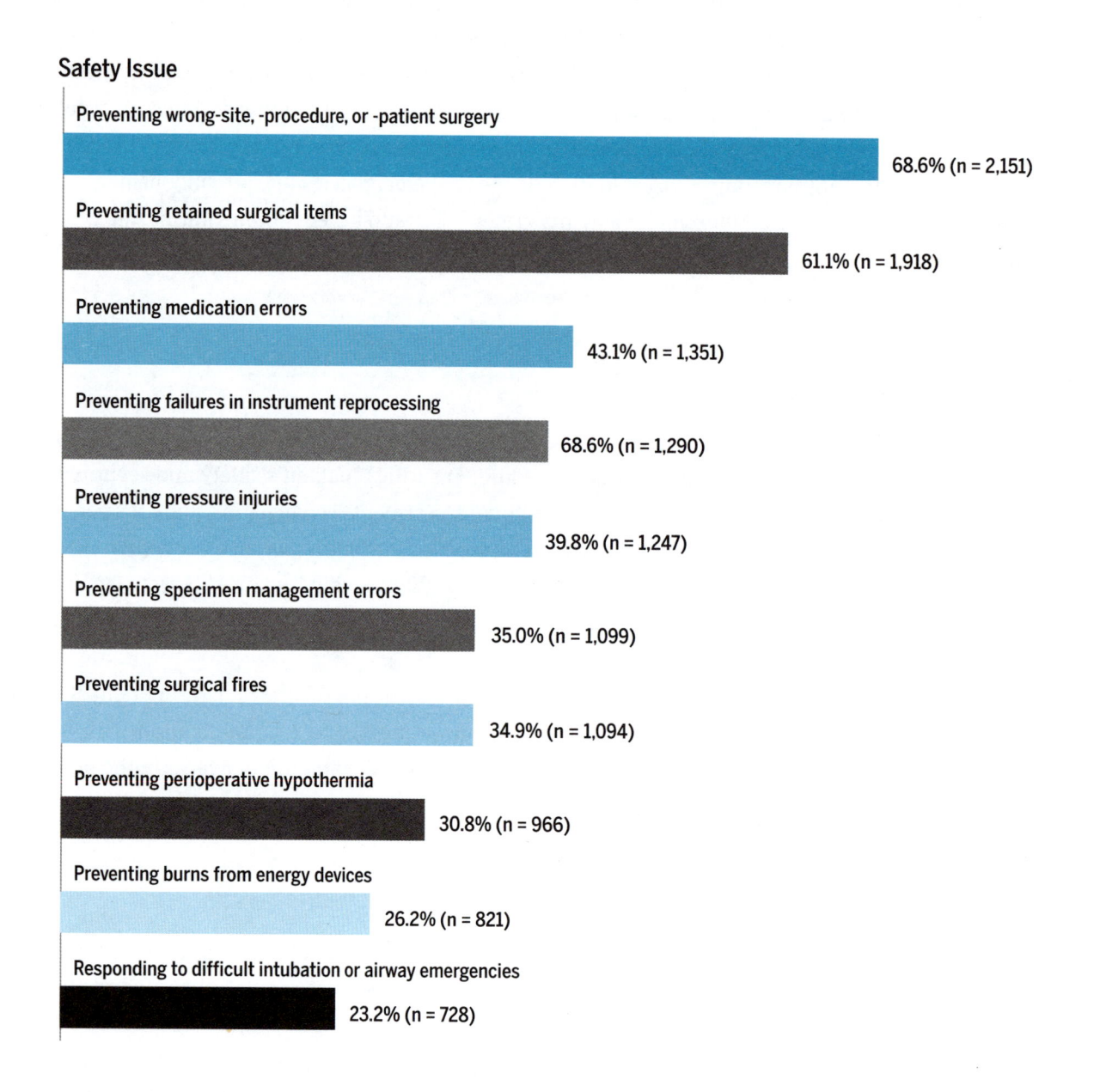

Safety Issue

Safety Issue	Percentage
Preventing wrong-site, -procedure, or -patient surgery	68.6% (n = 2,151)
Preventing retained surgical items	61.1% (n = 1,918)
Preventing medication errors	43.1% (n = 1,351)
Preventing failures in instrument reprocessing	68.6% (n = 1,290)
Preventing pressure injuries	39.8% (n = 1,247)
Preventing specimen management errors	35.0% (n = 1,099)
Preventing surgical fires	34.9% (n = 1,094)
Preventing perioperative hypothermia	30.8% (n = 966)
Preventing burns from energy devices	26.2% (n = 821)
Responding to difficult intubation or airway emergencies	23.2% (n = 728)

1. Steelman VM, Graling PR, Perkhounkova Y. Priority patient safety issues identified by perioperative nurses. *AORN J.* 2013;97(4):402-418.

ANAPHYLAXIS

Anaphylaxis is an adverse reaction to a known or unknown substance. Acute hemolytic reaction is a type of blood transfusion reaction in which transfused red cells react to the patient's circulating antibodies, which may cause intravascular hemolysis. It is imperative for health care providers to quickly identify the source and administer appropriate medications (eg, epinephrine, diphenhydramine, albuterol, cortisone). The perioperative team must conduct a thorough assessment of allergies before surgery, including food allergies (eg, banana, kiwi, avocado) that are implicated in increased risk for latex allergy as well as diseases (eg, spina bifida) requiring repeated urinary catheterizations. There are three types of reactions to natural rubber latex:

- IgE-mediated reactions (type I): true allergic reactions involving the immune system and they can be life threatening.
- Cell-mediated contact dermatitis (type IV): a type of latex allergy causing a delayed response 48 to 96 hours after exposure. Typically, this reaction is caused by the processing chemicals used in manufacturing natural rubber latex, but is not life-threatening.
- Irritant dermatitis: a non-allergic reaction that causes dry, irritated skin or linear-like skin lesions.

A safe environment of care includes removal from the room of all products that contain latex, posting signs on the doors of the OR, and including appropriate hand-over (ie, hand-off) communication that the patient has a latex sensitivity or allergy.[4] With the potential for increased prevalence of patients and employees with latex sensitivity or actual latex allergy, many health care facility managers have made their facilities completely latex free.

HEMORRHAGE

More than 80% of deaths in the OR and nearly 50% of deaths within the first 24 hours of injury are a result of exsanguination and coagulopathy.[5] **Hemorrhagic shock** is a pathophysiological state in which the circulatory system is unable to perfuse tissues adequately and thus meet the body's oxygen requirements. Patients who are bleeding require concurrent hemorrhage control and blood replacement therapy. In addition to the effective restoration of blood volume, the specific goal of transfusion management is to restore the patient's oxygen-carrying capacity.[6] As with all emergencies, when a hemorrhagic event is occurring, the universal action item for all members of the perioperative team is to call for help. Emergency actions may be performed by any member of the surgical team. All perioperative team members should

- know where the code buttons are located;
- adhere to professional practice parameters; and
- know and follow facility guidelines, protocols, policies, and procedures.[6]

The most important step for the surgical team in resuscitating a patient who is experiencing hemorrhagic shock is identifying and rapidly controlling the source of bleeding. In the OR, this may be accomplished by using a variety of methods, including the following:

- applying direct pressure to the source of bleeding,
- using electrosurgical or tissue-sealing devices,

- clamping and then ligating the bleeding vessels with suture, or
- applying hemostatic agents.[6]

The RN circulator and anesthesia professional carefully monitor the output of blood in suction canisters and saturation of laparotomy sponges on and off the field. Communication with the anesthesia provider is necessary to accurately estimate blood loss and enable both the surgeon and anesthesia personnel to make informed decisions regarding fluid replacement. The RN circulator should anticipate the need for crystalloid (eg, lactated Ringer's solution) or colloid solutions (eg, dextran, Hespan® [ie, hydroxyethyl starch]) for plasma volume expansion.[7]

A massive transfusion is defined as the need for more than 10 units of red blood cells within 24 hours of the start of treatment. A mass transfusion protocol is a standardized replacement of platelets and clotting factors in an optimum ratio to packed red blood cells, with a goal of increasing the speed and efficiency of transfusion. Initiation of the massive transfusion protocol is meant to improve communication among the surgeon, anesthesia professionals, perioperative nurses, laboratory personnel, and blood bank personnel, and to coordinate a systematic approach to the administration of large volumes of blood products.[6] Before surgery, perioperative nurses should determine whether any blood or blood products have been ordered, to include verifying whether the patient banked any of his or her own blood. The RN circulator should determine whether an intraoperative cell salvage machine is available.

CARDIOVASCULAR INSTABILITY

Patients undergoing surgery may be at risk for significant postoperative cardiac complications related to cardiac health, comorbidities, and length/type of the surgical procedure. Cardiac complications include

- unstable bradycardia or tachycardia;
- cardiac arrest for
    - asystole,
    - pulseless electrical activity,
    - ventricular fibrillation, or
    - ventricular tachycardia; or
- hypertension or hypotension.

General anesthesia and surgery contribute to major postoperative cardiac complications because of the potential for myocardial stress and decreases in central venous and arterial pressures as a result of volume shifts and blood loss. Blood pressure responses to surgery and anesthesia are dual faceted, and both hypotension and hypertension may occur in any phase of surgery. For example, induction of general anesthesia may lead to a substantial reduction in blood pressure and cardiac output, whereas endotracheal intubation, increased catecholamine release associated with surgical stress, and arterial vasospasm may significantly raise blood pressure; all of these factors are known to have a negative influence on cardiovascular physiology.[8]

MALIGNANT HYPERTHERMIA

Malignant hyperthermia is a hypermetabolic crisis in susceptible patients possibly triggered by anesthesia agents.[9] Although a thorough anesthesia history is crucial for identification of a potential crisis, every patient is considered as having a potential for **malignant hyperthermia** (MH).

- Discontinue volatile agents and succinylcholine (and notify the surgeon to halt the procedure ASAP).
- Call for help and additional personnel resources. (Call 911 if surgicenter.)
- Get dantrolene/MH cart.
- Hyperventilate with 100% oxygen at flows of 10L/min to flush volatile anesthetics and lower $ETCO_2$. If available, insert activated charcoal filters into the inspiratory and expiratory limbs of the breathing circuit. The [filter] may become saturated after one hour; therefore, a replacement set of filters should be substituted after each hour of use.
- Give IV dantrolene 2.5 mg/kg rapidly through a large-bore IV, if possible. Repeat as frequently as needed until the patient responds with a decrease in $ETCO_2$, decreased muscle rigidity, and/or lowered heart rate. Large doses (> 10mg/kg) may be required for patients with persistent contractures or rigidity.
- Obtain blood gas (venous or arterial) to determine degree of metabolic acidosis. Consider administration of sodium bicarbonate, 1 to 2 mEq/kg dose, for base excess greater than −8 (maximum dose 50 mEq).
- Cool the patient if core temperature is greater than 102°F (39°C) or less if rapidly rising. Stop cooling when the temperature has decreased to less than 100.4°F (38°C).[9]

> The Malignant Hyperthermia Association of the United States (MHAUS) has a website, research materials, and a 24-hour number to call for emergency help during an MH crisis:
> - 24-hour MH hotline: 800-644-9737
> - For emergencies only: www.mhaus.org/healthcare-professionals

The keys to success are early diagnosis, preparation with written protocols, and having MH supplies immediately available. (See Chapter 3 for a more in-depth discussion of MH risk factors, etiology, and signs and symptoms.)

> **⊙ EXAM TIP**
>
> At the onset of malignant hyperthermia symptoms, think "SHS-Cool"
> First action: **STOP** the inhalant anesthesia and **STOP** the surgery.
> Second action: **HYPERVENTILATE** the patient with 100% oxygen.
> Third action: **START** dantrolene.
> Fourth action: **COOL** the patient.

FIRE

Patients are at greatest risk of **fire** injury when all three elements of the fire triangle (Figure 7.2) are in close proximity, which occurs during surgery. Such proximity is particularly dangerous during surgery that is performed on the head, neck, and upper chest. Patient risk is high because these surgical areas are near the patient's airway, through which an endotracheal (ET) tube or mask delivers oxygen, thus producing an oxygen-enriched environment.[10]

The RN circulator should conduct a fire risk assessment at the beginning of each procedure and perform a fire time out with the entire surgical team before surgery is started. The RN circulator should ensure that if alcohol-based (ie, flammable) skin preparation solutions are used, they are used safely, according to manufacturers' instructions for use, and that team members allow adequate time for the solution to dry before draping the patient. The RN circulator should check drapes for pooling of flammable liquids after the surgical skin prep is complete, and remove drapes if needed. The surgical team should use all surgical devices and equipment safely according to manufacturers' recommendations. The RN should encourage communication among members of the surgical team, using the fire triangle as a guide by verifying whether

- open sources of oxygen are in use (ie, oxidizer);
- electrosurgical unit pencils, lasers, and other ignition sources have been stored properly (ie, ignition source); and
- combustible products (eg, drapes, sponges) are present (eg, fuel sources) and contained.

All members of the surgical team should plan how to manage a surgical fire. The first step is to fully understand the RACE method (Figure 7.3), which is a mnemonic used to recall the steps to take should a fire occur and in what order: rescue, alarm or alert, contain or confine, and extinguish or evacuate.

- *Rescue* those in immediate danger. Determine where the fire is. Is it inside or outside the surgical suite? Does it involve the patient's airway? All surgical team members should work cooperatively to turn off the oxygen and other gases, disconnect power sources, pour saline on drapes, move the back table, remove burning drapes, assess for secondary fires, and move the patient as needed.
- *Alarm* or *alert* others to the emergency. Personnel should pull the fire alarm, call the charge nurse, and get the word out that help is needed.
- *Contain* or *confine* the fire. Personnel should close the OR doors and put moistened towels at the bottom of the door to keep out smoke.
- *Extinguish* with a fire extinguisher, or pour normal saline on nonelectrical fires. Know your locations and the ABC classifications of your extinguisher. Class A is for wood, paper, cloth, and even rubber. Class B is for liquids and grease, including gasoline and flammable gases. Apply only class C extinguishers on electrical fires. Every person should be aware of the **evacuation plan** and be prepared to move horizontally first, staying behind designated fire doors, and then evacuating the patient as needed.

FIGURE 7.2 The Fire Triangle

FIGURE 7.3 The RACE Method

R Rescue
A Alarm/Alert
C Contain/Confine
E Extinguish/Evacuate

Resources such as the Council on Surgical and Perioperative Safety[11] and AORN's Fire Safety Tool Kit[12] are available for more information and support.

Surgical Classifications: Elective, Emergent, Urgent

In preparation for surgery, procedures are classified as elective, emergent, or urgent; however, every procedure has the potential to become emergent at any point. Emergency situations in the OR present in many ways: hypotension, hypertension, bradycardia, tachycardia, decreased respiration, or excessive bleeding from a wound. The RN circulator must pay attention not only to the patient and the sterile field but also to events occurring at the back table and behind the anesthesia screen. Patient outcomes are greatly enhanced by multidisciplinary communication, diligence in potential urgent and emergent situations occurring in the surgical suite, and appropriate actions in the presentation of trauma events.

Elective procedures are planned events that the patient, anesthesia professional, and surgeon have taken adequate time for in preparation for the surgery. The surgeon has completed a history and physical examination, ordered and received the results of preoperative tests, completed the informed consent process with the patient, and answered all of the patient's and family members' questions. The anesthesia professional and perioperative nurses have completed their assessments and all team members have gathered and prepared the necessary instruments, equipment, supplies, and medications.

Urgent procedures may not have allowed personnel the luxury of time in planning, and can quickly turn emergent, depending on multiple factors.

Emergent procedures are performed when a medical event occurs that is worsening and time becomes a factor in saving life or limb for a patient. In trauma, there is a **golden hour**, referring to the critical time after injury occurs during which rapid and definitive interventions can be most effective in reducing mortality and morbidity.[13]

Since 1963, the **American Society of Anesthesiologists** (ASA) has used a predictive system of classification for anesthetic outcomes for preoperative patients (Table 7.1).[14] The classification can range from ASA I (ie, a healthy individual) to ASA VI (ie, the patient is brain dead and is being prepared for organ donation). In later years, the ASA added an "E" for emergency; this designation has helped health care providers determine additional urgency needed in a patient's care. This preoperative information is the starting point for multidisciplinary teams to prepare for potential adverse outcomes during any surgical procedure.

The ABCs of Preparing for Emergencies

Emergencies are not planned and can occur at any time before, during, or even after a scheduled surgery. Preparation is the key to attaining positive outcomes in emergent situations. Surgical team members can use an alphabetical system to start a mental checklist to prepare for and gather needed items to deal with potential untoward events. The following discussion presents the A, B, C, D, and E (ie, airway, breathing, circulation, defibrillation, and emergency) components of emergency preparation and management.

TABLE 7.1 ASA Physical Status Classification System

ASA PS CLASSIFICATION	DEFINITION	EXAMPLES, INCLUDING BUT NOT LIMITED TO:
ASA I	A normal healthy patient	Healthy, nonsmoking, no or minimal alcohol use
ASA II	A patient with mild systemic disease	Mild diseases only without substantive functional limitations. Examples include (but are not limited to): current smoker, social alcohol drinker, pregnancy, obesity (30 < BMI < 40), well-controlled DM/HTN, mild lung disease
ASA III	A patient with severe systemic disease	Substantive functional limitations; one or more moderate to severe diseases. Examples include (but are not limited to): poorly controlled DM or HTN, COPD, morbid obesity (BMI ≥ 40), active hepatitis, alcohol dependence or abuse, implanted pacemaker, moderate reduction of ejection fraction, ESRD undergoing regularly scheduled dialysis, premature infant PCA < 60 weeks, history (> 3 months) of MI, CVA, TIA, or CAD/stents.
ASA IV	A patient with severe systemic disease that is a constant threat to life	Examples include (but are not limited to): recent (< 3 months) MI, CVA, TIA, or CAD/stents, ongoing cardiac ischemia or severe valve dysfunction, severe reduction of ejection fraction, sepsis, DIC, ARD or ESRD not undergoing regularly scheduled dialysis
ASA V	A moribund patient who is not expected to survive without the operation	Examples include (but are not limited to): ruptured abdominal/thoracic aneurysm, massive trauma, intracranial bleed with mass effect, ischemic bowel in the face of significant cardiac pathology or multiple organ/system dysfunction
ASA VI	A declared brain-dead patient whose organs are being removed for donor purposes	

ASA, American Society of Anesthesiologists; BMI, body mass index; DM, diabetes mellitus; HTN, hypertension; COPD, chronic obstructive pulmonary disease; ESRD, end-stage renal disease; PCA, postconceptual age; MI, myocardial infarction; CVA, cerebravascular accident; TIA, transient ischemic attack; CAD, coronary artery disease; DIC, disseminating intravascular coagulation; ARD, acute respiratory disease.

Note: The addition of "E" (eg, ASA III-E) denotes Emergency surgery: an emergency is defined as existing when delay in treatment of the patient would lead to a significant increase in the threat to life or body part.

Reproduced with permission of the American Society of Anesthesiologists, Schaumburg, IL.

AIRWAY

The potential exists for aspiration, **bronchospasm** and **laryngospasm**, dental damage, airway obstruction, swelling, and even loss of an airway during intubation and extubation.[7] During all ear, nose, throat, or facial surgeries, the surgical team must check that packing, sponges, or any other items used in these cavities have been removed. Any items that have the potential to fall in or be missed can obstruct the patient's airway. The team must remain attentive to the anesthesia professional for signs and symptoms of patient or anesthesia professional distress.

BREATHING

The anesthesia professional continually monitors the patient for hypoventilation, oxygen saturation, respiratory rates related to hypoxia, hypoxemia, hypercapnia, and hypercarbia. The postanesthesia care unit nurse continues this close observation for possible respiratory depression in the postoperative phase related to the effects of narcotic and anesthetic administration, or the neurological effects of regional (eg, spinal, epidural) anesthetics.[7]

CIRCULATION

Pulmonary embolism is a major cause of death in the intraoperative and postoperative phases.[7] The RN circulator monitors patients closely for venous stasis, particularly if the patient is in the OR for prolonged periods, and provides deep vein thrombosis prophylaxis with compression garments and devices. The surgical team continually monitors patients for hypotension, hypertension, and cardiac dysrhythmias, which can indicate the onset of a variety of complications. Cardiac arrest can occur at any stage in the preoperative, intraoperative, or postoperative phases of surgery. Resuscitative measures and appropriate chest compressions must be initiated within the first three to five minutes to prevent irreversible brain damage.[7] Most facility leaders require all health care providers to maintain competency in basic life support.

DEFIBRILLATION

All health care providers must know the location of the nearest crash cart whenever providing direct patient care. Perioperative nurses should periodically review the contents of the crash cart, to include determining whether a sternal saw and internal paddles are available if needed.

EMERGENCIES

The surgical team has to determine what injury has occurred and also identify the **mechanism of injury** (MOI) that caused it. The MOI could have been a blast, blunt, thermal, or iatrogenic injury.

   Blast injury. A blast injury is caused by a bomb, bullets, or a stabbing instrument that separates, stretches, compresses, or shears cells.[13] The extent of injury in these penetrating traumas is dependent on the nature of the foreign object (ie, bullet caliber, knife size) and velocity of the force used.[13] Debris, projectiles, and other secondary, tertiary, and even quaternary injuries may occur beyond the primary blast site.

Blunt injury. Often seen in motor vehicle collisions, sports injuries, and falls, blunt injuries represent acceleration, deceleration, shearing, compression, or any combination of forces that do not break the skin. Higher morbidity and mortality are related to difficulty in identifying these less obvious injuries.[13]

Thermal injury. Tissue or inhalation damage can occur from a fire or burn, or as a sole mechanism of injury.[13] One significant priority for the perioperative team is to work diligently at maintaining normothermia because burns compromise the protection that intact skin provides. When perioperative personnel are notified that a patient with a burn is coming to the OR, a separate room should be prepared in the preoperative area and postanesthesia care unit and the temperatures in those rooms should be raised. If separate rooms are not available, the surgical team should be prepared to accept the patient directly into the OR and to transfer the patient to the intensive care unit directly after surgery. The surgical team should raise the temperature in the OR and have warmed IV and irrigation solutions immediately available. The RN circulator should ensure that forced-air, temperature-regulating blankets are available and should be prepared to maintain the temperature of the patient's head and extremities if at all possible.

Iatrogenic injury. An **iatrogenic injury** is sustained while in a health care provider's care. For the most part, iatrogenic injuries are preventable. The RN circulator, as the patient's advocate, must regularly

- check the patient's positioning for presence of adequate padding,
- check that the patient's extremities are correctly aligned and free from injury,
- check the sterile field for instruments or personnel potentially pressing on the patient's body,
- monitor intubations and extubations for dental damage or corneal abrasions, and
- monitor the electrosurgical unit dispersive pad connections and other electrical devices making contact with a patient to prevent thermal injuries in the OR.

The RN circulator must remain vigilant throughout the surgical procedure to help prevent inadvertent injury of a patient under anesthesia, because "precaution is the best prevention of injury."[7(p639)]

Environmental Hazards and Natural Disasters

Environmental hazards and natural disasters are hard to predict, but easier to plan and prepare for. Know your facility's disaster plans and OR evacuation protocols. The priority is protecting the patient first, and then protecting resources, from environmental hazards and damage during disaster situations. Situations the perioperative personnel must consider when developing disaster plans and procedures include the following:

- preparing for extreme weather (eg, hurricanes, tornadoes, flash floods, earthquakes);
- determining the proper evacuation routes for a fire (ie, lateral, horizontal);
- locating the medical gases for the OR suite and communicating with anesthesia professionals before shutting off the flow if and when it becomes necessary;
- training teams for triage management during mass-casualty situations;
- identifying best practices for keeping patients and personnel safe during terrorist attacks; and
- following local, state, and hospital policies regarding actions during violence, hostage, and active shooter situations.

According to the World Health Organization's Emergency Triage Assessment and Treatment (ETAT), the term **triage** means to sort.[15] Triaging is a means of prioritizing attention to the critically ill into emergency (ie, immediate), priority (ie, rapid), and nonurgent (ie, can wait) categories,[15] which requires a shift in how injured patients are cared for:

> *Instead of being able to offer each patient immediate and comprehensive treatment, care should be prioritized to optimize the use of critical resources. Triage is the first step of the process. Triage is the process of sorting or prioritizing patients into specific care categories depending on the number and severity of casualties and the resources available at that time. The accepted concept is to do the greatest good for the greatest number, [and triage is the tool that guides this concept].*[16(p155)]

Diagnostic Tools

Assessment used in triage may be dependent on diagnostic tests such as **computed tomography** scans, diagnostic peritoneal lavage, **focused assessment with sonography in trauma** (ie, FAST), and ultrasound for the most accurate diagnosis (Table 7.2).

Computed tomography is a series of detailed, cross-sectional x-ray images that identify bone and soft tissue injury.[17] **Diagnostic peritoneal lavage** is performed by making a small incision in the abdomen and infusing saline to document intra-abdominal bleeding.[18] FAST is an acronym for the bedside ultrasound used in trauma. "The FAST examination, per [Advanced Trauma Life Support (ATLS)] protocol, is performed immediately after the primary survey of the ATLS protocol. Ultrasound is the ideal initial modality because it can be performed simultaneously with other resuscitative cares, providing vital information without the time delay caused by radiographs or computed tomography."[19]

System-Specific Situations, Complications, and Their Immediate Actions

Orthopedic and neurology specialties are often spoken of in combination, but are actually two separate areas of expertise. Neurology (eg, head and spine) and orthopedic (eg, skeletal) injuries are not always immediately apparent, and usually require additional examination and monitoring to determine the underlying pathology of the injury.

NEUROLOGY

A neurologist is a physician with specialized training in diagnosing, treating, and managing disorders of the brain and nervous system, such as Alzheimer's disease, stroke, migraine, multiple sclerosis, brain injury, Parkinson's disease, and epilepsy. The American Academy of Neurology (AAN), which was founded in 1948, now represents more than 30,000 members and is dedicated to promoting education, advocacy, and professional standards.[20]

Neurotrauma is a serious public health problem. According to the American College of Surgeons, "**traumatic brain injury** (TBI) accounts for almost 40% of all deaths from acute trauma."[16(p50)] There has been a significant decline in TBI mortality during the past three decades as understanding of the mechanism of

TABLE 7.2	Diagnostic Options
• Computed tomography scans to identify bone and organ injury
• Diagnostic peritoneal lavage to document internal bleeding
• Focused assessment with sonography in trauma to identify fluid accumulation

secondary injury has grown.[16] Often, forces of energy from the impact are tolerated by the rigid skull, but the soft tissue of the brain underneath is traumatized, resulting in the formation of subdural, epidural, or intracerebral hematomas.[13]

A baseline neurologic examination is extremely important. The trauma team uses the **Glasgow Coma Scale** to determine the severity of neurologic injury. The Glasgow Coma Scale has three components: the patient's eye opening and pupillary reactions, verbal responses (eg, incomprehensible words), and motor responses (eg, presence or absence of posturing). The Revised Trauma Score[21] adds the patient's respiratory rate and systolic blood pressure to the Glasgow Coma Scale information to further assess a patient's neurological status (Table 7.3).

The standard indicators of a possible cord injury are absence of rectal tone and bradycardia in the presence of hypotension.[13] Health care providers focus on maintaining head and spine stability, and carefully logrolling the patient when repositioning is necessary. An osmotic diuretic (eg, mannitol) can be used to treat increased intracranial pressure. Other interventions include elevating the head of the bed 30 degrees and keeping the patient's head midline to promote venous drainage.[13]

ORTHOPEDIC

Orthopedists are the primary medical specialty focusing on injuries and diseases of the musculoskeletal system (eg, bones, joints, ligaments, tendons, muscles, nerves) that allow the body to move, work, and be active. Originally founded in 1933, the American Academy of Orthopaedic Surgeons (AAOS) joined the American Association of Orthopaedic Surgeons and became the preeminent professional organization that provides continuing education to orthopedic surgeons throughout the world.[22]

The Greek etymology of the word "orthopaedics" is *ortho* (straight) and *pais* (child). Accounts of early orthopedic practice indicate treatments used to "make the child straight," which explains the traditional symbol of orthopaedics as a bent tree braced to a stake to make it grow upward and straight.[23] Orthopedic surgeons now perform numerous types of surgeries, including arthroscopies, joint fusions, internal and external fixation of bone fractures, joint replacements, osteotomies, and soft tissue repair.

The more complex the spectrum of injury, the more important the decision-making process becomes. For example, prompt stabilization of proximal long-bone fractures and spinal fractures can decrease inflammatory mediator production, catecholamine release, analgesic requirements, morbidity rate, and

TABLE 7.3 Revised Trauma Score (RTS)[1]

PHYSIOLOGIC VARIABLE	VALUE	SCORE
Respiratory rate (RR)	10-29	4
	> 29	3
	6-9	2
	1-5	1
	0	0
Systolic blood pressure (SBP)	> 90	4
	76-89	3
	50-75	2
	1-49	1
	0	0
Glasgow Coma Scale (GCS)	13-15	4
	9-12	3
	6-8	2
	4-5	1
	3	0

Note: The RTS triage tool is a physiological scoring system based on the data sets of three specific physiological parameters that are obtained from the patient: (1) respiratory rate (RR), (2) systolic blood pressure (SBP), and (3) the Glasgow Coma Scale (GCS). Values for the RTS are in the range of zero to 7.8408. A threshold of RTS < 4 has been used to identify patients who should be treated in a trauma center.[1]

1. Revised Trauma Score. TRAUMA.ORG. http://www.trauma.org/index.php/main/article/386/.

---

hospital costs.[16] The goal of fracture treatment is restoring function with a minimum of complications. Immobilization of fractures can be accomplished by casting, bracing, splinting, traction, or hardware fixation. Femoral fractures in particular can be associated with a high risk of hemorrhage and require traction before surgical repair.[13]

One complication of an orthopedic injury is **compartment syndrome**, a painful condition that occurs when pressure in the muscles builds to dangerous levels. This pressure can decrease blood flow, which prevents nourishment and oxygen from reaching nerve and muscle cells.[24] Swelling of the muscles below the fascia covering may compromise circulation and result in the eventual loss of the extremity because of tissue necrosis.[13] Compartment syndrome is a surgical emergency in which a surgeon typically needs to perform a fasciotomy (ie, an incision to cut open the affected area to release pressure). Often, the swelling is severe enough that the initial incision cannot be closed immediately, and a wound-healing vacuum-type device is placed to reduce the swelling and pressure until the swelling subsides. If the tissue still cannot be fully closed, a skin or even a tissue graft may be needed to facilitate closure of the wound.[24]

Perioperative-Specific Considerations

The surgical environment has special circumstances that require perioperative-specific knowledge. These topics include autotransfusion, rapid-sequence induction, and organ procurement.

AUTOTRANSFUSION

Ideally, in a planned procedure with medium to high expected blood loss, a patient may have the opportunity to bank his or her own blood. In both planned and unplanned situations where greater blood loss occurs, intraoperative **autotransfusion** (ie, blood salvaging) is an alternative to donor blood.

Various blood salvage devices are used to collect blood that is being rapidly lost, after which the blood is cleaned, filtered, and returned to the patient for additional transfusion. Although there are risks of contamination or fat embolism, the blood products that the patient receives from blood salvaging (ie, red blood cells) are the patient's own, so complications and potential risks (including the costs) from donor blood are subsequently reduced.

RAPID-SEQUENCE INDUCTION

In many emergent situations, a patient's NPO status is either unknown or there is not enough time for adequate stomach emptying. In these situations, the anesthesia professional may determine that **rapid-sequence induction (RSI)** is in the patient's best interest. In a trauma situation, health care providers assume that the patient's stomach is full and that the patient is at high risk for aspiration, and therefore, RSI is preferred (Table 7.4).[13] To reduce the risk of aspiration of stomach contents, basic principles include preparation with preoxygenation, pretreatment with paralytics, and positioning to ensure a quick and aspiration-free induction.

> **EXAM TIP**
>
> During RSI, the RN circulator should be available at the bedside to assist the anesthesia professional in whatever way is needed, whether it is providing cricoid pressure, suctioning, or reconnecting the endotracheal tube to the oxygen source.

TABLE 7.4 Rapid-Sequence Induction[1,2]

BASIC STEPS INVOLVED

- Preoxygenate with 100% oxygen.

- Induce anesthesia by administering neuromuscular agent to rapidly achieve loss of consciousness.

- Apply cricoid pressure[a] (ie, Sellick maneuver[b]) to help prevent the patient from aspirating stomach contents simultaneously while inserting the endotracheal tube.

- Inflate the endotracheal tube cuff.

- Verify endotracheal tube placement.

- Secure endotracheal tube.

- Release cricoid pressure only when the anesthesia professional states it is okay to do so.

- Verify ventilator settings.

- Monitor the patient according to routine.

a. Cricoid pressure is performed by gently pressing the thyroid cartilage downward to close the upper esophagus, thus decreasing the possibility of regurgitated stomach contents from entering the airway during intubation.
b. When performing the Sellick maneuver, the perioperative RN assists the anesthesia professional by applying cricoid pressure until placement of the endotracheal tube is verified.
1. Gawronski DP. Trauma surgery. In: Rothrock JC, ed. *Alexander's Care of the Patient in Surgery*. 15th ed. St Louis, MO: Elsevier; 2015:1104-1131.
2. Phillips N. Perioperative pediatrics. In: *Berry & Kohn's Operating Room Technique*. 13th ed. St Louis, MO: Elsevier; 2017:129.

ORGAN PROCUREMENT

Organ procurement is the process of evaluating and procuring donor organs for transplantation. Each state has different agencies and each facility different policies on procurement of organs following either brain or cardiac death. Perioperative personnel should review their facility's policies and procedures in referrals for organ procurement.

The National Organ Transplant Act of 1984 established the Organ Procurement and Transplantation Network to "maintain a national registry and improve the organ-matching and placement process [requiring] hospitals to develop policies and procedures to ensure that families are informed of the option to donate. Noncompliance endangers Medicare and Medicaid funding."[16(p161)]

Origins of Donated Organs

According to the American College of Surgeons, roughly 75% of donated organs originate from deceased donors, and more than 40% of cadaveric organ donors died because of trauma. This suggests that the trauma program plays a key role in organ donation by identifying potential organ donors, contacting organ procurement organizations, and providing critical care to potential organ donors to prevent cardiovascular collapse prior to organ donation.[1]

1. Committee on Trauma. Resources for Optimal Care of the Injured Patient 2014. American College of Surgeons. https://www.facs.org/~/media/files/quality%20programs/trauma/vrc%20resources/resources%20for%20 optimal%20care%20 2014%20v11.ashx.

Key Concepts and Review

Preparation, education, and training are key factors in successful responses to emergencies in the OR; adding multidisciplinary training consistent with the facility's acuity is ideal. Perioperative professionals' multidisciplinary teamwork, diligence in emergent situations, and accurate preparation for corrective actions are vital to the positive outcomes of all surgical patients.

Compliance with annual education and training for MH, fire safety, and AORN guidelines is expected by participation in seminars, webinars, and simulation laboratories.

Because of the unpredictability of surgery, checklists and preparations by the perioperative nurse can lead to appropriate action when an emergent situation arises. Attention to actions in the field, behind the anesthesia screen, and under the drapes can stave off worse events and outcomes.

Quality communication among all team members is the greatest emergency preventive technique a perioperative nurse can administer. At these most vulnerable moments, patients rely on their caregivers more than ever.

Case Study: Air Embolism Management

1. Mr. Johansen is a 62-year-old man undergoing a left shoulder arthroscopy and rotator cuff repair in the semi-sitting position. His medical history is unremarkable, and he has no known drug allergies. His preoperative laboratory studies, chest radiograph, and electrocardiogram are within normal limits. His preoperative vital signs are
   - blood pressure (BP) 104/68,
   - heart rate (HR) 72,
   - respiratory rate (RR) 16,
   - temperature 98.6°F (37°C),
   - peripheral capillary oxygen saturation (SPO_2) 98%, and
   - end-tidal carbon dioxide ($ETCO_2$) 36.
     › What are potential complications associated with the semi-sitting position?
     › What are potential contraindications to use of the sitting or semi-sitting position?
2. Mr. Johansen has been in the operating room for approximately 80 minutes when the anesthesia professional announces that the patient's $ETCO_2$, SPO_2, and BP have dropped to 28, 88% and 88/42.
     › What could be the cause of these vital sign changes?
3. The anesthesia professional states that the patient has a venous air embolism.
     › What actions should be taken by the perioperative team?

continues ›

Case Study: Air Embolism Management

ANSWERS TO CASE STUDY

1. Potential complications that may arise from the use of the sitting or semi-sitting positio pneumocephalus, quadriplegia, and compressive peripheral neuropathy. There is a risk for cerebrovascular insult and a risk for poor venous return from the lower extremities and pooling of blood in the pelvis. The sitting or semi-sitting position can also affect bispectral index values, which are used to evaluate depth of anesthesia and prevent patient awareness during surgery.

    Chronic obstructive pulmonary disease (COPD) is a potential contraindication to the use of the sitting or semi-sitting position because VAE is not well tolerated in patients with COPD. A known patent foramen ovale may also be a contraindication to the sitting or semi-sitting position because of the potential for a VAE to pass into the systemic arterial circulation.

2. The cause of these vital sign changes could be the result of a VAE that occurs when air is drawn into the circulation by the veins above the level of the heart. It is most likely to occur in patients undergoing neurosurgery or open shoulder surgery in the sitting or semi-sitting position. Venous air embolism can lead to cardiovascular collapse caused by obstruction of outflow from the heart with pulmonary hypertension and paradoxical air embolism. The embolism can pass into the systemic arterial circulation and lead to ischemia of vital organs.

3. Successful treatment of VAE requires prompt recognition and rapid and simultaneous implementation of multiple interventions by the perioperative team. If not diagnosed and treated immediately, VAE can be fatal. Venous air embolism should be managed by
    - ventilating the patient with 100% oxygen to maximize patient oxygenation, aid elimination of nitrogen, and reduce embolus volume;
    - controlling bone, dural sinus, and muscle bleeding to help prevent further entrainment of air;
    - filling the surgical wound with irrigation fluid or packing it with saline-soaked sponges to help prevent further entrainment of air;
    - placing the patient in left lateral and Trendelenburg position to help prevent air from traveling through the right side of the heart into the pulmonary arteries;
    - initiating cardiac compressions with the patient in supine and Trendelenburg position to break large bubbles into smaller ones and force air out of the right ventricle into the pulmonary vessels, thus improving cardiac output;
    - administering IV fluids and vasopressors to optimize myocardial perfusion, push the blocked airlock into the lungs where it can be absorbed, increase intravascular volume and central venous pressure, reduce further gas entry, and increase the force and speed of ventricular contractions;
    - implementing transesophageal echocardiography to confirm the diagnosis of VAE; and
    - using $ETCO_2$ to assist in assessing cardiac output and monitor the progression and resolution of VAE.

The goal of air embolism management is to prevent further air entry, reduce the volume of entrained air, and provide hemodynamic support.[1]

---

1. Guideline for positioning the patient. In: *Guidelines for Perioperative Practice*. Denver, CO: AORN, Inc; 2018:673-743.

References

1. Patient safety. Safe patient surgery. Why safe surgery is important. World Health Organization. http://www.who.int/patientsafety/safesurgery/en.
2. Steelman VM, Graling PR. Top 10 patient safety issues: what more can we do? *AORN J.* 2013;97(6):679-701.
3. Seifert PC, Yang Z, Munoz R. Crisis management of air embolism in the OR. *AORN J.* 2015;101(4):471-481.
4. Hughes AB. Implementing AORN recommended practices for a safe environment of care. *AORN J.* 2013;98(2):153-166.
5. Committee on Trauma. ACS TQIP Mass Transfusion in Trauma Guidelines. American College of Surgeons. https://www.facs.org/~/media/files/quality%20programs/trauma/tqip/massive%20transfusion%20in%20trauma%20guildelines.ashx.
6. Graling P, Dort J, Moynihan J. Crisis management of a hemorrhagic emergency in the OR. *AORN J.* 2014;99(4):510-516.
7. Phillips N. Potential perioperative complications. In: *Berry & Kohn's Operating Room Technique*. 13th ed. St Louis, MO: Elsevier; 2017:591-620.
8. Thanavaro JL. Cardiac risk assessment: decreasing postoperative complications. *AORN J.* 2015;101(2):201-212.
9. Managing an MH crisis. Malignant Hyperthermia Association of the United States. http://www.mhaus.org/healthcare-professionals/managing-a-crisis.
10. Seifert PC, Peterson E, Graham K. Crisis management of fire in the OR. *AORN J.* 2015;101(2):250-263.
11. Resources and tools for preventing surgical fires. Council on Surgical and Perioperative Safety. http://www.cspsteam.org/resources-and-tools-for-preventing-surgical-fires/?rq=fire%20safety.
12. Fire Safety Tool Kit. AORN, Inc. http://www.aorn.org/guidelines/clinical-resources/tool-kits/fire-safety-tool-kit.
13. Gawronski DP. Trauma surgery. In: Rothrock J, ed. *Alexander's Care of the Patient in Surgery.* 15th ed. St Louis, MO: Elsevier; 2015:1104-1131.
14. ASA Physical Status Classification System. American Society of Anesthesiologists. https://www.asahq.org/resources/clinical-information/asa-physical-status-classification-system.
15. *Emergency Triage Assessment and Treatment (ETAT) Manual for Participants*. Geneva, Switzerland: World Health Organization; 2005:3. http://apps.who.int/iris/bitstream/10665/43386/1/9241546875_eng.pdf.
16. Committee on Trauma. Resources for Optimal Care of the Injured Patient 2014. American College of Surgeons. https://www.facs.org/~/media/files/quality%20programs/trauma/vrc%20resources/resources%20for%20optimal%20care.ashx.
17. Tests and procedures: CT scan. Mayo Clinic. http://www.mayoclinic.org/tests-procedures/ct-scan/basics/definition/prc-20014610.
18. Diagnostic peritoneal lavage—series. US National Library of Medicine. MedlinePlus. https://www.nlm.nih.gov/medlineplus/ency/presentations/100159_2.htm.
19. Focused assessment with sonography in trauma (FAST). MedScape. http://emedicine.medscape.com/article/104363-overview.
20. AAN vision and mission. American Academy of Neurology. https://www.aan.com/membership/about-the-aan.
21. Champion HR, Sacco WJ, Copes WS, Gann DS, Gennarelli TA, Flanagan ME. A revision of the trauma score. *J Trauma*. 1989;29:623-629.
22. About us. American Academy of Orthopaedic Surgeons. http://orthoinfo.aaos.org/menus/orthopaedics.cfm.
23. About the AAOS. American Academy of Orthopaedic Surgeons. http://www.aaos.org/about/about.
24. Compartment syndrome. American Academy of Orthopaedic Surgeons. http://orthoinfo.aaos.org/topic.cfm?topic=a00204.

Additional Resource

AORN Emergency Preparedness Tool Kit. https://www.aorn.org/guidelines/clinical-resources/tool-kits.

Emergency Preparedness Rule. US Department of Health and Human Services, Centers for Medicare & Medicaid Services. October 23, 2017. https://www.cms.gov/Medicare/Provider-Enrollment-and-Certification/SurveyCertEmergPrep/Emergency-Prep-Rule.html.

Public Health Emergency. Hospital Preparedness Program. https://www.phe.gov/Preparedness/planning/hpp/Pages/default.aspx.

Practice Exam Questions

1. The _____ is an algorithm that guides EMS personnel through the following four decision points physiological parameters, anatomic parameters, mechanism of injury (MOI), and other special considerations.
    A. Triage Tree
    B. Medical Plan
    C. Decision Scheme
    D. Trauma Protocol

2. Massive hemorrhage is treated by transfusion that is equal to replacing _____ % of the patient's estimated blood volume in three hours or less.
    A. 15%
    B. 50%
    C. 25%
    D. 70%

3. Which of the following diagnostic procedures has the ability to be most specific when identifying a traumatic injury?
    A. Diagnostic Peritoneal Lavage (DPL)
    B. Computed Tomography (CT) Scan
    C. Chest x-ray
    D. Focused Assessment with Sonography in Trauma (FAST)

4. A disaster preparedness plan including the use of a command center, triage center, staffing plan, documentation, and communication should be held at least
    A. every three months.
    B. twice a year.
    C. yearly.
    D. every two years.

5. Management of a patient infected with anthrax includes using _____ precautions.
    A. droplet
    B. standard
    C. airborne
    D. contact

6. What component of the fire triangle does prepping solution represent?
    A. Oxidizer
    B. Liquid ignition
    C. Fuel
    D. Ignition source

7. Penetrating trauma is the result of _____ blast injuries common in explosions.
    A. initial
    B. tertiary
    C. primary
    D. secondary

8. The best way to preserve potential evidence on a trauma victim's hands is to
    A. place hands in plastic bags and tie at the elbow.
    B. wash hands and keep rinsed fluid in a sterile specimen container.
    C. cover hands with paper bags and tape at the wrist.
    D. have law enforcement conduct examination.

9. A 12-year-old child with a history of asthma is emerging from general anesthesia following a tonsillectomy. Upon extubation, the child begins wheezing, which rapidly progresses to stridor. The perioperative nurse can anticipate assisting the anesthesia professional with which of the following actions first?
    A. Suctioning the airway.
    B. Setting up an aerosol mask with 2.5% racemic epinephrine.
    C. Administering Solu-Medrol 2 mg/kg IV.
    D. Reintubating the child.

10. A patient is undergoing a procedure to remove vocal cord polyps using a carbon dioxide (CO_2) laser. During the procedure, the endotracheal tube (ETT) ignites. Which of the following actions should be undertaken first?
    A. Call for assistance.
    B. Remove the ETT.
    C. Pour saline into the patient's airway.
    D. Turn off the CO_2 laser.

Answers with Supported Rationales

1. Answer C is correct. The American College of Surgeons developed the Decision Scheme to assist EMS personnel with a plan to transfer patients to the health care facility that will provide the most effective care. Level I trauma centers demonstrate a 25% decreased risk of death for treatment of severe injuries. Reference: Gawronski DP. Trauma surgery. In: Rothrock JC, ed. *Alexander's Care of the Patient in Surgery*. 15th ed. St Louis, MO: Elsevier; 2015:1104.

2. Answer B is correct. Fifty percent of the estimated volume in three hours or less, or one or more blood volumes in 24 hours, should be replaced. Rapid infusion for massive trauma is consistent practice in many facilities. Reference: Gawronski DP. Trauma surgery. In: Rothrock JC, ed. *Alexander's Care of the Patient in Surgery*. 15th ed. St Louis, MO: Elsevier; 2015:1109.

3. Answer B is correct. Depending on the mechanism of injury, a CT scan can be completed on specific organs. A CT scan can be used diagnostically or as a screening tool. Reference: Gawronski DP. Trauma surgery. In: Rothrock JC, ed. *Alexander's Care of the Patient in Surgery*. 15th ed. St Louis, MO: Elsevier; 2015:1110, Table 28-4.

4. Answer B is correct. Disaster drills should be held twice a year to test the plans developed by the planning committee and to educate staff on roles and plans. Reference: Phillips N. Administration of perioperative care services. In: *Berry & Kohn's Operating Room Technique*. 13th ed. St Louis, MO: Elsevier; 2017:86.

5. Answer B is correct. Standard precautions should be used with special attention to containing any open or draining wounds. Reference: Spry C. Infection prevention and control. In: Rothrock JC, ed. *Alexander's Care of the Patient in Surgery*. 15th ed. St Louis, MO: Elsevier; 2015:85.

6. Answer C is correct. Prep solution is a type of fuel and will cause flames when exposed to an ignition source. Prep solution also poses high risk for chemical burns when pooling solution is not removed. Reference: Murphy EK. Patient safety and risk management. In: Rothrock JC, ed. *Alexander's Care of the Patient in Surgery*. 15th ed. St Louis, MO: Elsevier; 2015:16.

7. Answer D is correct. Secondary blast injuries result in penetrating trauma from shrapnel and debris that becomes airborne during the explosion. Reference: Gawronski DP. Trauma surgery. In: Rothrock JC, ed. *Alexander's Care of the Patient in Surgery*. 15th ed. St Louis, MO: Elsevier; 2015:1107.

8. Answer C is correct. A paper bag will preserve evidence without contamination from condensation, which may occur using plastic bags; and taping at the wrists prevents items from escaping the bag. Reference: Gawronski DP. Trauma surgery. In: Rothrock JC, ed. *Alexander's Care of the Patient in Surgery*. 15th ed. St Louis, MO: Elsevier; 2015:1115.

9. Answer A is correct. The first step is to attempt to remove the irritating substance. References: Odom-Forren J. Postoperative patient care and pain management. In: Rothrock JC, ed. *Alexander's Care of the Patient in Surgery*. 15th ed. St Louis, MO: Elsevier; 2015:274-275.

10. Answer B is correct. For fire in the airway or breathing circuit, the ETT should be removed immediately. Reference: DeRoy TJ. Otorhinolaryngologic surgery. In: Rothrock JC, ed. *Alexander's Care of the Patient in Surgery*. 15th ed. St Louis, MO: Elsevier; 2015:640.

8 Management of Personnel, Services, and Materials

📝 KEY TERMS

- Biological implants
- Cost containment
- Delegation
- Environmental sustainability
- Personal protective equipment (PPE)
- Preventive maintenance
- Product evaluation and selection
- Room turnover
- Scope of practice
- Spills
- Sterility of surgical supplies
- Terminal cleaning

✅ REQUIRED NURSING SKILLS

- Acquiring equipment
  - Performing preventive maintenance
- Complying with implant rules and regulations
  - Biological implants
  - Order, receipt, storage, implant, explant, wastage, and recording of implant process
- Environmental management
  - Environmental cleaning
  - PPE
- OR and non-OR personnel management
  - Acquiring personnel
  - Delegating to personnel within scope of practice
  - Supervising, educating, and training personnel
  - Supervising non-OR personnel roles

continues >

✅ REQUIRED NURSING SKILLS, CONTINUED

- Supply selection
  - Assessing availability and sterility of supplies
  - Cost-containment measures
  - Implementing sustainability practices

Wise use of resources, both human and material, benefits the patient, the perioperative health care team, the facility, and the environment. It is the perioperative registered nurse's (RN's) responsibility to ensure that equipment, supplies, and personnel are available to care for the patient in a safe, clean environment that maximizes the potential for a positive surgical outcome in a fiscally accountable manner. This chapter focuses on the perioperative nurse's role in

- providing oversight of OR personnel, vendors, and visitors;
- anticipating, obtaining, and managing surgical equipment and supplies;
- identifying factors that influence product evaluation and cost containment; and
- maintaining an optimal surgical environment.

Management of OR Personnel

The perioperative team includes the surgeon, anesthesia professional, RN circulator, and scrub person. The safety of the surgical patient is the primary focus of the entire perioperative team. The RN circulator, however, is the true gatekeeper for the perioperative environment. Safe patient care is affected by staffing levels, education and mentoring of the health care team, and the competence of every individual.

STAFFING

Workforce or staffing requirements for the perioperative setting are very different than for other nursing specialties. Although every facility should create staffing pattern policies based on current patient needs and availability of resources, every patient undergoing an operative or other invasive procedure should have a perioperative RN as circulator.[1] The priority for all staffing patterns must be safe perioperative patient care and a safe work environment. Perioperative patients present to the surgical or invasive procedure setting with a unique set of characteristics. Patients may also present with comorbidities that OR managers must take into consideration in the specific staffing patterns of procedures. In addition to creating staffing patterns that support each patient's individual needs, OR managers must take into consideration the technical requirements of the procedure (eg, robotic, minimally invasive, laser) as well as the competency level of personnel when determining staffing needs.[1] AORN has published a position statement[1] regarding safe staffing and on-call practices for the perioperative environment, which serves as a resource for best practices related to workforce planning and design.

EDUCATION AND MENTORING

Education in the perioperative setting should be based on current research. Evidence-based practice (EBP) is performance of nursing practice based on the most recent research available on a particular topic. EBP results in positive patient outcomes by implementing best practices. Managers and educators should focus on EBP when providing education and mentoring in the perioperative setting for both experienced and novice personnel. Educating perioperative personnel is costly and may be even more costly if a facility experiences a high attrition rate. "Research shows that health care providers who use [EBP] demonstrate a higher level of satisfaction in their work because they know that they are providing the very best care, and this in turn increases retention."[2(p378)]

Although facilities may have a formal educator for training in the perioperative environment, all perioperative RNs have a responsibility to mentor and precept new health care team members. Mentoring a new team member involves committing to a long-term relationship that demonstrates support and socialization into the new environment.[3] Typically, mentors have a great deal of experience and serve as a resource for all aspects of the perioperative RN role and future goals of the mentee. Preceptors, on the other hand, fulfill a short-term relationship with a new team member to complete a task-oriented plan for competency in the perioperative environment. The training provided by the educator, mentor, and preceptor should be based on the most current standards of practice. Selection of mentors and preceptors is an important process to promote a positive nursing work environment and develop skilled team members. Team members who have the most experience are not necessarily the best option for either preceptor or mentor. Consideration must be given to the skill, attitude, and commitment to national standards when choosing the individual who will be responsible for promoting the next generation of perioperative nurses.

SCOPE OF PRACTICE AND APPROPRIATE DELEGATION

It is essential for all perioperative RNs to be aware of their state Nurse Practice Act (NPA) to determine the specific scope of practice standards. (The perioperative RN's scope of practice is discussed in Chapter 9.) "The practice of nursing is a right granted by a state to protect those who need nursing care, and safe, competent nursing practice is grounded in the guidelines of the state NPA and its rules."[4(p40)]

The perioperative environment is highly collaborative. Many health care team members contribute to the care of the perioperative patient. The nursing leadership is responsible for the safety of all those who work in the OR and may supervise a variety of staff, to include perioperative RNs, surgical technologists, central processing technicians, and environmental services staff.

PERIOPERATIVE RN

The perioperative RN is responsible for the nursing process as it applies to patients undergoing surgical or other invasive procedures. "Using clinical knowledge, judgment, and clinical-reasoning skills based on scientific principles, the perioperative nurse plans and implements nursing care to address the physical, psychological, and spiritual responses of the patient having an operative or other invasive procedure."[5(p2)]

The perioperative nurse's role "encompasses supervision of unlicensed personnel who scrub in surgery, such as surgical technologists, and requires knowledge of practices and procedures performed under this title."[3(p2)] Both delegation and supervision are key responsibilities of the perioperative RN. **Delegation** is the act of transferring a task to another person who has demonstrated competency while adhering to the five rights of delegation (Table 8.1; see also Chapter 9).[6]

SURGICAL TECHNOLOGIST (ST)

The hallmark of the close relationship between the perioperative RN and ST is partnership and collaboration. The primary responsibility of the ST is to prepare and maintain the sterile surgical field during surgical and other invasive procedures. The ST works under the direction and supervision of the RN circulator. Preparation to become an ST may be completed through a certificate program or a college degree program. Similar to AORN, the Association for Surgical Technologists (AST) has a list of position statements. "Position statements address matters of professional concerns, such as collective bargaining, proper title and job descriptions."[7] Certification through one of several organizations is a requirement for employment at many health care facilities. As an organization, the AST supports an associate's degree as the entry level for STs.[8]

TABLE 8.1 The Five Rights of Delegation[1]

1	Right Task
2	Right Person
3	Right Circumstance
4	Right Communication and Direction
5	Right Supervision and Evaluation

1. Steelman VM. Concepts basic to perioperative nursing. In: Rothrock JC, ed. *Alexander's Care of the Patient in Surgery*. 15th ed. St Louis, MO; Elsevier; 2015:1-15.

CENTRAL SERVICE PERSONNEL

An important role in the perioperative environment is the central service (CS) personnel. "CS [personnel] are responsible for cleaning, decontaminating, sterilizing, and distributing medical and surgical instrumentation; they are among the most vital contributors to the delivery of safe, high-quality patient care."[9] This helps minimize the use of immediate-use steam sterilization (IUSS). It is important to note that IUSS should only be used when there is insufficient time to process the instrument in the preferred manner, and should never be used as a substitute for insufficient inventory or poor planning by perioperative personnel.[10] The International Association of Healthcare Central Service Materiel Management (IAHCSMM) is the professional organization for CS professionals. IAHCSMM offers two different certification exams for CS professionals: Certified Registered Central Service Technician (CRCST) and Certified Instrument Specialist (CIS). Some states required CS personnel to be certified.

ENVIRONMENTAL SERVICES (ES)

Many larger ORs have a team of several ES personnel to clean rooms and expedite **room turnover** times. ES personnel should be educated on the importance of their work in decreasing health care–associated infections (HAIs) and, in particular, on effective cleaning for high-touch areas.[11] Perioperative RNs should be familiar with the processes of cleaning and participate in the cleaning as indicated by the requirements of each facility.

Management of Non-OR Personnel

The perioperative environment has many highly technical facets; therefore, the presence of vendors or health care industry representatives (HCIRs) is essential to providing care with the most current equipment and techniques available. Often, students from many specialties (eg, nursing, medical, surgical technologists) are present for training or observation during a surgical or invasive procedure. It is important to support training for the future caregivers in the perioperative environment. An additional person who is not a member of the perioperative team who may be present in the perioperative environment is the patient's family member. Most often the family member is present for the birth of a child or for support with highly anxious pediatric patients.

HEALTH CARE INDUSTRY REPRESENTATIVE (HCIR)

Product vendor and HCIR presence in the perioperative environment is important because they fulfill the vital role of subject-matter experts for both surgeons and perioperative personnel related to instruments, equipment, and implants.[12] Advancing technology requires the collaboration of the health care team with vendors (or HCIRs) to support implementation of new and improved patient care techniques. There is an increased risk to patient safety when vendors are present in the OR. In addition to being a potential distraction to the perioperative team, vendors pose a risk related to legal exposure, lack of compliance with regulatory standards, and risk of infection secondary to more people in the OR or procedure room. Perioperative managers must ensure that facility-specific policies are in place to address the presence and supervision of vendors in the perioperative environment. Credentialing of vendors is a common practice in health care facilities. Credentialing ensures that vendors are compliant with regulatory standards and risk prevention, including vaccinations. Statements from both AORN and the American College of Surgeons (ACS) reflect the important safeguards that must be part of the facility responsibilities related to the presence of vendors in the perioperative environment. The vendor should

- not participate in decision-making related to medical or nursing practice,
- not be involved with the performance of surgery,
- not have any direct patient contact,
- never be scrubbed in on any procedure, and
- be monitored and supervised by the surgeon and RN circulator.[12]

AORN's position statement regarding the presence of HCIRs supports the need for them in the perioperative suite during specialized procedures.[13] However, the perioperative RN has additional responsibilities that may be relevant when HCIRs are in the OR (Table 8.2).

STUDENTS

Nursing students who are able to observe in surgery have a chance to interact with and learn from the entire perioperative team. Perioperative RNs have a great opportunity to support and encourage the next generation of nurses to become interested in perioperative nursing. Medical students who rotate through the various specialties may be present in the perioperative environment as well. A medical student could be working with a surgeon or anesthesia professional. It is essential that the RN circulator supervise the presence of all students to maintain the sterile field, patient safety, and patient privacy.

FAMILY MEMBERS

Allowing family members to be present in the OR is based on facility-specific policy. A common practice is for a single member of a patient's family to be present during a cesarean delivery. Some facilities allow a parent to be present during induction of a pediatric patient. A parent may be present in the

TABLE 8.2 Presence of Health Care Industry Representative (HCIR) in the OR[1]

NURSE RESPONSIBILITY	ROLE	ACTIONS
Patient advocate	Maintain patient privacy and dignity.	• Ensure that the HCIR is not present in the room during prepping and draping. • Verify that the patient has given written consent to presence of HCIR.
Competency	Verify that the team has had adequate training and education.	• Verify with the OR manager or educator that each team member has completed competency verification related to equipment use, necessary techniques, and new technology.
Materials management	Verify facility approval for HCIR presence and equipment use.	• Verify with the OR manager that each HCIR has current credentialing according to facility policy. • Ensure that each HCIR wears a name badge. • Verify with the OR, sterile processing, and biomedical department manager that all equipment has been checked by biomedical engineering personnel for safe use.
Infection prevention	Verify that equipment, personnel, and traffic patterns support patient safety related to risk of infection.	• Verify with the OR or sterile processing manager that loaner instruments have been sterilized in the facility before use. • Limit traffic in the room to decrease airborne contaminants. • Verify that each HCIR is wearing facility-approved clothing in the perioperative environment. • Monitor the HCIR's movement around the sterile field. • Ensure that the HCIR uses appropriate personal protective equipment correctly.
Collaboration	Assist the HCIR and perioperative team to work cooperatively to achieve the best patient outcomes according to facility policy.	• Monitor the HCIR's activities. • Facilitate interactions between the HCIR and the perioperative team.

1. AORN position statement on the role of the health care industry representative in the perioperative setting. AORN, Inc. April 2014. http://aorn.org/guidelines/clinical-resources/position-statements.

postanesthesia care unit to comfort pediatric patients postoperatively. It is up to the anesthesia professional and surgeon to determine the need for family presence in unusual situations and in accordance with hospital policy.

While the primary commitment and focus are on the patient, the RN circulator must be cognizant of the family member who is present. The RN circulator must monitor the family member for adherence to surgical attire and ensure that the family member does not interfere with care of the patient. The family member may also become ill during the perioperative experience. If a family member must be removed from the OR, it is important for the RN circulator to seek assistance in caring for the family member while maintaining the progress of the procedure and ensuring safety of the surgical patient.

Management of Supplies, Equipment, and Implants

Management of supplies and equipment and adherence to rules and regulations guiding the use of implants are additional responsibilities of perioperative nurses. The health care facility relies on its nurses' judicious use of supplies and equipment to help remain fiscally solvent. Although the OR is considered a revenue-generating department, it is also one of the most expensive in terms of capital and supply needs.

SUPPLIES AND EQUIPMENT

Managing the huge quantity of supplies and equipment available in the OR can be a daunting task. Perioperative staff, to include RNs, may have a role in the multidisciplinary product evaluation and selection process, ensuring and monitoring preventive equipment maintenance, ensuring the availability and sterility of supplies, implementing cost-containment measures, and implementing practical environmental sustainability practices (ie, reprocessing versus recycling).

PRODUCT EVALUATION AND SELECTION

Product evaluation provides an excellent opportunity for nurses to use their unique knowledge of the perioperative setting in the **selection** of equipment and supplies that the surgical team needs to provide safe, cost-effective, and high-quality patient care. Nurses should apply the principles of EBP to the product selection process when researching relevant current product literature, contacting end-users at other facilities, and talking with representatives from competing companies.[14] The nurse can then present this valuable information to the multidisciplinary product selection committee for use during the final selection process.

Being part of a multidisciplinary product selection committee carries with it the responsibility to objectively and knowledgeably evaluate products and supplies based on

- safety factors (eg, latex free, compliance with governmental/regulatory requirements, ergonomically correct, fire resistant),
- financial impact (eg, cost-effectiveness, direct and indirect costs, reimbursement potential, contract pricing, duplication of current products, compatibility with existing products),
- environmental impact (eg, compatibility with existing disposal and processing methods, disposable versus reusable, reprocessing capabilities),
- reliability factors (eg, clinical performance, estimated useful life of the product, outdates, repair history),

- quality patient care factors (eg, ease of use, patient- and end-user-related requirements),
- regulatory and standard-setting agency compliance factors, and
- vendor support and quality of training factors.[14]

Beyond negotiating contracts related to the purchase price, vendors serve as an important resource to end-users by providing just-in-time education and training for their equipment and supplies. Vendors provide information on current research related to the product, processing and reprocessing requirements, and individualized financial considerations (eg, consignment, partial purchase orders, shared inventory, or just-in-time purchase agreements), which are especially attractive to managers of facilities that have low volume or limited storage space.[14]

PREVENTIVE MAINTENANCE

Preventive maintenance is an important step in prolonging the useful life of equipment and should be taken into account during product evaluation and selection.[14] Aside from patient safety considerations, another issue is that warranties may expire prematurely or be voided if a piece of equipment has been abused or used for purposes other than intended. Checking equipment before it is used to ensure that it has met routine scheduled maintenance requirements conducted by qualified personnel according to manufacturers' recommendations is another way that perioperative nurses hold themselves and others accountable for providing safe patient care.

AVAILABILITY AND STERILITY OF SUPPLIES

Part of developing and implementing the patient plan of care is ensuring that the appropriate equipment and supplies are available at the correct time based on patient and surgeon needs.[6] Being prepared by ensuring the availability and **sterilty of supplies** makes efficient use of operative time, which has implications for cost, surgical and anesthesia-related complications, patient safety, and surgeon, personnel, and patient satisfaction. Planning ahead to ensure that instruments will be available when needed is one way to decrease the incidence of IUSS.

COST-CONTAINMENT MEASURES

Both direct and indirect costs should be taken into consideration during the product evaluation process. A reusable instrument may appear to be lower in cost, but when the cost of cleaning, packaging, and sterilizing the instrument is considered, along with safety issues to sterile processing personnel, perioperative personnel, and the patient, is factored into the total cost, a disposable instrument may be more cost-effective. Other **cost-containment** measures may include purchasing disposable products for items that are used infrequently or that have a short, useful life that requires frequent updates. Conversely, reusable items may be a better choice if shelf space is limited.[15] A sample of direct and indirect costs related to product purchases is presented in Figure 8.1.

Much of the waste generated in the OR is inappropriately treated as medical waste, increasing disposal costs to the facility and overwhelming regulated waste landfills.[16] Being fiscally responsible involves being an advocate not only for the patient but for the environment as well. This includes recycling when possible, opening supplies as needed, and separating biohazardous from medical waste for

FIGURE 8.1 Direct and Indirect Costs Associated with Product Purchase[1]

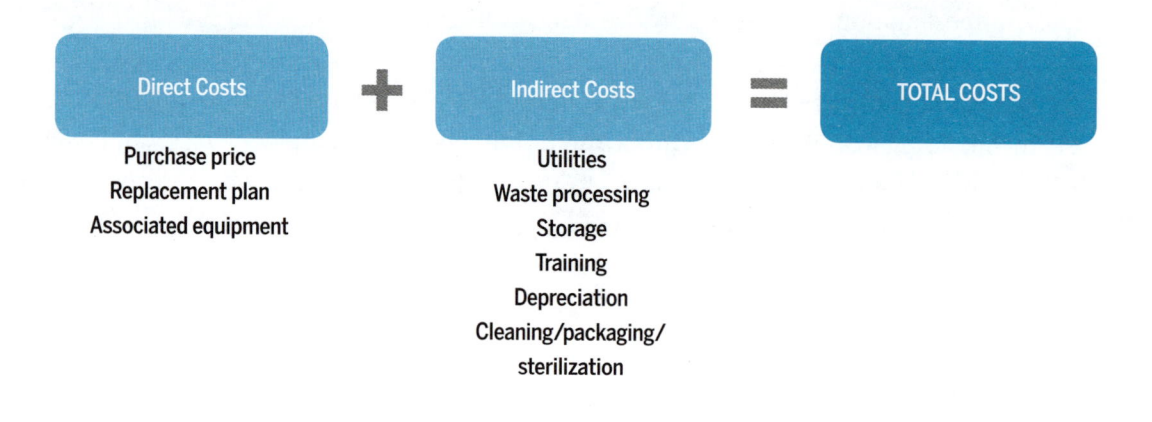

Direct Costs + **Indirect Costs** = **TOTAL COSTS**

Direct Costs:
- Purchase price
- Replacement plan
- Associated equipment

Indirect Costs:
- Utilities
- Waste processing
- Storage
- Training
- Depreciation
- Cleaning/packaging/sterilization

1. Guideline for product selection. In: *Guidelines for Perioperative Practice*. Denver, CO: AORN, Inc; 2017:184.

---

proper disposal. Periodic review of the contents of procedural packs to identify and remove unused items decreases the waste associated with opened, unused supplies.[14] Donating unused or no-longer-needed medical supplies and equipment to developing countries or for disaster relief purposes decreases medical waste while helping to promote global health.

Frequently, physicians have individual preferences for products, equipment, and supplies. Standardization of these items, however, can reduce costs, enhance inventory control, decrease storage requirements, and reduce end-user training time and errors related to the need to be competent on numerous items with the same function.[15] Nurses can facilitate the standardization process through sharing expert professional opinions as end-users during committee discussions and by assisting with the introduction of new products in the clinical setting.[3]

ENVIRONMENTAL SUSTAINABILITY PRACTICES

Reprocessing single-use devices (SUD) that previously were considered of onetime use or disposable is one way to engage in **environmental sustainability** but also another way to control costs and reduce medical waste. Reprocessing is possible within the guidelines and procedures established by the US Food and Drug Administration (FDA) under the 510(k) approval process. The FDA carefully monitors the types of products that can be reprocessed and requires health care facilities to comply with the same regulations for reprocessing as the original manufacturer does. Some facility managers may decide that using a third-party processor rather than in-house reprocessing is a better option because of these constraints.[11]

IMPLANT RULES AND REGULATIONS

Procedures involving implants require careful advance planning because these devices may not be stored in the facility but delivered as just-in-time inventory. Part of The Joint Commission's Universal Protocol is ensuring that the correct implants are available before the beginning of the procedure.[17] Implants may be size, site, and side specific. Not having the correct implant available may result in delay or cancellation of the procedure.

Often, implants used for orthopedic surgery (ie, screws, pins, plates, total joint prostheses) are delivered on consignment by manufacturer vendors. Unless processed in an FDA-approved instrumentation sterilization facility, reusable implants delivered to facilities must be processed in the same manner as in-house instrumentation: removed from the protective container or wrapper, then cleaned and sterilized according to manufacturers' instructions.[11] Implants processed or transported under unknown conditions cannot be considered sterile. Immediate-use steam sterilization should not be used for implantable devices except in cases of defined emergency.[11] Poor planning is not considered a defined emergency. If it is determined that there is no other alternative and IUSS must be used for sterilizing implants, biological and class V indicators must be run in the load.[11] Results of positive biological indicators must be reported to the surgeon and infection preventionist as soon as the results are known. As with other instrumentation sterilized through IUSS and not used, unused implants cannot be saved as sterile for future use.

The FDA requires special documentation for implants, regardless of type. If an issue is identified by the manufacturer (eg, sterility, packaging, sizing, etc.), there must be a mechanism in place to notify those patients involved and begin appropriate corrective action.[18] Conversely, if a patient develops a problem with an implant (eg, excessive or long-term pain, breakage), this information must be communicated to the manufacturer. Information to be documented on the patient's medical record and the implant registry includes

- patient identifiers;
- surgeon's name;
- date of procedure;
- manufacturer;
- lot, batch, model, and serial numbers;
- type and size of implant;
- site where the implant was placed;
- sterilizer load (if processed in-house); and
- any other information that would facilitate the manufacturer and facility in identifying a patient with a specific implant.[19]

Biological implants include both autograft (ie, the patient's own) and allograft (ie, from another source) implants. Organs (eg, heart, kidney, eye) and other body tissues (eg, cornea, heart valves, tendons) are common allografts. Bone is typically kept frozen until use. An additional responsibility of the perioperative nurse is to ensure that the freezer is monitored and kept at the appropriate temperature. Both donor and recipient identification information must be logged in the same manner as with other implants.[19] (See Chapter 3 for more discussion of implants.)

> **EXAM TIP**
>
> If a cranial bone flap is dropped and the decision is made to replant, rinse the graft with sterile normal saline using low-pressure pulsatile lavage on a separate sterile field. The wound classification should be changed to class III. The surgical team should be debriefed and a variance report completed.

Autologous tissue (ie, skin, cranial bone flaps) saved for autotransplantation at a later date must be stored in a manner that maintains the structural integrity and sterility of the tissue. Recommended storage mediums for a sampling of autologous tissues are presented in Table 8.3. Autologous tissue that is preserved and replanted within the same facility does not need to be registered with the FDA as an implant. If an autograft is transferred to another facility, documentation similar to that used for allografts must be provided so that the autograft can be traced to its final disposition. Unused autografts are disposed of in accordance with local and state regulations for biohazardous waste.[20]

Environmental Cleaning

Environmental cleaning is performed to decrease the incidence of surgical site infections by reducing the number of pathogens that can be transferred from inanimate objects to the patient and perioperative health care providers. It is the perioperative nurse's responsibility to ensure that the patient's environment is clean and safe throughout the entire surgical experience.[19]

Unlicensed assistive personnel who clean perioperative patient care areas need the same information on personal protective equipment (PPE), bloodborne pathogens, and standard and transmission-based precautions as do other members of the surgical team. The perioperative nurse can serve as a valuable resource in providing this education. Wearing the correct PPE is not only an important infection control measure but also serves to protect the worker from caustic cleaning chemicals. As with any other procedure requiring standard precautions, all personnel should wash hands after removing gloves and as soon as possible after hands are soiled.

Cleaning disinfectants should be hospital grade, specific for targeted organisms, and registered with the US Environmental Protection Agency (EPA). Alcohol, high-level disinfectants, and liquid sterilants should never be used as environmental surface disinfecting agents; they are not intended for this use and may damage the finish of metal furniture and equipment. Disinfectants should be applied with a low-linting cloth, clean reusable mop head, or single-use mop. Soiled cleaning materials are considered contaminated and should never be returned to the cleaning solution container or used for multiple patients.[21] Adequate time, expressed as dwell time, must be provided to allow environmental surface disinfectants to dry to reach their maximum effectiveness. Attempts to cut down on room turnover time by decreasing dwell time or beginning to clean the room before the patient is transferred to the postanesthesia care unit negate the efficacy of the cleaning process.

The tenacity of some pathogens and the continual evolution of drug-resistant organisms require careful attention to appropriate cleaning practices to prevent the spread of diseases that are becoming increasingly difficult to control. Extremely virulent pathogens (ie, *Clostridium difficile*, *Mycobacterium tuberculosis*, prions, multidrug-resistant organisms) require specialized environmental cleaning procedures. Recommended cleaning practices after caring for patients with suspected or diagnosed Creutzfeldt-Jakob disease are presented in Figure 8.2.

> **EXAM TIP**
>
> Before the first procedure of the day, damp dust all horizontal surfaces using a lint-free cloth to remove dust and pathogens that may have collected overnight.

TABLE 8.3 Management of Autologous Tissue Grafts[1]

TISSUE TYPE	RECOMMENDED STORAGE MEDIUM	COMMENTS
Avulsed tooth	• Hank's balanced salt solution • Milk • Store in water only if this is the only option to keep the tooth moist	• Tooth should be replanted as soon as possible.
Cranial bone flap	• Freeze • Cryopreserve	• Autologous bone should be stored at −4°F (−20°C) or colder for 6 months or less. • Bone flaps can also be stored in a subcutaneous pocket within the patient in an anatomical location determined by the physician.
Parathyroid tissue	• Cryopreserve	• Optimal storage temperature has not been determined.
Skin	• Normal saline • Cryopreserve	• Autologous skin should be stored between 32°F to 50°F (0°C to 10°C) for no longer than 14 days.
Vein	• Normal saline or lactated Ringer's and then refrigerated	• Autologous veins should be stored between 32°F to 50°F (0°C to 10°C) for no longer than 14 days. • Cryopreservation is not recommended.

1. Guideline for autologous tissue management. In: *Guidelines for Perioperative Practice.* Denver, CO: AORN, Inc; 2017:191-241.

SPILLS

Spills can occur at any time during the procedure. Spills pose a safety issue because personnel may slip and fall on wet surfaces or be exposed to caustic substances or noxious fumes. Spills involving biohazardous substances (eg, blood, body fluids) also serve as reservoirs for disease transmission when soiled clothing or shoes are worn outside the OR.

Spills should be dealt with as quickly as possible by the person who notices the problem. The type and amount of spill dictate the manner in which it is handled. Biohazardous spills or other potentially infectious substances should be removed with an absorbent cloth and the affected area then cleaned and disinfected. If a large amount of blood is involved in the spill, a disinfecting product registered with the EPA should be added to the spill before cleaning is begun.[21] Other spills should be cleaned based on recommendations found on the safety data sheets related to the substance involved in the spill. Personal protective equipment (ie, gloves, masks, eye protection, other impervious clothing as necessary) should always be worn when handling a spill.[22]

FIGURE 8.2 Enhanced Cleaning Protocol for High-Risk Procedures[1,2]

Creutzfeldt-Jakob disease (CJD) cleaning protocol

The prion associated with CJD is incredibly difficult to eradicate by current disinfection and sterilization methods. Currently, no EPA-approved disinfectant is available that inactivates prions; therefore, suspected or confirmed environmental contamination with high-risk tissue (ie, brain, spinal cord, eye tissue) requires special cleaning procedures. Personnel should wear personal protective equipment for standard and contact transmission-based precautions when handling equipment or instruments suspected of CJD contamination.

- Remove all equipment and supplies that will not be needed during the procedure. Only equipment, supplies, and personnel required for the procedure should be in the room.

⬇

- Cover work surfaces with disposable, impervious material. This includes pedals, cords, walls, OR bed, and floor.

⬇

- Cleaning and disinfection of surfaces contaminated with high-risk tissue involves the following steps:

➡

1. Remove gross tissue from surface.

2. Clean the area with a detergent.

3. Apply disinfectant solution (eg, sodium hypochloride [1:5 to 1:10 dilution with 10,000 ppm to 20,000 ppm available chloride]) to the area for 30 to 60 minutes.

4. Use absorbent material to soak up the solution and discard in biohazardous waste container.

➡

- Any cloth or paper product coming in contact with high-risk tissue should be treated as biohazardous waste and incinerated.

⬇

- Linens and environmental surfaces that have not been exposed to high-risk tissue may be cleaned using routine processes.

---

1. Guideline for environmental cleaning. In: *Guidelines for Perioperative Practice*. Denver, CO: AORN, Inc; 2017:19-20.
2. Karasin M. Perioperative care of the patient with Creutzfeldt-Jakob disease (Special Needs Populations). *AORN J.* 2014;100(4):391-407.

ROOM TURNOVER

Room turnover involves standardized practices that are performed at the conclusion of each operative or invasive procedure. Instruments, trash, and soiled linen are placed in fluid-impervious containers and transported to the appropriate processing area. Contents of suction containers may be poured down the drain unless contraindicated by local environmental regulatory agencies.[23] Room cleaning follows the same principle as performing patient skin antisepsis: move from the cleaner toward the more contaminated areas.

Surfaces that the perioperative team touches most frequently (ie, control panels, work stations, light switches, door handles, telephones) are also the most likely to transmit pathogens. These high-touch surfaces require extra attention during routine cleaning. The increased use of computers in the OR introduces a new cleaning challenge, because disinfectants may harm keyboards and monitors. Consider the use of keyboard covers, which can either be disinfected between patients or disposed of at the end of the procedure.[21] Clean reusable patient items and equipment after each patient's use. Single-use items should never be used for multiple patients. Ceilings and walls should be cleaned as necessary after each procedure.

> **EXAM TIP**
>
> Even with the most thorough cleaning practices, the floor of the OR should always be considered contaminated.

TERMINAL CLEANING

Terminal cleaning occurs after the last procedure of the day. The purpose of terminal cleaning is to provide a thorough, final disinfection of perioperative areas. The entire floor, including under the OR bed and any other equipment, should be either wet vacuumed or mopped. Clean all exposed surfaces, including wheels and casters. Remove, inspect, and clean mattress pads.[21] Cracked mattress or positioning pads harbor moisture and bacteria and should be discarded. The frequency of terminal cleaning for seldom- or lightly used areas has yet to be determined. Hospitals should develop and follow their own policies related to unused semi-restricted or restricted areas.[21]

Key Concepts and Review

An effective perioperative nurse is also an effective manager of personnel. Through supervision, delegation, and collaboration, the perioperative nurse puts diverse members of the surgical team (eg, surgical technologists, health care industry representatives, students, the patient's family) in the best possible position to assist the patient in achieving positive surgical outcomes. The delivery of nursing care is guided by ethical, legal, and moral principles while ensuring patient privacy, confidentiality, personal dignity, and safety.

Health care facility leaders rely on nurses' judicious use of supplies and equipment to remain fiscally solvent. Perioperative nurses are important end-users of products and as such are best qualified to provide input on the selection of products, equipment, and supplies that will be used in caring for patients. A standardized approach to product selection helps ensure that the safest, most cost-effective supplies and equipment are purchased. By sharing their knowledge and expertise, perioperative nurses have the opportunity to ensure that product quality, patient safety, cost-effectiveness, and environmentally responsible goals are met.

Ensuring that the correct instruments, implants, and equipment are available before the procedure is a major responsibility of the perioperative nurse. The surgical team's success in providing quality, cost effective, and safe patient care is dependent on the expertise of the perioperative nurse in providing the resources necessary for the unique needs of the patient.

The perioperative nurse is responsible for ensuring a safe, clean surgical environment for every patient. Knowledge of EBP for cleaning, infection control, and standard and transmission-based precautions is necessary to effectively manage a safe surgical environment.

References

1. AORN position statement on perioperative safe staffing and on-call practices. AORN, Inc. https://www.aorn.org/aorn-org/guidelines/clinical-resources/position-statements.
2. Martin KK. Meeting the challenge of perioperative education. *AORN J.* 2011;94(4):377-384.
3. Phillips N. Perioperative education. In: *Berry & Kohn's Operating Room Technique.* 13th ed. St Louis, MO: Elsevier; 2017:1-14.
4. Russell KA. Nurse practice acts guide and govern nursing practice. *J Nurs Regul.* 2012;3(3):36-42.
5. AORN position statement on one perioperative registered nurse circulator dedicated to every patient undergoing an operative or other invasive procedure. AORN, Inc. http://www.aorn.org/aorn-org/guidelines/clinical-resources/position-statements.
6. Steelman VM. Concepts basic to perioperative nursing. In: Rothrock JC, ed. *Alexander's Care of the Patient in Surgery.* 15th ed. St Louis, MO: Elsevier; 2015:1-15.
7. AST position statements. Association of Surgical Technologists. http://www.ast.org/AboutUs/Position_Statements_Guidelines/.
8. Statement on associate degree concept resolution (updated January 2013). Association of Surgical Technologists. http://www.ast.org/uploadedFiles/Main_Site/Content/About_Us/Resolution_Associate_Degree.pdf.
9. About IAHCSM. International Association of Healthcare Central Services Materiel Management. https://iahcsmm.org/about.html.
10. Guideline for sterilization. In: *Guidelines for Perioperative Practice.* Denver, CO: AORN, Inc; 2017:865-892.
11. Improvement stories: hospital environmental services staff are important drivers of the infection control agenda. Institute for Healthcare Improvement. http://www.ihi.org/resources/Pages/ImprovementStories/HospitalEnvironmentalSvcsStaffDriversInfectionControl.aspx.
12. Plonien C, Williams M. Vendor presence in the OR. *AORN J.* 2014;100(1):81-86.
13. AORN position statement on the role of the health care industry representative in the perioperative setting. AORN, Inc. April 2014. https://www.aorn.org/guidelines/clinical-resources/position-statements.
14. Plonien C, Donovan L. OR leadership: product evaluation and cost containment. *AORN J.* 2015;102(4):426-432.
15. Guideline for product selection. In: *Guidelines for Perioperative Practice.* Denver, CO: AORN, Inc; 2017:183-190.
16. Parham JC. Path to green: practice improvement in the OR. *AORN J.* 2011;93(6):792-795.
17. The Universal Protocol for Preventing Wrong Site, Wrong Procedure, and Wrong Person Surgery™. The Joint Commission. http://www.jointcommission.org/assets/1/18/UP_Poster.pdf.
18. Medical device tracking. US Food and Drug Administration. http://www.fda.gov/medicaldevices/deviceregulationandguidance/postmarketrequirements/medicaldevicetracking/default.htm.

19. Bowen B. Orthopedic surgery. In: Rothrock JC, ed. *Alexander's Care of the Patient in Surgery*. 15th ed. St Louis, MO: Elsevier; 2015:679-767.
20. Guideline for autologous tissue management. In: *Guidelines for Perioperative Practice*. Denver, CO: AORN, Inc; 2017:191-241.
21. Guideline for environmental cleaning. In: *Guidelines for Perioperative Practice*. Denver, CO: AORN, Inc; 2017:7-28.
22. Guideline for a safe environment of care, part 1. In: *Guidelines for Perioperative Practice*. Denver, CO: AORN, Inc; 2017:243-267.
23. Spry C. Infection prevention and control. In: Rothrock JC, ed. *Alexander's Care of the Patient in Surgery*. 15th ed. St Louis, MO: Elsevier, 2015:69-123.

Additional Resources

AATB Standards for Tissue Banking. 14th ed. McLean, VA: American Association of Tissue Banks; 2016. https://www.aatb.org/?q=content/standards-regulatory.

Medical device reporting. US Food and Drug Administration. http://www.fda.gov/medicaldevices/safety/reportaproblem/default.htm.

Position statement on environmental responsibility. AORN, Inc. http://www.aorn.org/guidelines/clinical-resources/position-statements.

Practice Exam Questions

1. A facility has a shortage of surgical technologists and is considering allowing radiology technologists to serve in the scrub role for interventional radiology procedures. What is the first step in determining the feasibility of this new role?
    A. Consult the state's standards of practice for radiology technicians.
    B. Determine if the radiology technician's educational program includes training on surgical scrub duties.
    C. Ask the perioperative nurse educator to develop an orientation plan.
    D. Develop a job description for the new role.

2. Which of the following products should be used for disinfecting environmental surfaces in the perioperative setting?
    A. Liquid chemical sterilants
    B. Hospital-grade Environmental Protection Agency (EPA)-registered disinfectants
    C. High-level disinfectants
    D. Commercial-grade bleach

3. The appropriate method for cleaning an operating room after a procedure includes
    A. disinfecting the back table and Mayo stand while the patient emerges from anesthesia to cut down on turnover time.
    B. starting at the center of the room and working toward the perimeter.
    C. starting at the top and working toward the bottom.
    D. flooding horizontal surfaces with alcohol.

4. Which of the following actions are appropriate for a health care industry representative (HCIR) who is present in the operating room during a surgical procedure?
    A. Providing technical support.
    B. Assisting with positioning the patient.
    C. Opening sterile supplies onto the sterile back table.
    D. Scrubbing in to assist the surgical team.

5. When delegating a task to unlicensed assistive personnel (UAP), the perioperative nurse retains _____ for that delegated task.
    A. responsibility
    B. accountability
    C. authority
    D. administration

6. The person responsible for granting permission for a parent to accompany a child into the operating room is the
    A. perioperative department manager.
    B. circulating nurse.
    C. anesthesia professional.
    D. child life specialist.

7. A new plastic surgeon has just joined the staff of an ambulatory surgery center. The surgeon requests a line of suture that is not carried by the facility. How can the nurse best respond in providing rationale for use of the facility's current brand of suture?
    A. "Standardization of products is one way our surgeons can help us control costs."
    B. "We don't have enough shelf space in the suture room to accommodate more boxes."
    C. "We don't have a contract with that suture company."
    D. "The rest of our surgeons won't use that type of suture."

8. A split-thickness skin graft is obtained for autotransplantation to occur in one week at the same facility. The best way to preserve the graft is to
    A. place the tissue in balanced salt solution.
    B. refrigerate the tissue in normal saline.
    C. sterilize the skin using ethylene oxide (ETO).
    D. sterilize the skin using steam sterilization.

9. A perioperative nurse is assigned to care for a patient with methicillin-resistant Staphylococcus aureus (MRSA). Which of the following cleaning practices can be anticipated to be required after the procedure?
    A. Closing the room for 28 minutes to allow for an adequate air exchange.
    B. Incinerating all disposable instruments.
    C. Incorporating enhanced environmental cleaning procedures.
    D. Incorporating routine environmental cleaning procedures.

10. A multidisciplinary team is evaluating a new brand of irrigation fluid. The empty container is recyclable. Which of the following will be affected if this product is chosen?
    A. The environment
    B. Patient safety
    C. End-user satisfaction
    D. Group purchasing contract

Answers with Supported Rationales

1. Answer A is correct. State laws regulate health care provider practices and establish legal qualifications for who can practice in a specific role. Reference: Steelman VM. Concepts basic to perioperative nursing. In: Rothrock JC, ed. *Alexander's Care of the Patient in Surgery*. 15th ed. St Louis, MO: Elsevier; 2015:7.

2. Answer B is correct. A hospital-grade EPA-registered disinfectant should be used for environmental surface disinfection in the perioperative setting. The manufacturer's instructions for use should be followed. Reference: Guideline for environmental cleaning. In: *Guidelines for Perioperative Practice*. Denver, CO: AORN, Inc; 2017:9.

3. Answer C is correct. Cleaning should progress from top to bottom areas, and from cleaner to dirtier areas. Reference: Guideline for environmental cleaning. In: *Guidelines for Perioperative Practice*. Denver, CO: AORN, Inc; 2017:10,15.

4. Answer A is correct. Because of their education, knowledge, and expertise, HCIRs have a valid but restricted role in the operative or other invasive procedure setting. The role of the HCIR includes providing technical support and education, but does not include providing patient care or directly participating in the performance of the surgical procedure. Reference: AORN Position Statement: Role of the Health Care Industry Representative in the Perioperative Setting. Denver CO: AORN, Inc; 2014.

5. Answer B is correct. Delegation transfers authority to a competent individual to perform the task while retaining accountability for the appropriate completion of that task. Reference: Steelman V. Concepts basic to perioperative nursing. In: Rothrock JC, ed. *Alexander's Care of the Patient in Surgery*. 15th ed. St Louis, MO: Elsevier, 2015:7.

6. Answer C is correct. Based on parental and child preoperative anxiety, anesthesia professionals may encourage parents to accompany the child through induction. Reference: Phillips N. Perioperative pediatrics. In: *Berry & Kohn's Operating Room Technique*. 13th ed. St Louis, MO: Elsevier; 2017:128.

7. Answer A is correct. Standardization of products can reduce costs. Reference: Guideline for product selection. In: *Guidelines for Perioperative Practice*. Denver, CO: AORN, Inc; 2017:185.

8. Answer B is correct. Autologous skin for delayed autotransplantation may be refrigerated and stored in normal saline. Reference: Guideline for autologous tissue management. In: *Guidelines for Perioperative Practice*. Denver, CO: AORN, Inc; 2017:212.

9. Answer C is correct. Enhanced environmental cleaning practices extending beyond routine cleaning practices to all high-touch objects should be implemented to prevent the spread of multiple drug-resistant organisms. Reference: Guideline for environmental cleaning. In: *Guidelines for Perioperative Practice*. Denver, CO: AORN, Inc; 2017:18-19.

10. Answer A is correct. The environmental effect of a product is influenced by whether it may be recycled. Reference: Guidelines for product selection. In: *Guidelines for Perioperative Practice*. Denver, CO: AORN, Inc; 2017:185.

9 Professional Accountability

KEY TERMS

- Accountability
- Altruism
- Autonomy
- Board of nursing
- Certification
- Code of Ethics
- Competency
- Delegation
- Duty
- Ethical practice
- Ethics
- Evidence-based practice (EBP)
- Excellence
- Fidelity
- Institute of Medicine (IOM)
- Just culture/culture of safety
- Nurse Practice Act (NPA)
- Patient advocacy
- Professional standards
- Professionalism
- Quality improvement
- Regulatory guidelines
- Research utilization
- Root cause analysis
- Scope of practice
- Sentinel event
- Shared governance
- Standards of practice
- Values

REQUIRED NURSING SKILLS

- Advocating for the patient
- Completing adverse event reports
- Complying with Health Insurance Portability and Accountability Act (HIPAA)

continues >

✓ REQUIRED NURSING SKILLS, CONTINUED

- Implementing current nursing research results
- Maintaining professional nursing competency
- Participating in continuous professional development
- Performing literature searches
- Promoting a culture of safety
- Promoting evidence-based practice
- Promoting standards of practice

The primary focus of perioperative nursing professionalism is dedication to the patient. The characteristics of a profession include a specialized knowledge base, self-imposed responsibility to serve the public, and regulation by a professional association. Professional accountability, as it applies to nursing, requires the perioperative registered nurse (RN) to be responsible for his or her specific behaviors. These include

- working within the perioperative scope of nursing practice,
- adhering to regulatory standards and guidelines,
- maintaining professional growth,
- participating in quality improvement practices,
- encouraging and supporting a culture of safety,
- delegating appropriate tasks,
- supporting risk management strategies, and
- supporting patient rights and advocating for the patient.

Nurses who participate in continuous professional development activities are better equipped to focus on and promote patient safety as well as ensure patient satisfaction.

Perioperative Nurse Scope of Practice

The foundation of all nursing practice is the provision of safe and ethical care to all clients, including responsible care of self. Professional standards and a legal framework provide guidance for implementing nursing care. The perioperative **scope of practice** is framed by a combination of laws, standards, and guidelines established by authoritative regulatory and professional organizations. Such organizations may be regulatory or a voluntary professional or membership groups.

Sources of Professional Standards

"**Professional standards** delineate activities related to performance, performance improvement, continuing education, ethical behavior, responsibility, and accountability."[1(p17)] Standards are developed by both regulatory agencies and professional organizations. Regulatory agency standards are legally binding, whereas professional organization standards, although recommended, are voluntary.[1] A summary of the purpose and key elements of regulatory agencies, as well as non-regulatory professional organizations, are included in Table 9.1.

TABLE 9.1 Regulatory Agencies and Professional Organizations

AGENCY/ORGANIZATION	PURPOSE	KEY ELEMENTS
Centers for Disease Control and Prevention (CDC) http://www.cdc.gov	Protects Americans from health, safety, and security threats.	• Sets guidelines for the prevention of health care–associated infections (HAIs) (eg, standard precautions, airborne precautions). • Provides infection prevention guidelines.
Centers for Medicare & Medicaid Services (CMS) https://www.cms.gov	Improves patient outcomes.	• Was previously called the Health Care Financing Administration (HCFA). • Focuses on decreasing fraud and abuse. • Establishes value-based incentive reimbursement. • Ties reimbursement to better patient outcomes. • Enforces compliance with the Health Insurance Portability and Accountability Act (HIPAA).
Occupational Safety & Health Administration (OSHA) https://www.osha.gov	Ensures a safe and healthy work environment for both workers and patients.	• Provides a list of patient and employer rights. • Publishes compliance standards. • Requires employers to comply legally.

REGULATORY AGENCIES

Regulatory agencies establish **regulatory guidelines** to define the boundaries of perioperative nursing practice. Two of the primary agencies that influence nursing practice are the Centers for Medicare & Medicaid Serves (CMS) and the Centers for Disease Control and Prevention (CDC).

CMS. Nurses are accountable for professional practice that demonstrates an ability to influence patient outcomes. Health care facilities depend on good patient outcomes for financial reimbursement. The CMS has oversight for enforcing conditions for participation that determine reimbursement fees and fee-for-service regulations.[2] The most notable aspect of the CMS fee-for-service and reimbursement regulations is related to patients who have hospital-acquired conditions (HACs). Acquiring an HAC is an adverse event, which is deemed preventable if current **evidence-based practice** (EBP) guidelines were followed.[3] The CMS lists 14 categories of HACs, which negatively affect reimbursement. Two of the most notable categories for the perioperative specialty are retained foreign objects and surgical site infections.

CDC. Health care–associated infections (HAIs) are a significant risk for perioperative patients. The CDC has created a list of recommendations for infection prevention related to HAIs. Causes of HAIs have been attributed to contact between the patient's skin and the contaminated hands of personnel and/or other patients as well as contaminated surfaces in the environment.[4] In September 2014, the CDC updated the guidelines for infection prevention focused on the outpatient setting. Perioperative nurses should be aware of the CDC recommendations for infection prevention, including

> **EXAM TIP**
>
> The perioperative nurse plays an important role in helping to prevent hospital-acquired conditions by implementing evidence-based practice guidelines.

- hand hygiene practices,
- environmental cleaning and disinfection,
- use of personal protective equipment (PPE),
- reprocessing standards, and
- respiratory hygiene.[4]

Most HAIs are preventable and may result in lack of reimbursement from the CMS; therefore, when possible, facilities should implement infection prevention bundling strategies outlined by the CDC. Bundled strategies apply to a variety of HAIs in the health care environment. Two HAIs that benefit from a bundled approach to infection prevention are central line–associated bloodstream infections and urinary tract infections.

ACCREDITING ORGANIZATIONS

A nurse can ensure that his or her practice is current by remaining cognizant of regulatory requirements and accreditation standards. Two of the accrediting organizations that affect perioperative practice are The Joint Commission (TJC) and the DNV GL (Det Norske Veritas [Norway] and Germanischer Lloyd [Germany]).

TJC accredits health care organizations for maintaining performance standards[5] and identifying best practices. In addition, TJC established both the National Patient Safety Goals (NPSGs)[6] and the Surgical Care Improvement Project (SCIP)[7] for improving patient safety. The NPSGs address specific patient safety concerns and patient safety risk areas with EBP strategies. For example, the NPSGs list patient identification as a potential risk for patient safety. This NPSG requires using a minimum of two specific patient identifiers to prevent patient-identification errors. The first set of NPSGs was published in 2003 and is updated annually. TJC safety advisory board decides whether to keep an established goal or retire the goal based on safety results for the previous year. The NPSGs are specific to the health care facility type. Both hospital and ambulatory NPSGs contain guidelines specific to the surgical specialty. The SCIP measures are specifically designed to improve surgical care by reducing surgical complications.[7] The SCIP measures are updated annually and nurses should be familiar with current core measure sets published by TJC.

DNV GL. In 2013, the DNV GL was formed as an international certification body and classification society.[8] The DNV GL has specific accreditation guidelines, and like TJC, the DNV makes survey visits. The focus of the DNV survey is on quality management projects that support consistent work processes. Direct care nursing personnel are supported in suggesting improved processes.

NURSING ORGANIZATIONS

Participation in professional organizations offers the perioperative nurse the opportunity to access educational resources as well as to collaborate with colleagues. The state Boards of Nursing (BONs), American Nurses Association (ANA), and AORN are the defining organizations for helping guide perioperative practice. Professional nurses should be familiar with these organizations and exhibit specific traits that promote professional practice (discussed later in this chapter).

State Boards of Nursing. The National Council of State Boards of Nursing (NCSBN) was established to protect the public by helping ensure that nurses practice in a safe and competent way.[9] The NCSBN is an independent, not-for-profit organization through which BONs act and counsel together on matters of common interest and concern affecting public health, safety, and welfare, including the development of nursing licensure examinations. Every state legislature has enacted a law known as the **Nurse Practice Act** (NPA). A provision of the NPA is the establishment of an individual BON for each state. Each state BON is responsible for creating rules and regulations that outline specific practices related to the NPA[10] that are unique to each state: "The NPA gives authority to regulate the practice of nursing and the enforcement of law to an administrative agency or BON that is charged with maintaining the balance between the rights of the nurse to practice nursing and the responsibility to protect the public health, safety, and welfare of its citizens."[11(p37)] It is the responsibility of every nurse to read and understand his or her particular state's NPA to ensure compliance with the laws regulating professional nursing practice. The general scope of nursing practice outlined in the NPA of the state in which the nurse is licensed and practices is the standard for the nursing care provided by an individual nurse.

ANA. The ANA is a membership organization that is responsible for creating and promoting nursing standards of care. The ANA publishes the *Code of Ethics for Nurses with Interpretive Statements*, which was updated in 2015. This version contains nine provisions with interpretive statements that address the role of the nurse in relation to patient, self, society, and the profession. The Code of Ethics guides nurses in providing patient care and in making patient care decisions.[12] All RNs are held to the same code of ethics regardless of specialty.

AORN. AORN is a membership organization that supports the perioperative nursing specialty by providing specialty education and resources for practice.[13] Delineating additional specific **standards of practice** for perioperative nurses is one focus of AORN through its evidence-based *Guidelines for Perioperative Practice*. The AORN guidelines present practice recommendations based on the latest research and EBP standards. The goal of the guidelines is to provide standards for perioperative nursing practice that promote patient safety and positive outcomes. Facility policies may not reflect the current guidelines. It is essential for perioperative nurses to stay current with the annual guidelines as published by AORN.

Specific to the perioperative scope of practice is AORN's Perioperative Explications for the ANA *Code of Ethics for Nurses with Interpretive Statements*.[14] AORN's Ethics Task Force expanded on all nine provisions of the ANA Code of Ethics (discussed earlier) to include perioperative explications (ie, real-life applicability) for the perioperative specialty. Based on the ANA Code of Ethics, AORN has developed these standards of perioperative nursing to outline the responsibility of RNs in providing ethical care that reflects the Code of Ethics for the nursing profession.[15]

AORN provides perioperative nurses with many opportunities to discuss current issues, trends, and opportunities in communication forums. The monthly *AORN Journal* (aornjournal.org) provides articles and columns focused on the latest topics related to perioperative practice. Continuing education opportunities are available in each issue to allow perioperative nurses to develop current knowledge. Additionally, AORN is involved at both the state and federal levels of government related to perioperative nursing. When legislative activities arise that have an effect on perioperative nursing or perioperative patient safety, AORN is the voice that government officials look to for the best standards of care.

Traits Exhibited by the Nursing Professional

Professionalism is the behavior and conduct that represent a commitment to and a belief in the profession of nursing.[16] Important traits of professionalism are presented in Figure 9.1.

Accountability is the willingness of a nurse to accept full responsibility for his or her professional practice.[17] One key aspect of professional nursing practice is the ability to make independent decisions based on scientific knowledge. Nurses can promote these independent decisions and **autonomy** by projecting confidence while working within their identified scope of practice.[18] There is no doubt that professional nurses display altruistic traits. Concern for the welfare of others is the hallmark definition of nursing behavior. The embodiment of true **altruism** is evidenced by the nursing profession being lauded as the most honest and trusted profession since 1990, other than that of firemen in 2001 after the World Trade Center attacks.[19]

Fidelity refers to a nurse's loyalty and faithfulness related to accountability and commitment to the profession. The perioperative nurse has a belief system based on personal **values** that are exhibited in nursing practice.

FIGURE 9.1 Traits of Nursing Professionalism

Nursing Professionalism: Accountability, Autonomy, Altruism, Excellence, Values, Fidelity

Nursing **excellence** is operationalized in nursing practice when the actions of nurses

- demonstrate consistent practice based on scientific knowledge and theory,
- challenge mediocrity,
- integrate patient perspectives, and
- align with continuous efforts to develop new knowledge.[17]

The development of new knowledge is enhanced through continuous exploration of current research data and familiarity with professional organization and regulatory guidelines (see earlier discussion).

The American Nurses Credentialing Center (ANCC) promotes nursing excellence through the credentialing process. The ANCC created the Magnet® Recognition program to promote the achievement of three primary goals:

1. promoting quality in a facility that supports professional practice,
2. identifying excellence in nursing care for patients, and
3. disseminating best nursing practices.[20]

Facilities that achieve Magnet status are recognized nationally as demonstrating best practices related to patient safety and satisfaction, a collaborative culture, and a primary focus on advancing nursing standards.

Professional Growth

Continuous professional development activities allow perioperative nurses to enjoy both personal and professional growth. Professional growth requires a commitment from perioperative nurses to develop their own professional development plan. Recommendations from the 2010 **Institute of Medicine** (IOM) report *The Future of Nursing: Leading Change and Advancing Health* addressed the nursing profession's commitment to safe quality patient care.[21] Aspects of a professional development plan are included in the key messages in the IOM report. A professional development plan may include

- participating in educational activities,
- maintaining competency,
- achieving specialty certification,
- seeking advanced degree credentials, and
- participating actively in professional organizations.

The IOM report includes four key messages:

1. *Nurses should practice to the full extent of their education and training.*
2. *Nurses should achieve higher levels of education and training through an improved education system that promotes seamless academic progression.*
3. *Nurses should be full partners, with physicians and other health professionals, in redesigning health care in the United States.*
4. *Effective workforce planning and policy making require better data collection and an improved information infrastructure.*[21(p4)]

This report is both a blueprint for individual nurses to advance personal professional development and a larger plan for improving patient care. Regardless of the nursing practice or specialty, all nurses can implement the key messages from the IOM report to improve the quality of patient care.

> **EXAM TIP**
>
> The purpose of a professional development plan is to outline the steps required to meet a personal and professional goal of lifelong learning to promote positive patient outcomes.

Educational activities are important for nursing professional growth. Activities include seeking continuing education, participating in facility-based training for equipment and technology, and committing to remaining current with EBP guidelines. These activities help perioperative nurses provide a safe level of nursing practice. Continuing education is required for nurses to stay current with the fast-paced changes in health technology and practice-based knowledge. The IOM report discusses the importance of lifelong learning as a commitment to improving patient outcomes.[21] Individual professional accountability includes participating in educational activities and maintaining competency.

Maintaining clinical competency is a standard of TJC.[22,23] Perioperative managers and educators should put competency assessment strategies in place to verify that personnel have the necessary skills and knowledge to provide safe patient care.[24] Managers and educators should implement assessment strategies for competency that evaluate the need for information pertinent to new hires, core job functions, newly implemented policies, changes in practice, and practices that demonstrate a high patient safety risk or are determined to be problematic.[25] Education related to competency standards is directly related to specialty certification.

Specialty certification is one way perioperative nurses can work to the full extent of their education and training as outlined in the IOM report. The American Nurses Credentialing Center (ANCC) defines **certification** as formal recognition of the specialized knowledge, skills, and experience demonstrated by the achievement of standards identified by a nursing specialty to promote optimal patient outcomes.[25] Increasing knowledge and experience is required to achieve and maintain specialty certification.[26] Nurses who seek specialty certification demonstrate a commitment to lifelong learning. Certification requirements include continuing education to stay up-to-date with the most current practice standards. Participation in lifelong learning validates that the perioperative nurse is committed to improving patient outcomes. Patient care needs are becoming more complex and require higher-level education and training to deliver necessary care. Findings in one particular study showed that certified perioperative nurses

- identify specialty certification as a personal accomplishment,
- have an increased level of personal satisfaction,
- identify certification as an indicator of professional growth, and
- demonstrate a commitment to the nursing profession.[27]

The IOM report recognizes major changes in the practice environment in which nurses work.[21] The nursing profession has multiple levels of entry related to education. Obtaining a baccalaureate education is becoming necessary to keep up with practice competencies required to provide more complex care.

Nurses are expected to provide care with a high level of critical thinking skills, collaborate across the health care continuum, use advanced technological tools, and use high-level information management systems.[21] According to the IOM report, it is important for nursing professionals to be involved with workforce planning and policy making.[21] For example, involvement with professional nursing organizations helps to set the stage for perioperative nurses to become involved in legislative action and research that will guide data collection and, ultimately, produce effective evidence-based policies to help improve patient care.

Quality Improvement

Quality improvement helps change practice based on the best evidence available.[28] Through activities like audits, processes are identified that do not meet the current standard of practice for patient care. Nursing research is the process of identifying and gathering evidence upon which practice should be based.[28] Through research utilization and the implementation of EBP standards, perioperative nurses can be assured that nursing practice is both current and contributes to improving patient outcomes.

The ability of perioperative nurses to perform a literature search will assist in identifying current EBP standards. Whether the perioperative nurse is seeking information related to a patient care issue or clinical practice, evidence is available through a literature search. **Research utilization** is the application of information discovered in one or more research studies in one's own practice. Nurses can apply new knowledge to real-life situations.[29] The Iowa Model of Evidence-Based Practice is commonly used to implement EBP changes that have been identified in an organization.[30] The model involves collaboration through a team approach to develop, evaluate, and plan the necessary changes in practice. Changes are based on an identified need followed by a literature search and research utilization. Although EBP appears to be similar to research utilization, it differs in that EBP is usually applied to a specific clinical problem.[30] When a clinical problem is identified, nurses seek research information and decide how that information can be applied to solve the problem.[29] Perioperative nurses have a responsibility to become involved in quality improvement activities to promote safe patient care practices.

Culture of Safety

Working in an environment that promotes a culture of safety or "just culture" contributes to better patient outcomes and satisfaction, lessens risk of medical errors, and decreases personnel turnover. A **just culture** is an environment built on trust, accountability, open and honest communication, integrity, and common goals and is free of retribution.[31] Behaviors that undermine a culture of safety may be obvious or subtle. Just a few examples are verbal outbursts, physical threats, refusing to participate in hand-over communications, rolling of the eyes, and gossiping. In 2008, TJC published an alert citing a research study with findings that 40% of health care workers chose not to speak up during patient care when in the presence of a known intimidator.[32] In January 2009, TJC published a leadership standard that discussed accountability for addressing behaviors that undermine a culture of safety. Three key parts of the leadership standard to address these behaviors are implementing a zero-tolerance policy for disruptive behaviors, educating all health care team members about the policy, and holding all team members accountable for their behaviors.[32]

Risk Management

The role of risk management in health care is to identify potential areas of patient health risk and implement strategies to prevent sentinel events. TJC defines a **sentinel event** as an alteration in safe patient care that results in death, permanent harm, or temporary harm requiring a life-sustaining intervention.[33] After a sentinel event occurs, the involved team members are required to complete an adverse event report.

The adverse event report is the first step in initiating a **root cause analysis** (RCA). An RCA is a comprehensive analysis of systems and processes that may have led to a sentinel event.[33] During an RCA, the health care team, in collaboration with the risk manager, works to identify factors that contributed to the sentinel event. Identification of strategies that can or should have been implemented to prevent the event is the primary goal of an RCA. TJC does not require sentinel events to be reported; however, voluntary reporting has several advantages, including presenting a just culture and an environment of transparency. TJC has multiple resources available to support facilities with an RCA, including patient safety specialists.[17,34] Patients have a right to expect safe care with positive outcomes during the perioperative experience.

> **EXAM TIP**
> Sentinel events require immediate action and should be reported.

Patient Rights and Advocacy

Patients have a specific bill of rights related to expectations of health care. During the perioperative experience patients are unable to advocate for themselves related to sedation and the inability to actively participate in decision-making during a surgical procedure. The perioperative nurse must act as the patient's advocate at all times but especially during the perioperative experience.

Patient advocacy applies to both the patient and the family. Perioperative nurses have many responsibilities in the role of patient advocate (Table 9.2). Nurses have a duty to patients that includes a commitment to providing safe, effective health care. Duty also refers to the nurse's obligation to serve the nursing profession by positively influencing the health of society as a whole.[17] **Ethical practice** is outlined in the ANA Code of Ethics. Ethics are the moral principles that guide the profession of nursing and help to guide the ethical behavior and practice of the perioperative nurse. One topic that is both a patient right and a duty for the patient advocate is protection of patient confidentiality. Patient confidentiality is protected through compliance with Health Insurance Portability and Accountability (HIPAA) regulations published by the CMS. Examples of HIPAA compliance include safety precautions when faxing patient information, discussing patient information in private areas, and never leaving computers displaying patient information unattended. Patient advocacy is both a duty and a responsibility of the perioperative nurse.

TABLE 9.2 Nurse's Role as Patient Advocate[1]

- Form a bond with the patient, family, and significant others that demonstrates sincerity and caring
- Promote the sharing of feelings
- Promote a safe environment for the patient, family, and significant others to ask questions
- Provide information on expectations to reduce anxiety
- Assist the patient with making informed decisions throughout the perioperative experience
- Share all pertinent patient information with the health care team
- Actively protect the patient throughout the perioperative experience by providing oversight of patient care activities
- Maintain communication with the family and significant others during the perioperative experience
- Protect the patient's rights by adhering to the patient's own advanced directives for patient care

1. Phillips N. Foundations of perioperative patient care standards. In: *Berry & Kohn's Operating Room Technique*. 13th ed. St Louis, MO: Elsevier; 2017:16.

Delegation

Delegation is when a nurse transfers certain tasks to a person who is competent to perform the task and within the five rights of delegation (Table 9.3). When nursing tasks are delegated the nurse still maintains accountability for the tasks performed. The NCSBN established guidelines for the delegation of nursing duties. The five rights have been identified as requirements when a nurse delegates a nursing duty to unlicensed assistive personnel.[35]

TABLE 9.3 The Five Rights of Delegation[1]

1	Right Task
2	Right Person
3	Right Circumstance
4	Right Communication and Direction
5	Right Supervision and Evaluation

1. Steelman VM. Concepts basic to perioperative nursing. In: Rothrock JC, ed. *Alexander's Care of the Patient in Surgery*. 15th ed. St Louis, MO; Elsevier; 2015:1-15.

Key Concepts and Review

Professional accountability describes the nurse's commitment to being held accountable for the care he or she provides and promoting behaviors that advance and positively influence the characteristics of nursing professionalism. The nursing profession is a calling that requires a specific knowledge base, intense academic preparation, and licensure. The IOM's *Future of Nursing* report lists four key messages that outline areas nurses should become more involved in to effect the change necessary for improved patient outcomes and advancing the nursing profession. Adherence to national standards and guidelines for practice is essential to provide safe patient care based on current research and EBP standards. A plan for continuous professional development is the foundation for all perioperative nurses to increase their knowledge base, obtain advanced degrees, maintain competency, obtain specialty certification, and challenge mediocrity while demonstrating professional accountability.

References

1. Phillips N. Foundations of perioperative patient care standards. In: *Berry & Kohn's Operating Room Technique.* 13th ed. St Louis, MO: Elsevier; 2017:15-35.
2. Privacy and security information. Centers for Medicare & Medicaid Services. Updated June 21, 2016. https://www.cms.gov/Regulations-and-Guidance/Administrative-Simplification/HIPAA-ACA/index.html.
3. Hospital-acquired conditions. Centers for Medicare & Medicaid Services. Updated August 18, 2015. https://www.cms.gov/Medicare/Medicare-Fee-for-Service-Payment/HospitalAcqCond/Hospital-Acquired_Conditions.html.
4. About OSHA. The Occupational Safety and Health Administration. https://www.osha.gov/about.html.
5. About The Joint Commission. The Joint Commission. http://www.jointcommission.org/about_us/about_the_joint_commission_main.aspx.
6. National Patient Safety Goals. The Joint Commission. 2017. http://www.jointcommission.org/standards_information/npsgs.aspx.
7. Surgical Care Improvement Project. The Joint Commission. http://www.jointcommission.org/assets/1/6/Surgical%20Care%20Improvement%20Project.pdf.
8. Hospital Accreditation. DNV-GL Healthcare. 2015. http://dnvglhealthcare.com/accreditations/hospital-accreditation.
9. About NCSBN. National Council of State Boards of Nursing. January 2016. https://www.ncsbn.org/about.htm.
10. Nurse Practice Act, rules & regulations. National Council of State Boards of Nursing. https://ncsbn.org/nurse-practice-act.htm.
11. Russell KA. Nurse Practice Acts guide and govern nursing practice. *J Nurs Reg.* 2012;3(3):36-42.
12. Code of Ethics for Nurses. American Nurses Association. http://nursingworld.org/codeofethics.
13. About AORN. AORN, Inc. http://aorn.org/about-aorn.
14. AORN's Perioperative Explications for the ANA *Code of Ethics for Nurses with Interpretive Statements.* 2017. https://www.aorn.org/guidelines/clinical-resources/code-of-ethics [member access only].
15. Standards of perioperative nursing. In: *Guidelines for Perioperative Practice.* Denver, CO: AORN, Inc; 2015: 693-708. http://www.aorn.org/guidelines/clinical-resources/aorn-standards.
16. Alidina K. Professionalism in post-licensure nurses in developed countries. *J Nurs Educ Pract.* 2013;3(5):128-137.
17. Stobinski JX. Professionalism. In: *The Surgical Services Management Certificate of Mastery Program.* Denver, CO: The Competency and Credentialing Institute; 2014:1-73.
18. Rachel MM. Accountability: a concept worth revisiting. *American Nurse Today.* 2012;7(3). https://www.americannursetoday.com/accountability-a-concept-worth-revisiting/.
19. Rifkin R. Americans rate nurses highest on honesty, ethical standards. *Social Issues.* December 18, 2014. http://www.gallup.com/poll/180260/americans-rate-nurses-highest-honesty-ethical-standards.aspx.
20. Magnet Recognition Program Overview. 2015. American Nurses Credentialing Center. http://www.nursecredentialing.org/Magnet/ProgramOverview.
21. Institute of Medicine. Committee on the Robert Wood Johnson Foundation Initiative on the Future of Nursing. *The Future of Nursing: Leading Change, Advancing Health.* Washington, DC: National Academies Press; 2010.
22. The Joint Commission 2009 Requirements Related to the Provision of Culturally Competent Patient-Centered Care Hospital Accreditation Program (HAP). The Joint Commission. http://www.jointcommission.org/assets/1/6/2009_CLASRelatedStandardsHAP.pdf.
23. Stobinski JX. Nursing's invisible architecture: individual responsibility for professional development. *AORN J.* 2015;102(4):324-328.
24. Wright D. *The Ultimate Guide to Competency Assessment in Health Care.* 3rd ed. Minneapolis, MN: Creative Health Care Management, Inc; 2005.
25. Certification. American Nurses Credentialing Center. 2012. http://nursecredentialing.org/Certification/CertMisc/WhyCertify.pdf.

26. Stobinski JX. Certification and patient safety. *AORN J.* 2015;101(3):374-378.
27. Schroeter K. The value of certification. *J Trauma Nurs.* 2015;22(2):53-54.
28. Melnyck BM, Fineout-Overholt E. *Evidenced-Based Practice in Nursing and Healthcare: A Guide to Best Practice.* Philadelphia, PA: Lippincott Williams & Wilkins; 2011.
29. Polit DF, Beck CT. *Essentials of Nursing Research: Appraising Evidence for Nursing Practice.* Philadelphia, PA: Lippincott Williams & Wilkins; 2010.
30. Brown CG. The Iowa Model of Evidence-Based Practice to Promote Quality Care: an illustrated example in oncology nursing. *Clin J Oncol Nurs.* April 2014;18(2):157-159.
31. Lockhart L. Does your organization have a just culture? *Nurs Made Incredibly Easy.* 2015;13(1):55.
32. Sentinel event data: behaviors that undermine a culture of safety. The Joint Commission. July 9, 2008. http://www.jointcommission.org/assets/1/18/sea_40.pdf.
33. Sentinel event policy and procedures. The Joint Commission. November 19, 2014. http://www.jointcommission.org/sentinel_event_policy_and_procedures.
34. Sentinel event data: root causes by event type 2004—3Q 2015. The Joint Commission. November 13, 2015. https://hcupdate.files.wordpress.com/2016/02/2015-11-se-root-causes-by-event-type-2004-q32015.pdf.
35. Steelman VM. Concepts basic to perioperative nursing. In: Rothrock JC, ed. *Alexander's Care of the Patient in Surgery.* 15th ed. St Louis, MO; Elsevier; 2015:1-15.

Practice Exam Questions

1. A _____ is an environment where actions are analyzed to determine accountability and reparations are enacted when appropriate.
    a. just culture
    b. culture of accountability
    c. culture of communication
    d. learning culture

2. Collecting and evaluating information to assess current processes are known as
    a. research utilization.
    b. change implementation.
    c. evidence-based practice.
    d. quality improvement.

3. The Joint Commission has provided guidance on _____ processes to address unexpected occurrences that have resulted or may result in patient injury or death.
    a. root cause analysis
    b. sentinel event
    c. error identification
    d. process analysis

4. *The Standards of Professional Perioperative Professional Practice* identifies key behaviors of a professional that include maintaining competency and current knowledge in the perioperative specialty and
    a. a pursuit of lifelong learning.
    b. an understanding of legislative matters.
    c. a commitment to precepting.
    d. an ability to identify patient outcomes.

5. The purpose of the _____ is that it contains statements related to ethical obligations, duties, standards, and a nurse's commitment to society.
    a. *Guidelines for Perioperative Practice*
    b. *Standards of Perioperative Nursing*
    c. *The Future of Nursing: Leading Change, Advancing Health*
    d. *Code of Ethics for Nurses with Interpretive Statements*

6. What professional nursing behavior is evidenced by mutual trust, recognition, and respect among all members of the health care team in a shared decision-making process?
    a. Conflict resolution
    b. Just culture
    c. Collaboration
    d. Advocacy

7. Which standard of perioperative nursing is represented by completing an individualized orientation based on identified learning needs and seeking experience to maintain skills and competency?
    A. Quality of practice
    B. Professional practice evaluation
    C. Education
    D. Evaluation

8. What type of research involves evaluating the link among patient characteristics, nursing care delivery, and the results of that care?
    A. Process
    B. Outcomes
    C. Implementation
    D. Results

9. What trait of professionalism is used to describe telling the truth and keeping promises?
    A. Honesty
    B. Veracity
    C. Fidelity
    D. Excellence

10. The Center for Transforming Healthcare is part of _____, which is dedicated to encouraging cultures of safety for patients and personnel.
    A. the World Health Organization
    B. The Joint Commission
    C. the Centers for Disease Control and Prevention
    D. the Institute of Medicine

Answers with Supported Rationales

1. Answer A is correct. A just culture allows for the discussion of errors in an environment free of fear of punishment. Such discussion includes risk factors and processes that may have contributed to the identified error. A culture of safety is when a facility promotes resources and education for safe patient care and includes the patient and family in the decision-making process. Reference: AORN Toolkit: Creating a Practice Environment of Safety. February 2011. AORN, Inc. https://www.aorn.org/guidelines/clinical-resources/tool-kits.

2. Answer C is correct. Evidence-based practice (EBP) is the process of obtaining and analyzing data to address process changes that may be needed to improve patient care. After the evidence is evaluated, a plan is created to use this evidence, a process known as research utilization (RU). Quality improvement is a process that uses both EBP and RU to improve quality measures and patient outcomes. Reference: Steelman VM. Concepts basic to perioperative nursing. In: Rothrock JC, ed. *Alexander's Care of the Patient in Surgery*. 15th ed. St Louis, MO: Elsevier; 2015:9.

3. Answer B is correct. Sentinel events, unexpected patient occurrences, signal the need for immediate investigation. The investigation is a root cause analysis (RCA). An RCA identifies changes in current performance standards that may have led to the occurrence. Reference: Murphy EK. Patient safety and risk management. In: Rothrock JC, ed. *Alexander's Care of the Patient in Surgery*. 15th ed. St Louis, MO: Elsevier; 2015:18.

4. Answer A is correct. A commitment to and pursuit of lifelong learning are part of AORN's description of professional practice as well as the Institute of Medicine's report *The Future of Nursing: Leading Change, Advancing Health*. Lifelong learning is necessary for perioperative nurses to stay current with the pace of technological change and to advance nursing professionalism. Reference: Steelman VM. Concepts basic to perioperative nursing. In: Rothrock JC, ed. *Alexander's Care of the Patient in Surgery*. 15th ed. St Louis, MO: Elsevier; 2015:390, 3.

5. Answer D is correct. The Code of Ethics for Nurses is focused on outlining the goals, values, and obligations to the profession of nursing. The foundation of professional nursing is ethics. Reference: AORN's Perioperative Explications for the ANA *Code of Ethics for Nurses with Interpretive Statements*. 2017. https://www.aorn.org/guidelines/clinical-resources/code-of-ethics [member access only].

6. Answer C is correct. Collaboration is an effort by the nurse and members of the interdisciplinary health care team to reach a common goal. The key aspect in collaborative cooperation for the team is an effective decision-making process. Reference: AORN's Perioperative Explications for the ANA *Code of Ethics for Nurses with Interpretive Statements*. 2017. https://www.aorn.org/guidelines/clinical-resources/code-of-ethics [member access only].

7. Answer C is correct. Acquiring and maintaining specialized knowledge and skills related to perioperative nursing practice are essential to representing the standard of perioperative nursing education. Reference: Standards of perioperative nursing. In: *Guidelines for Perioperative Practice*. Denver, CO: AORN, Inc; 2015:699. http://www.aorn.org/guidelines/clinical-resources/aorn-standards.

8. Answer B is correct. Outcomes research is a process that includes evaluating the process of implemented standards of care and helps to identify best practices. Reference: Steelman VM. Concepts basic to perioperative nursing. In: Rothrock JC, ed. *Alexander's Care of the Patient in Surgery*. 15th ed. St Louis, MO: Elsevier; 2015:5.

9. Answer C is correct. Fidelity is important for promoting a nursing work environment that is based on honesty and trust. When the health care team is able to believe in the word of nursing professionals, a sense of trust is built. Reference: Murphy EK. Patient safety and risk management. In: Rothrock JC, ed. *Alexander's Care of the Patient in Surgery*. 15th ed. St Louis, MO: Elsevier; 2015:44.

10. Answer B is correct. The Joint Commission's Center for Transforming Healthcare has found inadequate safety culture to be a significant contributing factor to adverse outcomes. Reference: The Joint Commission: Sentinel Event Alert: The essential role of leadership in developing a safety culture. https://www.jointcommission.org/assets/1/18/SEA_57_Safety_Culture_Leadership_0317.pdf.

Practice Exam

100-Question CNOR Practice Exam

The questions in this 100-question practice exam reflect the same percentage of questions by subject area and follow the same format as the actual CNOR exam. In some cases the practice questions explore concepts presented in this exam prep book in greater depth. In other cases, they reflect to what extent a topic or concept may be covered on the exam. As with any exam prep product, the content review and practice questions are based on careful analysis of the subject areas and the question format of the exam—not on exposure to the exam itself, which would be in violation of test development standards. Although the practice questions in this book are similar to the structure and content of the exam, they will not be used in the actual exam.

CNOR PRACTICE EXAM (100 QUESTIONS)

1. Aseptic technique is also known as
   A. clean technique.
   B. sterile technique.
   C. sterilization.
   D. decontamination.

2. An intrinsic factor that contributes to the development of a pressure injury is
   A. pressure.
   B. hypothermia.
   C. diabetes mellitus.
   D. general anesthesia.

3. Which of the following helps determine a patient's discharge destination?
   A. Written discharge instructions from anesthesiology and medical staff
   B. Risk of postoperative complications
   C. Standardized pain scoring
   D. General condition and readiness for discharge

4. Central nervous system (CNS) signs and symptoms of local anesthetic systemic toxicity (LAST) include
   A. hypertension.
   B. numbness of lips and tongue.
   C. respiratory depression.
   D. elevated temperature.

5. Autologous bone grafts should be stored at a temperature of
   A. 68°F (20°C).
   B. 32°F (0°C).
   C. −4°F (−20°C).
   D. −112°F (−80°C).

6. When providing patient education for a child, it is important to understand which learning characteristics of children?
   A. Children are self-directed.
   B. Children use intrinsic thought processes.
   C. Children respond to use of activities that follow transitions of maturity.
   D. Children respond to a trial-and-error approach.

246

7. Which of the following actions would decrease radiation exposure during fluoroscopy procedures?
    A. Positioning the patient as close to the tube as possible.
    B. Positioning the patient as far from the image intensifier as possible.
    C. Positioning the patient as far from the monitor as possible.
    D. Positioning the patient as close to the image intensifier as possible.

8. A perioperative nurse is assisting an anesthesia professional with a rapid-sequence induction by providing cricoid pressure using the Sellick maneuver. Which of the following is the most appropriate description of this technique?
    A. Exerting down-and-up pressure on the cricoid cartilage to compress the trachea.
    B. Palpating for the thyroid cartilage and exerting pressure on it with a dominant index finger and thumb to occlude the esophagus.
    C. Applying pressure on the cricoid cartilage to occlude the esophagus.
    D. Maintaining pressure on the thyroid cartilage until anesthesia verifies placement.

9. A diagnostic procedure that relies on radiofrequency waves to reproduce cross-sectional images of the body without exposing the patient to ionizing radiation is
    A. ultrasonography.
    B. positron emission tomography.
    C. computed tomography.
    D. magnetic resonance imaging.

10. Which of the following movements of a powered instrument is used to drill holes or to insert screws, wires, and pins?
    A. Reciprocating
    B. Oscillating
    C. Alternating
    D. Rotating

11. What is the most likely cause of a rapid decrease in blood pressure and heart rate for a patient being infused when 1.5% glycine is used for irrigation?
    A. Anaphylactic reaction
    B. Myocardial infarction
    C. TUR syndrome
    D. Pulmonary embolus

12. Preoperative teaching is most effective when patients have a readiness to learn and the perioperative nurse teaches from _____ different levels.
    A. two
    B. three
    C. four
    D. five

13. When caring for a patient with sickle cell anemia, the perioperative nurse should
    A. raise the temperature in the operating room to between 26.7°C and 29.4°C (80°F and 85°F).
    B. have relaxing music playing in the operating room to avoid overstimulation.
    C. administer a liter of normal saline prior to surgery to ensure that the patient is well hydrated.
    D. allow a family member or friend to sit with the patient in the preoperative area and in the postanesthesia care unit.

14. A _____ type of fire extinguisher should be used in an operating or procedure room.
    A. wet chemical
    B. carbon dioxide
    C. halogen
    D. dry powder

15. _____ requires purposeful, outcomes-directed thought and is driven by patient need.
    A. Critical thinking
    B. Assessment
    C. Diagnosis
    D. Planning

16. A hemoglobin value considered to be within normal limits for an adult woman is
    A. 10 g/dL to 14 g/dL.
    B. 12 g/dL to 16 g/dL.
    C. 14 g/dL to 18 g/dL.
    D. 16 g/dL to 20 g/dL.

17. What technique is the safest to use when securing the arms at the patient's sides?
    A. Drawing a sheet under the arms, over the patient, and using non-penetrating clamps to secure it to the opposite side.
    B. Drawing a sheet over the arm and then sliding it between the mattress and the bed.
    C. Drawing a sheet over the arm and tucking it between the patient and the mattress.
    D. Wrapping the patient's arm with padding and securing it to the body with a safety belt.

18. Which of the following intraoperative medication orders would prompt a perioperative nurse to have a urinary catheter readily available?
    A. Levetiracetam 1gm IV after incision
    B. Cefepime 2 g/100 mL IV infusion within 30 minutes of incision
    C. Ketorolac 20 mg IV push before incision
    D. Mannitol 10% 10 g/100 mL after incision

19. Which of the following is defined as the process of teaching adults?
    A. Pedagogy
    B. Andragogy
    C. Cognition
    D. Orientation

20. Personal protective equipment that must be worn when mixing and inserting methyl methacrylate bone cement includes
    A. head coverings.
    B. latex gloves.
    C. goggles.
    D. shoe covers.

21. Which of the following nursing actions would best support a positive outcome for a nursing diagnosis of potential for alteration in skin integrity?
    A. Place a warming blanket on the OR bed prior to the patient coming into the operating room.
    B. Obtain an appropriate positioning device that will aid in redistribution of pressure.
    C. Place a several layers of linen material on the OR bed.
    D. Position the patient in a supine position with arms tucked at sides and palms facing down to protect the ulnar nerve.

22. Which of the following describes point-of-use cleaning of a surgical instrument?
    A. Prior to the procedure, the instrument is cleaned with a moist sponge.
    B. During the procedure, the instrument is cleaned with a moist sponge after each use.
    C. After the procedure, the instrument is cleaned with a moist sponge in the sterile processing area.
    D. Continually clean the instrument with a sponge moistened with saline.

23. Venous air embolism is most likely to occur when the patient is in the _____ position.
    A. supine
    B. sitting
    C. lithotomy
    D. lateral

24. A subjective sign of the existence and intensity of postoperative pain is the patient's
    A. self-report.
    B. change in blood pressure.
    C. facial expression.
    D. protective guarding behavior.

25. A nursing diagnosis that considers a patient is at risk means the nursing interventions
    A. are directed at prevention.
    B. will not affect the patient's outcome.
    C. should be performed only as needed.
    D. may put the patient at risk.

26. Signs of a blood transfusion reaction include which of the following?
    A. Hypotension, hemoglobinuria, hyperthermia
    B. Weak pulse, hemoglobinuria, hypertension
    C. Hypothermia, weak pulse, tachycardia
    D. Hypothermia, hemoglobinuria, tachycardia

27. When performing time out, which of the following should be verified?
    A. Laboratory studies
    B. Instruments
    C. Suture
    D. Procedure

28. Pneumatic tourniquets should be deflated under the direction of
    A. the surgeon and the scrub person.
    B. the anesthesia professional and the circulating nurse.
    C. the circulating nurse and the surgeon.
    D. the surgeon and the anesthesia professional.

29. Which organization should be consulted about a perioperative RN's scope of practice related to administration of medications for moderate sedation?
    A. Association of periOperative Registered Nurses
    B. The Joint Commission
    C. State board of nursing
    D. Centers for Medicare & Medicaid Services

30. A perioperative nurse is monitoring a patient under local anesthesia during a hernia repair when the patient reports a strange taste in the mouth. What is the most appropriate response by the perioperative nurse?
    A. Reassure the patient that it is a common sensation and will resolve soon after surgery.
    B. Check the patient's hemoglobin and hematocrit.
    C. Ask the patient to confirm nothing by mouth status.
    D. Call for help.

31. A 47-year-old Spanish-speaking male presents with abdominal pain. He does not speak or understand English. How should the nurse communicate with the patient?
    A. Use a family member to interpret.
    B. Use a trained medical interpreter.
    C. Speak loudly and slowly to the patient.
    D. Ask a bystander to interpret.

32. Which of the following actions terminates the direct perioperative nurse-patient relationship?
    A. Evaluating the degree of attainment of expected outcomes.
    B. Performing the postoperative assessment or follow-up telephone call.
    C. Attending conferences with the patient's physician and/or other caregivers.
    D. Suggesting comfort measures to help calm the patient.

33. Operating room floors should be cleaned with
    A. dry mops.
    B. brooms.
    C. vacuums.
    D. damp or wet mops.

34. A coworker in the operating room asks to see the patient's chart for the nurse's next case, stating that the patient is her neighbor. The nurse should
    A. state this would be a violation of the patient's privacy.
    B. hand over the patient's chart because they are neighbors.
    C. consult with the doctor about letting the coworker see the chart.
    D. ask their director to make the decision.

35. Surgery of the liver requires incising the external covering referred to as
    A. Glisson's capsule.
    B. Gerota's fascia.
    C. porta hepatis.
    D. hepatic fascia.

251

36. Which of the following is the most appropriate recommendation for hair removal prior to surgery?
    A. A depilatory should be used in the operating room.
    B. The patient should shave at home the night before surgery.
    C. A wet shave should be done in the operating room.
    D. The patient's hair should be clipped in the preoperative area.

37. Joey is a 4-year-old scheduled to have surgery. During preoperative teaching, the perioperative nurse knows that Joey's age-specific needs can best be met by
    A. allowing his parent or caregiver to explain what will happen.
    B. providing him privacy whenever possible.
    C. allowing him to handle the oxygen mask and ride in the wagon that will later take him to the OR.
    D. giving him a thorough explanation of everything that will happen.

38. "Flammable" antiseptic solutions differ from "combustible" ones in that
    A. flammable solutions have a flash point above 101.5°F.
    B. flammable solutions will not ignite.
    C. combustible solutions have a flash point above 100.0°F.
    D. combustible solutions will not ignite.

39. Which of the following is the most important action by the circulating nurse to reduce specimen error?
    A. Seeking clarification from the surgeon about the specimen site and side
    B. Calling the laboratory to confirm the proper storage solution for the specimen
    C. Asking the scrub person to verify the specimen
    D. Paging the surgical assistant postoperatively to identify the specimen

40. Using the nursing process, nursing interventions lead to
    A. planning.
    B. implementation.
    C. assessment.
    D. outcome identification.

41. Which of the following statements on wearing safety glasses is true?
    A. Eye protection must be worn if splashes, spray, or droplets of potentially hazardous materials can be reasonably anticipated.
    B. Corrective lenses fulfill the personal protective equipment requirements for ocular safety.
    C. Safety glasses enhance the visual field of the wearer.
    D. Wearers of corrective lenses are not permitted to wear either contacts or eyeglasses with their safety glasses.

42. When delegating a task, the circulating nurse should
    A. verify the task is within the scope of practice of the designee.
    B. provide a minimum of instructions on how to complete the task.
    C. give feedback to the designee based on personal experiences.
    D. assume the designee has the skills to perform the task.

43. A medication that should be administered for treatment of local anesthetic systemic toxicity crisis is
    A. lidocaine.
    B. epinephrine.
    C. 20% lipid emulsion.
    D. propofol.

44. Hospital policy should include the requirement of PPE for all personnel that are likely to come in contact with blood or infectious materials based on
    A. OSHA regulations.
    B. TJC standards.
    C. AORN Guidelines.
    D. CDC recommendations.

45. When double gloving, personnel should wear
    A. gloves one size larger for the first layer.
    B. gloves one size smaller for the first layer.
    C. gloves that are the same size for both layers.
    D. hypoallergenic gloves for the outer layer.

46. When preparing the skin for head and neck surgery, the circulating nurse understands that
    A. chlorhexidine gluconate should not be used for facial preps because corneal damage can occur if the cleanser is accidently introduced into the eye(s).
    B. cotton applicators should not be used for cleaning the external ear canal because they can puncture the inner ear.
    C. facial skin surfaces should be cleansed within 1 to 2 inches of the hair line.
    D. shaving the eyebrows should be avoided unless medically ordered.

47. Medication errors related to _____ may be prevented by the medication reconciliation process.
    A. procuring and prescribing
    B. transcribing and procuring
    C. prescribing and monitoring
    D. transcribing and prescribing

253

48. Deviation from a standardized procedure that is hospital policy suggests the need for
    A. a root cause analysis.
    B. a verbal warning.
    C. an evaluation of the procedure or staff.
    D. better communication.

49. A patient reports to the ambulatory surgery center for local anesthesia without sedation and claims that the surgeon gave him permission to drive himself home. The most appropriate action for the perioperative nurse is to
    A. cancel the surgery and reschedule when the patient has a ride.
    B. contact the social worker to assist in finding transportation for the patient.
    C. check for an order stating that the patient may drive himself home.
    D. allow the patient to leave when his postoperative Aldrete score is 10.

50. Which of the following are methods of sterilization?
    A. Chemical, mechanical, and biological
    B. Decontamination, disinfection, and pasteurization
    C. Thermal, chemical, and radiation
    D. Low-level disinfection, intermediate-level disinfection, and high-level disinfectionl

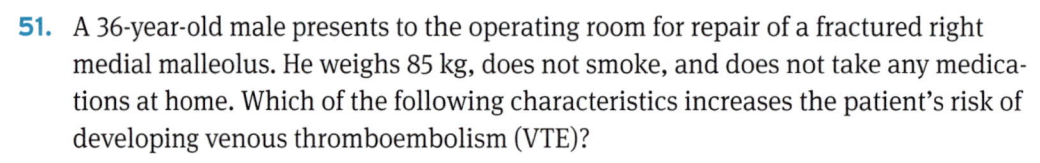

51. A 36-year-old male presents to the operating room for repair of a fractured right medial malleolus. He weighs 85 kg, does not smoke, and does not take any medications at home. Which of the following characteristics increases the patient's risk of developing venous thromboembolism (VTE)?
    A. His age
    B. His injury
    C. His weight
    D. His smoking status

52. During the preoperative assessment of an 82-year-old malnourished woman, the RN circulator determines that the patient is at an increased risk of
    A. postoperative hyperthermia.
    B. unplanned hypothermia.
    C. ineffective peripheral tissue perfusion.
    D. excess fluid volume.

53. Gelatin pads used for hemostasis absorb in
    A. 7 to 10 days.
    B. 10 to 20 days.
    C. 20 to 40 days.
    D. 60 to 90 days.

54. A collection of blood in a body cavity or space caused by uncontrolled bleeding or oozing is called
    A. hematoma.
    B. pseudoaneurysm.
    C. varicosity.
    D. contusion.

55. Policies and procedures for standardized transfer of care should reflect rules and recommendations from regulatory agencies and accreditation agencies as well as
    A. a contingency plan should a patient's status change.
    B. verbal confirmation via read-back of cardiac monitoring and oxygen needs.
    C. use of a checklist to ensure all parameters for transfer of patient care have been met.
    D. approval of regulatory agencies for transfer of patient care processes, as documented in the institution's policies and procedures.

56. A perioperative nurse is reviewing a patient's chart and notes that the patient will undergo a brain biopsy for symptoms of progressive dementia. Which of the following suspected pathogens would prompt the nurse to take additional actions during the perioperative period of this patient's care?
    A. Treponema pallidum bacteria
    B. Culex tritaeniorhynchus virus
    C. Neuro-Cutaneous Leishmania protozoa
    D. Proteinaceous prion

57. When a discrepancy is identified in the surgical count, the perioperative RN should
    A. organize the sterile field.
    B. perform a methodical wound exploration.
    C. remain in the room until the item is found.
    D. call for assistance.

58. A health care industry representative should
    A. not participate in direct patient care.
    B. bring additional equipment that was not requested.
    C. check in with materials management.
    D. open requested implants.

59. Which of the following demonstrates nursing professional development?
    A. Arriving to work on time every day.
    B. Assisting with room turnover between cases.
    C. Helping a coworker with his portfolio.
    D. Achieving certification.

60. The perioperative nurse identifies the patient's medical history in which phase of the nursing process?

   A. Assessment
   B. Diagnosis
   C. Planning
   D. Evaluation

61. Most complications occur within the first _____ after surgery.

   A. 4 hours
   B. 12 hours
   C. 48 hours
   D. 72 hours

62. The hand-over/hand-off report should be a standardized transfer of patient information from the current caregiver to the receiving caregiver. Strategies to avoid breakdown in hand-over communication include

   A. ensuring that the person reporting has had a rest break.
   B. documenting the unit personnel receiving the report.
   C. using a standardized documentation format such as SBAR (Situation, Background, Assessment, Recommendation).
   D. asking the anesthesia professional to confirm the accuracy of the hand-over report.

63. For which of the following should an incident report be completed?

   A. Surgeon arriving late for scheduled surgery
   B. Equipment malfunctioning during procedure
   C. Sponge, sharps, and instrument counts correct
   D. Scrub person not relieved for lunch break

64. Preprocedure verification should include confirmation of the

   A. presence or absence of surgical complications.
   B. complete and signed history and physical by attending physician.
   C. surgical count status.
   D. estimated blood loss.

65. When correcting a patient care entry in the electronic health record, the perioperative nurse should

   A. highlight the correction in a different color.
   B. double strike through the incorrect entry.
   C. add a rationale for the correction.
   D. enter corrected information at the end of the document.

66. A superficial surgical site infection (SSI) is defined as
    A. an infection of an organ/space that is routinely evident on x-ray film and that occurs within 30 days of surgery.
    B. an infected burn wound may that extends into the fascial and muscle layers.
    C. purulent drainage originating from proximate organs or compartments.
    D. an infection with purulent incisional drainage involving only skin or incisional subcutaneous tissue that occurs within 30 days of the surgical procedure.

67. Which of the following is a measure of the Surgical Care Improvement Project (SCIP)?
    A. Performing strict hand hygiene protocols.
    B. Administering the prophylactic antibiotic within 1 hour of surgical incision.
    C. Damp-dusting prior to the first case of the day.
    D. Performing a surgical count prior to the start of surgery.

68. Which of the following statements regarding radiation safety is true?
    A. All personnel in the operating room should wear wrap-around lead aprons when ionizing radiation is used.
    B. When a C-arm is in use, radiation emanates from the top part of the C-arm that is over the patient.
    C. Time, distance, and shielding are important components of radiation safety.
    D. When only one x-ray badge is worn, the proper placement is underneath the lead apron and along the neck line.

69. At the end of the case, loaned instruments should be
    A. disassembled, cleaned, decontaminated, inspected, and returned to the lending facility.
    B. disassembled, cleaned, decontaminated, inspected, sterilized, and returned to the lending facility.
    C. disassembled, decontaminated, sterilized, inspected, reassembled, and returned to the lending facility.
    D. placed in a biohazard plastic container, sealed, labeled, and returned to the lending facility.

70. Postoperative phone calls to the patient
    A. should be documented on the intraoperative record.
    B. should be made after the first week to accurately assess for complications.
    C. should not be part of a quality improvement initiative due to possible HIPAA violations.
    D. can be used to measure patient satisfaction.

71. The relative humidity in a restricted area should be maintained within a range of
    A. 15% to 60%.
    B. 15% to 70%.
    C. 20% to 60%.
    D. 20% to 70%.

72. What are the five rights of delegation?
    A. Right task, right circumstances, right practice, right communication and direction, and right supervision and evaluation
    B. Right task, right circumstances, right person, right communication and direction, and right supervision and evidence
    C. Right task, right circumstances, right person, right communication and direction, and right supervision and evaluation
    D. Right assignment, right circumstances, right person, right communication and direction, and right supervision and evaluation

73. An oxygen-enriched environment is present when the oxygen concentration in the operating room is greater than
    A. 21%.
    B. 22%.
    C. 26%.
    D. 28%.

74. Which of the following forms of protection is not considered part of standard precautions?
    A. Gloves
    B. Eye protection
    C. Head covers
    D. Sharps safety

75. Oxidized cellulose is a hemostatic agent that is absorbable but is contraindicated to be left in place after closure on
    A. bone.
    B. organs.
    C. vessels.
    D. ovaries.

76. When a surgical item is left in the patient, which of the following is a potential result of ensuing litigation?
    A. The surgical team could be found guilty of assault and battery.
    B. The surgical team could be found liable under the doctrine of respondeat superior ("let the master answer").
    C. The facility could be found liable under the doctrine of corporate negligence.
    D. The surgical team could be found liable under the doctrine of res ipsa loquitur ("the thing speaks for itself").

77. Corrective measures that may be implemented based on a multidisciplinary risk assessment following a variance in the parameters of the heating, ventilating, and air conditioning (HVAC) system include
    A. taking no action.
    B. discarding all disposable surgical supplies.
    C. terminal cleaning of the entire perioperative area.
    D. inventorying all perioperative supplies.

78. Marking the surgical site for procedures that involve laterality
    A. should be performed after the patient is anesthetized and positioned in the OR.
    B. can use different methodology depending on surgeon preference.
    C. should use marking that is clear and unambiguous.
    D. can be performed by any member of the surgical team.

79. When using a medical interpreter to speak with a patient, the perioperative nurse should
    A. maintain eye contact with the interpreter.
    B. speak loudly to ensure understanding.
    C. talk directly to the patient.
    D. smile at the interpreter for reassurance.

80. Which of the following factors should be considered when selecting products for use in the operating room?
    A. Indirect costs, and reimbursement potential
    B. Reimbursement potential and group purchasing organization contract pricing
    C. Direct costs and group purchasing organization contract pricing
    D. Direct costs, indirect costs, reimbursement potential, and group purchasing organization contract pricing

81. What is a desirable characteristic of antimicrobial skin cleansing agents?
    A. Broad spectrum
    B. Slow acting
    C. Abrasive
    D. Pathogen specific

82. When a parent is present during induction of a 6-month-old patient, the perioperative nurse explains the sequence of events and the atmosphere of the operating room. This is done to
    A. ensure cooperation of the child.
    B. decrease the parent's anxiety.
    C. comply with the surgical consent.
    D. minimize anesthesia distractions.

83. Which type of indicator should be used to validate air removal in an sterilizer cycle
    A. Class I
    B. Class II
    C. Class III
    D. Class IV

84. Shock resulting from anaphylaxis or sepsis is _____ shock.
    A. hemorrhagic
    B. cardiogenic
    C. vasogenic
    D. neurogenic

85. How many personnel are required to transfer an unconscious supine patient from the OR bed to a patient bed when a lifting frame or patient roller is used?
    A. Two
    B. Three
    C. Four
    D. Five

86. Which action should be taken when moisture is noted on the outside of a wrapped instrument tray?
    A. Open the tray starting with the closest flap.
    B. Leave the tray until it has cooled.
    C. Open the tray and return for reprocessing.
    D. Consult with the surgeon.

87. When should discharge teaching begin?
    A. In the PACU
    B. During preoperative teaching
    C. On the day of discharge
    D. In the surgeon's office prior to surgery

88. Which of the following is true about chromic suture?
    A. It is used most often as a fine suture material for the eye.
    B. It should be used immediately after removal from the packet.
    C. It is well suited for closing skin edges.
    D. It is a synthetic absorbable suture produced from strands of polymers.

89. The Agency for Healthcare Research and Quality (AHRQ) is one of the 12 agencies within the Department of Health and Human Services (DHHS). They are committed to safety and quality, effectiveness, and
    A. equality.
    B. culture.
    C. public information.
    D. efficiency.

90. A body mass index (BMI) equal to or above _____ kg/m² is considered obese.
    A. 22 kg/m²
    B. 28 kg/m²
    C. 30 kg/m²
    D. 40 kg/m²

91. A surgical blood loss of 750 mL to 1,500 mL is categorized as
    A. minor.
    B. moderate.
    C. major.
    D. catastrophic.

92. When preparing a room for the next patient after use by a confirmed tuberculosis (TB) patient, in addition to performing routine environmental decontamination, the air exchanges should be _____% complete.
    A. 99%
    B. 50%
    C. 65%
    D. 85%

93. When using a skin preparation solution that contains isopropyl alcohol, drape application should occur
    A. after wiping the area dry.
    B. after the skin and hair have dried.
    C. immediately after applying the prep.
    D. after waiting five minutes.

94. Before the patient's discharge and transfer to the surgical unit, the nurse completes a final
    A. assessment.
    B. evaluation.
    C. hand-off/hand-over report.
    D. standardized scoring.

95. Critical items should be processed by
    A. low-level disinfection.
    B. high-level disinfection.
    C. intermediate-level disinfection.
    D. sterilization.

96. The biggest risk associated with the supine position for obese patients is
    A. respiratory distress.
    B. spinal pressure.
    C. foot drop.
    D. shearing.

97. What is the correct workflow traffic pattern for instrument processing?
    A. Decontamination area, set assembly room, sterile processing, sterile storage, and case cart packing room
    B. Set assembly room, sterile processing, sterile storage, case cart packing room, and decontamination area
    C. Case cart packing room, decontamination area, set assembly room, sterile processing, and sterile storage
    D. Decontamination area, sterile processing, set assembly room, sterile storage, and case cart packing room

98. Ventricular fibrillation is characterized by
    A. an ectopic focus in the ventricles, causing the heart to beat prematurely.
    B. a rapid heartbeat caused by ventricular ischemia or irritability.
    C. an impulse originating in the ventricles and traveling to the rest of the myocardium.
    D. a total disorganization of ventricular activity.

99. Evidence-based practice (EBP) is a systematic, thorough process to identify a _____ issue, collect and evaluate evidence, design and implement a change, and evaluate the process.
    A. personal
    B. clinical
    C. corporate
    D. non-clinical

100. When the patient's arms are extended on arm boards, the palms should be positioned face up to decrease pressure on the
    A. brachial plexus.
    B. median nerve.
    C. ulnar nerve.
    D. radial nerve.

ANSWERS AND SUPPORTED RATIONALES for CNOR PRACTICE EXAM

1. Answer A is correct. Aseptic technique refers to clean methods of containing microbial contamination in the environment. The environment cannot be sterilized. Reference: Phillips N. Principles of aseptic and sterile technique. In: *Berry & Kohn's Operating Room Technique*. 13th ed. St Louis, MO: Elsevier; 2017:249.

2. Answer C is correct. An intrinsic factor is related to the health of the patient. Diabetes mellitus is an intrinsic factor that contributes to the development of a pressure injury. Heizenroth PA. Positioning the patient for surgery. In: Rothrock JC, ed. *Alexander's Care of the Patient in Surgery*. 15th ed. St Louis, MO: Elsevier; 2015:157.

3. Answer B is correct. The choice of discharge site is based on patient acuity, access to follow-up care, and the potential for postoperative complications. Reference: Hoch CR. Postoperative care. In: Lewis SL, Dirksen SR, Heitkemper MM, Bucher L. *Medical-Surgical Nursing: Assessment and Management of Clinical Problems*. 10th ed. St Louis, MO: Elsevier; 2017:344.

4. Answer B is correct. CNS symptoms of LAST include circumoral and tongue numbness. All other options are not considered part of the CNS. Reference: Guideline for care of the patient receiving local anesthesia. In: *Guidelines for Perioperative Practice*. Denver, CO: AORN, Inc; 2017:622.

5. Answer C is correct. Maintaining storage temperatures within recommended parameters of −4°F (−20°C) helps ensure that autografts are maintained in optimal conditions for successful replantation. Reference: Guideline for autologous tissue management. In: *Guidelines for Perioperative Practice*. Denver, CO: AORN, Inc; 2017:225.

6. Answer D is correct. When teaching children, using a trial-and-error approach is effective. Child learners are task-oriented, use extrinsic thought processes, and value self-esteem. Reference: Phillips N. Perioperative education. In: *Berry & Kohn's Operating Room Technique*. 13th ed. St Louis, MO: Elsevier; 2017:3, Table 1-2.

7. Answer D is correct. The x-ray beams originate from the tube and are captured by the image intensifier. Multiple studies have demonstrated that positioning the patient closer to the image intensifier results in a significantly decreased dose of radiation. Reference: Guideline for radiation safety. In: *Guidelines for Perioperative Practice*. Denver, CO: AORN, Inc; 2017:348.

8. Answer C is correct. The Sellick maneuver, more commonly known as cricoid pressure application, involves exerting downward pressure on the cricoid cartilage with the thumb and index finger of one hand to compress the esophagus. The Sellick maneuver is used to prevent potential aspiration during induction of anesthesia. Reference: Campell BD. Anesthesia. In: Rothrock JC, ed. *Alexander's Care of the Patient in Surgery*. 15th ed. St Louis, MO: Elsevier; 2015:140.

9. Answer D is correct. Magnetic resonance imaging stimulates disequilibrium in the nuclei of hydrogen atoms and the water of body cells. As nuclei return to their original state, they emit radiofrequency signals. Reference: Phillips N. Diagnostics, specimens, and oncologic considerations. In: *Berry & Kohn's Operating Room Technique*. 13th ed. St Louis, MO: Elsevier; 2017:388.

10. Answer D is correct. Rotary movement is used to drill holes or to insert screws, wires, or pins. Reciprocating and oscillating movements are used to cut or remove bone. Alternating movement should not be used. Reference: Phillips N. Surgical instrumentation. In: *Berry & Kohn's Operating Room Technique*. 13th ed. St Louis, MO: Elsevier; 2017:341.

11. Answer C is correct. The patient is most likely experiencing TUR syndrome associated with excessive glycine absorption. Reference: Guideline for minimally invasive surgery. In: *Guidelines for Perioperative Practice*. Denver, CO: AORN, Inc; 2017:636.

12. Answer B is correct. There are three different levels of preoperative teaching: information, psychosocial support, and skill training. Information should include explanations of procedure and what to expect throughout the phases of perioperative care. Psychosocial support includes encouraging the patient to share anxiety and supporting coping mechanisms. Skill training allows the patient to learn the skills required to function after the procedure and provides confidence and understanding. Reference: Phillips N. Preoperative preparation of the patient. In: *Berry & Kohn's Operating Room Technique*. 13th ed. St Louis, MO: Elsevier; 2017:371.

13. Answer A is correct. The sickle cell patient must be kept warm to prevent hypothermia and meet increased demands for oxygen. Reference: Phillips N. Potential perioperative complications. In: *Berry & Kohn's Operating Room Technique*. 13th ed. St Louis, MO: Elsevier; 2017:612.

14. Answer B is correct. The National Fire Protection Association recommends using either a water mist or carbon dioxide extinguisher for extinguishing fires in the operating room. Reference: Guideline for a safe environment of care, part 1. In: *Guidelines for Perioperative Practice*. Denver, CO: AORN, Inc; 2017:249.

15. Answer A is correct. Scientific nursing interventions, critical thinking and clinical reasoning, and caring, comforting behaviors are at the heart of perioperative nursing. Critical thinking is a thoughtful process important in the performance of perioperative nursing care versus being part of the nursing process. Reference: Steelman VM. Concepts basic to perioperative nursing. In: Rothrock JC, ed. *Alexander's Care of the Patient in Surgery*. 15th ed. St Louis, MO: Elsevier; 2015:2.

16. Answer B is correct. Normal hemoglobin values are 12 g/dL to 16 g/dL for women and 14 g/dL to 18 g/dL for men. Reference: Phillips N. Potential perioperative complications. In: *Berry & Kohn's Operating Room Technique*. 13th ed. St Louis, MO: Elsevier; 2017:611.

17. Answer C is correct. A safe and effective way to prevent nerve injury of the upper extremities is to secure the patient's arms by smoothly wrapping the draw sheet over the arm and then tucking it under the patient's body to prevent arm slippage during surgery. Heizenroth PA. Positioning the patient for surgery. In: Rothrock JC, ed. *Alexander's Care of the Patient in Surgery*. 15th ed. St Louis, MO: Elsevier; 2015:163.

18. Answer D is correct. Hypertonic mannitol is a nonosmotic diuretic that is often used during brain surgery to promote diuresis and therefore decrease intracranial pressure. Reference: Krizman Germanovich SJ. Neurosurgery. In: Rothrock JC, ed. *Alexander's Care of the Patient in Surgery*. 15th ed. St Louis, MO: Elsevier; 2015:777.

19. Answer B is correct. Teaching and learning processes related to mature adults are known as andragogy. Reference: Phillips N. Perioperative education. In: *Berry & Kohn's Operating Room Technique*. 13th ed. St Louis, MO: Elsevier; 2017:1.

20. Answer C is correct. Methyl methacrylate can penetrate many latex compounds. Methyl methacrylate fumes may irritate the eyes; therefore, eye protection must be worn when mixing and inserting methyl methacrylate bone cement. PPE is defined as any clothing or other equipment that protects a person from exposure to chemicals. PPE may include gloves, aprons, chemical splash goggles, and impervious clothing. Reference: Guideline for a safe environment of care, part 1. In: *Guidelines for Perioperative Practice*. Denver, CO: AORN, Inc; 2017:258.

21. Answer B is correct. Warming blankets and extra layers of material should not be placed under the patient. The goal is to use equipment that is designed to redistribute pressure and that decreases the risk for positioning injuries. Palms should face the patient when the arms are tucked. Reference: Guideline for positioning the patient. In: *Guidelines for Perioperative Practice*. Denver, CO: AORN, Inc; 2018:688.

22. Answer B is correct. One type of point-of-use cleaning of a surgical instrument is when the instrument is cleaned with a sterile, water-soaked sponge after each use during the procedure. Point of use cleaning also occurs when an instrument is cleaned at the point of use immediately following the procedure. Saline should not be used for point of use cleaning. Cleaning at the point of use prevents bioburden from building up on the instrument and helps maintain the life of the instrument. Reference: Phillips N. Surgical instrumentation. In: *Berry & Kohn's Operating Room Technique*. 13th ed. St Louis, MO: Elsevier; 2017:343.

23. Answer B is correct. Venous air embolism can occur when air or gas is drawn into the circulation by the veins above the level of the heart and is most likely to occur during neurosurgery or open shoulder surgery in the sitting or semi-sitting position Reference: Guideline for positioning the patient. In: *Guidelines for Perioperative Practice*. Denver, CO: AORN, Inc; 2017:2018:713.

24. Answer A is correct. A subjective sign is what the patient states. Objective signs include results of physical assessment or observation. Reference: Odom-Forren J. Postoperative patient care and pain management. In: Rothrock JC, ed. *Alexander's Care of the Patient in Surgery*. 15th ed. St Louis, MO: Elsevier; 2015:271, Box 10-2.

25. Answer A is correct. For perioperative patients, nursing diagnoses that consider a patient at risk for an outcome mean the problem has not yet occurred, and the interventions are directed at prevention. Reference: Steelman VM. Concepts basic to perioperative nursing. In: Rothrock JC, ed. *Alexander's Care of the Patient in Surgery*. 15th ed. St Louis, MO: Elsevier; 2015:5.

26. Answer A is correct. A blood transfusion reaction reflects vasomotor instability and is evidenced by hypotension, hemoglobinuria, and hyperthermia. Many common signs are not readily obvious when a patient is under anesthesia. Reference: Spry C. Infection prevention and control. In: Rothrock JC, ed. *Alexander's Care of the Patient in Surgery*. 15th ed. St Louis, MO: Elsevier; 2015:38.

27. Answer D is correct. Ensuring correct-site surgery requires affirmation of the following: correct patient, position, site, procedures, equipment, images, and implants (if required). Reference: Phillips N. Foundations of perioperative patient care standards. In: *Berry & Kohn's Operating Room Technique*. 13th ed. St Louis, MO: Elsevier; 2017:21.

28. Answer D is correct. Hemodynamic changes may occur when the tourniquet is deflated. As the tourniquet cuff deflates, the anesthetic agent may be released into the circulatory system, causing systemic effects. Coordination among members of the perioperative team under the direction of the surgeon and the anesthesia professional can

facilitate management of the patient's physiologic status during this period of rapid change. Reference: Guideline for care of patients undergoing pneumatic tourniquet-assisted procedures. In: *Guidelines for Perioperative Practice*. Denver, CO: AORN, Inc; 2017:169.

29. Answer C is correct. The professional registered nurse's scope of practice is defined by the individual state board of nursing. Reference: Guideline for care of the patient receiving moderate sedation/analgesia. In: *Guidelines for Perioperative Practice*. Denver, CO: AORN, Inc; 2017:661.

30. Answer D is correct. The patient's symptom may represent a local anesthetic systemic toxicity (LAST), which would require urgent treatment under the direction of a qualified health care provider such as an anesthesia professional or a code team. In addition to altered taste (eg, metallic taste), other symptoms of LAST are consistent with neurologic (eg, numbness, confusion, seizures) and/or cardiovascular collapse (eg, bradycardia/hypotension). Reference: Guideline for care of the patient receiving local anesthesia. In: *Guidelines for Perioperative Practice*. Denver, CO: AORN, Inc; 2017:623.

31. Answer B is correct. Using a trained medical interpreter decreases errors and misunderstanding of the explanations of care. Using a family member may cause either the family member or patient to not be truthful to the care provider due to embarrassment. Using a bystander to interpret is a violation of HIPAA. Reference: Lenart J. Health disparities and culturally competent care. In: Lewis SL, Dirksen SR, Heitkemper MM, Bucher L. *Medical-Surgical Nursing: Assessment and Management of Clinical Problems*. 10th ed. St Louis, MO: Elsevier; 2017:31.

32. Answer B is correct. The postoperative assessment or follow-up telephone call terminates the direct perioperative nurse-patient relationship. Reference: Phillips N. Postoperative patient care. In: *Berry & Kohn's Operating Room Technique*. 13th ed. St Louis, MO: Elsevier; 2017:790.

33. Answer D is correct. Wet and moist mopping produce fewer aerosols and are most effective in reducing organic soil in the environment. Reference: Guideline for environmental cleaning. In: *Guidelines for Perioperative Practice*. Denver, CO: AORN, Inc; 2017:11.

34. Answer A is correct. The federal Health Insurance Portability and Accountability Act (HIPAA) granted patients significant rights in respect to how their health information is used. Only health care personnel involved in direct patient care should have access to patient information. Reference: Murphy EK. Patient safety and risk management. In: Rothrock JC, ed. *Alexander's Care of the Patient in Surgery*. 15th ed. St Louis, MO: Elsevier; 2015:41.

35. Answer A is correct. The covering of the liver is made up of dense connective tissue called Glisson's capsule. Reference: Neil JA. Surgery of the liver, biliary tract, pancreas, and spleen. In: Rothrock JC, ed. *Alexander's Care of the Patient in Surgery*. 15th ed. St Louis, MO: Elsevier; 2015:350.

36. Answer D is correct. When necessary, hair at the surgical site should be removed in an area outside of the procedure room and in a manner that minimizes injury to the skin, such as by clipping or depilatory methods. Reference: Guideline for preoperative patient skin antisepsis. In: *Guidelines for Perioperative Practice*. Denver, CO: AORN, Inc; 2017:56.

37. Answer C is correct. The preschooler needs to explore and interact with his environment. Allowing him to familiarize himself ahead of time with some objects he may encounter can help ease anxiety. Reference: DiFusco LA. Pediatric surgery. In: Rothrock JC, ed. *Alexander's Care of the Patient in Surgery*. 15th ed. St Louis, MO: Elsevier; 2015:1013.

38. Answer C is correct. The threshold between flammable and combustible solutions is the flash point of 100.0°F, with flammable ones being below this temperature and combustible ones being above. All saturated flammable solutions should be removed prior to draping the patient. Fumes from volatile or combustible solutions may ignite without a direct connection to the source of ignition. Reference: Guideline for a safe environment of care, part 1. In: *Guidelines for Perioperative Practice*. Denver, CO: AORN, Inc; 2017:247.

39. Answer A is correct. The surgeon is the person with the most accurate information about the site/side of the specimen, how the specimen should be handled (eg, specific storage solution), and what kinds of tests should be requested of the pathology department. Reference: Guideline for specimen management. In: *Guidelines for Perioperative Practice*. Denver, CO: AORN, Inc; 2017:447.

40. Answer D is correct. Outcome identification describes the desired patient condition that can be achieved through nursing interventions. Reference: Steelman VM. Concepts basic to perioperative nursing. In: Rothrock JC, ed. *Alexander's Care of the Patient in Surgery*. 15th ed. St Louis, MO: Elsevier; 2015:5.

41. Answer A is correct. Health care personnel must wear eye protection when splashes, spray, spatter, or droplets of blood or other potentially infectious materials can be reasonably anticipated. Reference: Guideline for prevention of transmissible infections. In: *Guidelines for Perioperative Practice*. Denver, CO: AORN, Inc; 2017:517.

42. Answer A is correct. When delegating tasks, the circulating nurse must verify that the person being assigned the task can perform them within their scope of practice. Clear instructions and appropriate feedback are vital to ensuring safe execution of the task

being delegated. Reference: Phillips N. Administration of perioperative patient care services. In: *Berry & Kohn's Operating Room Technique*. 13th ed. St Louis, MO: Elsevier; 2017:89.

43. Answer C is correct. A medication that should be administered for treatment of local anesthetic systemic toxicity is 20% lipid emulsion. The lipid emulsion is used to draw the local anesthetic out of the bloodstream. Reference: Guideline for care of the patient receiving local anesthesia. In: *Guidelines for Perioperative Practice*. Denver, CO: AORN, Inc; 2017:623, Table 3.

44. Answer A is correct. OSHA regulations require the use of PPE for any person that may encounter blood or infectious materials. Hospital policy must comply with the OSHA regulations. Reference: Spry C. Infection prevention and control. In: Rothrock JC, ed. *Alexander's Care of the Patient in Surgery*. 15th ed. St Louis, MO: Elsevier; 2015:105.

45. Answer A is correct. Using an inner glove that is one size larger allows for an air pocket that will prevent constriction when the outer glove is applied. If hypoallergenic gloves are worn, these should be donned as the first pair, with generic sterile gloves worn as the outside pair. Reference: Phillips N. Coordinated roles of the scrub person and the circulating nurse. In: *Berry & Kohn's Operating Room Technique*. 13th ed. St Louis, MO: Elsevier; 2017: 455.

46. Answer A is correct. Facial preps can risk injury to the eyes and ears in particular. Chlorhexidine gluconate can cause corneal and inner ear damage if the agent enters these areas. Cotton applicators can be used (with caution). Eyebrows should not be shaved as they are likely to grow back incompletely and/or unevenly. The hair should not be included in the prep unless the area is part of the sterile field. Reference: Phillips N. Positioning, prepping, and draping the patient. In: *Berry & Kohn's Operating Room Technique*. 13th ed. St Louis, MO: Elsevier; 2017:503-504.

47. Answer D is correct. The medication reconciliation process has been implemented to help prevent transcribing and prescribing errors. Reference: Guideline for medication safety. In: *Guidelines for Perioperative Practice*. Denver, CO: AORN, Inc; 2017:305.

48. Answer C is correct. Standardization of procedures helps staff develop skill and efficiency. Policies and procedures based on standards and guidelines help to incorporate evidenced-based practice into patient care. Deviation from those policies should lead to an evaluation of the processes and staff involved to discover if the process needs to be improved. Reference: Phillips N. Foundations of perioperative patient care standards: In: *Berry & Kohn's Operating Room Technique*. 13th ed. St Louis, MO: Elsevier; 2017:17.

49. Answer C is correct. It may be permissible for the patient to drive himself home if the surgery was performed under local anesthesia without sedation and if there is a physician's order. Reference: Phillips N. Ambulatory surgery centers and alternative

surgical locations. In: *Berry & Kohn's Operating Room Technique*. 13th ed. St Louis, MO: Elsevier; 2017:193.

50. Answer C is correct. Sterilization processes are either physical (eg, steam), chemical (eg, ethylene oxide gas), or radiation (eg, x-ray). Reference: Phillips N. Sterilization. In: *Berry & Kohn's Operating Room Technique*. 13th ed. St Louis, MO: Elsevier; 2017:301.

51. Answer B is correct. Procedure-related VTE risk factors include ankle fracture. The patient is less than 40-years, does not smoke, and is not obese. Reference: Guideline for prevention of venous thromboembolism. In: *Guidelines for Perioperative Practice*. Denver, CO: AORN, Inc; 2018:776-777.

52. Answer B is correct. The preoperative patient assessment should include factors that may contribute to unplanned hypothermia, including patient-related factors such as age (ie, above 65 years of age), sex (ie, female), low body-surface area or weight, and preexisting medical conditions (eg, malnourishment). Reference: Guideline for prevention of unplanned patient hypothermia. In: *Guidelines for Perioperative Practice*. Denver, CO: AORN, Inc; 2017:569.

53. Answer C is correct. Absorbable gelatin is treated to retard absorption, which allows the hemostatic agent to absorb 20 to 40 days after placement. The gelatin pad absorbs 40 times its weight and may be used wet or dry. Reference: Phillips N. Wound healing and hemostasis. In: *Berry & Kohn's Operating Room Technique*. 13th ed. St Louis, MO: Elsevier; 2017:566.

54. Answer A is correct. Hematomas form when there is uncontrolled bleeding or oozing into a body space or cavity. The hematoma may cause pain and require drainage. Reference: Phillips N. Wound healing and hemostasis. In: Berry & Kohn's Operating Room Technique. 13th ed. St Louis, MO: Elsevier; 2017:565.

55. Answer A is correct. Should a patient's status change, having a contingency plan in place has been shown to improve the effectiveness of the transfer of patient information in settings with high consequence for failure. Reference: Guideline for transfer of patient care information. In: *Guidelines for Perioperative Practice. Denver*, CO: AORN, Inc; 2017:714.

56. Answer D is correct. Prions are proteinaceous infectious agents that are resistant to routine sterilization and disinfection practices. Reference: Guideline for cleaning and care of surgical instruments. In: *Guidelines for Perioperative Practice*. Denver, CO: AORN, Inc; 2017:835.

57. Answer D is correct. When a discrepancy is identified in the count, the perioperative RN should call for assistance. The scrub person should organize the sterile field. The surgeon and first assistant should perform a methodical wound exploration.

The surgeon should remain in the room until the item is found or determined not to be in the patient. Reference: Guideline for prevention of retained surgical items. In: *Guidelines for Perioperative Practice*. Denver, CO: AORN, Inc; 2017:402.

58. Answer A is correct. Sales representatives should never participate in patient care and must not enter the sterile field. Only the requested equipment is brought in, and sales representatives must check in and out with the appropriate hospital staff. Reference: Phillips N. Administration of perioperative patient care services. In: *Berry & Kohn's Operating Room Technique*. 13th ed. St Louis, MO: Elsevier; 2017:92.

59. Answer D is correct. Certification is defined as documented verification of an individual's professional achievement of knowledge and skill in identified standards. The ANA supports certification as part of the individual nurse's professional development. Reference: Phillips N. The perioperative patient care team and professional credentialing. In: *Berry & Kohn's Operating Room Technique*. 13th ed. St Louis, MO: Elsevier; 2017:54.

60. Answer A is correct. Assessment is the collection and analysis of relevant health data about the patient. Reference: Steelman VM. Concepts basic to perioperative nursing. In: Rothrock JC, ed. *Alexander's Care of the Patient in Surgery*. 15th ed. St Louis, MO: Elsevier; 2015:3.

61. Answer C is correct. Most complications occur within the first 48 hours after surgery; therefore, a registered nurse should call to check on the patient's progress and to reiterate postoperative instructions the next day or, at most, within 2 days of discharge. Reference: Phillips N. The perioperative environment. In: *Berry & Kohn's Operating Room Technique*. 13th ed. St Louis, MO: Elsevier; 2017:194.

62. Answer C is correct. A standardized format for passing on crucial patient information from the operative staff to the staff of the receiving unit (eg, PACU staff) facilitates communication. Communication breakdown is the root cause of many sentinel events according to The Joint Commission. Reference: Phillips N. Legal, regulatory, and ethical issues. In: *Berry & Kohn's Operating Room Technique*. 13th ed. St Louis, MO: Elsevier; 2017:47.

63. Answer B is correct. Accidents or unusual occurrences involving a patient, employee, or property should be reported according to facility policy. Unusual situations requiring an incident report include falls, needlesticks, fire, theft, malfunctioning equipment, medication error or reaction, and retained surgical items. Reference: Phillips N. Legal, regulatory, and ethical issues. In: *Berry & Kohn's Operating Room Technique*. 13th ed. St Louis, MO: Elsevier; 2017:48.

64. Answer B is correct. Transfer-of-patient information for the preoperative phase includes verification of correct patient, evidence of site marking, and required clinical

documentation (eg, complete and signed history and physical by attending physician). Reference: Guideline for transfer of patient care information. In: *Guidelines for Perioperative Practice*. Denver, CO: AORN, Inc; 2017:712.

65. Answer C is correct. Any correction to the patient health record should include providing the rationale for the correction above the inaccurate entry (if room is available) or adding it to the margin of the document. Reference: Guideline for patient information management. In: *Guidelines for Perioperative Practice*. Denver, CO: AORN, Inc; 2017:604.

66. Answer D is correct. SSIs are defined according to specific criteria into three categories, including superficial incisional, deep incisional, and organ/space. The correct answer is defined as a superficial incisional infection. Reference: Phillips N. Surgical asepsis and sterile technique. In: *Berry & Kohn's Operating Room Technique*. 13th ed. St Louis, MO: Elsevier; 2017:252-253, Table 15-1.

67. Answer B is correct. Administering the prophylactic antibiotic within 1 hour of the surgical incision is the only option that is a SCIP measure. Reference: Spry C. Infection prevention and control. In: Rothrock JC, ed. *Alexander's Care of the Patient in Surgery*. 15th ed. St Louis, MO: Elsevier; 2015:77.

68. Answer C is correct. For all x-ray procedures, time, distance, and shielding affect dose levels sustained. Reference: Patton RM. Workplace issues and staff safety. In: Rothrock JC, ed. *Alexander's Care of the Patient in Surgery*. 15th ed. St Louis, MO: Elsevier; 2015:64.

69. Answer A is correct. Loaned instruments should be disassembled, cleaned, decontaminated, and inspected before they are returned to the vendor or lending facility. The instruments do not have to be sterilized as they will have to be undergo sterilization at the lending facility. Reference: Guideline for cleaning and care of surgical instruments. In: Guidelines for Perioperative Practice. Denver, CO: AORN, Inc; 2017:819.

70. Answer D is correct. Postoperative phone calls can be used to measure patient satisfaction, outcomes, and QI data. Reference: Phillips N. Ambulatory surgery centers and alternative surgical locations. In: *Berry & Kohn's Operating Room Technique*. 13th ed. St Louis, MO: Elsevier; 2017:195.

71. Answer C is correct. The relative humidity in a restricted area should be maintained within a range of 20% to 60%. Reference: Guideline for a safe environment of care, part 2. In: *Guidelines for Perioperative Practice*. Denver, CO: AORN, Inc; 2017:279.

72. Answer C is correct. The Five Rights of Delegation are the right task, right circumstances, right person, right communication and direction, and right supervision and evaluation. Perioperative nurses must continually be involved in the assessment, evaluation, and

judgment needed for perioperative patient care. Reference: Steelman VM. Concepts basic to perioperative nursing. In: Rothrock JC, ed. *Alexander's Care of the Patient in Surgery*. 15th ed. St Louis, MO: Elsevier; 2015:8, Box 1-5.

73. Answer A is correct. An oxygen-enriched environment is present when the oxygen concentration is greater than 21% by volume. In an oxygen-enriched environment, the temperature and energy required for fuels to ignite is lower than that of ambient or medical environments. Reference: Guideline for a safe environment of care, part 1. In: *Guidelines for Perioperative Practice*. Denver, CO: AORN, Inc; 2017:248.

74. Answer C is correct. Standard precautions include gloves, masks, eye protection, face shields, and sharps to avoid injury and contamination. Head covers are not impervious, are considered as part of the surgical attire, and are not part of standard precautions. Reference: Spry C. Infection prevention and control. In: Rothrock JC, ed. *Alexander's Care of the Patient in Surgery*. 15th ed. St Louis, MO: Elsevier; 2015:83.

75. Answer A is correct. Oxidized cellulose left on bone inhibits regrowth and can interfere with healing. Reference: Phillips N. Wound healing and hemostasis. In: *Berry & Kohn's Operating Room Technique*. 13th ed. St Louis, MO: Elsevier; 2017:566.

76. Answer D is correct. Res ipsa loquitur ("the thing speaks for itself") is a doctrine likely to be invoked in cases involving retained surgical items, to prove medical negligence and making the litigation nearly indefensible. Reference: Phillips N. Legal, regulatory, and ethical issues. In: *Berry & Kohn's Operating Room Technique*. 13th ed. St Louis, MO: Elsevier; 2017:39.

77. Answer A is correct. Based on the risk assessment, corrective measures may include rescheduling or redirecting procedures to areas of the surgical suite where the HVAC system is functioning within parameters, delaying elective procedures, limiting surgical procedures to emergency procedures only, closing the affected OR(s), or taking no action. Discarding disposable surgical supplies, terminal cleaning of the perioperative area, and inventorying perioperative supplies are measures that may be taken to restore the surgical suite to full function after the HVAC system variance has been restored. Reference: Guideline for a safe environment of care, part 2. In: *Guidelines for Perioperative Practice*. Denver, CO: AORN, Inc; 2017:277.

78. Answer C is correct. Marking the surgical site must occur so that the intended site of incision or insertion is clear and unambiguous. Procedures that involve left/right distinction, multiple structures, or multiple levels (spinal surgery) require specific marking. Initials, a "yes," or a line at or near the incision site are all acceptable examples of unambiguous marking. The marking methodology should be consistently used throughout the facility. Reference: Spry C. Infection prevention and control. In: Rothrock JC, ed. *Alexander's Care of the Patient in Surgery*. 15th ed. St Louis, MO: Elsevier; 2015:29.

79. Answer C is correct. Speaking directly to the patient shows respect for the patient and allows the perioperative nurse to view body language and facial expression. The perioperative nurse should also speak slowly, use simple language, avoid raising their voice, and obtain verbal feedback to be certain the patient understands. Lenart J. Health disparities and culturally competent care. In: Lewis SL, Dirksen SR, Heitkemper MM, Bucher L. *Medical-Surgical Nursing: Assessment and Management of Clinical Problems*. 10th ed. St Louis, MO: Elsevier; 2017:31.

80. Answer D is correct. The financial impact analysis should include cost of the product, replacement strategy, associated equipment, training, depreciation, reimbursement potential, and group purchasing organization (GPO) contract pricing. Reference: Guideline for product selection. In: *Guidelines for Perioperative Practice*. Denver, CO: AORN, Inc; 2017:184.

81. Answer A is correct. The following are desirable characteristics of antimicrobial skin cleansing agents: broad spectrum, fast acting, effective, non-irritating and nonsensitizing, and prolonged action (ie, leaves an antimicrobial residue on the skin to temporarily prevent growth of microorganisms). Reference: Phillips N. Appropriate attire, surgical hand hygiene, and gowning and gloving. In: *Berry & Kohn's Operating Room Technique*. 13th ed. St Louis, MO: Elsevier; 2017:274.

82. Answer B is correct. During induction, a parent will watch his or her child go from being animated to lethargic to anesthetized. This gives the appearance of helplessness or death and can be upsetting to parents. Walking parents through the process helps to manage their expectations and decrease their anxiety. Reference: Phillips N. Perioperative pediatrics. In: *Berry & Kohn's Operating Room Technique*. 13th ed. St Louis, MO: Elsevier; 2017:129.

83. Answer B is correct. Class II chemical indicators are used as sterilizer test packs. They are used to test for air removal during the cycle. Reference: Phillips N. Sterilization. In: *Berry & Kohn's Operating Room Technique*. 13th ed. St Louis, MO: Elsevier; 2017:302.

84. Answer C is correct. Anaphylaxis and sepsis from infection are the most common types of vasogenic shock. Reference: Phillips N. Potential perioperative complications. In: *Berry & Kohn's Operating Room Technique*. 13th ed. St Louis, MO: Elsevier; 2017:616.

85. Answer C is correct. A minimum of four people is required to safely move the patient when using a lifting frame or patient roller. Reference: Phillips N. *Berry & Kohn's Operating Room Technique*. 13th ed. St Louis, MO: Elsevier; 2017:470.

86. Answer C is correct. Any sterile item that has any type of moisture on it is considered contaminated. The item/s must be opened—to prevent others from mistakenly

thinking the item is sterile—and sent back for reprocessing. Reference: Phillips N. Sterilization. In: *Berry & Kohn's Operating Room Technique*. 13th ed. St Louis, MO: Elsevier; 2017:322.

87. Answer B is correct. The patient needs to know preoperatively when to get assistance with discharge care if needed. Reference: Phillips N. *Berry & Kohn's Operating Room Technique*. 13th ed. St Louis, MO: Elsevier; 2017:371.

88. Answer B is correct. Surgical gut suture is wet-packaged in an alcohol solution to provide maximal pliability and should be used immediately after removal from the packet. When a gut suture is removed from its packet and is not used at once, the alcohol evaporates, which causes the strand to lose its pliability. Reference: McCarthy J. Sutures, needles, and instruments. In: Rothrock JC, ed. *Alexander's Care of the Patient in Surgery*. 15th ed. St Louis, MO: Elsevier; 2015:188.

89. Answer D is correct. The overall focus of AHRQ activities is: safety and quality, effectiveness, and efficiency. Safety and quality reduces the risk of harm. Effectiveness improves healthcare outcomes with the use of research. Efficiency then transforms research into practice. Reference: Murphy EK. Patient safety and risk management. In: Rothrock JC, ed. *Alexander's Care of the Patient in Surgery*. 15th ed. St Louis, MO: Elsevier; 2015:21.

90. Answer C is correct. A patient is not clinically obese until the BMI is over 30 kg/m^2. BMI equal to or above 40 kg/m^2 is considered extremely obese. Reference: Heizenroth PA. Positioning the patient for surgery. In: Rothrock JC, ed. *Alexander's Care of the Patient in Surgery*. 15th ed. St Louis, MO: Elsevier; 2015:166.

91. Answer B is correct. Blood loss is categorized at four different levels. A surgical blood loss of 750 mL to 1,500 mL is categorized as moderate (ie, 15% to 30% of total blood volume). Reference: Phillips N. Potential perioperative complications. In: *Berry & Kohn's Operating Room Technique*. 13th ed. St Louis, MO: Elsevier; 2017:609.

92. Answer A is correct. Before the next patient is brought into a room with known TB exposure, the air exchanges must be 99% complete. This may take 20 to 30 minutes. Personnel should wear appropriate filtration masks during room cleaning. Reference: Phillips N. Care of the perioperative environment. In: *Berry & Kohn's Operating Room Technique*. 13th ed. St Louis, MO: Elsevier; 2017:202.

93. Answer B is correct. Solutions used for skin prep must dry before application of surgical drapes. Reference: Murphy EK. Patient safety and risk management. In: Rothrock JC, ed. *Alexander's Care of the Patient in Surgery*. 15th ed. St Louis, MO: Elsevier; 2015:34.

94. Answer A is correct. Before a patient can be discharged, the registered nurse completes a final assessment to verify patient status for discharge to the next level of care. Reference: Odom-Forren J. Postoperative patient care and pain management. In: Rothrock JC, ed. *Alexander's Care of the Patient in Surgery*. 15th ed. St Louis, MO: Elsevier; 2015:286.

95. Answer D is correct. Critical items contact sterile tissue or the vascular system and thus require sterilization. Reference: Phillips N. Decontamination and disinfection. In: *Berry & Kohn's Operating Room Technique*. 13th ed. St Louis, MO: Elsevier; 2017:289.

96. Answer A is correct. Obese patients have a decreased respiratory reserve and are at an increased risk for rapid respiratory distress in the supine position. Reference: Heizenroth PA. Positioning the patient for surgery. In: Rothrock JC, ed. *Alexander's Care of the Patient in Surgery*. 15th ed. St Louis, MO: Elsevier; 2015:166.

97. Answer A is correct. First, the instruments must be decontaminated and disinfected prior to use. Then they are assembled in sets/trays and sterilized per manufacturer's instructions for use and care. Next, they are transported to sterile storage where they are rotated out to be placed on case carts for posted procedures. Reference: Phillips N. Decontamination and disinfection. In: *Berry & Kohn's Operating Room Technique*. 13th ed. St Louis, MO: Elsevier; 2017:284-285.

98. Answer D is correct. Ventricular fibrillation is characterized by total disorganization of ventricular activity. Because the impulse does not travel via the rapid, specialized conduction system, depolarization of both ventricles takes longer and is not simultaneous. Reference: Phillips N. Potential perioperative complications. In: *Berry & Kohn's Operating Room Technique*. 13th ed. St Louis, MO: Elsevier; 2017:598.

99. Answer B is correct. EBP is a systematic, thorough process to identify a clinical issue, collect and evaluate best evidence, design and implement a practice change, and evaluate the process. EBP uses research to guide practice, utilizing scientific evidence rather than opinions to implement practice changes. Reference: Steelman VM. Concepts basic to perioperative nursing. In: Rothrock JC, ed. *Alexander's Care of the Patient in Surgery*. 15th ed. St Louis, MO: Elsevier; 2015:9.

100. Answer C is correct. Placing the patient's palms up decreases pressure on the ulnar nerve. Arm boards should be at less than 90 degrees, padded, and with the patient's arms/wrists in neutral alignment. Reference: Guideline for positioning the patient. In: *Guidelines for Perioperative Practice*. Denver, CO: AORN, Inc; 2018:697.

APPENDIX: TAKING THE CNOR EXAM

Successfully passing the CNOR exam has two essential keys. First, a comprehensive and robust body of knowledge and skills required for competent and safe clinical practice. The second key for success is understanding the test-taking process. Successful CNOR exam preparation includes

- understanding the examination process,
- creating a personal study plan,
- understanding strategies for completing multiple-choice questions, and
- identifying day-of-testing requirements.

Finally, valuable information related to successfully completing the CNOR certification exam includes understanding the scoring methods and the requirements for maintaining certification.

Examination Process

The knowledge and skills required for competent and safe clinical practice are the basis for the questions on the CNOR certification exam. Knowledge and skills can be achieved through a combination of formal study, independent study, and experience. The certification exam is written for perioperative RNs with a minimum of two years of perioperative experience.

The CNOR exam has 200 multiple-choice questions. The test score achieved at the end of the exam is based on 185 questions. Your final score does not include 15 pretest questions that are spread throughout the exam. The exam is given on a computer at a local testing center. There are multiple versions of the CNOR exam to ensure the utmost quality and security of the exam process. Computer experience is not required to take the exam. Before taking the exam, you have the option to complete a tutorial. The test taker has three hours and 45 minutes to complete the actual exam.

There are nine subject areas related to the overall practice of perioperative nursing. The nine subject areas are further broken down into specific terms/concepts and skill requirements for each subject area. Each of the nine subject areas has a designated percentage of practice application for the perioperative

RN role. This percentage is then calculated as a set number of questions on the exam (see Table I.1 in the Introduction). For example, subject area three is Intraoperative Care, which has the highest role participation. The 27% assigned to subject area three translates into 50 questions on the exam.

Study Plan

The decision to take the CNOR certification exam demonstrates a commitment to promoting safe patient care and nursing excellence. Studying for the exam may seem daunting, but putting together a plan that is specific to your learning needs is very helpful. Identifying the necessary resources for the study plan is essential. After the resources are identified, it is important to complete an honest self-assessment of current knowledge and skills. The success of every test taker is directly related to his or her personal investment in studying for the exam. There is no magic book that will give all the answers. The suggested length of study before taking the exam is three months. This book is a comprehensive guide that presents an overview of content, the exam process, and test-taking strategies.

Study resources for the CNOR certification exam include the *Guidelines for Perioperative Practice*, published by AORN annually, *Alexander's Care of the Patient in Surgery*, and *Berry & Kohn's Operating Room Technique*. The majority of test questions are written from these three resources. Regardless of which resources you use, it is imperative that you use the most current edition. Additional resources are listed in the *CNOR Candidate Handbook* available for free download on the CCI website (www.cc-institute.org).

A well-thought-out study plan is a key to success on the CNOR certification examination. The CCI website has a number of resources to facilitate the making of that study plan (www.cc-institute.org/cnor). The certified nurses at CCI collaborate with other CCI staff to maintain the resources found on the website and ensure this information is current and accurately reflects the exam content. Nurses taking the CNOR exam would be well-served to familiarize themselves with the resources on the site, which include the job analysis findings on which the certification exam is based, webinars, sample study plan, and other study aids.

The recommended study period to successfully pass the CNOR certification exam is three months. Working backward from the date selected as test day, choose the amount of time to study in each of the subject areas. Keep in mind how many questions or what percentage of the exam is contained within each of the subject areas being studied. A calendar and written plan of study will help you stay on track. Make appointments on your calendar that can be devoted to study. Be realistic about the time commitment and balance your time with family, work, and other responsibilities. Studying in small increments of a time versus a cramming session every two weeks will increase comprehension and retention of the content.

Study groups are another way to prepare for the exam. Groups require a commitment to study and provide an additional support team. Every day at work in the practice setting is an opportunity to study. Take the time to talk to the anesthesia team about the medications used for induction. Ask about the properties, dosages, and potential adverse effects of commonly used medications. While you are learning, you can create study tools. Create your own flash cards. Buy some index cards and color code them according to the subject area. While reading content related to task and knowledge statements, write your own question and include the reference. Use the flash cards to quiz your study partners or use in the morning huddle. Study tools are all around you. It is important for you to take advantage of all the opportunities available.

Multiple-Choice Questions

Answering multiple-choice questions takes some skill. The skill developed to take multiple-choice questions successfully is based on knowledge of the structure and format of the question. Expert perioperative nurses write the questions to assess important knowledge and skills that are required for competent perioperative nursing practice. After the question has been written, it goes through many reviews by subject matter experts for quality and accuracy. Multiple-choice questions are not written to trick the test taker. Every question is straightforward. Those test takers who understand the content will answer correctly.

Every question on the CNOR certification exam is multiple-choice with one single correct answer. For each question, there are four possible answers (ie, A, B, C, or D). There is only one correct answer for every question. There are no multiple correct answers. The multiple-choice questions on the exam are written to measure either basic knowledge or a skill that is required to apply that basic knowledge.

Question format is important to understand. Each multiple-choice question on the exam is considered an item. The question part of the item is the stem. Three of the answers are called distractors. Distractors may be plausible but not correct. A perioperative nurse has the ability to critically think through the options and identify the correct response. The fourth answer is the correct option. Information within the stem should contain all the necessary content to answer the question correctly. Questions are written in one of two formats. The first format is an open-ended question (Table A.1). Open-ended questions are similar to a fill-in-the blank format. The answer will complete the stem. Closed-ended questions ask a complete question and end with a question mark (Table A.2).

Certain strategies are helpful when taking multiple-choice exam questions. The first strategy is to eliminate the distractors. Determine why the distractors are not the correct answer. Keep in mind that the answer is based on current best practice as published in the literature. The answer is not based on what you or your facility may currently be doing. A second strategy is to try to answer the question without looking at the options. Practice putting your hand over the choices, then see if

TABLE A.1 Sample Open-Ended Question

Pain can be categorized as acute, chronic, neuropathic, and ← STEM/QUESTION

- A. nociceptive. ← CORRECT ANSWER
- B. complex. (distractor)
- C. regional. (distractor)
- D. superficial. (distractor)

TABLE A.2 Sample Closed-Ended Question

Which of the following is an example of an opioid analgesic? ← STEM/QUESTION

- A. Aspirin (distractor)
- B. Acetaminophen with codeine ← CORRECT ANSWER
- C. Ketorolac (distractor)
- D. Celecoxib (distractor)

the answer you thought of is an option. Third, you can eliminate options that have absolutes within the answer. There is rarely an answer that is "always," "only," or "never" based on the knowledge and skill application of perioperative nursing.

Finally, many test takers make common errors when taking the exam. Avoiding the identified errors will help you successfully pass the exam. Following are some of the errors most commonly committed.

- Do not read into the stem or overthink the question. The exam is written for a perioperative nurse with two years of experience. Thinking back along your long career is not the reference material for answering the question. Taking too much time to answer each question can be a problem. Reading into the stem requires spending too much time on each question and answer option. Each question should take approximately one minute to answer.
- The stem of the question may contain a quantifier like "most," "most appropriate," "primarily," "first," or "initially." Do not be in such a hurry that you miss the quantifier in the stem of the question.
- You may find that as you progress through the test, a future question helps you to answer a previous question. If this is a confident decision, go ahead and change the previous answer. But changing the answers on multiple questions is not a good idea.
- Do not leave questions blank. Blank questions are marked wrong.

The multiple-choice questions on the CNOR certification exam are unique to the exam. You will never find a duplicate of a study question on the exam. Practice taking multiple-choice questions and online formatted exams. This will best prepare you for success.

Day-of-Testing Requirements

Being prepared on the day of testing is essential to successfully passing the CNOR certification exam. The best preparation is a completed study plan and knowing what to expect on the actual day you go to the testing center.

Several strategies can help to eliminate added stress on the day of testing. Start with knowing the directions to the testing center. Drive there before the day of testing to make sure you know the route and will arrive on time. If you arrive late for your scheduled appointment, many testing centers will lock the door and not allow you to test. This can be disruptive to other test takers who were on time and are currently testing.

You are required to have a current, government-issued ID that has both your photo and your signature. An additional requirement is your Authorization to Test (ATT) email. Your name in the ATT email must match your identification. If you have recently changed your last name, make sure to call CCI to update your personal profile and also to call Prometric to update your name in the Prometric system account, so they match.

Avoid last-minute cramming and get a full night's sleep before testing. Another very important strategy is to have a good breakfast on the morning of testing. Hunger can be distracting. Arrive 30 minutes early to be prepared for any issues or delays. There are extensive security measures at the testing site. Visit (www.prometric.com) to understand all day-of-testing requirements.

Understanding Your Score

The score for the CNOR certification exam is a scaled score. A scaled score is transformed from the raw test score (ie, the number of test questions answered correctly). The process is something like converting height (ie, your test performance) from centimeters (ie, your raw score) into inches (ie, your scale score). Possible scores range from 200 to 800. A score of 620 is required to pass. You will know if you passed immediately after you complete the exam. If you did not pass, you will receive an email with a link from Prometric to your score report. Please keep this report for future reference.

Maintaining Certification

Obtaining CNOR certification is a personal and professional commitment to nursing excellence. Creating a professional development plan that includes maintaining the CNOR certification demonstrates a commitment to lifelong learning.

This exam prep guide is a great place to start on your journey to CNOR certification. The content overview contained within this book is your jump start to studying essential information that is crucial to your commitment to the highest quality of perioperative nursing practice.

LIST OF CONTRIBUTORS

LEAD CONTRIBUTORS

Julie Mower, MSN, RN, CNS, CNS-CP, CNOR
Nurse Manager, Education Development
Competency & Credentialing Institute
Denver, CO

Dawn Whiteside, MSN-Ed, RN-BC, CNOR, RNFA
Director, Education
Competency & Credentialing Institute
Denver, CO

CONTRIBUTORS

Joan C. Blanchard, MSS, BSN, RN, CNOR, CIC
Clinical Presenter, Independent Consultant
Littleton Adventist Hospital
Denver, CO

Melanie L. Braswell, DNP, RN, CNS-CP, CNS-BC, CNOR
Advanced Practice Provider
IU Health Arnett
Lafayette, IN

Heather Burrell, MSN, RN, CNOR
Assistant Professor
Jamestown Community College
Per Diem OR Staff Nurse
Olean General Hospital
Olean, NY

Julie A. Conrardy, MSN, RN CCNS, CNS-CP, CNOR
Perioperative Nurse Program Director-EAST
Senior Nurse DSS
Naval Hospital Jacksonville
Jacksonville, FL

Terri Goodman, PhD, RN, CNOR
Owner
Terri Goodman & Associates
Dallas, TX

Lesia Hatlestad, MSN, RN CNOR
Clinical Practice Specialist for Perioperative Services
Lutheran Medical Center
Wheat Ridge, CO

Brenda G. Larkin, MS, RN, ACNS-BC, CNS-CP, CNOR
Perioperative Clinical Nurse Specialist
Aurora Health Care
Milwaukee, WI

Ramie K. Miller, MSN, RN, CNOR
Night Charge Nurse
University Medical Center New Orleans
New Orleans, LA

INDEX

AAMI, 170
abdomen, prepping, 81, 84
abuse, behavioral/verbal/physical, 78
accountability, 209, 233, 236, 238
    professional, 229, 235, 239
advance directives, described, 7
Advanced Trauma Life Support (ATLS), protocol of, 193
air embolism, 183
airflow, 60, 170
Aldrete scoring, 144
Alexander's Care of the Patient in Surgery, 246
allergies, 6, 13, 79, 98, 124, 141, 143, 168, 174, 185
allow natural death (AND), 7, 40
American Academy of Neurology (AAN), 193
American Academy of Orthopaedic Surgeons (AAOS), 198
American Association of Blood Banks, storage and, 65
American Association of Orthopaedic Surgeons, 194
American Board for Specialty Nursing Certification (ABSNC), xi
American College of Surgeons (ACS), 193, 196, 212
American Congress of Obstetricians and Gynecologists, 79
American National Standard for Safe Use of Lasers (ANSI), 59-60
American National Standards Institute, 83
American Nurses Association (ANA), 73, 232
American Nurses Credentialing Center (ANCC), 234, 235
American Society of Anesthesiologists (ASA), 49, 189
American Society of PeriAnesthesia Nurses (ASPAN), 143, 144
analgesics, administration of, 68-69
anaphylaxis, 184, 185
anesthesia, 7, 9, 28, 33, 66, 70, 72, 73, 129, 141, 143, 187, 191
    general, 61-62, 72, 128, 186
    hypotensive, 73
    management, 61-62
    sampling of, 63 (table)
    screen, 189

anesthesia professionals, 54, 64, 120, 128, 141, 191, 194, 197, 209, 214
    communication and, 122, 186
    RN circulators and, 62, 64-65, 98-99, 119
antibiotics, 6
    prophylactic, 29, 30 (table)
antiseptic agents, 78, 79
anxiety, 39, 72, 90, 118
    education and, 121
    reducing, 28, 29, 71-72
    undertreated/unacknowledged, 28
anxiolytic medication, 29, 71, 72
AORN, 9, 10, 11, 49, 73, 88, 199, 209, 211, 212, 233
    Fire Safety Tool Kit by, 51, 189
    Guideline for Medication Safety by, 123
    model by, 24
    Patient Hand-off/over Tool Kit by, 138
    publications by, 232
    Safe Patient Handling Tool Kit by, 58
    Sharps Safety Tool Kit by, 59
    transfer of care and, 138
AORN Journal, 233
as low as reasonably achievable (ALARA), 52
aseptic medication delivery methods, 69 (table)
assessments, 1, 35, 122, 137, 140, 141
    perioperative, 3-4, 13-14
    preoperative, 4, 5, 6, 12, 14
Association for Surgical Technologists (AST), 211
Association for the Advancement of Medical Instrumentation, 83
Authorization to Test (ATT) letter, 248
autologous tissue, 88-89, 218, 219
autotransfusion, 62, 64, 196

bacteria, 78-79, 62, 82, 163
behavior, 41, 70-73
    accountability for, 237
    ethical, 229
    patient/family, 24, 25
    recognizing, 28-29
Berry & Kohn's Operating Room Technique, 246
bill of rights, patient, 237
bioburden, removal of, 160
biofilm, 158, 160

biohazardous materials, 87-88, 171, 173, 216, 218, 219, 221
biological indicators, 164, 168, 168, 169
blood banks, 63-64, 186
blood flow, 26, 62
blood gas, obtaining, 187
blood loss, 63, 64, 73
blood products, 63, 64, 186
blood replacement therapy, 185-186
blood transfusions, 64, 73, 185, 186
Boards of Nursing (BONs), 232
body piercings, 6, 14, 37, 140
bowel surgery, performing, 86
Bowie-Dick air removal test, 168, 169
bradycardia, 71, 97, 186, 189, 194
brain biopsy sets, 161
bronchoscopy, 73

carbepenem-resistant enterobacteriaceae (CRE), 162
enterobacteriaceae (CRE), 166
cardiac arrest, 186
cardiac instability, 187, 195
cardiovascular instability, 187, 186-187
Centers for Disease Control and Prevention (CDC), 30, 67, 84, 163, 230, 231
    surgical wounds and, 94
    transmission-based precautions and, 31
Centers for Medicare & Medicaid Services (CMS), 29, 67, 230, 231
central service (CS) personnel, 211
certification, xiii
    CNOR, xi, 249
    maintaining, 245, 249
    specialty, 234, 235, 236
Certified Instrument Specialist (CIS), 211
Certified Registered Central Service Technician (CRCST), 211
Certified registered nurse anesthetist (CRNA), 141
chemical indicators (CI), 163, 166, 169, 172, 173
    types of, 168
chemicals, 34
    cleaning, 218
    handling, 50-51
    hazardous, 171, 174

cleaning, 157-164, 171
    environmental, 218-221
    high-risk procedures and, 220 (fig.)
    products, 159 (table)
    ultrasonic, 160
CNOR Candidate Handbook, xiii, 246
CNOR exam
    quality/security of, 245
    questions on, 245, 247, 248
    scoring methods for, 245
    subject areas of, xi-xii, xii (table)
    taking, 245-249
Code of Ethics for Nurses (ANA), 74, 232, 233, 237
collaboration, 40, 60, 118, 222
    clinical, 41
communication, 61 67, 88 236
    anesthesia professional and, 186
    assertive, 114, 115, 119, 123
    barriers to, 117-118, 120
    effective, 114, 115-122, 127, 129, 137, 138, 148, 188
    hand-over, 122, 141, 143, 237
    ineffective, 11, 114, 114 (table), 114, 137, 138, 139, 142, 143
    information management, 125-127
    intraoperative, 122-125
    listening and, 114-115
    nonverbal, 114, 115, 120
    skills, 4, 114, 121, 127, 137
    transfer-of-care, 123, 124, 137, 139, 140
    written, 140, 149-150
Competency & Credentialing Institute (CCI), xi, xiii
    job analysis of, xii-xiii
    testing partner of, xii
complications
    positioning, 56-57 (table)
    system-specific, 193-194
computed tomography, 193
confidentiality, 39, 119, 127, 238
considerations, 196-198
    age-specific, 25, 27, 28-29, 33, 35-36, 39-41
    cultural, 23, 25, 32, 34, 38-39, 74, 122
    ethical, 40-41
    ethnic, 32
    moral, 41
contamination, 79, 83-84, 221
    cross-, 67, 171
    microbial, 161
    preventing, 84-85, 163, 169, 171
Council on Surgical and Perioperative Safety, 189
Creutzfeldt-Jakob disease (CJD), 161, 219
    cleaning protocol for, 220 (fig.)
critical thinking, 41, 127, 236

decision-making, 29, 41, 119, 120, 121, 124, 125, 186, 194
decontamination, 157-163, 169, 171
delegation, 210
    rights of, 238, 238 (table)
Det Norske Veritas and Germanischer Lloyd (DNV GL), 231, 232
diagnosis, 3, 5, 10, 123, 140, 193, 194
diagnostic peritoneal lavage, 193
disaster plans, 192, 193
discharge instruction sheets, 146-147, 150
discharge planning, 144-147, 148
disinfection, 157, 158, 162, 174
    high-level, 163

process, 160, 161
    products, 221
do not resuscitate (DNR), 7, 40
documentation, 10-11, 147, 149-150, 165, 168, 174
    instrument cleaning/disinfection, 162 (table)
    perioperative, 90, 147
    transfer of care, 147, 149-150
drains, 95, 143
duodenoscopes, 162, 163
durable power of attorney, described, 7

education, 70, 74-77 (table), 194, 209-210, 236
    anxiety and, 121
    continuing, 229, 233, 235
    family, 38-40
    patient, 38-40, 146, 147, 150
    teach-back method of, 38, 122, 140, 146, 147, 150
electrocardiogram monitors, 115
electronic health record (EHR), 126, 146, 147, 150
electronic medical record (EMR), 128, 146
electrosurgery, 140, 185
electrosurgical unit (ESU), 89
emergency, 185
    preparation, 189-192, 197
emotions, 71, 116-117, 118, 120, 125
end tidal carbon dioxide (ETCO$_2$), 65, 66, 187
endoscopes, cleaning/disinfecting, 159-165
endoscopic retrograde cholangiopancreatography (ERCP), 162
environmental controls, monitoring of, 165-166
environmental factors, 16, 60-62, 183, 216
environmental hazards, 34, 183, 192-193
environmental services (ES), 165, 210, 211
equipment, 143, 145
    cleaning/disinfecting, 157-164
    contaminated, 85
    management of, 214-218
    procedure-specific, 58-60
    safety, 58, 7
    sterilizer, 165
    See also personal protective equipment
ethical issues, 72, 73, 222, 237
Ethics Task Force, 232
ethylene oxide (EO), 163, 166-167, 169
evacuation protocols, 186, 192-193
evidence-based practice (EBP), 209-210, 231, 235
    knowledge of, 222
    standards for, 236, 239
eyewear, 59-60, 159

Face, Legs, Activity, Cry, Consolability (FLACC), 33
FACES, 33
fasciotomy, 195
Federal Patient Self Determination Act (1990), 40
fire, 187
    risk of, 35, 51-52, 54, 188, 189
    prevention strategies for, 36 (table)
Fire Safety Tool Kit, 51, 189
fire triangle, 51, 188, 188 (fig.)
Five Ps (Patient, Plan, Purpose, Problem, Precautions), 117, 138
focused assessment with sonography in trauma (FAST), 193
Food and Drug Administration (FDA), 90, 84, 157, 162, 165, 167, 173, 216, 218
    sterilization and, 165, 167

Future of Nursing: Leading Change and Advancing Health, The, 234, 239

Glasgow Coma Scale, 194, 195 (table)
gloving, 83-84
gowns, sterile, 83-84
Guidelines for Perioperative Practice (AORN), 232, 233, 246

hair removal, 37-38, 78
hand-held devices, rules governing, 61
hand hygiene, performing, 29, 78, 82-83, 159, 164
hand overs, 121, 137, 138, 140, 142 (table), 143, 147
hazardous waste, 174
health care-associated infections (HAIs), 157, 211, 231
health care industry representatives (HCIRs), 211, 212
    presence of, 213 (table)
health care teams, 34, 210, 235, 237
    HCIRs and, 212
Health Insurance Portability and Accountability Act (HIPAA), 126-127, 147, 230 (table), 237
health literacy, 120
heating, ventilation, and air conditioning system (HVAC), 60, 61
hematoma, 91
hemodynamics, 63-65, 143, 145, 149, 183
hemorrhage, 183, 185-186, 194
hemostasis, 64, 91, 94-97
hemostatic agents, 93-94 (table), 186
herbs, 32, 139
    surgery and, 33 (table)
high-efficiency particulate air (HEPA), 52
high-risk procedures, cleaning protocol for, 220 (fig.)
homeopathic substances, 32
homeostasis, level of, 149
hospital-acquired conditions (HACs), 231
Hospital National Patient Safety Goal 2: 137
hydrogen peroxide, 86, 164, 167, 169, 174
hypertension, 97, 186, 189, 191, 194
hyperventilation, 187
hypotension, 65, 186 193, 195, 198
hypothermia, 25, 54, 65, 73, 98
hypoventilation, 191

I PASS THE BATON (Introduction, Patient, Assessment, Situation, Safety Concerns, Background, Actions, Timing, Ownership, Next), 117, 138
I-SBAR (Introduction, Situation, Background, Assessment, Recommendation), 117, 125, 138
identification, 3, 8-9, 141, 141, 143, 148, 248
    patient, 90
    specimen, 123
immediate-use steam sterilization (IUSS), 88, 157, 161, 166, 171, 211, 215, 217
implants, 88-89, 141, 165, 170, 171, 212
    management of, 214-218
infection, 30, 31, 81, 174
    health care-associated, 157, 211, 231
    prevention strategies, 25, 29, 157, 165
    rates, 91
    surgical site, 25, 29, 37, 59, 66, 78, 81
information, 4, 70, 125-127, 137
    accuracy of, 117, 142
    contact, 147, 149

286   Index

critical, 113, 129
management of, 125-127, 128, 236
providing, 140
sharing, 122, 125, 127, 142
informed consent, 6-7, 75, 143
injuries, 10, 91, 165
blunt, 196
brain, 195, 198
iatrogenic, 196
orthopedic, 193, 19
positioning in, 35, 55, 58
preventing, 50, 55, 173, 196
thermal, 196
Institute of Medicine (IOM), 234, 235, 236
instructions for use (IFU), 54, 60, 163, 167, 163-164, 169, 173
following, 51, 160
manufacturers, 170, 171, 172, 178
instrument cleaning/disinfection, documentation of, 166 (table)
instruments, 157-158
cleaning/disinfecting, 157-164
contaminated, 84, 173
industry reps and, 170
intraocular ophthalmic, 160
sterilization of, 86-88, 165-168, 170-174
storing, 170
surgical, 85-86, 157
transporting, 161, 173
International Association of Healthcare Central Service Material Management (IAHCSMM), 211
interventions, 66
complementary care, 71-72
definitive, 189
nursing, 23, 24, 25, 65, 67
intraoperative care, 4, 143, 246
transfer to, 142 (table)
intraoperative nurse, 148
postoperative nurse and, 139, 143-144
preoperative nurse and, 139, 140-143
intraoperative phase, 139, 191
preoperative phase and, 140-141
introductions, 9, 12, 122
Iowa Model of Evidence-Based Practice, 236

Joint Commission, The (JC), 9, 11, 49, 67, 137, 150, 231, 232, 235
discharge planning guidelines and, 144
effective communication and, 115
leadership standards and, 237
RCA and, 237
Surgical Care Improvement Project of, 67
surgical counts and, 125
Transitions of Care Portal by, 250
Universal Protocol of, 128, 141, 217
WHO and, 8
knowledge, 157, 247, 248
developing, 23, 233
practice-based, 235
laparotomy, 89, 91, 96, 124, 186
laryngoscopes, cleaning, 160
lasers, 35, 52, 59, 188
listening, 138
communication and, 114-115
living will, described, 7
local anesthetic systemic toxicity (LAST)
described, 70
signs/symptoms of, 71 (table)
low-temperature hydrogen peroxide gas plasma, 167, 169

Magnet Recognition program (ANCC), 234
malignant hyperthermia (MH), 66, 124, 187, 191-193, 201
Malignant Hyperthermia Association of the United States (MHAUS), 66, 191
management, 209-212
anesthesia, 61-62
cultural preferences and, 72
equipment, 214-218
implant, 214-218
information, 125-27, 236
medication, 66-68, 13
pain, 33, 69-70, 146
risk, 229, 237
supply, 161, 170, 178, 214-218
wound, 91, 92-96

material safety data sheets (MSDS), 34, 50
mechanism of injury (MOI), 191
Medicaid, 128, 201
medical antishock trousers (MAST), 94
medical record review, 4, 6-7
Medicare, 126, 148, 196
medication reconciliation, 4, 146, 150
performing, 7-8
medications, 123
management of, 25, 31-34, 66-68, 123
over-the-counter, 32, 139
mental health care team, education/mentoring of, 209
microorganisms, 84, 157, 158, 160, 164, 165
monitored anesthesia care (MAC), 68
monitoring, 165-158
moral principles, 41, 221, 237
multidrug-resistant organisms (MDROs), 157
multiple-choice questions, xii, 245, 247-248
close-ended, 247, 247 (table)
open-ended, 247, 247 (table)
mycobacterium tuberculosis, 32, 158, 218

NANDA International, nursing diagnoses and, 10
narcotics, overdosing, 67
National Commission for Certifying Agencies (NCCA), xi
National Council of State Boards of Nursing (NCSBN), 232, 238
National Council on Radiation and Protection Measurements, 59
National Healthcare Safety Network, 84
National Organ Transplant Act (1984), 196
National Patient Safety Goals (NPSGs), 67, 231, 232
natural disasters, 183, 192-193
needles, 99, 173
neurology, 143, 193, 194
Nurse Practice Act (NPA), 210, 232
nursing care, 139, 144, 234, 235
components of, 3, 3 (fig.)
description of, 24, 138
perioperative, 229
preoperative, 141
transcultural, 32
nursing diagnoses, 10, 65
perioperative, 11 (table)

obesity, 27, 35-36, 97, 190
Occupational Safety and Health Administration (OSHA), 34, 50, 59, 80, 83, 169

contamination and, 171
occupational exposure limits and, 34
opioids, 33, 62-63, 68
Organ Procurement and Transplantation Network, 198
orthopedics, 194-195
outcomes, 3, 5, 8, 66
anesthetic, 189
improving, 28, 90, 157
patient, 23, 28, 41, 66, 83, 147, 239
positive, 40, 174, 232, 237

packaging, 86, 157, 163-167
pain, 10
chronic, 32-33
management of, 33, 68-69, 144
physiological effects of, 33
psychological effects of, 33
response to, 34
pathogens, 218, 219
bloodborne, 171, 218
drug-resistant, 158 (table)
transmission of, 31, 221
patient beliefs, cultural/spiritual/ethical, 72-78, 74-77 (table)
patient care, 24, 116-117, 126, 138, 149
coordinating, 146, 157, 193
evidence-based, 29
improving, 235, 236
individualization of, 89
intraoperative, 11
perioperative, 49
preoperative, 11
quality, 34, 72, 215
safe/quality, xiv, 41, 113, 116, 117, 121, 123, 215, 235, 236
patient discharge instruction, 143-147
patient-focused model, perioperative, 24 (fig.)
Patient Hand-off/over Tool Kit, 138
patient health information (PHI), 125-127
patient rights, 40-41, 237-238
Patient Self-Determination Act (PSDA), described, 7
perineum, 81
Perioperative Explications for ANA Code of Ethics for Nurses, 73, 232
perioperative nurses, 3, 65, 89, 145, 169, 186, 212, 229, 231
anesthesia professionals and, 63
as patient advocates, 238 (table)
responsibilities of, 23, 49, 55, 70, 209, 210, 214, 236
standards for, 232
Perioperative Nursing Data Set (PNDS), 10
Perioperative Patient Focused Model, 24
personal protective equipment (PPE), 59, 60, 82-83, 157, 168, 174, 218, 221, 231
chemical safety and, 50
using, 30-31, 34, 81, 159
physical examination, 4, 5-6
Physical Status Classification System (ASA), 190 (table)
physician orders for life-sustaining treatment (POLST), described, 7
physiological responses, 25-28, 41, 65-68
physiology, 6, 92, 98
plan of care, 23, 138, 145, checklist for, 26-27 (fig.) cyclical nature of, 23 (fig.) patient-centered, 24-36

Index **287**

positioning, 128
complications from, 56-57 (table) surgical, 54-55, 56-57 (table), 58
postanesthesia care unit (PACU), 68, 120, 125, 143, 145, 149, 191
postoperative care, 4, 145, 147, 149
postoperative nurse, intraoperative nurse and, 139, 143-144
postoperative phase, 138, 143, 191
povidone-iodine, 79
potential harm from, 79 (table) power of attorney, 9
practice errors/preventing, 119
scope of, 210, 229
standard of, 236
precautions, 30, 192
transmission-based, 31, 32 (table)
preoperative care, 4, 143 transfer of, 142 (table)
preoperative nurse, 149
intraoperative nurse and, 139, 140-143
preoperative evaluation provider and, 139-140
STs and, 211
preoperative phase, 138, 191 intraoperative phase and, 140-141
privacy, 4
patient, 127, 212
providing for, 71
procedure verification, 4, 8-10
steps of, 10 (table)
product purchase, 214-215
direct/indirect costs associated with, 216 (fig.)
professional development, xi, 23, 229, 234, 235, 236
professionalism, 13, 198, 229, 231, 232
nursing, 233-234, 239
traits of, 233-234, 233 (fig.)
psychosocial status, 5, 99, 121, 144, 147

quality improvement, 90, 236
Quick Safety, 137

RACE method, 188, 188 (fig.)
radiation hazards, 34-35, 52, 59
radiation safety, 35, 53 (table), 171, 174
rapid-sequence induction, basic steps of, 196 (table)
regulatory agencies, 147, 215, 230-231, 230 (table)
respiratory rate, 191, 194
retained surgical items (RSIs), 89, 90 91
Revised Trauma Score (RTS), 194, 195 (table)
RN circulators, 63, 93, 100, 119, 125, 127, 129, 143, 150, 186, 200, 209, 214
anesthesia and, 196
anesthesia professionals and, 65, 101, 118
communication and, 120, 124, 126
fire risks and, 192
hand-over report by, 145
responsibility of, 35, 37, 68, 87, 122-123
scrub persons and, 124
sterilization and, 91
surgeons and, 92, 122
room turnover, 211, 221
root cause analysis (RCA), 237

Safe Patient Handling Tool Kit (AORN), 58
safety
body piercings and, 14
chemical, 50-51

culture of, 114, 117, 125, 229, 236-237
electrical, 54
ensuring, 34, 214
fire, 51-52
high-priority, 183, 184 (table)
laser, 52, 54
medication, 66-67
patient, 23, 24, 29, 41, 49, 50-54, 58, 71, 99, 116, 117, 123, 129, 137, 183, 212, 215, 222, 232, 233
perioperative, 25
personnel, 50-54
radiation, 52, 59
sharps, 59
spills and, 219
safety data sheets (SDS), 50, 171, 221
scope of practice, 229, 233
scrub persons, 118, 123, 124, 127, 141, 149, 209
communication and, 122
instruments and, 157-160
sterilization and, 89
sedation, 61, 63 (table), 68, 72, 237
Sellick maneuver, 62, 98
sharps, 59, 89, 173
Sharps Safety Tool Kit (AORN), 59
single-use devices (SUD), 165, 216, 221
site marking, 8, 9, 38, 128, 141
skills, xii-xiii, 247, 248
communication, 4, 114, 121, 127, 137

skin antisepsis, performing, 78-81
Society for Hospital Epidemiology of America (SHEA), 161
special needs, 25, 26-27, 29, 36
specimens, 123
handling, 87-88
standards of practice, 232, 233, 236
State Boards of Nursing, 232
sterile drape, 84, 85
sterile field
maintaining, 84-85, 212
movement within, 85 (table)
sterile processing, 160-163, 165, 171, 173
sterilization, 59, 83, 85, 89, 157-163, 165, 170, 218
dry heat, 167, 169
dynamic air-removal, 169
EO, 163, 166-167, 169
event-related, 86
hydrogen gas plasma, 167
immediate-use steam, 88, 157, 161, 166, 171, 211, 215, 217
monitoring, 165-170
ozone, 164, 167, 169, 172
parameters of, 86, 164, 169
prevacuum, 161
steam, 161, 165-166, 167, 168, 217
types of, 86, 160, 165-168
sterilizers, 161, 165-168
biological monitoring of, 172-173 (table)
strategies
fire, 36 (table)
infection, 25, 29, 157, 165
test-taking, 245, 246
stress, reduction of, 29, 120
study plan, creating, 245, 246-247, 248
supplies
management of, 157, 165-168, 214-218
sterility of, 162, 166, 215
surgery, 141
herbs and, 33 (table)

psychological responses to, 24
unpredictability of, 199
wrong-site, 9, 38, 129, 141, 183, 184 (table)
surgery safety checklist (WHO), 8 (fig.)
surgical attire, wearing correct, 81, 80-81 (table)
Surgical Care Improvement Project (SCIP), 29, 66, 142, 232
surgical counts, 89-90, 123, 183
surgical procedures, 35, 85, 157, 183
education about, 38
intervention during, 66
parental consent, 12
surgical products, sterility of, 85-86
surgical site infection (SSI), 25, 29, 37, 60, 66, 78
surgical sites, 58
preparing, 9, 37-38, 78
surgical team
gender preferences for, 38
sign-in and time-out process and, 49
surgical technologists (STs), 119, 210, 211, 221
sutures, nonabsorbable, 98, 99

teach-back method, 38, 120, 146, 150
temperature, 60
controlling, 25, 65-66
terrorist situations, 183, 188
Test Specifications Committee, xii
time out, 8, 9-10, 49, 122-123, 128-130
tissue perfusion, 26, 27, 28, 66
toxic anterior segment syndrome (TASS), 160, 161 (table)
traffic patterns, types of, 60
training, 215, 235
transfer of care, 138
documentation of, 149-150
patient-centered, 146-148, 150
perioperative, 141-146
by phase, 140, 141 (fig.)
Transitions of Care Portal (JC), 150
traumatic brain injury (TBI), 198
triage, 193
ultra-low particulate air (ULPA), 52
Universal Protocol, 4, 8-10, 38, 49, 128, 141, 216
components of, 8
US Department of Defense Patient Safety Program, 138
US Environmental Protection Agency (EPA), 218, 221
US Nuclear Regulatory Commission, 59

verification, 49 (table), 90, 128, 137, 141
See also procedure verification
vials, multiple-dose, 67
vital signs, 6, 7, 12, 97, 142, 143, 144

World Health Organization (WHO), 11, 49, 66
Emergency Triage Assessment and Treatment of, 193
JC, The, and, 8
surgical safety checklist by, 8 (fig.), 9
wound healing, 66, 97, 98, 146
wound management, 91 (fig.), 92, 96-97,
wrong-patient, wrong-site, wrong-procedure events, 9, 38, 129, 141, 183, 184 (table)